An American Revolution

GAY POWER

DAVID EISENBACH

CARROLL & GRAF PUBLISHERS
NEW YORK

Dedicated to Joanne, George, and Charity Eisenbach

GAY POWER:
AN AMERICAN REVOLUTION

Carroll & Graf Publishers
An imprint of Avalon Publishing Group, Inc.
245 West 17th Street, 11th Floor
New York, NY 10011

AVALON
publishing group incorporated

ISBN-13: 978-0-78671-633-0

Printed in the United States of America
Interior design by Maria Torres

CONTENTS

Foreword

AN AMERICAN REVOLUTION

On a Sunday afternoon in June 2005, fans in Boston's Fenway Park witnessed a scene that was unimaginable just a few years earlier. With the Green Monster looming in the background, the cast of television's *Queer Eye for the Straight Guy* threw out the first pitch before a World Champion Red Sox game. In honor of Gay Pride Week, the *Queer Eye* cast had been invited to Fenway to promote their show's season premier, which featured the Fab Five giving style make-overs to a few Boston Red Sox stars. Prior to the game, Jai Rodriguez, the so-called "culture vulture" of the *Queer Eye* cast, sang the national anthem. Throwing the ceremonial first pitch is a privilege usually reserved for civic heroes. In the same ballpark just two days before, the first pitch was thrown by an Army Sergeant who lost his right arm while serving in Iraq. A Boston journalist had complained that the Fab Five were not "family friendly" enough for Fenway and had speculated that Ted Williams must be "spinning in his freezer," but when the *Queer Eye* cast hit the field, the crowd greeted them with warm applause. "There were a lot of families there who were accepting and fantastic," one of the cast members observed. "Boston and the Red Sox welcomed us into their family and could not have been more gracious. I think the whole event was very positive."

Six months after the famously gay men from *Queer Eye* received a friendly reception from tens of thousands of baseball fans, Americans flocked to movie theaters throughout the United States to see *Brokeback Mountain*, a major motion picture about a love affair between two ranch hands in Wyoming. *Brokeback* opened to the highest per-screen average attendance of any movie released in 2005. A multiplex in Plano, Texas sold more advance tickets for the so called "gay cowboy movie" than it did for a much-hyped blockbuster remake of *King Kong*. A month later *Brokeback* won four Golden Globe awards including Best Drama, Best Director and Best Screenplay and was nominated for eight Academy Awards including Best Picture. "The culture is finding us," James Schamus, the movie's producer told *USA Today*. "Grownup movies have never had that kind of per-screen average. You only get those numbers when you're vacuuming up enormous interest from all walks of life." Advertisements for the movie hailed *Brokeback*'s appeal to Middle America, citing glowing reviews from newspapers across "the Heartland."

The growing acceptance of homosexuality throughout the nation has had remarkable political effects. During the 2004 presidential election, the news media focused on the gay marriage controversy and the debate over the Federal marriage amendment, but the presidential candidates themselves displayed a notable consensus in favor of gay rights. All the Democratic aspirants supported most of the key points on the gay rights agenda: sexual orientation nondiscrimination laws, an increase in funding for HIV/AIDS services, lifting the military ban on homosexuals, hate crimes laws, and the recognition of domestic partnerships. Three candidates supported gay marriage while four openly opposed it, including the Party's nominee John Kerry. Kerry's stance on gay marriage was typical of his many torturously nuanced positions. The Massachusetts Senator claimed he supported state laws that prohibited same-sex marriages, but he also opposed the federal constitutional amendment that banned gay marriage nationally. Despite disagreements over gay marriage, the ten Democratic contestants comprised the most pro-gay field of candidates ever.

The Republican ticket was also surprisingly supportive of gay rights. In an ABC-TV interview days before the election, President Bush said he disagreed with the Republican Party platform opposing civil unions of same-sex couples: "I don't think we should deny people rights to a civil union, a legal arrangement, if that's what a state chooses to do so." When the interviewer pointed out that the Republican Party platform opposed civil unions for gays, Bush replied, "Well, I don't." Vice President Dick Cheney took the defense of gay rights a step farther. Asked about gay marriage at a Republican campaign rally, Cheney said, "Lynne and I have a gay daughter, so it's an issue our family is very familiar with. With the respect to the question of relationships, my general view is freedom means freedom for everyone. . . . People ought to be free to enter into any kind of relationship they want to." While stiff opposition still resists granting gays equal rights, particularly the push-button right to marry, the American political mainstream has embraced much of the gay rights agenda, including recognition of civil unions.

This political and social sea change did not begin five or ten years ago. It began four decades ago when a few brave activists set out to challenge a vast anti-homosexual matrix of stereotypical media images, discriminatory laws, and repressive social mores. *Gay Power* explores the history of this American revolution.

Before the gay rights movement, the media commonly depicted homosexuals as insane deviants and sexual predators. The movement's revolutionary aim was to create a positive image for homosexuals in the media. Gay rights activists in the 1960s and 1970s understood that only after the public saw that homosexuals were not threats to society could gay rights make any political and legal progress. By manipulating the media and forcing more sympathetic characterizations of homosexuals on television shows, the gay rights movement offered powerful challenges to common stereotypes. Drawing upon over two dozen interviews with former activists, this book investigates how the gay rights movement exploited the unique power of the American entertainment and news media to humanize the homosexual in the popular imagination.

New York City is the primary setting of this investigation because the movement in the media capital of the world was able to generate media events and images that had a nationwide reach. Stories in New York newspapers were often picked up by national publications and local newspapers. If the story involved a controversial subject like gay rights, syndicated columnists weighed in, thereby drawing national

viii   FOREWORD

attention to an event. More than in any other city, reports on the gay rights movement in New York triggered chain reactions throughout the nation's media, transforming local events into major "happenings" on a national scale. By setting off what I call "media triggers," the New York gay rights movement broke through the stifling atmosphere surrounding homosexuality in mid twentieth century America. Through news reports about the New York movement, Americans saw gay people who were Ivy League students, tough rioters capable of battling the NYPD, and committed activists willing to take a beating for a cause and literally fight for their rights. Closeted gays throughout the United States knew the old stereotypes were being challenged. Some became emboldened to come out proudly while others found themselves compelled to reveal their sexuality. The gay rights revolution won important victories in Los Angeles and San Francisco, but the movement in New York had the most significant impact on the entire American political and social scene.

In the early 1970s New York activists used the "zap" to force media corporations and politicians into complying with their agenda. Zaps were theatrical demonstrations designed to disrupt corporate offices or political events like campaign rallies. Activists stormed the offices of broadcasters, newspapers and magazines and demanded more sympathetic coverage of gay rights and homosexuality. By stealing the limelight, they turned high priced political fundraisers into highly visible gay rights demonstrations. Zaps forced some of the country's most powerful politicians in the 1970s to advocate publicly, for the first time, equal rights for homosexuals, thereby provoking a national political debate over gay rights.

The period from 1960 to 1980 was an auspicious time for the Gay Power activists. The sexual revolution and the feminist movement simultaneously posed powerful challenges to social mores, sex roles and standards of behavior for both women and men. The style and ideals of the counterculture redefined what it meant to be a "real man" and "ladylike." At this time, American liberals had begun vigorously defending the rights of minorities. Once gay rights activists pushed the media to define homosexuals as a minority group, liberals were vulnerable to demands for recognition of the rights of the "homosexual minority." Liberals were also at the height of their power and capable of meeting those demands and pushing them into the mainstream political discussion.

The media was another ripe—and powerful—target for gay power activists. In the 1960s and 1970s, the three networks held a near monopoly on the American viewing audience. Television shaped the way most Americans viewed everything from fashion and music to social mores and politics. Gay activists could reach millions of Americans by directing zaps on the offices of the three New York-based networks and a handful of influential newspaper and magazine publishers. Activists in the 1960s and 1970s were unhampered by the webs of security that today would prevent someone from zapping a talk show or coverage of a political debate.

The movement's success between 1960 and 1980, however, unleashed a powerful conservative backlash that continues to shape contemporary American politics. After the liberals took up the cause of gay rights and the media began presenting a more sympathetic view of homosexuals, conservative leaders introduced a counter argument to the national political dialogue: Any progress toward legal recognition of gay rights was a threat to "the American family." This book explains how homosexuality and gay power came out of the national closet and took center stage in the American political drama of the past three decades.

The political battle over gay rights and homosexuality entered a brutally dark phase in the 1980s with the outbreak of AIDS. The story of Gay Power suddenly took a Hegelian turn backward when the old association of homosexuality with sickness once again flooded the American consciousness in the persistent news reports about the so called "gay cancer." Right wing pundits blamed "the excesses of gay liberation" for the new plague and its *literal* threat to the health of American families. The growing political and public health menace, however, revived gay rights activism, which had declined in the wake of its success in the 1970s, and a new generation of activists joined gay rights veterans in the AIDS awareness movement. Former gay liberation activists founded Gay and Lesbian Alliance Against Defamation (GLAAD) to monitor media reports on the disease and press the media for more balanced coverage. A bold organization called ACT-UP revived the powerful zap to pressure the federal government and pharmaceutical companies to expand access to life-extending drugs. *Gay Power* explores how AIDS activists successfully applied lessons and tactics learned during the first decades of the gay rights struggle to save their own lives.

Polls taken in the first decade of the 21st century reflect the revolutionary legacy of the Gay Power movement. According to the 2000 National Election Study, 56 percent of Republican voters, 70 percent of independents and 75 percent of Democrats supported sexual orientation nondiscrimination laws. Another poll revealed significant majorities of Americans supported treating same-sex couples equally under Social Security policy (68 percent) and laws governing inheritance (73 percent). A 2002 Gallup poll found that 86 percent of respondents thought homosexuals should have equal rights in terms of job opportunities. Three years later, 76 percent of respondents to a Harris poll said they strongly agreed that employees should be measured by their job performance not their sexual orientation. By the middle of the decade, nearly nine in ten Americans in some sense supported gay rights.

As is often the case, popular culture has been a barometer of the new zeitgeist. Every week *Queer Eye* viewers have witnessed a straight guy enthusiastically welcome five gay men into his home so he could learn how to become a better lover and potential husband. Audiences for *Brokeback Mountain* have finally seen on the big screen something they have always known; homosexuality is everywhere, not just New York and San Francisco, but the Heartland as well. Critical attention generated by the movie also has exposed Americans, on an unprecedented scale, to non-stereotypical images of gay men—a goal that gay power activists began pursuing four decades earlier. Even the archetype of American masculinity and national identity, the cowboy, has been swept up in the Gay Power revolution.

David Eisenbach
March 2006

chapter one

"THE GREATEST HOMOSEXUAL POPULATION IN THE WORLD"

The gay New Yorker in the mid-twentieth century inhabited a strange world of freedom and oppression. Living amid what the *New York Times* called "the greatest homosexual population in the world," he enjoyed unparalleled sexual and social opportunities.[1] If he were talented and smart, he also had access to positions of power and influence in every professional field, from business and the arts to religion and politics. Wealth and status provided the gay New Yorker with obvious advantages but also might have forced him to maintain two lives: a straight one at work and sometimes at home, and another in the bars, the subway station men's rooms, or out on Fire Island. Although he lived this double life alone, he learned through the "gay grapevine" of other powerful, closeted New Yorkers, among them Republican Party heavyweight Roy Cohn, and Philip Johnson, one of the world's most famous architects. He even heard rumors about the archbishop of New York, Cardinal Francis Spellman, and the Broadway chorus boys whom His Eminence was said to favor. While the New York gay elite did not quite constitute "a community," the midcentury gay New Yorker found some consolation in knowing that so many others shared in his secret, exciting, dangerous world.

The gay New Yorker's professional position provided financial security but also made him vulnerable to the harrowing web of police harassment and Mafia extortion that stretched throughout Gotham. Behind every new encounter with the thousands of young men roaming the city's bars, parks, and baths might lurk a cop or a Mafioso who could destroy his career or subject him to years of blackmail.

In numerous books and articles, the gay New Yorker read that the American Psychiatric Association officially categorized his homosexuality as a sickness, along with pedophilia, transvestitism, exhibitionism, voyeurism, sadism, and masochism. Psychiatric experts informed him that he and millions of other "perverts" were turned into homosexuals at a young age by "close-binding, intimate" mothers and "absent, weak, detached, or sadistic" fathers.[2] No matter how happy or successful he might be, he was "sick," according to expert medical opinion. Only by undergoing therapies designed to convert him to heterosexuality could he be "cured."[3]

When the gay New Yorker read novels about "the homosexual," he found caricatures with mincing gaits and sex addictions. Almost daily, he saw newspaper headlines announcing police sweeps of "deviates" from the city's parks and streets. In the 1950s, nearly every reference to lesbians and gays in New York City's newspapers was connected to crime.[4] Between the end of the Second World War and the dawn of the 1960s, more than half of the state legislatures in America passed sexual psychopath laws that officially designated homosexuality as a threat to society.[5] Negative characterizations of homosexuals were so common in the media that it was impossible for even the most self-confident and successful gays and lesbians to completely escape feelings of inferiority.

The gay New Yorker constantly heard comedians and politicians dredging up and exploiting the stereotypes of the effete homosexual and the predatory deviant, which he found painful but also strangely comforting. Although the stereotypes were unjust and hurtful, he knew they helped him maintain his double life. As long as he did not look or act like the silly fop or the insane "pervert," he was straight in the eyes of his coworkers and maybe his wife. Before the gay rights movement challenged the stereotypes by forcing the media to offer realistic depictions of homosexuals, the caricatures, jokes, and diagnoses remained his greatest protection from oppression and his greatest obstacle to liberation.

One of the main forces promoting gay stereotypes was the federal government. In the early 1950s, Republicans, led by Senator Joseph R. McCarthy and his closeted young assistant Roy Cohn, waged a crusade against the State Department, which they said was dominated by "cookie pushers" with "striped pants" who lacked the toughness to stand up to the enemy. Along with accusing Secretary of State Dean Acheson of harboring communists in his department, Congressional Republicans and many Democrats raised questions about the influence of sexual deviants in the halls of government. McCarthy crudely combined the accusations when he jokingly told members of the press that "if you want to be against McCarthy, boys, you've got to be a communist or a cocksucker." Right-wing syndicated columnist John O'Donnell claimed in a 1950 edition of the New York *Daily News* that "the foreign policy of the United States even before World War II was dominated by an all-powerful, super secret inner circle of highly educated, socially highly placed sexual misfits in the State Department, all easy to blackmail."[6] O'Donnell also asserted that of the first twenty-five hundred letters McCarthy received in response to his campaign against the State Department, "A preliminary sampling of the mail shows that only one out of four of the writers is excited about the red infiltration into the higher branches of the government; the other three are expressing their shocked indignation at the evidence of sex depravity." The Republican Party quickly exploited the popular anxiety about homosexuals by painting the Democrats as tolerant of sexual deviants, a strategy that the GOP continued to employ over subsequent decades.[7]

Homosexuality became a hot subject of a Congressional investigation in 1950 after the head of the Washington, D.C., morals squad, Lieutenant Roy E. Blick, testified that 3,750 "perverts" worked in the U.S. government. Questions immediately arose about the vulnerability of these homosexuals to being blackmailed by foreign agents. The Senate Committee on Expenditures in Executive Departments conducted an investigation and issued a report on "Employment of Homosexuals and Other Sex Perverts in Government." "Contrary to common belief," the Congressional report intoned, "all homosexual males do not have feminine mannerisms." However, continued the report, they were "not proper persons to be employed in government" because "they are generally unsuitable" and "they constitute security risks." Under the subtitle "General Unsuitability of Sex Perverts," the report asserted that "those who engage in overt acts of perversion lack the emotional stability of normal persons. In addition there is an abundance of evidence to sustain the conclusions that indulgence in acts of sex perversion weakens the moral fiber of an individual to a degree that he is not suitable for a position of responsibility." Homosexuals were a "corrosive influence" in government, according to the Congressional report, because they "frequently attempt to entice normal individuals to engage in perverted practices. . . . One homosexual can pollute a government office."

The Congressional report further warned that homosexuals were security risks because their "lack of emotional stability" and the "weakness of their moral fiber" made them "susceptible to the blandishments of a foreign espionage agent."

> Perverts are vulnerable to interrogation by a skilled questioner and they seldom refuse to talk about themselves. Furthermore most perverts tend to congregate at the same restaurants, night clubs, and bars, which places can be identified with comparative ease in any community, making it possible for a recruiting agent to develop clandestine relationships which can be used for espionage purposes.[8]

Even as late as 1965, the *Washington Post* reported that intelligence and security officials thought homosexuals were special security risks because along with being prime targets for blackmailers, "they are emotionally immature and unstable, talk too much and are highly susceptible to flattery."[9] In the mid-twentieth century, characterizations of homosexuality as an unstable, subversive, and corrosive influence on government fed common fears about homosexuals and shaped public policies.

Shortly after his first inauguration in 1953, Dwight Eisenhower signed an executive order listing "sexual perversion" as sufficient grounds for disbarment from federal jobs. To assist in the "purge of perverts" from government service, the U.S. Park Service launched a "Pervert Elimination Campaign" in the parks of Washington, D.C., arresting thousands of men for solicitation.[10] Well into the 1960s, State

Department officials made an annual appearance before Congressional appropriations committees that required them to reveal how many homosexuals were fired from the department the previous year. The annual rite became a sad routine by 1968, when the *Washington Post* commented that just as "the ancient Aztecs or Mayas used to sacrifice virgins, annually, to propitiate the gods and to gain favors from them . . . the State Department sacrifices homosexuals, annually, to propitiate the House Appropriations Committee, and to gain money from them."[11] At the height of the Cold War, the State Department fired many more homosexuals than communists.[12]

FBI director J. Edgar Hoover used Washington's antihomosexual hysteria to expand the reach of his power throughout the halls of government. FBI agents secretly cut deals with many high-ranking, closeted homosexuals in other governmental agencies. The Bureau would agree to suppress information it uncovered about the officials' sexual activities, if they became FBI informants. "In other words," according to one of Hoover's former aides, "if we found out that so and so was one, and most of them were quite covert about their activities, that person would be 'doubled' and would become a listening post for the FBI." Ironically, while Hoover managed the capital's most extensive homosexual blackmailing scheme, he often found it necessary to dispatch agents to intimidate people who spread rumors about his own alleged homosexuality.

Widely publicized depictions of the homosexual as both the weak-willed fop and the insane criminal had severe consequences for gays. Such images seeped into the consciousness of the many who could not escape feeling flawed and afflicted with a perversion. But the stereotypes also provided camouflage for the closeted homosexual who could pass for straight simply by defying the stereotypical image of gays.[13] When a gossip columnist threatened to expose Rock Hudson's homosexuality, his agent arranged a marriage between the movie star and his secretary. Although the marriage lasted less than three years, it was enough to save Hudson's acting career.[14] A closeted celebrity had to be wary of the use of certain buzzwords when he was described in the press. After J. Edgar Hoover read a couple of references to his "mincing step" and "fastidious dress" in *Collier's Magazine*, the second most powerful man in Washington reflexively lengthened his stride.

Even Liberace feared being described in the press as "mincing." The man who later spent a career performing in sequin-covered jumpsuits and feather boas was flabbergasted when the *London Daily Mirror* referred to him in 1959 as "this deadly, winking, sniggering, snuggling, chromium plated, scent-impregnated, luminous, quivering, giggling, fruit-flavored, mincing, ice-cream covered heap of mother love . . . the summit of sex—the pinnacle of masculine, feminine and neuter." Liberace denied he was a homosexual and sued the *Mirror* in the British courts because its words "made him appear to be one."

American newspapers closely followed the trial, which turned on the question of whether references to effeminacy meant homosexuality. On the witness stand, Liberace's lawyer asked him if he engaged in homosexual acts. Liberace, dressed in a conservative dark suit, replied, "My feelings are the same as anybody else. I am against the practice because it offends convention and offends society." The performer complained that, since the words had appeared in print, "When I went on the stage, there were cries from the audience of 'queer' and 'fairy' and such things as 'go home, queer.' " To bolster his case that a few words in a newspaper could be so harmful, Liberace explained how effeminacy and homosexuality were connected in the public mind.

> Ask millions of people. People in England and all parts of the world where I am dependent on making a livelihood have given it that interpretation. It has caused untold agonies and embarrassment and has made me the subject of ridicule . . . it has cost me many years of my professional career. . . . This article only means one thing, that I am a homosexual and that is why I am in this court.

In the closing argument, Liberace's lawyer asked the jury, "if the article did not mean that Mr. Liberace is a homosexual, what on earth did it mean? Can there be any doubt that this master of language chose these particular phrases to convey the impression that Mr. Liberace is a homosexual?" Nothing about Liberace's costumes, mannerisms, or campy sense of humor mattered; *words* that connoted effeminacy labeled him a homosexual. *The Mirror*'s lawyer argued that the words did not mean that he was a homosexual; they were intended to explain his sex appeal to both men and women. "The plaintiff has homosexuality on the brain," the lawyer added. The judge instructed the jury that they had to decide whether the words *sniggering, quivering, giggling, fruit-flavored,* and *mincing,* "in ordinary and natural meaning mean that the plaintiff was a homosexual." The jury ruled that the words did indeed mean that Liberace was a homosexual and awarded him 8,000 pounds ($25,000). American newspapers reported that after Liberace announced to the press that he was "delighted that his reputation had been vindicated," he "walked jauntily out of court" and was "immediately mobbed by a cheering crowd of women fans who shouted 'jolly good' and 'well-done.' "[15]

Roy Cohn was representative of many men in his generation who were so steeped in the idea that a homosexual was a "quivering, giggling, mincing" type that they did not regard themselves as homosexual despite their intense attraction to men. As he told one interviewer in 1978, "Anybody who knows me and knows anything about me or who knows the way my mind works or knows the way I function . . . would have an awfully hard time reconciling ah, ah, reconciling that with ah, ah, any kind of homosexuality. Every facet of my personality, of my, ah, aggressiveness, of my toughness, of everything along those lines, is just totally, I suppose, incompatible with anything like that."[16] Stereotypes helped most mid-twentieth-century American gays hide their homosexuality from their families, colleagues, friends, and even themselves. Like Roy Cohn, many did not accept their own homosexuality simply because they were tough and aggressive. The camouflage afforded by the stereotypes allowed many homosexuals, such as Cohn, to achieve professional and social success while they enjoyed a vigorous, and in certain contexts, flamboyant gay life. But while sexual secrecy enabled the closeted homosexual to succeed in the mid-twentieth century, it also made him vulnerable to blackmail.

The 1950 Congressional report on the employment of homosexuals in government noted that "many cases have come to the attention of the police where highly respected individuals have paid out substantial sums of money to blackmailers over a long period of time rather than risk the disclosure of their homosexual activities." The largest known extortion scheme ran from 1961 to 1966, ensnaring hundreds of gay movers and shakers in cites throughout the United States. The

"Chickens and Bulls" operation, as it became known, sent a young man, or "chicken," to a hotel or airport bar to look for a well-dressed older man. After striking up a conversation, the chicken lured the victim to a hotel room, where one of two scenarios would ensue. A couple of phony cops might burst into the room to arrest the pair, whereupon the hundreds of businessmen, professors, and doctors who fell prey to the scheme invariably offered a bribe to the officers to look the other way. In other cases, the chicken assaulted the victim in the hotel room and stole his wallet. The victim's driver's license and other identification were then sent to ring members in his hometown. Weeks later, extortionists posing as police officers showed up at the victim's office informing him that his driver's license was found in the possession of a male prostitute and that he must testify about the theft. After threatening to arrest the victim if he did not testify, the bogus cops would agree to drop the investigation in exchange for a large cash payment.

The "Chickens and Bulls" ring had a nationwide reach with branches in Phoenix, Portland, Los Angeles, Miami, and Chicago. A New York businessman who was beaten up and robbed in Chicago was visited weeks later by two phony police officers who shook him down for two thousand dollars. A wealthy Midwest schoolteacher paid the ring $120,000 over a four-year period, while a man from Tucson, Arizona, handed over $25,000. When one businessman refused to pay off the extortionists, they informed his wife that he was a homosexual. The couple soon divorced.

After a nuclear scientist from California was ensnared by the ring, two men posing as detectives visited the nuclear plant in which he worked and gained admittance to his office. Fooled by the disguise, the scientist began negotiating a payoff. When his supervisor entered the room, the victim diffused the awkwardness by introducing the officers as his friends from New York and asked if he could give them a tour of the facility. His supervisor approved and the blackmailers were shown around the high security plant. New Jersey Congressman Peter Frelinghuysen was so frightened when extortionists showed up at his Capitol Hill offices that he immediately escorted them out of the building, caught a flight to New Jersey, and withdrew a hefty payoff from his personal account.

Admiral William Church, brother of Idaho Senator Frank Church, was in his Pentagon office when extortionists arrived to collect their hush money. After handing over five thousand dollars, the admiral thought his troubles were over. But when prosecutions of the ring members began, a grand jury subpoenaed Church to appear as a witness. The admiral became so distraught the night before he was scheduled to testify that he drove to a hotel in Bethesda, Maryland, and blew his brains out with his service pistol. Recalling the suicide decades later, his son, the Reverend Forrest Church, told the *New York Post*, "It was a great tragedy. The family never knew why because he left no note, nothing. It was a great mystery at the time." When at last the ring was uncovered, according to prosecutors, it had extorted more than $1 million from nearly seven hundred victims, including a U.S. Congressman, an admiral, two generals, a "much admired television personality," a well-known musician, a Princeton dean, a head of the American Medical Association, several clergymen, and hundreds of lawyers, teachers, writers, and businessmen from all over the United States, Canada, and Mexico.

In 1966 the New York district attorney launched an investigation that resulted in the arrest and conviction of thirty ring members on local and federal charges. However, many of the accused escaped prosecution because witnesses were afraid to testify. Robert Morgenthau, the United States Attorney, found "the most difficult part of this investigation is getting cooperation of the victims." According to the *New York Times*, when authorities tried to convince the "much admired television personality" to testify against the extortionists, he refused, saying, "I can afford to lose the money."[17]

The Chickens and Bulls scheme was just one of many extortion operations in New York City. One law enforcement official told the *New York Times*, "Extortion of money from well-known persons who are homosexual or bisexual is a persistent problem."[18] After mob extortionist Ed "The Skull" Murphy served a short prison sentence for his involvement with the Chickens and Bulls, he took a job at a run-down Greenwich Village dance club in which Wall Street executives fell prey to another profitable blackmailing operation. (The name of that club was the Stonewall Inn.)

New York City was the perfect setting for extortion schemes. State laws prohibited everything from serving alcohol to homosexuals to

cross-dressing. In 1959, the New York State Liquor Authority transferred sixteen upstate investigators to the city to help wage a campaign
against bars that catered to homosexuals. Investigators closed the
Grapevine Restaurant on East Twenty-eighth Street because it
employed homosexuals and "a substantial portion of the patronage
included lesbians and homosexuals, some of whom were observed
committing indecent acts." The Kildare Restaurant on Sixth Avenue
had its liquor license revoked for "permitting homosexuals and degenerates on the premises." Chez Elle was one of twelve taverns closed
according to the *New York Times* for "encouraging a homosexual clientele." The Prospect Tavern & Restaurant lost its liquor license for
being a "notorious congregating place for homosexuals and degenerates." The State Liquor Authority closed dozens of bars in 1959 alone
just for serving homosexuals.

The Mafia exploited prohibitions against serving alcohol to homosexuals by opening illegal enterprises that satisfied the large demand for
gay nightlife in New York City. A high police official told the *Times*:
"The Mafia has long been in a lot of gay bars. They're in for a quick
turnover now. They buy a 'straight' bar that is losing money, redeco-
rate and bring in a couple of tame homos to lure the others. When it
starts making money they sell it. It's a quick-buck operation." Eventually Mafia operators learned to maintain their investments by paying
protection money to the police. Cops "on the take" ignored the mob-
run joints and issued summonses for real and phony violations to places
without Mafia protection. According to one gay bar operator, "It is
impossible to open a joint in the Village and stay in business without a
Mafia partner."[19] The mob collected millions of dollars from its gay
bars in 1963 alone.[20] By the mid-1960s, the Genovese crime family
controlled most of the gay bars and nightclubs in Greenwich Village
and on Manhattan's fashionable East Side and began extending operations to Long Island.[21]

Mafia ownership of gay bars with police consent allowed for more
than just the sale of overpriced, watered-down drinks; it facilitated
extortion. The *New York Times* reported that "most of the bars that
cater to male and female homosexuals are Mafia operations and some
are bases for blackmail of deviates from wealthy families." The combination of oppressive state liquor laws and police corruption gave Mafia

extortionists control of the city's gay night life—a situation that resembled putting a wolf in charge of the sheep pen.

The New York state penal code also regulated consensual sex between homosexuals by making it an offense if "any person, with the intent to provoke a breach of the peace . . . frequents or loiters about any public place soliciting men for the purpose of committing a crime against nature or other lewdness." The NYPD enforced this law by assigning young, sharply dressed undercover detectives to cruise the city's gay bars, public men's rooms, and bathhouses.[22] During a licensing hearing for Julius, a bar accused of indecency by the State Liquor Authority (SLA), Patrolman Stephen C. Chapwick testified that he would wear natty sports clothes when on special assignment to catch solicitors. According to Chapwick's testimony, one night he sat in Julius observing several males who "spoke in a high shrill voice," had "limp wrists," "wore tight clothes," and "walked with a mincing gait." Eventually a young man engaged him in a friendly conversation and made an "indecent proposal to him." The patrolman did his duty and arrested the young man. Although the defendant was found not guilty in criminal court, the SLA suspended Julius's liquor license because it permitted homosexuals "to conduct themselves in an indecent manner."[23] The New York City police department assisted the SLA in its crusade against gay bars by hanging "Raided Premises" signs on the doors of bars in which homosexuals were arrested for "indecency." After a raid on the Cherry Lane Tavern, a hot spot for tourists and male prostitutes, however, the "Raided Premises" sign served more as a titillating advertisement than a scarlet letter.[24]

According to an ACLU spokesman, the New York City police also sent large numbers of officers into the parks and streets "dressed in tight pants, sneakers and polo shirts . . . to bring about solicitations."[25] The *New York Times* reported that between 1959 and 1963, one thousand to thirteen hundred men were arrested annually in New York City for overt homosexual activity. About two-thirds of those arrested were charged with soliciting male partners under the disorderly conduct statute.[26] The NYPD intensified its longstanding practice of arresting homosexuals for loitering and solicitation on the street in 1964 after Edward Koch, the Greenwich Village Democratic Leader, demanded a drive to rid the Village of what the *New York Times* called "degenerates and other undesirables." Koch, whose own sexuality was questioned when he ran for mayor in the 1970s, proudly announced after the 1964 police sweeps that the NYPD had assured him more effective measures would be taken to curb activity of homosexuals in the Village.[27] The *Times* reported a few days later that a policeman on a motor scooter was added to the force patrolling Washington Square Park to aid in the removal of "drunks, hoodlums and flagrant homosexuals."[28]

Men arrested for propositioning an officer were frequently beaten by the police. One patrolman recalled in 1969, "We used to have the feeling that the public wanted us to keep pushing around homosexuals and other perverts." A rookie policeman said "one of the older men advised me that if the courts didn't punish a man, we should."[29] Those beaten by the police were reluctant to register official complaints. A spokesman for the Mattachine Society, the main gay rights organization in New York in the 1950s and 1960s, explained that "the last thing homosexuals are going to do is complain about something. They'll just sit there like a possum, they're so afraid of their families finding out or losing their jobs."[30]

There is another, more complex explanation for the refusal of many of those beaten by the police to complain. News reports depicting homosexuals as criminals and traitors shaped the views and prejudices of not only straights but of homosexuals themselves. Many gays believed that antihomosexual discrimination was not without justification. Perhaps the most horrible effect of the stereotypes and misrepresentations was how they made millions of gay Americans hate themselves.[31]

Fortunately psychiatrists, journalists, politicians, and comedians did not have a monopoly on the subject of homosexuality. A book appeared in 1951 that questioned the barrage of antigay stereotypes, police practices, and laws that pounded American homosexuals. *The Homosexual in America*, written by Edward Sagarin under the pseudonym Donald Webster Cory, offered an analysis of the condition of homosexuals from the viewpoint not of a psychiatrist or a criminologist but of a gay man. For the first time, a nonfiction book was not demonizing, diagnosing, or patronizing the homosexual. Instead, Cory celebrated him for his unique perspectives and talents and assigned him a central role in the defense of America's liberty.

Cory offered his heterosexual readers a look into the "gay" world and its language. He explained how the word "gay" derived from the sixteenth-century French word *gaie*, which made its way into English by the beginning of the twentieth century.[32] Cory also disclosed how in the gay argot heterosexuals were called "straights," effeminate homosexuals, "camps," and hypermasculine gays were "rough trade."[33] In an attempt to demystify gay life, Cory described cruising practices, bar scenes, and tactics of concealment. He argued that not only were gays and lesbians worthy of understanding and respect, they possessed a special "homosexual creativity, so often freed from conventional thought, with imagination unbound and unfettered . . . present in men of science and industry, in educators, religious leaders, inventors."[34] Cory did not dismiss the differences between straights and gays. But unlike every previous nonfiction book on homosexuality, Cory's did not attribute the idiosyncrasies of gay life to mental illness or moral weakness. Instead it described a gay culture that contributed to the glorious diversity of American culture. At a time when homosexuals were being hounded out of the State Department and "swept" from public parks, Cory's observations on the value of being gay had a revolutionary impact on his readers.

When *The Homosexual in America* was published, the psychiatric community was enthusiastic about using psychoanalysis to convert homosexuals to heterosexuality. Cory himself had undergone years of psychiatric treatment, including sexual conversion therapy, and came away convinced that homosexuals could not be "converted" into heterosexuals. Instead he called upon unhappy homosexuals to follow his lead and work with their therapists to achieve self-acceptance. He also made the then revolutionary suggestion that homosexuals should form groups in which ten to twenty homosexuals would gather weekly under the guidance of a therapist to discuss "their personal and psychological problems, their fears and their phobias, their frustrations and humiliations" along with less personal topics like "the meaning of a new novel." Participants in these meetings would find a kind, liberating atmosphere in which they could be free of "the burden of secrecy and shame."[35] Cory suggested that the groups be restricted to homosexuals so that no one would feel inhibited. (Almost twenty years later, gay liberationists would practice a form of such group therapy in what were called consciousness-raising sessions.)

Along with questioning the psychiatric establishment, Cory excoriated the government and media for trapping homosexuals in a "vicious circle." As a gay New Yorker, Cory knew how laws that prohibited socializing in gay bars and consensual sex unjustly transformed good citizens into criminals. News reports about arrests of "criminal deviants" fed into stereotypes that were used to justify the laws.[36] Fear of arrest and loss of employment made the homosexual vulnerable to blackmail, turning him into a victim of both the law and the extortionist. He could not turn to the authorities or the courts because "the price for making the struggle is public disgrace and further economic discrimination."[37] In the end, the American homosexual faced a dilemma. "If he does not rise up and demand his rights, he will never get them, but until he gets those rights, he cannot be expected to expose himself to the martyrdom that would come if he should rise up and demand them."[38] Cory, however, offered a way to break the vicious circle.

First, he suggested that all Americans needed to recognize gays and lesbians as a minority. Cory argued that homosexuals, like blacks and Jews, were an oppressed group that suffered discrimination from the dominant society because of what they were, not just what they did. Sexual impulses were not a choice but a characteristic that was as much a part of people as their skin color. Cory concluded that criminalizing consensual homosexual acts was therefore absurd and unjust. Like all oppressed minorities, homosexuals confronted daily reminders of their inferior status, but according to Cory their experience packed a unique bitterness:

> Ethnic groups could take refuge in comfort and pride of their own, in the warmth of family and friends, in acceptance of themselves among the most enlightened people around them. But not the homosexuals. Those closest to us, whose love we are in extreme need of, accept us for what we are not. Constantly and increasingly we carry a mask, and without interruption we stand on guard lest our secret, which is our very essence, be betrayed.[39]

One of the worst aspects of antihomosexual discrimination, Cory maintained, was that it was usually experienced alone. For the homosexual to feel free to remove his mask to his family, friends, and colleagues, society had to change its attitudes toward homosexuality.

To achieve this change, Cory hoped to enlist the support of the American liberal who had begun to champion equal rights for racial and ethnic minorities aggressively in the early years after World War II. He noted how groups like the American Civil Liberties Union had shown little interest in fighting laws that discriminated against homosexuals, but he hoped that liberals would soon realize that gays and lesbians, like all other minorities, were worthy of equal rights.[40] Cory's claim to minority status for homosexuals was a revolutionary moment for both the gay rights movement and American liberalism. Previous appeals for homosexual rights called for understanding and compassion. Cory demanded social justice. Liberals could no longer defend equal rights for all minorities without including homosexuals.

While enlisting the support of liberals was essential to the movement for reform, Cory understood the most significant and perhaps most difficult step toward gay rights would be the political involvement of homosexuals themselves. The ability to wear a mask and avoid detection was a blessing for many successful gays and lesbians, but it was a curse for the homosexual minority:

> The inherent tragedy—not the saving grace—of homosexuality is found in the ease of concealment. If the homosexual were as readily recognizable as are members of certain other minority groups, the social condemnation could not possibly exist. Stereotype thinking on the part of the majority would, in the first instance, collapse of its own absurdity if all of us who are gay were known for what we are. Secondly, our achievements in society and our contributions to all phases of culture and social achievement would become well-known. . . . The laws against homosexuality could not be sustained if it were flagrantly apparent that millions of human beings in all walks of life were affected. Blackmail, naturally enough, would be non-existent as a problem facing the invert.[41]

For the majority of homosexuals to be comfortable enough to lift their masks, newspapers, magazines, and broadcast media had to present

serious and sympathetic discussions of homosexuality to the public.
"The answer is to be found in the liberalization of our newspapers,
radio, and theater, so that homosexuality can be discussed freely as any
other subject and within the confines that circumscribe any other type
of discussion."[42] Cory observed that in the 1940s and early 1950s, a
"conspiracy of silence" about homosexuality began to be broken by
novelists like Gore Vidal and James Baldwin along with Tennessee
Williams and other playwrights. Cory wanted the subject of homosexuality to move beyond book clubs and Broadway. He knew that only
the mass media could bring the issue of homosexuality into America's
living rooms and spur "the interchange of opinion, the conflict and the
controversy, which alone can establish truth."[43] Once the mass media
started presenting serious discussions of homosexuality and gay rights,
the American public would begin to consider the legitimacy of rights
for homosexuals.

Cory did not want to surrender the discussion about homosexuality to straights. He called for the right to publish gay books and
magazines without the interference of the police and demanded that
homosexuals have access to "the main channels of communication,
the leading newspapers, magazines and the air for the expression of
a viewpoint in the spirit and traditions of American freedoms. . . .
We need freedom of expression to achieve freedom of inversion."[44]
A gay press would enable homosexuals themselves to break the
stranglehold that the mainstream media had over the image of the
homosexual.

Along with support of the liberals and access to the media, Cory saw
the need for a "gay hero" who could counteract the stereotypes. "In
identifying a great personality with a minority, the members of the
group are actually identifying themselves to a large extent with their
hero's greatness. . . . By displaying the positive rather than the negative stereotype, they hope, furthermore, to counteract the unfavorable
propaganda to which homosexuals are subject."[45] The homosexual
minority needed a hero or a group of heroes who defied the common
perception that all gays had mincing gaits and limp wrists. A serious,
tough gay hero would force straights to reconsider their assumptions
about homosexuals and perhaps make them more comfortable with
gay rights.

Further, once the gay rights movement enlisted the liberals, busted the conspiracy of silence, and found its heroes, it would not only begin rescuing millions of homosexual Americans from discriminatory laws, it would help preserve the liberty of the American Republic. Cory observed how both Stalin and Hitler

> utilized the bias against homosexuality as a smoke screen to cover up their own deficiencies, to rally the outraged populace against opposition, to arouse the fury of hatred by linking personal and political opposition with this sexual practice. These dictators were carrying on in the traditions of those who had linked homosexuality with heresy and sorcery in the Middle Ages; whereas here in the United States the charges of sex-perversion in the government were used as a basis for an attack upon the foreign policy of the Truman Administration, when support for such an attack could not be obtained on the basis of the logic of relevant argumentation.[46]

The great obstacles to totalitarianism in the United States were the "minorities in our culture, whether of a sexual or religious or ethnic character. . . . No force will be able to weave these groups into a single totalitarian unity which is the unanimity of the graveyard." Cory argued that "fortunately but unwittingly" homosexuality "must inevitably play a progressive role" in American society by broadening "the base for freedom of thought and communication." He predicted a gay rights movement "will be a banner-bearer in the struggle for liberalization of our sexual conventions and will be a pillar of strength in the defense of our threatened democracy."[47] If only to help preserve their own liberty, Cory called upon straights to join the fight for gay rights.

The Homosexual in America went through seven hardcover printings, was translated into French and Spanish, and appeared as a mass-market paperback in 1963. Over the years, Cory received thousands of letters of praise and gratitude from ministers, parents, professors, scientists, and writers, including Norman Mailer.[48] In the introduction to the 1959 edition of the book, Cory wrote about the many "homosexuals, their friends, their parents, their husbands or wives" who expressed "one continuous refrain: Thank you for speaking up, for saying what had to be said."[49] Cory's book inspired a generation of gay rights activists who adopted his ideas and tactics in the 1960s and bestowed him with the title, "father of the homophile movement."

Over the subsequent quarter century, Cory's vision directly and indirectly shaped the gay rights movement. In the early 1960s two of Cory's most enthusiastic readers, Frank Kameny and Jack Nichols, formed a gay rights group in Washington, D.C., where they took the fight for the minority status of homosexuals into the federal courts and the Congress. In the late 1960s and early 1970s, the gay liberation movement built on Kameny's successes by challenging the stereotypes and targeting the media and liberals just as Cory had suggested. The following chapters recount how in less than two decades the gay rights movement achieved much of Cory's program and transformed the American social and political landscape.

chapter two

BREAKING THE "CONSPIRACY OF SILENCE"

The *New York Times* ran a story in 1963 disclosing "the city's most sensitive open secret—the presence of what is probably the greatest homosexual population in the world and its increasing openness." The *Times* was particularly amazed with the "openness" of "the minority of militant homosexuals" in the city's two gay rights organizations, the Mattachine Society of New York and the Daughters of Bilitis.[1] While American homosexuals were playing cat and mouse with the press, the mob, and the cops, a small number of gay heroes followed Donald Webster Cory's call to action in *The Homosexual in America* and waged campaigns against the government, the police, and the "conspiracy of silence."

The organized gay rights movement in the United States began with the founding of the Mattachine Society in Los Angeles in 1951, the same year Cory's book was first published. The principal founder of the Mattachine Society was Henry Hay, a fervent Communist Party member who convinced fellow gay leftists to form an organization of homosexuals that would combat oppression by generating a group consciousness free of negative attitudes toward homosexuality. Hay named his new organization after a traditional European folk dance called *les Mattachines,* which was performed in medieval France by groups of unmarried clerics who wore masks while they danced, sang, and satirized the rich and powerful. Hay hoped his modern group would also speak the truth even if its members had to live in disguise.[2]

Like Donald Webster Cory, Hay and the other Mattachine founders celebrated the unique gay identity and its contributions to society. Hay argued that homosexuals met the five principles of the Stalinist definition of a minority: they shared common language, territory, economy, psychology, and culture. Hay hoped that someday gays would take pride in their culture and straights would view homosexuals not as criminals or psychological deviants but as minorities deserving of legal protections.[3]

The Communist Party's strategies and ideology had a great impact on the Mattachine in its formative years. The structure of the early Mattachine even resembled the cell structure of the Communist Party so that the identity of members would be less likely to be compromised.[4] Because the Mattachine founders believed social change required action by masses of activists, they looked to mobilize a large gay constituency that was capable of militancy if necessary. The first step they took to create a mass gay rights movement was to make homosexuals aware of themselves as a "class." Unless homosexuals began to view themselves as proud members of a class, rather than as sinners or "deviates," they would not connect themselves with a gay rights movement. According to a 1951 mission statement, the goal of the Mattachine Society was to create a "new pride—pride in belonging, a pride in participating in the cultural growth and social achievements of . . . the homosexual minority."[5] To generate such homosexual pride, the Mattachine set up semipublic discussion groups that affirmed the self-worth of participants.

Within two years of its founding, chapters of the Mattachine Society opened in Berkeley, Oakland, and San Francisco. To break the silence about homosexuality in the press, one of the Los Angeles Mattachine members in 1953 created *One*, a gay-run and -edited newspaper. Donald Webster Cory, who saw the creation of a gay press as essential to the homosexual rights movement, became a contributing editor.[6] *One*, echoing ideas that Cory presented in *The Homosexual in America*, published editorials stating that "homosexual acts between consenting adults are neither anti-social nor sinful; legal attempts to regulate such behavior violate principles of American freedom," and "Solutions must be found for the present minority status of millions of American men and women who refuse any longer to tolerate suppression, subjection and abuse from every side. As citizens they have their rights." *One* was however careful to emphasize that it was trying to provoke ideas and discussion rather than political action: "Let no one rashly assume that the magazine is now going into politics. Nothing could be further from its intentions. It has its field: the homosexual and homosexuality."[7] *One*'s sales quickly climbed to over 2,000 copies per month. As second- and thirdhand copies made their way to Denver, Chicago, and New York, gays and lesbians nationwide discovered that a homosexual movement was on the rise.

The incorporation of new chapters and members into the Mattachine quickly undermined the consensus of the organization and generated challenges to its founding ideals. Some newcomers began to argue that the goal of the Mattachine should not be the celebration of a homosexual identity but the integration of homosexuals into the mainstream society as citizens who happened to be gay. At the annual Mattachine convention in 1953, member Marilyn Reiger condemned the characterization of homosexuals as a separate minority and declared that equality for homosexuals would come "by integrating . . . not as homosexuals, but as people, as men and women whose homosexuality is irrelevant to our ideals, our principles, our hopes and aspirations." New Mattachine members began abandoning Henry Hay's vision of a homosexual minority that was proud of its distinct culture in favor of the idea that homosexuals were only different from straights in the limited realm of sexual interest.

The new members of the Mattachine also viewed Hay's plans for mass social revolution as naive. Hal Call, the gruff leader of the San Francisco Mattachine, dismissed Hay and the founders as "pie in the sky, erudite and artistically inclined. . . . We saw Mattachine as here-and-now, practical. . . . Public protests were not part of our program. Not at all. . . . We knew that if we were going to get along in society, we were going to have to stay in step with the existing and predominant mores and customs." For Call, change would "come about by holding conferences and discussions, and becoming subjects of research" conducted by sympathetic experts.[8]

As the Mattachine Society grew and became more visible, the

founders' connections with the Communist Party began to threaten the organization. After Hay and the organization's lawyer were subpoenaed to appear before the House Un-American Activities Committee, the *Los Angeles Mirror* speculated that homosexuals, "scorned" by the hetero-sexual majority, "might band together for their own protection. Even-tually, they might swing tremendous political power. A well-trained subversive could move in and forge that power into a dangerous polit-ical weapon."[9] In response to the uproar, Hal Call and the San Francisco delegation to the 1953 annual Mattachine conference made a motion to amend the Society's constitution with "a very strong statement con-cerning our stand on subversive elements."[10] Call complained that "we are already being attacked as Communistic." The proposed resolution, he promised, "guarantees us that we will not be infiltrated by Commu-nists." Pressures from the new members became too much for Henry Hay, who left the groundbreaking organization he had created.

With Hay gone, the Mattachine moved toward a program that mil-itant gay rights activists would later dismiss as "accomodationalist." The new leadership abandoned the idea of the homosexual minority and adopted the view that "the sex variant is no different from anyone else except in the object of his sexual expression." Instead of creating a mass organization of militants proud of being members of the homo-sexual minority, the Mattachine would rely on appeals to the public through experts. The Mattachine's "greatest and most meaningful contribution . . . will consist of aiding established and recognized sci-entists, clinics, research organizations and institutions . . . studying sex variation problems." The decision to focus on mobilizing sympathetic experts rather than on radicalizing a gay constituency inhibited the Mattachine from taking provocative actions. When members of the Los Angeles chapter called upon its leaders to launch a campaign against police entrapment of homosexuals, they were rebuffed with the warning that the organization was "not yet strong enough" to push an "aggressive program." Instead Mattachine would provide entrapment victims with the names of sympathetic lawyers.[11]

Without the stirring rhetoric and inspiring radicalism of the old leadership, the Mattachine membership began to slump. Hal Call, a professional journalist, knew that communicating the moderate mes-sage was key to boosting his sputtering organization, and in 1955 he founded *Mattachine Review* to promote a more conciliatory approach to gay rights. In a statement on the "Aims and Principles of the Mattachine Society," Call wrote that the organization would act in a "law-abiding" manner and "was not seeking to overthrow existing institutions, laws, or mores, but to aid in the assimilation of *variants*" (italics added), a term the *Mattachine Review* used for gays.[12]

Although the Mattachine Society was open to men and women, it never attracted large numbers of lesbians, many of whom gravitated toward the Daughters of Bilitis (DOB). The absence of a social outlet for lesbians outside of the bar scene was the main motive behind Del Martin's and Phyllis Lyon's decision to create the DOB in 1955 as a social club for San Francisco lesbians. The Daughters of Bilitis, named after the lesbian heroine in Pierre Louys's *Songs of Bilitis*, offered a safe environment in which women could meet each other, talk, and dance. When Martin and Lyon broadened the DOB's mission to education and public information about lesbianism, some members rejected this more political mission and quit. The DOB was even less radical in its politics than the Mattachine Society. Its mission statement called the Daughters of Bilitis "a home for the Lesbian. She can come here to find help, friendship, acceptance, and support. She can help others understand themselves, and can go out into the world to help the public understand her better." The DOB would not be a mass organization agitating for social reform; it would be a support group that would encourage lesbians to make individualistic contributions to the creation of a more tolerant society. Its newspaper, *The Ladder* eschewed political commentary and devoted most of its space to poetry, fiction, history, and biography.[13]

Under Martin and Lyon, the Daughters of Bilitis joined the Mattachine Society in what was called the "homophile movement." The label "homophile" was chosen because it was ambiguous enough not to arouse suspicion in a society increasingly anxious about homosexuality. Both the Mattachine and the DOB used their journals to push their "accommodationalist" views on how to achieve equal rights. Stories and editorials downplayed differences between gays and straights and criticized homosexuals who did not fit the respectable image that both the Mattachine and DOB were trying to offer the general public.[14] *The Ladder* published a letter from a reader claiming, "the kids in fly front pants and with butch haircuts and mannish manner are the worst publicity that we can get." In response, the editor unequivocally reaffirmed the writer's sentiment with a simple: "Very true."[15] An issue of *Mattachine Review* claimed that "the homosexual adjusts best who can make the greatest compromises with his own social and sexual needs, and the best adjusted individuals are those with the fewest contacts in the homosexual world."[16] For the homophiles of the mid-1950s, the road to gay rights began with self-reformation into "acceptable citizens" rather than joining forces as a "class" and making a revolution.

One, Mattachine Review, and *The Ladder* did not completely cower in the face of the straight hegemony. As Donald Webster Cory hoped, the gay press critiqued the stereotypical images of homosexuals that frequently appeared in the mainstream media and offered news that straight publications ignored.[17] The gay press broke the conspiracy of silence that kept serious discussions of homosexuality and gay rights off the pages of mainstream publications. One story the homophile publications closely monitored was the British government's reevaluation of the effect of laws against homosexual acts. The result of that investigation, the 1957 Wolfenden Report, called for the repeal of criminal penalties for private consensual acts between adults. To the homophile press, this development offered hope for a future when sympathetic allies and enlightened experts would conduct a similar re-evaluation of antisodomy statutes in the United States.

Regardless of whether the homophile press pushed positions that were too moderate or too naive, its very existence was a significant accomplishment. As Rodger Streitmatter wrote in his history of the gay press, "lesbians and gay men could, for the first time, speak above a whisper about issues fundamental to their lives. The magazines gave an oppressed minority the chance to express thoughts that previously had been barred from public discourse."[18] Streitmatter aptly compared the homophile publications of the 1950s to the first African-American newspaper, *Freedom's Journal,* founded in 1827, which marked the beginning of a national movement to secure black civil rights. Just as *Freedom's Journal* facilitated the exchange of ideas and the building of ties among African-American women and men all over the country, *One, Mattachine Review,* and *The Ladder* likewise laid the foundation for a national gay and lesbian community.[19]

There is another reason why the homophile publications of the 1950s were so significant. In an age when most Americans received their news from mass media rather than from word of mouth, social and political movements needed mass-media coverage to gain legitimacy. Even though the homophile movement in the 1950s was reporting on itself, its publications brought an air of importance and credibility to its organizations and positions. When readers picked up issues of *One, Mattachine Review,* or *The Ladder,* they discovered the words of openly gay and lesbian writers in print. The same ideas that had been heard for years in speeches and barroom conversations suddenly gained a new weight. To people who saw the media as a filter that separated the extraneous and false from the pertinent and "newsworthy," publication bestowed credibility upon ideas. If something was worthy of being published, it was worthy of discussion and consideration. The early gay press brought such credibility to the homophile cause. Throughout its history, the gay rights movement has continued to use media, both gay and mainstream, to build its credibility as a serious social and political force.

In the mid-1950s, branches of the DOB opened in New York, Los Angeles, Chicago, and briefly in Rhode Island, while the Mattachine added chapters in New York, Boston, Denver, Philadelphia, Detroit, and Chicago. But by the end of the decade the Mattachine only had 230 members; the DOB, 110. Such limited membership resulted from a combination of intimidation and apathy. Many gays and lesbians were understandably concerned about adding their names to membership lists because of the danger of exposure, while the absence of widespread political group consciousness also stymied recruitment. As Donald Webster Cory and Henry Hay argued, homosexuals first needed to see themselves as an oppressed minority before they would become active in a movement for social change. The homophile groups of the 1950s did little to generate such loyalty and confidence. When a Boston Mattachine member suggested that his chapter might work to repeal the Massachusetts sodomy statute, the Mattachine leadership in San Francisco rejected the proposal because such a public campaign might provoke a backlash.[20] The moderate views of the West Coast leadership continued to dominate the Mattachine Society until the mid-1960s, when a challenge arose from groups in New York and Washington, D.C.

The Mattachine Society of New York (MSNY) was the creation of Tony Segura and Sam Morford. Segura, a Cuban émigré and research chemist, was introduced to the idea of a homosexual rights movement when he found a copy of Cory's *The Homosexual in America* on a business trip to Cleveland. "Everything in Cory's book excited me. It gave me a strong sense of the existence of homosexuals as a group which I had never thought about before." When Segura returned to New York, he formed a discussion group about homosexuality that met on the Lower East Side. One of the regulars at the discussions was Sam Morford, a clinical psychologist. After getting the approval of the Mattachine leadership in San Francisco, Segura and Morford formed a New York Mattachine in December 1955.

Access to "the greatest homosexual population in the world" enabled the New York Mattachine to surpass the San Francisco branch as the largest of the Society's chapters by 1960. Nevertheless a significant portion of the money the New Yorkers collected from membership dues had to be sent to the national office in San Francisco, leading to charges of fiscal irregularities between the New York and San Francisco delegations. Conflicts over money and control led Hal Call, the head of the San Francisco office, to convince the Mattachine board to dissolve the national organization in 1961. Without the support of the national organization, the Boston and Denver chapters dissolved. The Philadelphia group underwent a restructuring and changed its name to the Janus Society. The New York Mattachine became an independent organization and retained its name despite Call's demands that it no longer be associated with the Mattachine Society.[21]

Freed from the constraints of the West Coast groups, the New York Mattachine embarked on a less "accommodationist" program. Changes in American politics and law had given many in the homophile movement hope that a more aggressive campaign could secure equal rights. Gays and lesbians saw how African-Americans had begun to assert their rights through the heroic and well-publicized civil rights movement. Starting in 1959, the Supreme Court began rendering decisions that limited the power of governmental authorities to censor films, books, and magazines that were previously deemed "obscene." Even *One* magazine successfully fought a U.S. Postal Service ban in the Supreme Court. Suddenly there was freedom of expression about sexuality in general. More importantly, such high-profile legal decisions gave many gays hope that government was no longer the force of zealous repression that it had once been. The 1960 election of John Kennedy, who was known to be a close friend of Gore Vidal, gave many homosexuals the feeling that a more socially liberal environment had taken over the halls of government while Kennedy's rhetoric of service and political participation galvanized masses of people, including many homosexuals, to become active in various civil rights causes.[22] The new political and social atmosphere was particularly inspiring to the East Coast homophile activists, who revived the call for recognition of homosexuals as a minority.

Although the New York Mattachine demanded minority rights for homosexuals, it rejected Henry Hay's vision of the Mattachine as a mass organization of homophiles focused on political action. In 1962 Curtis Dewees of the New York Mattachine offered a program for how the homophile movement could achieve their goals without enlisting masses of homosexuals. He looked to the Homosexual Reform Society of Great Britain, which had been the main gay organization behind Britain's decriminalization of consensual sex acts between adults. According to Dewees, the British organization "consisted of some of that country's most respected citizens. It was definitely not a group of organized homosexuals who pressed for legal reform." Dewees believed that "organized homosexuals" in Britain or the United States would only generate "indignation, horror, and a general demand to crush such a despicable monster." For a gay rights movement to work, it had to be led "by pillars of the community. . . . Strategically placed individuals can do more to change public opinion in the next decade than many times that number of persons picked at random from society." While the New Yorkers began enlisting "pillars of the community" in the homophile cause, Frank Kameny of the Washington, D.C., Mattachine Society began advocating more radical tactics.[23]

Frank Kameny grew up in a middle-class Jewish family in the Bronx. Toward the end of the Second World War he served in a mortar crew that saw fierce combat in Holland and Germany. After the war, he received a PhD in astronomy from Harvard and moved to Washington, D.C., where he taught briefly at Georgetown University. The U.S. Army Map Service hired him a year later and sent him to observatories

around the country to calculate the distances between points in the
United States and abroad so the military could target the interconti-
nental ballistic missile system.[24] Shortly after he joined the map service,
the Soviet Union launched *Sputnik,* the first space satellite. In the
United States, a widespread public outcry went up for a massive commitment of public resources to win the space race. Suddenly Kameny,
a Harvard-trained astronomer, found his skills and knowledge in great
demand. But two months later, his Army superiors discovered that
three years prior to entering the Map Service Kameny was arrested for
disorderly conduct in a San Francisco men's room. They noticed he did
not list the arrest on his job application and accused him of falsifying a
government document. When confronted with evidence of homosexual behavior, most federal workers of the time would have decided
to resign quietly. Frank Kameny, the combat veteran, chose to fight.[25]

Kameny charged the Army Map Service with discrimination before
the civil service commission and the federal courts. He based his case
on Donald Webster Cory's claim that homosexuals constituted a
minority like blacks and Jews. Therefore denial of security clearances to
homosexuals was a violation of minority rights.[26] After the civil service
commission rejected his appeal Kameny began looking for a new job in
his field, but without security clearance no one would hire him. While
surviving on handouts from the Salvation Army, he appealed to the
federal courts to redress his grievances as a member of a minority
group. When the Supreme Court rejected his final appeal, Kameny
concluded, "I felt I'd gone as far as I could go acting as an individual
and that the time had come to act through an organization." He
decided to start a homophile group in Washington, D.C., so he would
not have to wage his crusade for equal rights alone.

Kameny found a partner in his mission to create a new gay rights
group when he met a handsome twenty-two-year-old named Jack
Nichols. Nichols, like so many other homophile leaders, had been
introduced to the idea of a gay movement by Cory's *The Homosexual
in America:*

> Cory made a powerful case for self-esteem under the most
> grueling circumstances. He helped me to see poor self-
> images not as a product of homosexuality, but as the result

of the prejudices internalized. At that moment, I was determined to stand outside the condemning culture and, with the healthy pride of a teen, to claim my rightful place as an individual.[27]

After coming out to his friends at Bethesda-Chevy Chase High School in Maryland, Nichols gave each of them a copy of Cory's book. A couple of his friends indicated they were also gay while "the rest found the company of admitted homosexuals too interesting to disparage."[28]

One night in 1960, Nichols found himself alone and bored at a late-night party when he heard a voice rise above the din, saying, "Donald Webster Cory, who wrote *The Homosexual in America*, has made an excellent case for our rights." Nichols stood up from the couch and searched for the voice. He found a thin, balding man with an intense manner who introduced himself as Frank Kameny.[29] The two quickly became close friends and decided to form a chapter of the Mattachine Society in Washington.

In an attempt to counterbalance the West Coast Mattachine's power with another East Coast group, the New York Mattachine gave Kameny its mailing list for the Washington area. Sixteen men met at the Hay-Adams Hotel in late 1961 to form the Washington Mattachine with Kameny as its president. At the first meeting, someone noticed Lieutenant Louis Fouchette of the Washington Police Moral Division, an officer notorious for entrapping gay men in parks and theaters. When Kameny asked Fouchette to identify himself, the officer muttered something about being invited and shuffled out of the room.[30] Somehow the Washington, D.C., vice squad had got on the New York Mattachine Society's mailing list.[31]

Kameny's fledgling organization received much needed publicity when John Dowdy, a conservative Texas Congressman and chairman of the House District of Columbia Committee, introduced a 1963 bill that specifically sought to revoke the Mattachine's fund-raising permit in Washington, D.C. The bill also sought to prohibit the district commissioners from issuing permits to any group not deemed beneficial to "the health, welfare and morals" of the city. A year later Dowdy opposed the Civil Rights Act of 1964, which he labeled a "totalitarian" and "vicious bill" that "would destroy freedom for all of us and put shackles on liberty." One Texas state senator said of Dowdy, "He's against Negroes and queers and down here that's unbeatable."[32]

Kameny used the Congressional hearings on Dowdy's bill as an opportunity to defend and publicize the Washington Mattachine. In keeping with Cory's idea that homosexuals needed to speak publicly for themselves, Frank Kameny became the first openly gay person to testify before a Congressional committee.[33] In four hours of testimony spread over two days, he tried to explain the Mattachine's intention to protect homosexuals from discrimination. Dowdy, however, ignored questions about the legitimacy of the organization's work and focused on "perverts," "homosexual orgies," and a bizarre rumor of men gaining weight on "a diet of semen."[34] At one point, the Texan interrupted Kameny's testimony to add that "down in my country if you call a man a 'queer' or a 'fairy' the least you can expect is a black eye." When Kameny noted that Texas also had its share of homosexuals, Dowdy replied, "Maybe, but I never heard anyone brag about it."[35] Dowdy brushed aside the question of whether specifically targeting the Mattachine Society was unconstitutional by noting that Congress had passed laws designed to smite the Communist Party. "As far as I know all the security risks that have deserted the United States have been homosexuals. Do you place them on a higher plane than the Communists?"[36] Dowdy and Kameny may have been talking about the same subject, but they were speaking a different language. Dowdy spoke about homosexuality with the paranoid stereotypes of the 1950s. Kameny used the language of the 1960s: minority status and equal rights.[37]

After Dowdy's committee favorably reported the bill to the House, the ACLU reversed its policy of ignoring discrimination against homosexuals and sent telegrams urging the bill's defeat to one hundred Congressmen.[38] Nine representatives responded by issuing a minority report condemning Dowdy's bill as "ill-considered, unnecessary, unwise and unconstitutional."[39] In an editorial entitled "Legislating Morality" the *Washington Post* called Dowdy's legislation "a paragon of bad bills" that could not be passed "without abandoning the Constitution and as is very often the case, common sense as well."[40] The House passed an amended version of Dowdy's bill in August 1963 only to see it fail in the Senate.

Amazingly, Kameny and the Washington Mattachine emerged

victorious from the battle with Dowdy. Publicity surrounding the hearings bolstered the group's reputation in Washington, while homosexuals throughout the country discovered that rather than living in a monolithic, repressive society, they had allies in the Congress, in the legal and academic communities, and even in the media. Homophile groups nationwide were so thankful for Dowdy's failed crusade that they honored him at a national conference for being the public official "who has caused more attention to be called to the homosexual's problem than any one else."[41]

Kameny's experiences battling the government shaped the philosophy of the Washington Mattachine. As a PhD, he was not in awe of the wisdom of the experts. His group would fight their own battles.[42] As Kameny said on the issue of homosexuality, "we are the experts, we are the authorities."[43] While other Mattachine chapters sponsored debates by medical experts on causes and cures for homosexuality, the Washington Mattachine sent its members to educate straight audiences.

The Washington Mattachine focused its early energy almost entirely on Kameny's favorite cause, the discriminatory employment policies of the federal government.[44] The group wrote Congressional representatives, senators, Supreme Court justices, cabinet secretaries, and President Kennedy, requesting meetings to discuss their grievances. After only two liberal Congressmen, William Fitts Ryan of Manhattan and Robert Nix of Philadelphia, offered to meet with the Mattachine, Kameny knew he needed more allies.[45]

Taking his cue from Donald Webster Cory, Kameny worked to enlist the liberals. He appealed, in 1962, to the local chapter of the America Civil Liberties Union to join the crusade for employment rights. At first the ACLU leaders were "very queasy about the subject," Kameny recalled, but in 1964 they adopted a resolution that called upon the federal government to "end the policy of rejection of all homosexuals." That same year, the Washington ACLU also pressed its national organization to publicly denounce the criminal penalties against sexual behavior between consenting adults.[46] At Kameny's request, the ACLU took up the case of Bruce Scott, a Mattachine secretary who was refused employment by the Pentagon because of "convincing evidence of homosexual conduct." The homophile movement won its first victory in the fight against employment discrimination in 1965 when the

U.S. Court of Appeals ruled that the Pentagon's reasons for rejecting Scott were too vague.

Kameny's confidence as a leader swelled and his more aggressive approach evolved into a philosophical stance. He told the Washington Mattachine, "It is absolutely necessary to be prepared to take definite, unequivocal positions upon supposedly controversial matters. We should have a clear, explicit, consistent viewpoint and we should not be timid in presenting it." Kameny dismissed the "genteel, debating society approach" in which old guard homophiles felt "impelled to present impartially both or all sides." Polite, balanced appeals would do no good when "[o]ur opponents will do a fully adequate job of presenting their views, and will not return us the favor of presenting ours; we gain nothing in virtue by presenting theirs, and only provide the enemy . . . with ammunition to be used against us."

Kameny called upon the entire homophile movement to start consistently framing the issue of homosexual rights in terms of minority status:

> We cannot ask for our rights from a position of inferiority, or from a position, shall I say, as less than WHOLE human beings. . . . I do not see the NAACP and CORE worrying about which chromosome and gene produce a black skin, or about the possibility of bleaching a Negro. I do not see any great interest on the part of the B'nai B'rith Anti-Defamation League in the possibility of solving problems of anti-Semitism by converting Jews to Christians. . . . We are interested in obtaining rights for our respective minorities AS Negroes, AS Jews, and AS HOMOSEXUALS. Why we are Negroes, Jews or Homosexuals is totally irrelevant, and whether we can be changed to Whites, Christians, or heterosexuals is equally irrelevant.[47]

Kameny tried to convert the New York Mattachine members to his new style of activism by explaining the folly of relying "solely on an intellectually-directed program of information and education . . . to change well-entrenched, emotionally based attitudes. . . . The prejudiced mind is not penetrated by information, and is not educable." It had to be impressed by something more emotionally powerful. Kameny raised the example of the civil rights movement: "The Negro tried for 90 years to achieve his purposes by a program of information and education. His achievements in those 90 years, while by no means nil, were nothing compared to those of the past ten years, when he tried a vigorous civil liberties, social action approach." Kameny called for public gay rights protests that would draw media attention to anti-homosexual discrimination and inspire apolitical gays and indifferent straights to support the homophile movement.

Like Hal Call, Kameny began presenting his views on the gay rights movement to a wider audience through his own publication, *The Homosexual Citizen*, first printed in 1966. Kameny sent copies to President Lyndon Johnson, members of the U.S. Congress, the Supreme Court, and J. Edgar Hoover. Soon after the FBI director received his first copy, agents contacted Kameny and ordered him to remove Hoover from the mailing list. Kameny agreed on the condition that the FBI cease maintaining files on the Mattachine Society. The FBI did not respond to Kameny's offer, and Hoover continued to receive copies of *The Homosexual Citizen*.[48]

While Kameny was molding Donald Webster Cory's ideas into a new ideology and program for the homosexual rights movement, one of his friends, a New Yorker named Randy Wicker, began attacking one of Cory's favorite targets, the media. Wicker first learned about the homophile movement when he came across a copy of *One* as a student at the University of Texas in Austin. His interest in the civil rights struggle, which was generating headlines and news reports daily during his college years in the 1950s, convinced him that the media could be a powerful tool in the fight for gay rights. After graduation Wicker moved to New York in search of a vibrant, politically active gay community. Instead he encountered hostility among most gays to the homophile movement:

> I couldn't understand why every homosexual did not actively support gay groups. . . . I was belittled. "There's Miss Mattachine," they would say. They didn't want to hear about it. They would give you arguments: "We don't want people to know we [look like] everybody else. As long as

they think everyone's a screaming queen with eyelashes, we're safe. We're not suspected. We don't want publicity."[49]

Wicker realized that one of the impediments to homosexuals becoming gay rights activists was the ability to hide behind the camouflage of the gay stereotypes. Those who could pass as straight seemed to have nothing to gain and everything to lose by disclosing their sexuality. Wicker concluded that the only way to drag hidden homosexuals out of their complacency was by presenting nonstereotypical homosexuals to the public through the media. Images of serious, tough, politically savvy gays would counter the stereotypes and lift the camouflage that hid covert homosexuals. As news reports and broadcasts introduced straights to homosexuals who spoke, dressed, and looked like everyone else, there would be less squeamishness toward homosexuals and gay rights. Wicker offered his ideas on the use of media to the leadership of the New York Mattachine, but Curtis Dewees and his lover Al de Dion, who was the group's president, feared a well-publicized movement would generate an antigay backlash. Frustrated, Wicker dropped out of Mattachine and became a one-man organization called the Homosexual League of America.

Wicker launched his media campaign in April 1962 after hearing a group of psychiatrists discuss homosexuality on the radio. As the self-appointed public relations director of the Homosexual League of America, Wicker contacted the radio station and demanded equal time for a call-in show in which homosexuals offered their own ideas about themselves. When the station agreed, he found some willing gay participants and sent press releases to all of the New York media announcing the broadcast. Wicker's call-in program triggered a flurry of news articles. The *New York Times* pronounced the program "the first time that the subject had been presented on the air by homosexuals in this area."[50] *Newsweek* praised Wicker and the broadcast in a full-page story, while the *Times* followed with two positive reviews. After Jack O'Brien, a conservative columnist for the *New York Journal American*, condemned the broadcast and dismissed Wicker as an "arrogant card carrying swish," Wicker gratefully took a copy of O'Brien's column to the press desks of other publications and generated even more publicity. With his new media profile, Wicker was able to persuade the *Village Voice* to print a series of articles on gay life in Greenwich Village, including one article featuring himself and the homophile movement.

Wicker also convinced the editors of *Harper's Magazine* to run a story in the spring of 1963 about the New York gay scene and provided the *New York Post* with an inside look into homosexuality for a series on sex and the law. As the media began to present Wicker as a spokesperson of the homophile movement, he received invitations to speak at the American Humanist Association, the New York Ethical Culture Society, and Rutgers University. The *New York Times* ran a story about Wicker's appearance at the City College of New York, quoting him as saying, "we are only interested in educating the public, not in converting anyone to homosexuality. . . . Most homosexuals live fearful, ghettoized lives. The homosexual's biggest problem is the lack of adequate communication with others."[51] Newspaper articles spread Wicker's name around the country and letters of support poured in from as far away as Massachusetts, Illinois, Florida, and Oregon.

Kameny's and Wicker's noisy approach presented a serious challenge to the homophile old guard. While Kameny had abandoned the deferential attitude toward sympathetic experts and officials, Wicker's media campaign exposed aspects of gay subculture that belied the "respectable" image the old guard wanted to present. The two radicals acquired a forum to market their aggressive strategies to other East Coast homophiles in 1963 when Kameny organized the East Coast Homophile Organization (ECHO), a coalition of the MSNY, the Washington Mattachine, and the Janus Society of Philadelphia. A year later ECHO officially declared that homosexuals constituted "the second largest minority group" in the United States and therefore deserved federal protections against discrimination particularly in jobs.[52] While the old guard homophiles just wanted to be left alone by the government, homophile militants like Kameny and Wicker chose to enlist government in the struggle for equal rights. At ECHO meetings, activists learned of Kameny's new projects and Wicker's media blitz. Dick Leitsch and Julian Hodges of the New York Mattachine were soon consulting Kameny and Wicker on how to push their organization toward more aggressive positions and tactics.

ECHO conferences frequently hosted speakers who challenged the old guard positions, including the acceptance of the sickness diagnosis of homosexuality. One of the speakers at the second annual ECHO conference in 1965 was George Weinberg, a young straight psychologist. In a speech entitled "The Dangers of Psychoanalysis," Weinberg condemned his colleagues' use of scientifically suspect diagnoses of homosexuality as a sickness: "With the aid of pseudoscientific literature, superadded to our early cultural bias to loathe the homosexual, too many of us are able to take his time and money while treating him as deranged, without any evidence that he is." Throughout the 1960s, Weinberg continued to write books and articles attacking the medical community's approach to homosexuality. One gay journalist called him "the greatest ally we have ever had."[53]

One of the young radicals inspired by Weinberg's speech at the 1965 ECHO meeting was Barbara Gittings, founder and first president of the New York Daughters of Bilitis. Like most of her fellow activists, Gittings had been introduced to the gay rights movement by Cory's *The Homosexual in America*. She wrote to Cory, who informed her about the Mattachine Society, and later visited San Francisco, where the founders of the Daughters of Bilitis, Del Martin and Phyllis Lyon, "provided me with a much better sense of lesbianism and the lesbian community than I'd ever had before." She created a New York chapter of DOB in 1958 and held its presidency for three years until she became the editor of *The Ladder*. While attending an ECHO meeting in 1963, Gittings approached Kameny, whom she described as "the first gay person I met who took firm, uncompromising positions about homosexuality and homosexuals' right to be considered fully on a par with heterosexuals. He was more positive than any other gay activist on the scene."[54] Recalled Gittings, "Until I met Frank, I had only a muddled sense of what we could do as activists. Frank crystallized my thinking."[55] Soon she was using *The Ladder* to push the DOB toward Kameny's aggressive positions:[56] "I discovered the power of the press, the power to put in what you want in order to influence readers."[57]

Gittings expanded *The Ladder*'s political reportage and offered radical opinion pieces. *The Ladder* stopped urging readers to eschew "fly fronted pants" and "butch haircuts" in favor of more socially acceptable dresses and skirts. "Pants are proper!" the magazine informed readers in 1964. "This season you can wear pants absolutely anywhere—

which means dandy pants for town and fancy pants for evening. Combine with a champion swimmer hairdo sleeked back behind your ears and cropped coat." Gittings altered the cover of *The Ladder*, adding the subtitle *A Lesbian Review* to encourage lesbians to openly embrace their sexuality. "Adding those words to the cover," she later recalled, "helped our readers gain a new sense of identity and strength. That subtitle said, very eloquently I thought, that the word *lesbian* was no longer unspeakable." Gittings gradually altered the cover of *The Ladder* so that the title shrunk while the new subtitle grew larger. At the urging of her lover, Kay Lahusen, Gittings also replaced the abstract art and shadowy pictures that previously graced *The Ladder*'s covers with full-faced pictures of lesbians. Photos of lesbians were important, Gittings explained, because "heterosexuals, as well as many lesbians themselves, had weird ideas of what most lesbians looked like. We wanted to show everyone that lesbians were normal, happy, wholesome women—every mother's 'dream daughter.' "[58] Gittings's attempt to raise the visibility of lesbians alarmed the conservative DOB leadership, who dismissed her from the editorship in 1965. Free from the restrictions of the DOB, she and Lahusen became independent activists who fully embraced Kameny's approach to homosexual rights.[59]

By the mid-1960s, visible militants like Kameny, Nichols, Wicker, and Gittings presented a stark alterative to the homophile leaders who had taken over the gay rights movement a decade earlier. They rejected the need for sympathetic straight spokespeople, embraced the minority status of homosexuals, and used the media to spread their message. By incorporating the radical ideas of Donald Webster Cory into their ideology, the homophile radicals set the stage for the revolutionary rise of the gay liberation movement of the late 1960s and 1970s.

One strategy that Cory did not prescribe, the use of street protests, would prove to be the militant homophiles' most effective tactical contribution to the evolution of the gay rights movement. The occasion for the first homophile demonstration came in April 1965 when newspapers began reporting that the Cuban government was expelling homosexuals from the universities and packing many gays into labor camps. The Cuban newspaper *El Mundo* described homosexuality as a legacy of capitalism and declared that "the virility of our peasantry does

not permit that abominable vice. But in some of our cities, it is rampant." The Castro revolution therefore had to fight to eliminate
homosexuality from "our virile country which is locked in a fight for
life or death with Yankee imperialism. . . . No homosexuals represent
the revolution, which is a movement of he-men."[60] On one thing San-
tiago and Washington could agree: homosexuals were a threat to
national security. Jack Nichols's young lover, Army Lieutenant Lige
Clarke, became incensed by the reports from Cuba, and he convinced
Nichols to organize a protest to draw attention to Castro's oppression.
Since Cuba did not have diplomatic relations with the United States
and there was no Cuban embassy to picket in the nation's capital, the
Washington Mattachine decided to target the White House with the
rationale that the federal government also discriminated against homosexuals.[61] The evening before the protest, Lige Clarke returned home
from his job editing top secret messages at the Pentagon and began
hand-lettering signs that read: "Fifteen Million U.S. Homosexuals
Protest Federal Treatment" and "Cuba's Government Persecutes
Homosexuals. U.S. Government Beat Them to It." Lt. Clarke decided
not to participate in the demonstration out of fear he would be identified as a homosexual and dishonorably discharged. The next morning
he dropped off Jack Nichols and the signs near the White House and
drove off to his highly sensitive army post at the Pentagon.[62]

The seven men and three women who hoisted Clarke's signs and
marched in the picket outside the White House set the gay rights
movement on a bold new path. No longer would gay rights be
restricted to soliciting the support of sympathetic experts and waging
court battles. Over the next decade the gay rights movement would
strategically deploy press-worthy protests that would counter stereotypes and inspire homosexuals to join the cause.

Much to the disappointment of Kameny and Nichols, the initial
White House protest in April 1965 attracted little media attention.
Only the *Washington Afro-American* covered the event. They decided
to launch a series of better publicized protests at the Pentagon, the
State Department, and the Civil Service Commission followed by a
return visit to the White House, this time with more reporters. The
Mattachine Society laid down strict restrictions on the attire of pro-
testors to manage their image for the news media: "Picketing is not an

occasion for an assertion of personality, individuality, ego, rebellion, generalized non-conformity or anti-conformity." Smoking and talking on line were prohibited. To further emphasize the peaceful, law-abiding nature of the pickets, public statements always referred to gays and lesbians as "homosexual citizens." To maximize media attention, press releases announcing the pickets were hand-delivered to editors and TV news producers. At the protests, leaflets explaining the demonstrations were distributed to passersby, and after each demonstration more press releases announced the number of protestors.

By the end of the protest series, the Washington Mattachine had received coverage by all the major news wires and television networks. The protest at the State Department spurred a member of the Washington press corps to ask Secretary of State Dean Rusk during a press conference why homosexuals were barred from his department.[63] As media attention increased, the numbers of protestors grew. The Civil Service Commission picket in June 1965 drew twenty-five participants, and four months later the second White House protest attracted forty-five activists, some from as far away as Florida. One man who reluctantly joined the second White House protest became so moved by the event that he allowed himself to be interviewed on CBS-TV. Through his very public revelation, he later recalled, he "gained a little piece of his soul."[64] Lilli Vincez, editor of the *Homosexual Citizen*, described the importance of the media images generated by the well-dressed Mattachine protestors:

> People had no idea that homosexuals look just like everyone else. And we went out of our way to dress properly—skirt and stockings for the women, suits and ties for the men—so that no one could say we were disgusting rabble, the way they did about the anti-Vietnam protesters. We were well dressed and well groomed. So we defied all the myths. Pedestrians just stopped and stared at us. They were absolutely awe-struck.[65]

Many gays, however, reacted to the public presence of "normal looking" homosexual protestors with discomfort. Leroy Adams, a closeted reporter for the *Washington Post*, was listening to the police radio when he heard about the White House demonstration. "I thought they must be totally reckless or weird," he recalled years later. Suddenly homosexuals were threatening his compartmentalized life. "What does this have to do with me? I had my job, I had my gay life." Another homosexual who had been denied a State Department job in the 1950s said "we were alarmed by them. Wouldn't touch them with a ten-foot pole."[66] For closeted homosexuals, the militant gay heroes threatened the stereotypes and the silence that had helped so many avoid detection.

After the second White House protest, Kameny, Jack Nichols, Craig Rodwell of the New York Mattachine, and a few others celebrated over a late lunch in a coffee shop. As people began to express sadness that the protest series was over, Rodwell jumped in, "It doesn't have to be over!" He then proposed that the homophile movement stage a demonstration every Fourth of July in front of Independence Hall in Philadelphia. "We will create like a gay holiday. We can call it the Annual Reminder—the reminder that a group of Americans still don't have their basic rights to life, liberty, and the pursuit of happiness." The next year, thirty-nine well-dressed activists solemnly walked a picket outside Independence Hall to mark the first annual reminder. Coverage of the demonstration appeared on the local TV news and on the front page of the *Philadelphia Inquirer*. Every Fourth of July dozens of gay rights protestors continued to appear in front of Independence Hall until the Annual Reminder was superseded by the Stonewall commemorations of the 1970s.[67]

In addition to bringing direct action tactics to the homophile movement, the Washington Mattachine challenged the idea that homosexuality was a sickness. During his years battling the federal government for a security clearance, Frank Kameny learned that federal officials rarely raised the fear of blackmail when they justified their discrimination against homosexuals. Instead they cited the medical opinion of the psychiatric establishment that all gays were mentally unstable. When Kameny addressed the New York Mattachine Society in the summer of 1964, he declared the sickness diagnosis the main impediment to equality for homosexuals and demanded an aggressive effort to eliminate it. "The entire homophile movement is going to stand or fall upon the question of whether homosexuality is a sickness, and upon our taking a firm stand on it."[68]

Jack Nichols had been concerned with the sickness diagnosis of homosexuality ever since the day, during his teenage years, that his aunt called him "sick." For the first time, he had been directly branded with the label that had been stamped on homosexuals for decades. In response, Nichols tried to commit suicide by swallowing a fist full of aspirin. After recovering from a bad stomachache, he read everything he could about the subject of homosexuality and pathology and assembled psychological studies and news reports that challenged the diagnosis of homosexuality as a sickness.[69] Kameny encouraged Nichols to present his impassioned critique of the medical diagnosis to the executive board of the Washington Mattachine.

At Nichols's urging in 1965, the Washington Mattachine published the most radical statement on the sickness question yet issued by any homophile group: "The Mattachine Society of Washington takes the position that in the absence of valid evidence to the contrary, homosexuality is not a sickness, disturbance, or other pathology in any sense, but is merely a reference, orientation, or propensity, on par with, and not different in kind from, heterosexuality."[70] Leaders of other Mattachine groups such as Hal Call of San Francisco and Curtis Dewees of New York dismissed the Washington Mattachine's rejection of the sickness diagnosis as wrongheaded and dangerous.[71] The old guard hoped to achieve legal protections for homosexuals by enlisting medical and psychiatric experts who would argue that persecuting psychologically sick people was cruel, unjust, and impractical. The old guard thought a challenge to the medical diagnosis of homosexuality would push the homophile movement into an extraneous debate that would antagonize the few sympathetic medical authorities who supported the rights of "deviants." The sickness question struck at the heart of the divide between the homophile radicals and the old guard. Unlike debates about tactics or style, the sickness debate was a question of truth. There could be no compromise or grudging acceptance of a diversity of opinion; one side was right. One side would win.

The debate over the sickness designation had a great impact on the New York Mattachine's 1965 elections. For years the MSNY leadership had been hoping society would be more sympathetic to homosexuals if they were considered sick rather than criminal or sinful.[72] Al de Dion even published a letter in the *Washington Post* calling the Mattachine Society a "research organization working in the field of sexual deviation and to the protection of the *sexual deviates*' civil liberties"[73] (italics added). While the old guard New York homophiles offered to continue "helping the individual homosexual adjust to society," a group of radicals led by candidates Julian Hodges and Dick Leitsch rejected the idea that homosexuality was a sickness and promised to imitate Kameny's "program of militant action" if elected.

The MSNY old guard did not surrender without a fight. To add weight to their slate of candidates they enlisted the "Father of the Homophile Movement," Donald Webster Cory. Since publishing *The Homosexual in America* in 1951, Cory had reversed himself on a number of key issues. He now claimed in articles and speeches that homosexuals were indeed disturbed and in need of a cure. In the new preface for the 1959 edition of *The Homosexual in America*, Cory wrote that while he still thought homosexuals "should not be persecuted" he did "not mean that their way of life is a desirable or a mentally healthy one." He argued that "homosexuals and their friends have made a grave mistake in seeking to deny the psychological disturbances in order to fight the social cruelties." Cory also began to advocate sexual conversion therapy: "Change toward acceptance of the heterosexual life, rather than change toward suppression of the homosexual one, is aided by freedom from guilt and fear, and hence becomes far less difficult than I have anticipated in the original text. Inasmuch as this is a subjective study, I am happy to say that I found such change not only possible, but personally rewarding." After the Washington Mattachine passed its 1965 resolution declaring that homosexuality was not a sickness, Cory told Dick Leitsch that he would "quit the society" if the New York Mattachine ever passed a similar statement. In a letter to Cory, Kameny could not hide his contempt:

> You have left the mainstream for the backwaters . . . you have fallen by the wayside, lost most of your effectiveness . . . you have become no longer the vigorous Father of the Homophile Movement, to be revered, respected and listened

to, but the senile Grandfather of the Homophile Movement,
to be humored and tolerated at best; to be ignored and dis-
regarded usually; and to be ridiculed, at worst.[74]

Leitsch who was running for the vice presidency of the New York Mattachine, exploited the sickness issue during the election with a campaign flyer quoting Cory designating homosexuals as "disturbed
individuals" and "borderline psychotics." In 1965, such language was
offensive to the many homophiles who had come to embrace the radical ideas in Cory's *The Homosexual in America*.

Hodges and Leitsch trounced Cory and the old guard, winning
two-thirds of the vote. An elated Jack Nichols sent Dick Leitsch a letter
of congratulations: "It is very much a victory for all of us who are
working hard and who don't want to see the clock turned backwards
by the stick-in-the-muds and the 'sickniks.' " Cory also congratulated
the new vice president. "Well, Dick," Cory said, "they call me 'the
father of the homophile movement,' and homosexuals always turn on
their fathers, so I should have expected this."

Cory left the Mattachine and three years later aired his views on the
Mattachine in a book published under his real name, Edward Sagarin.
Reverting to his original name allowed Cory to write about the Mattachine Society and the homophile movement in the guise of an unbi-
ased social scientist. *Odd Man In: Societies of Deviants in America*,
presented a much different view of the homosexual and the homophile
movement than was to be found in *The Homosexual in America*. While
The Homosexual in America celebrated the gay identity, Cory's new
book described gay life as filled with "an extraordinary amount of male
prostitution and compulsive searching for partners . . . homosexual
pornography has a wide market; sexual interest in strangers, particularly adolescent strangers, knows hardly any bounds."[75] Homosexuality, according to Cory, was a psychological sickness, "not an 'equally
good' way of life; it is not 'on a par' with heterosexuality any more than
blindness, claustrophobia, and epilepsy are on a par with the absence
of these states."[76] Cory also criticized Frank Kameny's challenge to the
sickness model as an unscientific, dishonest ploy to attract members.

Cory's first book hoped for an America that valued the homosexual
minority for its contribution to the diversity and freedom of the nation.

His new book suggested that social acceptance of homosexuality might have devastating social effects on young people:

> What is not yet known is the effect on ambivalent young people of propaganda that maintains that the "gay" life is "just as good" or "on a par" with any other. Youths striving to find the sexual way are in a stage that may be called ambisexual or even pansexual. It is entirely possible that they can be influenced away from the normative path. To this Mattachine members privately shrug their shoulders. "So what?" they ask. "Why make a value judgment? Why isn't our way just as good?"[77]

Cory warned that if young people were not inhibited from homosexuality during the formative years they might increasingly choose homosexuality over family life. "Whether [homosexuality] can ever be or should be placed on par with heterosexuality, without endangering the continued existence of the family, is more than questionable."[78] A decade later, a conservative backlash against the gay rights movement would loudly echo the idea that social equality for homosexuals contributed to the breakdown of the American family.

While Cory underwent his metamorphosis into Edward Sagarin during the mid-1960s, the New York Mattachine Society embarked upon a more aggressive program under the new leadership of Hodges and Leitsch. MSNY president Hodges tried to generate publicity for the gay rights movement by inviting the press to a fully catered conference in a midtown hotel. The liquor bill alone exceeded MSNY's treasury. Hodges was convinced the conference would generate so much media attention that MSNY would be flooded with donations. Fully confident in his plan, he covered the expenses with his credit cards. When news reports failed to appear and donations did not arrive, he quietly passed his presidency to Dick Leitsch and skipped town, never to be heard from again.[79] A newcomer from the Kentucky horse country, Leitsch quickly learned to use his dark looks, sharp wit, and southern charm to disarm critics and dominate the New York gay rights movement.

In 1965, the same year Leitsch assumed the presidency of MSNY, John Lindsay won his first term as mayor of New York. Lindsay, the dashing liberal Congressman from the Upper East Side, epitomized cosmopolitan society. For many homosexuals, Lindsay's election held the promise of relief from the police harassment that reached absurd extremes under his predecessor, the devout Catholic Robert Wagner.[80] While Mayor Wagner maintained a policy of noninterference with police procedure during his three terms in office, Lindsay declared that *he* would have the final say in police affairs.[81] Leitsch hailed Lindsay's election as a harbinger of "hope for New York City to become a free and open society in which the rights of minority groups and the rights of those who are different will be protected and respected."[82] Shortly after taking office, Lindsay gravely disappointed Leitsch by approving a police sweep of Times Square in an attempt to remove what the *New York Times* called "honky tonks, promenading perverts, homosexuals, and prostitutes." The following month, the police waged a campaign against "undesirables" in Greenwich Village where they focused on the western edge of Washington Square Park, known to gays as the "meat rack."

Leitsch alerted the New York ACLU, which promptly called upon the police to cease "confusing deviant social behavior with criminal activity." Lindsay, "upset by complaints that his administration was acting illiberally," agreed to meet in a Bleecker Street restaurant with the local ACLU director, Dick Leitsch, and Beat poet Allen Ginsberg, who headed a committee of artists, writers, and coffeehouse owners opposed to the petty restrictions of the city's licensing department. Determined to demonstrate that he was not a "crack down, clean up mayor," Lindsey sipped a Bloody Mary and assured everyone that he opposed entrapment of homosexuals "in policy and in practice." When discussion turned to licensing of cabarets, Allen Ginsberg asked, "Is there anyone hip in the license department?" After Lindsay pointed to the only representative of the department at the meeting, Ginsberg pressed, "Is he hip?" Without skipping a beat, the mayor replied with a flat "No," and the whole place erupted in laughter. By the end of the meeting, Lindsay had charmed everyone. "It was a civil liberties happening, a great meeting," the executive director of the New York Civil Liberties Union gushed, "I've never seen anything like it."[83]

A week later, police commissioner Howard Leary issued orders that police officers could no longer entice homosexuals into breaking the law and were to make every effort to find a witness whenever an arrest involved sexual advances toward undercover detectives. Officially, the NYPD practice of entrapping homosexuals had ended. Leitsch told the

New York Times that Lindsay's order was "the best thing that ever happened. Most homosexuals like the Mayor and [police commissioner] Mr. Leary—they're tremendous men. We were taken aback when the big cleanup started in Greenwich Village and Times Square, but since then they've shown good faith. If things keep on this way, we'll vote 100 percent for Lindsay next time."[84] Leitsch discovered he could influence powerful liberals like Lindsay in polite, behind-the-scenes meetings. For Leitsch, securing rights for the homosexual community was just a matter of winning over the liberals with charm and votes.

Having won a ban on entrapment, the New York Mattachine Society turned its sights on the Mafia-controlled gay bars by challenging the legal restrictions on serving alcohol to homosexuals. Inspired by the Sit-Ins of the media-savvy heroes of the civil rights movement, Leitsch organized a "Sip In" on April 21, 1966. Leitsch, Craig Rodwell, and John Timmons invited reporters from the *New York Times*, the *New York Post*, and the *Village Voice* to observe them ordering drinks as announced homosexuals at the Ukrainian-American Village Restaurant in the East Village, an establishment infamous to many gay New Yorkers for the hand-lettered sign that hung above the bar, "If you are gay, Please Go Away." Leitsch figured his openly gay party would be refused service, and he could then bring a test case of discrimination to the State Liquor Authority. Someone, however, must have tipped off the restaurant because when Leitsch and his crew arrived, they found the place locked.

The group moved on to a Howard Johnson's known for its "cruisy" men's room in the basement. Before ordering drinks, Leitsch read a statement identifying himself and the others as homosexuals. The manager doubled over with laughter and asked, "How do I know you are homosexuals?" After having a waiter serve up three bourbons, the manager said he knew of no regulation against serving homosexuals and if it existed he did not agree with it. "I drink," he told the reporters, "and who's to say whether I'm a homosexual or not."

After downing the bourbon, the activists and the reporters proceeded up the block to the Waikiki Bar, where the manager assured them that he "would serve anybody, so longs as he doesn't annoy anybody." More drinks were poured. The "Sip In" seemed to be a washout. Leitsch wanted to demonstrate the absurd oppression of the state liquor laws, but instead he got good-humored service. From the

Waikiki, the group trundled two blocks down to Julius, a famous gay bar that had been temporarily closed the previous year by the State Liquor Authority for "permitting homosexuals to remain on the premises and conduct themselves in an offensive and indecent manner contrary to good morals." Julius had much more to lose than the other bars if the authorities learned that it again had served known homosexuals. When Leitsch walked in, he announced to the bartender, "We are homosexuals and we would like a drink." The bartender hesitated. "I don't know what you're trying to prove." Hoping for a confrontation, Leitsch asked, "You can't serve us if we are homosexuals?"[85] When the bartender sheepishly replied, "No, I think it's the law," Leitsch finally got his test case—in a gay bar of all places. Fellow activist John Simmons was even more relieved than Leitsch. "Another bourbon and water," he later recalled, "and I would have been under the table."[86]

The next day, the *New York Times* ran a story about the "Sip In," and Leitsch filed a discrimination complaint against Julius with the State Liquor Authority. Although the SLA refused to take any action against Julius for *refusing* to serve homosexuals, the New York City Commission on Human Rights said it would use its power to end such discrimination.[87] A month after the Sip In, the police commissioner announced his department would no longer hang "Raided Premises" signs on establishments after just one arrest or "on reasonable grounds for suspicion." Under the new guidelines, division commanders could designate an establishment as a "raided premises" only after three patrons were arrested leading to convictions for solicitation over a three-year period.[88] The next year, the New York State appellate court ruled in two separate cases that "substantial evidence of indecent behavior" was necessary to revoke the liquor licenses of gay bars. The SLA could no longer close a bar because two same-sex customers kissed or a gay patron solicited an undercover cop. Raids and bar closings became less frequent, and soon non-Mafia investors, who had previously shunned the gay bar scene because it was too risky, began to open legitimate establishments.

The mob, however, was making too much money to loosen its grip on the city's gay nightlife. After selling their holdings in gay bars to legitimate businessmen, the crime syndicates reinvested their money in private clubs immune from State Liquor Authority control. Private clubs enjoyed the same legal sanctuary as homes against police inspection without court warrants. Plainclothes detectives could not get past the bouncers to gather evidence that the courts needed to issue search warrants. Police found it difficult to act against any of the clubs' violations, including unlicensed liquor sales and prostitution. For an annual fee of one hundred dollars, club members in the Mafia joints had access to special rooms for assignations, leaving many homosexuals vulnerable to extortion schemes. (One of the new Mafia-run gay clubs was a divey joint on Sheridan Square called the Stonewall Inn.)[89]

Victories over City Hall and the federal government generated substantial publicity for the New York and Washington Mattachine Societies. Media attention attracted new members, but it also raised the stakes on future action. Some homophiles began to argue that since the media was watching, there needed to be centralized control over the various activist groups throughout the country. The homophile movement had finally acquired some bold, well-spoken, clean-cut heroes. If a group of reckless radicals suddenly stole the spotlight, the old stereotypes would be revived, and the movement might lose its tenuous support among liberals. According to a homophile named Foster Gunnison Jr., a national organization would prevent "fringe elements, beatniks, and other professional non-conformists" from becoming the center of the media's attention.

Paunchy, cigar smoking, and middle aged, Gunnison appeared to epitomize the staid, bourgeois Ozzie Nelson type. But below his frumpy attire and mellow demeanor there raged a fervent gay activist. Gunnison worked briefly for his father's construction firm in Florida until he acquired enough investments to become financially independent. He then devoted his time to pursuing two master's degrees in philosophy and singing in barbershop quartets. When he read Cory's *The Homosexual in America*, he discovered a new passion.[90] After attending an East Coast Homophile Organizations conference and talking to Nichols and Kameny, Gunnison concluded that the breakup of the Mattachine Society as a national organization was a mistake. He soon began delivering speeches to homophile audiences on the need for a national confederation of homophile groups that would coordinate their messages and efforts. At a homophile conference in San Francisco during the summer of 1966, Gunnison gave a keynote address in which he called for a national organization that would abandon the secrecy that allowed the image of homosexuals to be shaped by psychiatrists, news reporters, and comedians. As a political conservative, however, he warned against "flamboyant" direct action and "violating the law" that would bring discredit to the movement. "It won't be necessary to trot down to city square, climb up on the statue of General Sheridan, and wave a banner" to achieve equality. For Gunnison, the key to securing gay rights was organization, not direct action.

When the question of the national organization arose at the San Francisco conference, the assembly rejected the idea of a centrally controlled national organization and voted instead to create North American Conference of Homophile Organizations (NACHO), a confederation of groups in what Foster called "a sort of U.N.–type forum for ideas." One impediment to the creation of a national organization was the increasing influence of the women's movement on Del Martin and others from the Daughter of Bilitis who began to distrust the ability of the male homophiles to understand feminism and address the needs of lesbians. Another hindrance to homophile unity was Dick Leitsch's reluctance to surrender the power and autonomy of the New York Mattachine.[91] By the summer of 1966, Leitsch was confident in his new influence with the Lindsay administration. A mass organization, he reasoned, might alienate powerful, sympathetic liberals like the mayor. Leitsch decided that MSNY would remain aloof "as much as possible" from a national organization: "If this means MSNY is isolationist, so be it. I believe it is better to be alone and effective than to be part of an ineffective crowd."[92] Neither Leitsch nor Gunnison could have predicted how the next few years would render them both ineffective and irrelevant.

By the time the North American Conference of Homophile Organizations met at its annual conference in 1968, Leitsch, Kameny, and the other radical homophiles were brimming with confidence. After winning well-publicized battles against the U.S. Congress, the NYPD, and the New York State Liquor Authority, there seemed to be no limit to the progress that they would achieve. Meeting in Chicago just weeks after the tumultuous Democratic National Convention, the air hummed with revolution. As a way to force politicians to break the conspiracy of silence and make formal statements about homosexuality, the conference declared that all candidates for public office should be questioned about their views on sodomy laws. The conference also adopted a "Homosexual Bill of Rights" and urged local organizations to exert pressure on police officials, state legislatures, and the federal government to put it into effect. Among the rights were the legalization of private sex acts between consenting adults and lifting of bans on homosexuals from federal security clearances, visas, citizenship, military service, and employment.[93]

At Kameny's suggestion, the 1968 NACHO conference also adopted a new slogan for the gay rights movement. Inspired by Stokely Carmichael's "Black is Beautiful," Kameny realized that homosexuals, like blacks, needed a catchphrase to counter decades of negative news stories, jokes, and stereotypes. Kameny later recalled how "black" had previously been "universally equated with everything bad, undesirable, dirty, ugly, and otherwise negative in every way," while homosexuality was equated with perversion, sin, mental illness, and criminality.[94] After rejecting the use of "homosexual" in the new slogan as too clinical and abandoning "Gay is Great" as a bit of an overstatement, Kameny came up with "Gay is Good," a slogan that would soon frame the way a new generation of gays and straights saw homosexuality.[95]

chapter three

PRIDE OF LIONS

In May of 1967, Columbia University's undergraduate newspaper, the *Spectator*, published the following from a letter written by an anonymous student.

> In editorially condoning homosexuality, *Spectator* has lowered itself into a slime of degradation. Homosexualism and lesbianism are unnatural. . . . To say homosexuality is justifiable because humans engage in it, is to justify stealing, lying, murder and the like, because they too are tendencies of many people. Police records show that drug addiction and homosexual forms are invariably linked. Furthermore, homosexuals and lesbians believe theirs is a higher form of life, and they subtly teach their disgusting, repulsive habits to children, before the natural drives of the innocents can emerge. History repeatedly shows that any people adopting homosexuality soon becomes a conquered people.[1]

This bit of vitriol was prompted by the *Spectator*'s endorsement of the Student Homophile League (SHL), founded at Columbia University in 1966. Many opponents of SHL feared a homosexual group would corrupt the young men of Columbia and spread "homosexualism" like an epidemic throughout the campus. Despite fierce opposition from alumni, administrators, journalists, and even leaders of the homophile movement, SHL became the first gay student group to be officially recognized by an American university administration and quickly evolved into the first gay liberation organization in the United States.

If the liberation movement had a single founder, it was Bob Martin, a bright twenty-year-old whose primary interests were gay rights, sex, and the Navy. His father, the son of Italian and German immigrants, graduated from the U.S. Naval Academy in 1942 and served as a naval officer for twenty years. Robert Jr. described his father as a man who "frowned on display of emotion—control, duty and responsibility emphasized." Martin's mother, Lois, was "an English, Scottish Texan, artistic, free-spirited, emotional, impulsive," a woman who resented the frequent moving and rigidity of Navy life.[2] She divorced Robert's father in 1953 and abandoned their two sons, not contacting them again until 1964.[3] In 1956, when Martin was ten years old, his father remarried. Two years later, the young adolescent was sent to an elite boarding school in Berlin, where he began to engage in sexual activity with his male classmates.[4] After three years in Germany, Martin returned to the United States to attend high school in a New Jersey suburb where the precocious teen excelled academically and finished first in his graduating class of eight hundred. Ironically, he was a politically conservative youth who considered joining the Young Americans for Freedom (YAF) but was so uptight he first checked with J. Edgar Hoover by letter to inquire whether the YAF was

> a communist organization, communist subverted, or in danger of becoming either? I believe that YAF most definitely is not, but my parents will accept only your authority or a statement by some Congressional committee responsible or the Justice Dept. etc. By the way, I want you to know that millions of young Americans agree with your remarks to the women's press club in New York recently.[5]

Hoover sent Martin a note back praising his concern about communism and then opened an FBI file on the boy.

In the summer of 1965, Martin went to Florida to live with his mother after an eleven-year separation. When Lois discovered young Robert was having an affair with a Cuban man, she decided to punish her son by outing him in letters to her ex-husband and to Columbia University, which Martin had planned to attend in the fall. Assuming that his father would cut off financial support and that Columbia would refuse to enroll him, Martin ran away to New York City.[6] There, the young runaway soon encountered Julian Hodges, then president of the Mattachine Society of New York (MSNY) who provided a place to stay and introduced him to the New York gay scene and the homophile agenda.[7] Through Hodges, Martin met several leading members of the Mattachine Society, including Frank Kameny and Dick Leitsch. The young man later reminisced about his summer with Hodges, "I began gay life with instruction from a movement activist."[8] He was soon taking part in Mattachine meetings and making "a favorable first impression on the powers-that-be."[9]

In late August 1965, Martin decided to attempt to enroll at Columbia University despite his mother's disclosure of his homosexual activity to the administration. He had a social worker call the dean's office to ask whether Columbia would register a known homosexual. The administration took two weeks to respond to the unprecedented inquiry.[10] Martin later recalled that "when the decision came down it was this: the student would be allowed to register, on condition that he undergo psychotherapy and not attempt to seduce other students."[11] The administration's response reflected the commonly held view that homosexuality was a sickness spread by predatory homosexuals.[12] The administrators may not have realized the significance of the decision to accept this particular applicant, but Martin understood he was "a precedent case";[13] he was "the first officially recognized homosexual student to be tolerated."[14] Because he wanted to be openly bisexual yet did not want to injure the reputation of his father, who taught mathematics at Rider College in New Jersey, Martin adopted the pseudonym Stephen Donaldson.[15]

Martin's freshman year was difficult. To his great frustration, he could not find any other gay students or faculty members.[16] He began the year living with three other students in a dorm suite, but in December his roommates told the college dean David Truman that they felt uncomfortable living with a homosexual. The dean relocated

Martin to a single room in another dorm.[17] "This traumatic event," he later wrote, "was largely responsible for motivating me to form SHL."[18]

The origins of the Student Homophile League can be traced to the summer of 1966, when Martin began a relationship with Frank Kameny, who arranged a Congressional internship for the young man and provided a place to live in Washington, D.C. "Frank gave me a complete education both in homosexuality and in the homophile movement, instructing me also in how to respond to attacks from psychiatry, religion, the law, etc., etc. He largely shaped my gay ideology and continued to influence me even after I split with him ideologically in '68–'69."[19] In August 1966, Kameny took Martin to Fire Island's Cherry Grove, where Dick Leitsch, Hodges's successor as president of MSNY, had begun a protest movement against Suffolk County's policy of arresting men for "tricking" in the dunes.[20] While Leitsch was introducing the "the campy, boozing sensibility of the Grove" to political activism, Martin began a friendship with a Columbia senior, James Millham.[21] Martin was thrilled to meet another gay Columbia student and to learn that Millham lived with his lover, a New York University student, in one of Columbia's dormitories. When Martin returned to school in September, he, Millham, and five other students formed a small, supportive gay clique that they called "the family."[22]

Not long after school started, Martin and Millham had a conversation over coffee about the homophile movement. During the discussion, Martin began "thinking of my freshman year experiences (and lack of them)" and suggested that there needed to be a gay rights organization at Columbia.[23] Martin envisioned the club as a political group that would provide himself and gay students with access to a gay social life, which he lacked during his freshman year. He also hoped the student group would be the vanguard of a wider university gay rights movement that would reach across the United States.[24] He and Millham understood the importance of the "academy" for the Civil Rights movement and saw a national student homophile league as a means to involve straight intellectuals in the gay rights movement.[25]

Martin knew the administration could not expel him for being gay. Thanks to his meddlesome mother, it had already acknowledged and therefore tacitly accepted his sexuality. Martin was therefore free to take the lead in the creation of the group. " 'The family,' " Martin recalled, "supported the idea with varying degrees of enthusiasm and 'keep me out of it' and was finally won over with a promise of complete anonymity"—for the rest of them. Only he and Millham would be known to the Columbia authorities.[26] The reluctance of the other students to reveal even their pseudonyms might have stemmed from a rumor that circulated around the campus in the mid-1960s. According to the story, one evening a Columbia boy was peering through binoculars into the windows of an all-female Barnard College dormitory and happened to spy two young women having sex. He promptly reported the incident to administrators, who expelled the women and congratulated the Peeping Tom. In her memoir *Lavender Menace*, Karla Jay recalls how this rumor frightened her into posing as a heterosexual throughout her years at Barnard.[27]

Martin's public assumption of the gay rights cause was a by-product of his political transformation during his years at Columbia.[28] The boy who wrote a fan letter to J. Edgar Hoover became a young radical who experimented with marijuana and LSD.[29] While he was a self-proclaimed "full-fledged hippy-valued radical," who "was ordained in the psychedelic church," he refused to conform to the fashions of the counterculture and maintained both his short-cropped hair and passionate adoration for the Navy.[30] In 1966, he had his mother write to the Pentagon to ask if his homosexuality would prevent him from being able to enlist. The Navy's negative response was a "crushing blow," but he was "still determined to get in" one way or another.[31] Martin bought a sailor's uniform and spent countless evenings cruising the city in his white cap and tight bell-bottoms. He even went on an excursion to a naval base in Pensacola, Florida, where he pretended to be a serviceman and spent a night in the midshipmen's barracks. The next day he dressed in full flight gear and marched with a group of enlisted men. Unfortunately, an officer noticed him enjoying a carton of chocolate milk in the middle of the march and promptly had the impostor ejected from the base.[32] (Martin would once again experience the joys of Navy life when he officially enlisted after graduation in 1970.)

On October 30, 1966, Martin submitted a request to the university's Committee on Student Organizations (CSO) for official recognition of his "Student Homophile League." The CSO was composed of two students, a faculty member, and two administrators who were

responsible for granting recognition to university groups. The requirements for recognition were simple. An organization had to submit
copies of its bylaws, its constitution, and the names of four officers and
one regular member.[33] Martin and Millham were prepared to submit
their own names, but the other members of SHL refused to identify
themselves publicly because they feared being investigated by the
FBI.[34] After a long negotiation, the CSO agreed to a hearing on their
requests for both recognition and anonymity.

In a statement submitted to CSO on February 13, 1967, Martin
played to the liberals on the committee by citing Columbia's "noble tradition of granting freedom of speech, assembly and the press and its reputation as a liberal, tolerant and academically free institution."[35] He also
attempted to placate conservatives by promising that "no possible activities of SHL would infringe upon rights of others or the unimpeded functioning of the University." At a time of increasing student unrest over the
Vietnam War, such a promise was undoubtedly welcomed by the
Columbia administration. "Because we do not court public exposure of
our identity—such exposure would ruin our lives and our careers—we
have little interest in such activities as picketing. We will incite no riots,
block no doorways. We won't even show dirty films." Martin pledged
SHL's "activities [would be] primarily intellectual and educational rather
than activist." The group would not organize mass demonstrations or
confrontations; it would focus on "correspondence, academic research,
white papers, newsletters, and the like."[36] Martin concluded SHL's statement of purpose with a line typed in capital letters. "IT IS NOT THE
PURPOSE OF THIS SOCIETY TO ACT AS A SOCIAL GROUP OR
AGENCY OF PERSONAL INTRODUCTIONS."[37] By the spring of
1968 SHL had broken all of these promises.

The group's statement of purpose was not entirely nonconfronta-
tional. "The homosexual," it boldly asserted, "is being unjustly, inhu-
manly and savagely discriminated against by large segments of
American society. . . . The homosexual should feel free to declare himself as such without risking ostracism, expulsion from school or loss of
employment" and he should be permitted to "live free from unwel-
comed pressure to conform to the prevailing heterosexuality." Martin
envisioned SHL as a vehicle that would bring these rights to Columbia
and other universities.

While Martin waited for a response from the CSO, he sought advice on organizing SHL from Foster Gunnison, the driving force behind the creation of the North American Conference of Homophile Organization. Gunnison, a Columbia alumnus, was pleased to hear about a student group that would encourage gay students at his alma mater to embrace their sexuality. As a Columbia student in the 1930s, Gunnison was so uncomfortable with his sexuality that when he was propositioned by a fraternity brother he seized a mop and chased the young man from the room. Except for one sexual encounter in his forties, Gunnison reportedly maintained a life of celibacy.[38] When SHL was first initiated, Gunnison sent the administration a letter of support and made a cash contribution to the group.

Martin and Gunnison soon began an intense friendship that would last decades. Although the two could not have been more disparate— Gunnison the frumpy, middle-aged, cigar-smoking celibate; and Martin the Dionysus in a sailor suit—they wrote each other weekly. Martin became an important adviser to Gunnison on the organization of NACHO, while the elder activist guided the student through the founding of SHL. Gunnison even proposed a way to use the membership list requirement to "get the administration over a barrel" and force the university to recognize SHL.[39]

Martin mentioned to Gunnison that SHL might be able to convince nongay students and prominent campus leaders to become pro forma members as a way of asserting the civil liberties of all students. Gunnison suggested that Martin lead the administration to believe SHL would never be able to provide a membership list and then "get them to use this as their only excuse for turning [SHL] down." Gunnison figured that if the administration thought SHL could not submit the required names, recognition would be denied "purely based on the objective grounds of inability to meet the specified requirements rather than subjective concern over [SHL's] aims." Martin could then "hit them" with another application with the sympathizers' names. The administration would have no choice but to grant recognition.[40]

As Gunnison predicted, the Committee on Student Organizations withheld recognition because SHL would not provide names.[41] Undaunted by the refusal, Martin first obtained the ironclad assurance that if SHL submitted a list of students' names there would be no other barriers to recognition. He then convinced Dotson Rader, who later became a well-known writer, and John Ward, chairman of the College Citizenship Council, to submit their names as officers. After the Committee on Student Organizations confirmed that the names on the list belonged to students, the university vice president had no choice but to grant SHL official recognition as a student group.[42] Thanks to Gunnison's advice and Martin's maneuvering, on April 19, 1967, SHL became the first gay student organization to be officially recognized by an American university.

Martin had assured the administration that publicity would be kept to a minimum, but once recognition was granted he launched an aggressive public information campaign about SHL and homosexuality.[43] As a staff member of WKCR, the university's radio station, he made sure the morning broadcast mentioned SHL and he sent at least three press releases to several large newspapers, wire services, and magazines with national and international distribution.[44]

Martin's press releases were more than just announcements of SHL's recognition. One countered the stereotype of the effeminate homosexual: "Can't you tell homosexuals by the way they look? Certainly not. Only a small minority of homosexuals are in any way effeminate, but because these are highly visible, they form the public stereotype. The great majority pass as heterosexuals." Another press release attacked the sickness model of homosexuality that Frank Kameny and the Washington Mattachine had renounced the previous year.[45] In a third public statement, Martin called for the repeal of laws that prohibited homosexual acts, and the termination of government policies that abused the civil liberties of homosexuals. He cited the efforts of the federal government to support civil rights for blacks while the "same government hypocritically does its best to persecute the homosexual American citizen." The statement also condemned the government's practice of denying homosexuals security clearances and criticized military policies, such as forcing homosexuals to accept 4-F classification and discharging homosexual servicemen.[46] Martin understood the potential media attention that might result from Columbia's recognition of a homophile organization. In his wide-ranging press releases he attempted to use that attention to publicly contest antihomosexual stereotypes and discrimination outside of the university. In addition he wanted to challenge the more conservative approach of the older generation of gay rights activists. Martin later reflected on SHL's early statements on homosexuality:

> In our insistence on the "goodness" of gayness and the thoroughness of our application of this principle we worked out the basic principles and approaches of what came later to be known as "gay liberation," but a couple of years before Stonewall. These ideas filtered out into the rather conservative homophile movement and did much to pave the way to Stonewall. Any historian of the ideas of the gay movement who neglects the pioneering intellectual work of SHL has missed a key element of gay history.[47]

Whether SHL indeed "worked out the basic principles of gay liberation" or was the first organization to promote them publicly is debatable. But in either case, its formation and evolution over the subsequent two years mark the transition in the gay rights movement from homophile to gay liberation.

Despite Bob Martin's numerous press releases, the only media to report on the organization's recognition by the university were the *Columbia Spectator* and the radio station, WNEW.[48] SHL may have gone largely unnoticed if it had not been for Murray Schumach, a columnist and reporter for the *New York Times*. Schumach, who supported gay rights, happened to notice the *Spectator* article and decided to write a piece for the *Times*.[49] His article entitled "Columbia Charters Homosexual Group" appeared on the front page of the May 3, 1967, edition, two weeks after recognition was granted. Martin later recalled the importance of the *Times*' coverage:

> The world . . . ignored us for a week; then somebody at the *New York Times* saw the *Spectator* story and decided it was news, never mind that they had ignored my press release. A front-page story began with the headline: "Columbia Charters Homosexual Group." The *Times* decides what is news. That afternoon the *World Journal Tribune* did a big, sensational story. All the TV stations, radio stations suddenly

were doing stories, the next couple of days were frantic as
media which had all ignored the press release suddenly
wanted the information I had already given them. The story
spread abroad: incoming mail told us of an article in Paris'
Le Monde, various London papers and newspapers in Australia, Japan and other distant points.[50]

The dean of Columbia College, David Truman, also saw Schumach as the
key to SHL's unexpected fame, albeit in a very different light. He informed
one alumnus "the publicity was stimulated by the group itself and strengthened by a reporter who was determined to misread the facts."[51]

Schumach did more than just report the basic story of the recognition process. He related Martin's story of being kicked out of his
freshman dorm because of his homosexuality and he publicized SHL's
intentions to open chapters on other campuses such as Stanford University and the University of California, Berkley.[52] He even helpfully
quoted from SHL's declaration of principles: "The homosexual has a
fundamental right to live and to work with his fellow man as an equal
in their common quest for the betterment of human society. . . . The
homosexual has a fundamental human right to develop and achieve his
full potential and dignity as a human being and member of human
society." Schumach revealed his motive for promoting SHL in a piece
he wrote in the *New York Times* "Morals" column on May 5, 1967:
"When word got out last week that Columbia University had become
the first collegiate organization in the nation to issue a charter to an
organization seeking equal rights for homosexuals, it brought a few
rays of sunshine to the twilight world that alternates between the
furtive and the flagrant."[53] Like Martin, the *Times* reporter wanted to
confront the public with the issue of gay rights.[54] Columbia's recognition of SHL offered both men the opportunity to do so.

The Schumach article was sent via the *Times* wire service around the
country and became the basis for articles printed in a dozen other
newspapers. Condensed versions of the Schumach piece appeared in
Long Island's *Newsday* ("Homosexual Rights Backed at Columbia"),
in the *Chicago American* ("University Charters Homosexuals
Group"), and in the *Milwaukee Journal* ("Homosexual Rights Group
Gets Charter)." The *Chicago Sun Times* ran a UPI story ("More Units

Proposed by Homophile League"), while the *Gainesville Sun* placed the entire text of the sympathetic Schumach article under the incongruous headline "Student Group Seeks Rights for Deviates." The Schumach article had triggered a chain reaction in the American media. Without this *media trigger,* the founding of SHL would have had little consequence beyond the Columbia College student body.

Two newspapers outside New York interviewed administrators at their local universities about SHL. Under the headline "New York College Group Bomb to Trinity, UConn," the *Hartford Times* ran a story that repeated much of the information in the Schumach piece but in a negative light. The article reported the reactions of an administrator at one of the Connecticut universities: "This is like deciding what we would do if one of our students built an atom bomb. We would approach such an issue cautiously at all levels."[55] When asked if the University of Connecticut would form a SHL chapter, the university's dean of students said the administration "would have to investigate the legal purposes of it." Although the dean admitted the Connecticut student community of 11,000 "probably has its fair share of deviates," he believed most students would oppose the formation of a homophile league. "We would," he added, "try to get reaction from reliable student leaders if we had severe reservations ourselves."[56] The *San Francisco Chronicle* ran a story entitled "A Campus Society for Homosexuals," which specifically mentioned SHL's plan to open chapters at Stanford and the University of California at Berkley. The *Chronicle* quoted Berkeley's assistant dean of students, who said he "felt sure that such a group would be able to get a charter if it applied."[57] After reading articles in local newspapers, homosexual students at various other colleges and universities immediately began to contact Martin to inquire how they could form SHL chapters.[58] Once the media trigger was set off, Bob Martin's message hit his intended targets in universities all around the country.

Murray Schumach's *New York Times* report also triggered at least six different editorial writers from around the country to comment on SHL. Those editorials reveal some commonly held attitudes toward homosexuality. On May 10, the *Herald News* of Passaic, New Jersey, condemned recognition of SHL in an editorial titled "A Strange Thing Happened at Columbia." The *Herald News* described homosexuals as sexual predators who "hunt" innocent students: "In the minds of the Columbia authorities there may be no reason [to deny recognition] but it will be impossible to convince the public that no reason exists to withhold what amounts to a license to hunt on the campus."[59] An editorial on SHL in the *Christian Science Monitor* also exhibited the fear of solicitation: "There is a growing conviction among those who have studied the problem most closely that many persons become homosexual only through solicitation. Anything which makes such solicitation easier through lending it an air of social acceptability can only facilitate the spread of what is both a personal and social tragedy."[60] On top of the fear of solicitation, the *Christian Science Monitor* raised another objection. Officially sanctioning a homophile organization would release students from the guilt and shame that would and should discourage homosexual activity:

> It should be plain that in granting this charter (whatever its motive may have been in doing) Columbia has in the eyes of many students thrown a cloak of respectability and sanction over homosexuality which it did not have before. To a very considerable degree, an impressionable student could now be tempted to say: the university sees nothing wrong or harmful in this, why should I?[61]

Without sexual repression, according to the *Christian Science Monitor*, students might be tempted to experiment sexually and consequently become homosexuals.

Four editorials about SHL depicted homosexuality as a sickness. Keynon Roberts wrote in the *Los Angeles Daily Journal*, "One does not persecute sick people because they are sick, and on the medical and counseling level, homosexuality is an ailment to be treated as best we can like other ailments." An Indiana radio station declared, "In our opinion, this league is not a bona fide 'student' organization, because not a single member can ever have a sane mind in a sane body, unless he relinquishes his perversion, let's raise our voices in protest before it is too late."[62] The *Providence Journal* supported recognition but also viewed homosexuality as a sickness:

As with abortion, drug addiction, and alcoholism, homosexuality is no longer a taboo subject banned in polite discussion. Columbia's action recognizes this fact. By permitting the Student Homophile League to function as an approved campus organization, the University had tacitly condemned the social ostracism of persons who, most doctors agree, are suffering from an emotional affliction.[63]

Only one editorial questioned whether homosexuality was a disease. In the *Pittsburgh Post Gazette*, columnist Henry W. Pierce defended Columbia's action. Under the title, "Homosexuality—A Disease or Way of Life?," Pierce wrote, "these homosexuals [members of SHL] are asking that they be accepted much the way Republicans accept Democrats, doctors accept lawyers, and baseball fans accept stamp collectors. 'To each his own' is their cry. The homosexuals are asking that they not be thought of as 'sick' in any sense. They are asking to be thought of merely as people with rather special preferences."[64] Pierce reiterated the argument of gay rights activists who attributed the emotional pain of many homosexuals to society's discrimination rather than their sexual nature.[65] The recognition of SHL and the Schumach article provided the occasion for Pierce to challenge his readers to adopt a more tolerant view of homosexuality.

While Pierce's editorial was one of only a few that supported SHL, all the articles and editorials, negative or positive, wittingly or unwittingly, promoted gay liberation. Before Stonewall, gays in America existed in the eyes of the larger society as sinners, criminals, and lunatics. Morty Manford, who became a famous liberation activist in the early 1970s, recalled the turmoil he felt as a result of these popular conceptions of homosexuals:

> It was a personal civil war. I remember extremely intense mental activity all the time. The conflict was over trying to repress my homosexuality in order to conform to society's values. The whole society was telling us a homosexual was a flaky, vacuous, bizarre person. If you wanted to insult somebody, you accused him of being a faggot. The newspapers always referred to homosexuals and perverts as if they were

one and the same. The official line from psychiatrists was
that homosexuals were inherently sick. Homosexual acts
were illegal. People referred to homosexuality in terms of
sinfulness. This attitude was pervasive. People didn't realize
the impact such positions and attitudes had on gay men and
women. They affected the way you thought and lived, what
you felt, and how you thought of yourself. If you were gay
and you accepted those societal norms, then you were at war
with yourself.[66]

All the positive and negative news reports and editorials about SHL
countered the idea that homosexuals were "flaky, vacuous, bizarre"
people simply by offering a counterexample of gays who were politically active Ivy League students. And as Martin expected, homosexuals
who saw the articles were encouraged by the Columbia students' bold
assertion of rights.[67] Manford was a senior at Bayside High School in
Queens when he read Schumach's *New York Times* article. He had
been accepted to Columbia and was very excited to learn that there
was a gay group there. One of the first things he did upon arrival on
campus was call SHL from an off-campus phone booth. Two members
showed up at his dormitory and took Manford to a coffee shop, where
they convinced him to attend one of the meetings.[68]

Of course, not everyone who read about SHL was as enthusiastic as
Manford. Articles and editorials about SHL provoked alumni and concerned citizens to flood the Columbia administration with letters of
complaint. The vice president of the university, Lawrence Chamberlain, later told Martin, "the University received more mail over SHL
than any issue he had seen in his 20-odd years at Columbia."[69] Of the
thirty-eight letters in the Columbia University archives, only four supported SHL. An examination of the thirty-four negative letters that the
administration received in the month after recognition reveals
common fears about how a gay student group would affect the university.[70] Several of the letter writers feared members would "proselytize" homosexuality.[71] Dr. Bertram Selverstone, professor of
neurosurgery and neurosurgeon in chief at the Tufts University School
of Medicine, wrote to Columbia's president:

As you doubtless know, many homosexuals proselytize among students and other young people, and it seems to me unfortunate that they will now be given an opportunity to say that their activities have the imprimatur of Columbia University. I believe along with many others that the proselytizing activities of these unfortunate individuals leads a substantial number of otherwise normal young people into a way of life which must, in most cases, bring them a great deal of unhappiness.[72]

The fear of "proselytizing" arose from the commonly held theory that homosexuality was caused when a heterosexual youth was introduced to it at a sexually ambiguous age.[73] In an open letter printed in the *Columbia Spectator* on May 9, 1967, Anthony Philip, director of counseling services at Columbia, defined homosexuality and discussed its causes:

A person who is a "homosexual" is one who prefers homosexuality as a sexual way of life, and has engaged in overt homosexual activity habitually over a long period of time. The vast bulk of students who have homosexual concerns or may have had even a few overt homosexual experiences are young men at a particular developmental stage in their lives, who perhaps more so than others their age are troubled by questions of masculinity, sexuality and more generally with their sense of personal identity. If there is one thing such students can certainly do without, it is the mythology that they really are homosexuals whose "latent homosexuality" needs only to be "brought out" by the sympathetic, tutorial attention of the Student Homophile League.[74]

One anxious alumnus expressed a similar concern about giving students too much freedom to explore realms of their sexuality. In a letter to the university president, the alumnus argued that a homophile club would present sexually ambiguous youths with "temptations" and a "sympathetic," nonjudgmental atmosphere in which they would explore their "latent homosexuality."[75] The university, he argued, had the responsibility to stifle such sexual experimentation.

Many letter writers expressed the common view that homosexuality was a sickness.[76] Alumnus Dr. Bertram Selverstone wrote,

> It is still the opinion of a great many physicians that homosexuality is a mental disorder, and that the difference between homosexuals and heterosexuals is not simply analogous to that between Republicans and Democrats as the homosexuals would have us believe. Frankly I can find no more justification for a Student Homophile League than for a Student League of Schizophrenics or perhaps of Sadists.[77]

An anonymous letter reflects how even many homosexuals saw themselves as mentally ill:

> Would you also charter a leper group which sought status on your campus? Perhaps yes, judging from the recent performance. Your statement that you saw no reason is amazing, sir, amazing. Now perhaps a little shock is in store. I myself am a latent Homosexual, seeking to get rid of this loathsome thing. Your action makes me sick and very discouraged. I would urge you to reconsider this stupid action in the light of modern day psychiatric sanity.[78]

The comparison of SHL to a "leper group" was typical of how the view of homosexuality as a mental illness led to comparisons with physical sickness. In a letter to Kirk, another alumnus asserted, "Homosexuality is a thing which should be eliminated just as much as cancer or tuberculosis—or crime."[79] The stereotypical view of homosexuals as dangerous deviants who spread their sickness led some people to conclude that homosexuals not only needed to be cured, they should be quarantined, or "eliminated."

Obviously, alumni were concerned with the impact of SHL on Columbia's image, its recruitment of prospective students, and its fund-raising.[80] In a letter written to college dean David Truman, an alumnus expressed his opposition to recognition not because it was immoral or illegal but because it was bad for public relations.[81] The alumni's fears about the effect of the SHL controversy on fund-raising were legitimate.

Grayson Kirk received a note reporting that his office assistants were "getting some phone calls in the [fund-raising] Campaign office from alumni who [were] enraged by the 'homosexual bit.' And some of whom say they certainly will not now give any money to our cause."[82]

The articles, editorials, and letters infuriated and embarrassed the university president, Grayson Kirk.[83] The portly, pipe-smoking, sixty-three-year-old president of one of America's most prestigious universities grew up on a farm in Jeffersonville, Ohio: population eight hundred. As a young man, Kirk left a bucolic life and embarked upon a career in academics and government. During the Second World War, he headed the State Department's security section and in 1944 he served on the United States staff at the Dumbarton Oaks Conference. When Dwight Eisenhower left the presidency of Columbia to become President of the United States, Kirk took over and oversaw a $300 million increase in Columbia's endowment and the construction of more than a dozen buildings. For Kirk, SHL presented a serious challenge to the university's fund-raising and growth. Regarding SHL, he wrote to an alumnus, "There is far too much hostility toward established authority and resistance to accepted standards on American campuses today."[84] Kirk saw student radicals of all sexual orientations as a small group of nihilists who were intent on destroying the very institutions that enabled him, a farm boy from Jeffersonville, to become a distinguished university president living in Scarsdale. SHL made Kirk particularly uncomfortable because of his own feelings toward homosexuality. In a letter to an alumnus concerned about SHL, Kirk wrote:

> As a parent myself, I can understand why parents of prospective students might view the matriculation here of their sons and daughters with reluctance and I trust you will reassure them that they will find here no temptations not existing everywhere in contemporary society. No unpalatable or distasteful temptations have ever been encouraged on this campus and they will not be encouraged in the future.[85]

He exclaimed in another letter, "I agree wholly with the sentiments expressed by you and your fellow alumni and find this development personally distasteful and repugnant."[86]

Behind the scenes, Kirk asked Henry W. Proffitt, a member of the Columbia Board of Trustees and a partner in the law firm Thatcher, Proffitt, Prizer, Crawley & Wood, to investigate whether the New York State antisodomy law could be used to justify repealing recognition.[87] Proffitt found that the law designated anal intercourse and oral to genital contact as "acts against Nature," which were misdemeanors and in certain cases felonies even if they occurred between consenting adults. However, he informed the administration there was no proof that SHL members were committing sodomy, soliciting in public for the purpose of committing an immoral act, endangering the morals of minors, conspiring to commit misdemeanors, or engaging in any activity that openly "outrages public decency."[88] Proffitt concluded that membership in SHL was legal and could not be prevented by the administration. Reverend John Cannon, the university chaplain who had advised SHL, disclosed the nature of Proffitt's investigation to Martin, who was further radicalized by the administration's attempt to disband his group.[89]

Kirk and the other university administrators decided to counter the negative reaction to SHL with a coordinated public information campaign designed to distance the university from the student group.[90] Kirk personally sent a letter to the editor of the *Christian Science Monitor*. "May I emphasize that it is not the intent of the league—and surely not the intent of the University—to project an aura of sanction over homosexuality."[91] All the university's attempts to use publications like the *Christian Science Monitor* to disassociate itself from SHL, however, further fed the mini media frenzy that the Schumach article triggered.

Columbia College dean David Truman expressed his frustration with SHL in an interview with a *Spectator* reporter: "My personal view is that this is a quite unnecessary thing. It is highly unlikely that the sort of meeting activity that is usually the reason for the existence of such a group would not be available to them through existing organizations." Truman also said the extensive publicity " 'sure as hell won't help' the college fund drive, admissions or recruiting. The Dean stated that once Columbia receives bad publicity 'it can never catch up.' " When the *Spectator* reporter asked if Columbia could become "a Mecca for homosexual applicants," Truman declined to comment. "He also declined to conjecture on what the admissions office would do if faced with an applicant who had admittedly applied to Columbia because of the existence of the Homophile League."[92]

Truman's comments, in addition to Proffitt's investigation, incited Bob Martin, who responded to Truman in an open letter to the *Spectator*:

> In suggesting that we may have distorted to the press our relationship to the University, you have either made very serious charges without checking them, or you have deliberately sought to misrepresent the truth. We assume the former, but in either case something is seriously and inexcusably wrong. . . . In criticizing the extensive publicity which we have received—without stimulus on our part—in general media, you have engaged in a subtle attack on the principle of free propagation of ideas, a cornerstone of academic freedom. Such attacks do not become a responsible member of this University.[93]

Here was the outraged voice of a new generation of gay rights activists who would not be cowered by authority whether it was in the form of deans, politicians, or cops.

Thanks to newspaperman Murray Schumach, Martin's voice found a megaphone in the *New York Times*. The reporter submitted another article on SHL for the May 11, 1967, edition. Headlined "Criticism by Two Officials at Columbia Angers Leaders of Student Homophile League," the piece was largely based on Martin's open letter to the dean and quoted his statement that "the Dean's comments not only demonstrate anew the need for this organization, but also reveal again the irresponsible tendency of the Deans to stick their heads in the sand and try to ignore the problems we are raising."[94] The publicity generated by this second *New York Times* report on SHL now attracted the attention of Dick Leitsch and the leadership of the New York Mattachine Society.

Like Kirk and Truman, the board of the MSNY and its president, Dick Leitsch, resented the media attention that SHL had generated. Leitsch did not want to share the spotlight with another New York gay rights group, especially one led by unpredictable young radicals who might antagonize the movement's hard-won liberal supporters.

Immediately after Martin's strident criticism of the Columbia administration appeared in the *Times*, the MSNY board voted unanimously to have Leitsch contact Frank Hogan, the Manhattan District Attorney and a Member of the Columbia Board of Trustees, to advise him on how to undermine SHL.[95] Leitsch wrote Hogan a confidential letter suggesting how the university could quietly dissolve SHL: "For reasons I shall enumerate later, I want the group packed away, quietly and unobtrusively, without newspaper headlines." Leitsch warned Hogan, "If you oppose them under the law they will litigate, and you're the villain. If you oppose them on moral grounds, you'll look a fool with the churchmen against you. The only possible outcome of a public fight will be either the continuance of the group, as it is, but with more strength gained from having beaten down a District Attorney; or the end of the group, but strong opinion on their side."

Instead of publicly opposing the group "and thus giving them headlines and sympathy," Leitsch suggested Hogan wait until summer recess, "state [his] objections to the group at a trustee's meeting and swing a vote against the group. Thus come fall, a fait accompli, several months old, and no press interest."[96] After years of using the media for his own group's purposes, Leitsch understood its power. "Now, so close on the heels of the first news-break—and on the front page of the *Times* at that—you'd be bound to get too much press coverage."

In the letter, Leitsch claimed the reason for his opposition to SHL was Bob Martin himself.[97] The MSNY president wrote to Hogan:

> The man using the pseudonym Stephen Donaldson is known to me and to the Mattachine Society as an irresponsible, publicity-seeking member of an extremist political group. We have grave doubts as to his sincerity in his stated aim as helping homosexuals, and feel that he may be, instead, a bigoted extremist, interested upon wrecking the homophile movement. Our single experience with him was his attempted obstructionism of our Annual Business meeting last May, which almost led to our having to call the police to have him removed from the premises. A similar disruption had not been witnessed since the Nazi party attempted to disrupt a conference we sponsored in Washington, D.C.,

several years ago. Because of this irresponsibility, and his
alleged membership in a group well and widely known for
its animosity towards homosexuals, we fear that his intent
may be the ruination of the reforms we have achieved in
New York City—reforms which I am certain you, like all
reasonable men, consider valuable and needed.[98]

An investigation of Martin's personal papers, including his diary,
reveals no evidence of an affiliation with an antihomosexual group or
any exhibition of antihomosexual sentiment. The previous November,
Leitsch received a letter from Barbara Gittings and Frank Kameny, who
defended Martin from these rumors and criticisms. The two giants of
the homophile movement praised Martin for his tireless work on behalf
of gay rights and denied that he was a member of the John Birch
Society or sympathetic to it.[99] Foster Gunnison acknowledged that
Martin possessed "tendencies toward arbitrariness and manipulation"
but was "a sort of diamond in the rough."[100] Gunnison trusted him
enough to nominate him as his successor to the chair of the NACHO
Credentials Committee.

Leitsch's true motive for opposing SHL was his fear that Martin and
SHL would continue to attract media attention and emerge as rivals for
leadership of the gay rights movement in New York. After listing
Columbia's openness to homosexuals and Martin's antihomosexual
extremism as reasons for opposing SHL, Leitsch confided:

> Our third reason appears selfish, and probably is; however, I
> believe in it as a political necessity. A minority group speaks
> loudest if it speaks with a unified voice. The Negro move-
> ment is dead because it is so fragmented; the peace move-
> ment is ineffectual because there are more "leaders" than
> followers. I want our movement to avoid this pitfall, and to
> unify—preferably around MSNY. There are no campus
> problems at Columbia—to my knowledge—in the area of
> homosexuality. Thus there is no reason why any student
> interested in changing the sodomy law, ending police
> abuses, and fighting prejudice against homosexuals should
> not join MSNY and speak through our voice.[101]

Leitsch's reference to the fragmentation of the civil rights movement is significant. He thought the younger, more radical generation
of civil rights activists who had emerged in the mid-1960s had undermined the efforts of the older, more moderate leaders to appeal to liberal whites. Leitsch feared Martin and SHL would become his Stokely
Carmichael and SNCC, the radical civil rights organization that had
recently begun criticizing the more moderate positions of Martin
Luther King Jr. Just as Kameny, Hodges, and Leitsch replaced the old
guard homophile leaders in the early 1960s, Martin might contest
Leitsch's leadership in the late 1960s. Leitsch's concern about the
impact of the new generation of gay rights activists on his power and
influence would soon prove prophetic.

As Leitsch feared, Martin was not content to follow the leadership
of the Mattachine Society. He envisioned SHL as an "activist and militant" group that would promote its own ideology and philosophy.
Martin understood that members of his generation matured in a more
liberated atmosphere and consequently were more confident and optimistic than Leitsch's contemporaries: "Having escaped the struggles of
the past and seeing long futures ahead of them, students will want to
be in front of the movement with the issues of tomorrow, impatient
with those who are still fighting on the terms of yesterday's battles."
Like the young militants in the civil rights and feminist movements,
Martin and the new gay rights activists would not defer to their elders.
As he wrote, "we will not be content to sit back and let others inform
us of what the decisions are—we will be asking for a voice in these decisions, and asking loudly."[102] This new aggressive attitude was the
essence of gay liberation.

From the beginning, SHL assumed an activist and social character
rather than the "intellectual and educational" orientation that Martin
had emphasized in his appeal to the administration for recognition.
Martin and other members of SHL resented the antihomosexual sentiment of many people in the New Left so they crashed a major antiwar
march in Washington, D.C., and distributed thousands of leaflets that
"called the left to task for its anti-gay positions."[103] SHL also supported
a student campaign to rid Columbia of the NROTC. Martin submitted
an open letter in which he described the antihomosexual policies of the
Navy and questioned how the Columbia University could justify

allowing a discriminatory group to operate on campus. Discrimination in armed forces became one of SHL's primary objects of protest probably because of both Vietnam and Martin's fascination with the Navy.

SHL members also began to assert themselves as homosexuals in campus social life. To receive official university recognition, Martin had promised the administration that SHL would not be a social organization. But he and Millham began SHL partly because the campus lacked a gay social life. Martin kept his promise to the administration by organizing informal parties to which SHL members were coincidentally invited.[104] Members also attended parties in the student center and in dormitories where they danced together. At first the "Dance-Ins" created a sensation, but eventually men dancing together was accepted. Martin later crowed, "it was part of our consciousness raising effort as well as fun."[105] The integration of dances exposed other students to overt homosexuality and showed them that homosexuals were not predators or contagious. This exposure and integration was a major step toward students' acceptance of gays on campus.

Through Dance-Ins and its public profile, SHL inspired closeted students to come out. Homophile leaders saw coming out as a selfless act for the good of the movement and they rarely encouraged others to endure public exposure.[106] Martin saw coming out as a political act that had great personal benefit. He held regular office hours in the university chaplain's office, where he "did a lot of counseling mostly with students who were just 'coming out' (a process triggered by exposure to us in many cases)."[107] SHL became a consciousness-raising group in which participants shared experiences and began to see their difficulties, not as individual problems but as results of a shared oppression. Historian Neil Miller called such consciousness-raising groups "the building block of gay liberation."[108] Those who opposed SHL probably viewed the new openness of the gay Columbia students as confirmation of their fears that SHL would spread "homosexualism."

While SHL did not spread "homosexualism," it did drag the subject of homosexuality into the open on the campus. The Student Homophile League concluded its first official year of existence by inviting Frank Kameny to Columbia to lecture on "The Homosexual Dilemma: What Every Heterosexual Should Know."[109] Although SHL only had about fifteen to thirty members, nearly two hundred attended Kameny's lecture in the main Columbia University Library.[110] After the lecture, the standing-room-only audience enthusiastically applauded Kameny.[111] In the spring of 1968, SHL held "floor rap sessions" in the dormitories, where discussion leaders "exposed students to the fact fellow students might be gay."[112] SHL introduced heterosexuals on campus to facts about homosexuality to disabuse them of the stereotypes and fears that preclude acceptance. Later gay liberationist groups would try to do the same for the general public through mass media.

Martin advertised the new openness of gay life on campus in a statement he submitted to be included in the information packet for the incoming class of freshmen and their parents in the fall of 1968. The statement declared that "homosexuality was not a sickness but a way of life comparable in nature to heterosexuality; that the homosexual has a moral right, in our pluralistic society to be homosexual."[113] He concluded with a "Note to Homosexuals from Stephen Donaldson," aka Bob Martin.

> The homosexual student coming to Columbia will be relieved to know that the University does not discriminate against homosexuals. Those who feel themselves to be homosexual or bisexual or who are uncertain about their sexual orientation can expect sympathetic and confidential consideration from most of the religious counselors and the staff of the Columbia Counseling service, as well, as from S.H.L itself. We cannot at this time extend that statement to the College Dean's office.

Martin's note attracted the attention of top administrators, who swiftly removed it from the freshmen orientation materials.[114]

By 1968, Martin ambitiously spread SHL's influence within the larger gay rights movement. He represented SHL in the North American Conference of Homophile Organizations (NACHO), of which he became treasurer, chair of the credentials committee, chair of the committee on youth, head of the radical caucus, and secretary of the regional organization.[115] Of course Martin was never one to separate business from pleasure. During a NACHO conference, he seduced

Gunnison and interrupted the chairman's "decades-old celibacy."[116] Through Martin's participation in NACHO, SHL became a radicalizing force within the umbrella organization.[117] Richard Inman, founder of the Athenium Society of America, the first state-chartered homophile group in the South, feared Martin and the younger activists were "taking over the movement."[118]

Martin also began forming a national Student Homophile League after a student from the University of Hartford contacted him about forming an SHL chapter.[119] One weekend Martin hitchhiked up to Hartford to advise the new chapter on organizing.[120] He also formed contacts with students at Stanford, the University of Pittsburgh, Wayne State, City College of New York, and Monmouth College.[121] The writer Rita Mae Brown, then a student, founded a SHL chapter at NYU, and Martin convinced the chaplain at Stanford University and antiwar activist the Reverend Philip Berrigan at Cornell University to support the creation of SHL chapters on their campuses.[122] Martin had begun to realize the vision that he had shared with Millham over coffee in the spring of 1966; SHL had become "the first chapter of a spreading confederation of student homophile groups." As *The Stanford Daily* reported, "The Stanford group is part of a nationwide campus movement begun last May at Columbia University. Stanford's fledgling league hopes to charter a group similar to Columbia's."[123] In late 1968, the first non-SHL student gay group in the nation was established at the University of Minnesota. Martin later claimed the founder of the Minnesota group "was much influenced by the SHL literature I had sent him, and that he considered the SHL to be the true founder of 'Gay Liberation.' "

Martin wrote university president Grayson Kirk an ironic, slightly patronizing letter in February 1968 regarding the foundation of a Student Homophile League at Stanford.

> It may be of some relief to you that Columbia is no longer alone in having an active homophile organization on campus; we hope that before too long this will be commonplace and no longer a source of pressure for harassed administrators. For the problems that SHL's birth here have caused for you and the University, we are of course sorry

and sympathetic, but at the same time they are in a sense a tribute to Columbia's greatness.

Martin knew Kirk had enlisted legal advice on how to force SHL to disband. He must have enjoyed telling the university president that "before too long this will be commonplace." The letter continued,

> We would also like to give you credit for an increasing enlightenment in your public pronouncements on the subject of homosexuality. As the academic world was in the forefront of the struggle for equal rights for the Negro, so we hope the same intellectual elite will take up the effort to enlighten the public on homosexuality long before other elements of society are able to do so.[124]

By 1971 sixty American universities had officially recognized gay rights student organizations, and many more gay student groups existed without official recognition.[125]

While SHL was expanding its influence, the tumultuous atmosphere of 1968 and the psychedelic counterculture fueled its radicalization. Martin recalled "nobody who was at Columbia in the spring of 1968 can ever forget that year. In certain ways, the atmosphere in those days was a lot freer than it is now [in the 1980s] in respect to gay people. Experiments, including sexual deviations, were encouraged by the psychedelic culture, love and a benevolent attitude toward people with different lifestyles was part of the time."[126] On March 22, 1968, SHL announced new goals and activities including organizing social functions and picketing "programs with anti-homosexual points of view in order to show up the fallacies presented." The previous year, Martin assured the Columbia administration that "because we do not court public exposure of our identity—such exposure would ruin our lives and our careers—we have little interest in such activities as picketing." By 1968, Martin and SHL no longer limited their political activism or hid their social activity. The student group declared "being in the public eye and working with SHL enables our members to express their own personalities, to help their fellow human beings, to learn more about themselves and the gay subculture, to realize their own potentials and take pride in themselves."[127] Martin's determination to "take pride" personally can be seen in his refusal to use his pseudonym after 1968.[128] More than a year before Stonewall, he and SHL had begun to internalize and advocate "Gay Pride."

SHL also orchestrated the first ever demonstration against the psychiatric establishment and its diagnosis of homosexuality as a sickness. One day in the spring of 1968, Martin noticed advertisements for a panel discussion about homosexuality at the Columbia medical school. He and other members of SHL considered only one of the scheduled panelists to be "remotely favorable, all the others were psychiatrists known to be hostile" to homosexuals, so they decided to provide some balance "by showing up and asking pointed questions."[129] With the aid of Frank Kameny, SHL prepared a statement that asserted that the problems of the homosexual were not inherently medical.[130] "They are problems of prejudice and discrimination. These problems are not intrinsic to their homosexuality, but arise from the practical effects of society's attitudes toward them and from the damaged self-image and self-esteem arising therefore, and which usually accompanies the minority condition." SHL attacked the belief that homosexuals were heterosexuals who were converted during their sexual development.

> Despite what you may be told, little is known in regard to the causes of homosexuality, nor will it be known as long as it is looked at separately and out of context, from the viewpoint of something having gone "wrong." . . . In particular we wish to point out that the entire theory which alleges that homosexuality is some sort of "fixation" at an immature developmental state is a misrepresentation of a cultural artifact, unsupported by valid evidence.

The statement also called for the inclusion of the voices of gays in public discourse on homosexuality.

> In this setting it is obvious that heterosexuals alone can no more speak with authority upon homosexuality than can whites alone speak upon the plight of the Negro, or Christians alone upon anti-Semitism. We feel that the time has

passed for homosexuals to function as a mere passive battlefield, across which conflicting "authorities" parade and fight
out their questionable views, prejudices, and theories. We
intend, increasingly, to be participants in considerations of our
condition and in the disposition of our fate. It is time that talk
stopped being about us, and started being with us.[131]

SHL refused to rely on sympathetic heterosexuals to carry their argument in public discussions; these young gay liberation activists were
going to be heard. When the medical school administrators learned of
the planned protest, however, they announced that admission to the
conference would be restricted to medical students.

On the morning of April 23, 1968, members of SHL formed a
picket outside the forum. They handed their statement to medical students, several of whom stopped to read it and talk with SHL members.
A few students gave their tickets to the protestors. Martin recalled that
the Q&A after the discussion was "overwhelmingly on our side."[132]
"Flushed with success," SHL returned to campus, where they learned
students had taken over a university building and were holding the
dean of the college hostage. The 1968 Columbia student uprising had
begun.

A few weeks later Martin was elected to the university student
council. He later recalled that "since everyone on campus knew who I
was, I considered the election a triumph for non-discrimination."[133]
Martin used his position on the student council to promote the gay
rights agenda on campus. On March 19, 1969, he submitted a resolution condemning the "policy under which the Columbia University
chapter of NROTC discriminates against students with homosexual
tendencies, making them liable for less than honorable discharge." After
the student council approved the resolution, SHL sent the university
administration a letter demanding the abolishment of the campus
NROTC program because of the Navy's policy of discharging homosexuals. The letter warned the administration, "It is your responsibility
to end this injustice; we will be watching."[134] The university's decision
to shut down the NROTC program in the spring of 1969 stemmed
more from antiwar sentiment on campus than concern for the rights of
gays. But over the subsequent decades the university continued to

maintain the ban on NROTC purely because of the Navy's discriminatory policies toward homosexuals.

SHL issued four press releases in the spring of 1969 that exhibited a political radicalism that would define the new generation of gay activists. A statement written "on behalf of America's second largest minority," addressed the New York antisodomy law by appealing to members of the university community to support SHL's "efforts to end laws against acts in private with mutual consent."[135] Another statement criticized the federal government, especially the Defense Department, for not granting security clearances to homosexuals.[136] A third statement not only condemned the military for discharging discovered homosexuals but suggested how antihomosexual discrimination could be used to the advantage of someone interested in dodging the draft.[137] Before the foundation of the Gay Liberation Front, Martin and SHL had combined gay rights and antiwar activism.

At the close of the spring 1969 semester, SHL presented the administration with a bold memo titled "Our Demands." One of their demands was the creation of an Institute of Homosexual Studies that would offer "a wide program of studies of sex, sexual orientation, the gay subculture, and the relationships between the oppressed subculture and the majority heterosexual society." Not only did SHL promote gay studies before Stonewall, the group insisted "the institute should be controlled by a board having at least equal representation from the homosexual/bisexual and the heterosexual communities." The statement ended with a threat: "Should the University continue to ignore these demands as it has the requests of the past, you may be sure that the Columbia chapter of SHL will see to it that they cannot be ignored!"[138] Arthur Felson, a Columbia student and future member of the Gay Activists Alliance, later recalled SHL's change of character by the spring of 1969: "Something was happening. The lion was growing and learning. Columbia was teaching us something. It was teaching us to fight. It was teaching us not to be afraid. It was teaching us to hate."[139] Members of the SHL were both experiencing and promoting a new militancy that just a few months later would incite a revolutionary battle on an unlikely battlefield—a run-down gay dance club called the Stonewall Inn.

chapter four

FROM *BOYS IN THE BAND* TO
STREET FIGHTING MAN

An October 1969 *Time* magazine cover story on "The Homosexual in America" presented two conflicting images of "the homosexual." The article opened with a description of an exclusive San Francisco Halloween ball:

> In couturier gowns and elaborately confected masquerades: the couples will whisk around the floor until 2 A.M. while judges award prizes for the best costumes and the participants elect an "Empress." By then the swirling belles will sound more and more deep-voiced and in the early morning hours, dark stubble will sprout visibly through their Pan-Cake Makeup. The celebrators are all homosexuals.

Although *Time*'s depiction of the "swirling belles" evoked the effeminate stereotype, the article proceeded to offer readers a very different image from the previous June's Stonewall riot: "Hurling rocks and bottles and wielding a parking meter that had been wrenched out of the sidewalk, homosexuals rioted last summer in New York's Greenwich Village." The battle between the police and homosexuals outside the Stonewall Inn triggered many such news accounts that countered the stereotype of the "swirling" gay. The image of "the homosexual" in the popular imagination would never be the same.

The Stonewall riot occurred at a time of increasing public visibility for homosexuals. The 1969 *Time* cover story noted that "though they seem fairly bizarre to most Americans, homosexuals have never been so visible, vocal or closely scrutinized by research. They throw public parties, frequent exclusively 'gay' bars (70 in San Francisco alone) and figure sympathetically as the subjects of books, plays and films." As Donald Webster Cory had hoped, by the late 1960s the American mass media had been liberalized to the point that the subject of homosexuality was no longer taboo. Still, even the most sympathetic articles, plays, and films tended to reinforce the old stereotypes.

Typical of the new visibility was Mart Crowley's *Boys in the Band*, which opened on Broadway in 1968 and was made into a film in 1970. The action of the play takes place in a single evening at a birthday party attended by sharp, effeminate, depressed gay men. One character introduces himself with the line, "What I *am*, Michael, is a thirty-two-year-old, ugly, pocked-marked Jew fairy—and if it takes me a while to pull myself together and if I smoke a little grass before I can get up the nerve to show my face to the world, it's nobody's goddamn business but my own." The same character later snaps at the host, "You are a sad and pathetic man. You're a homosexual and you don't want to be. But there is nothing you can do to change it—not all your prayers to your god, not all the analysis you can buy in all the years you've got left to live." In its October cover story on homosexuality, *Time* magazine quoted from Crowley's play to support one of its many generalizations on homosexuals: "Homophile activists contend that there would be more happy homosexuals if society were more compassionate, still, for the time being at least; there is a savage ring of truth to the now famous line from *The Boys in the Band*: 'Show me a happy homosexual, and I'll show you a gay corpse.' "[1]

The legendary *New York Times* theater critic Clive Barnes pronounced *The Boys in the Band* "the frankest treatment of homosexuality I have ever seen on stage." It was also the first truly sympathetic depiction of homosexuals on Broadway.[2] Writing for the *Times*, Rex Reed called *Boys* a "breakthrough" because the gay characters "are human beings and, like human beings, they have fun too. They don't kill themselves or want to get married or spend the rest of their lives tortured by conscience. The only way they 'pay' is to know who they are."[3] The show was so popular that the black market traffic in tickets prompted the producers to double the price of seats in the first seven rows.[4]

Not everyone appreciated *Boys* however. Reviewing it for *Screw* magazine, Washington Mattachine veterans Jack Nichols and Lige Clarke called the play a "morbid collection of vomit-producing comments from a roomful of bitchy, guilt-ridden, self-pitying creeps."[5] While Rex Reed approved of how the play tried to evoke sympathy for the characters coming to terms with their sexuality, Nichols and Clarke saw no reason for sympathy. To them, being homosexual was something to be celebrated and enjoyed. Gay was good.

In 1968, the same year *Boys* opened on Broadway, Jack Nichols and Lige Clarke published the inaugural installment of "The Homosexual Citizen," in Al Goldstein's *Screw*, the first pornographic publication to feature full frontal shots of nude women and men. Goldstein, who wanted to celebrate and promote sexual liberation for everyone, hoped Nichols and Clarke would introduce *Screw*'s mostly straight audience to the gay rights movement. After rejecting Goldstein's suggestion that they title their column "Cornhole Corner," Clarke and Nichols settled on the much more dignified "Homosexual Citizen," taken from the Washington Mattachine newsletter of the same name.[6]

Placed within the pages of a straight porn monthly, the "Homosexual Citizen" reached a readership of 150,000. Although only a percentage of *Screw* "readers" actually read the column, their numbers still dwarfed the aggregate circulations of the homophile publications, *One, Mattachine Review,* and *The Ladder,* which may have reached 15,000 readers combined at their peak.[7]

Nichols and Clarke became the most celebrated and recognizable gay couple in America and a fixture on the New York scene.[8] Abandoning the suits and ties that the homophiles thought were essential to the image of the "normal" homosexual, Nichols and Clarke grew their hair long and donned beads and bell-bottom jeans. In the waning days of the movement's first wave, they embodied and voiced the attitudes and aspirations of gays who came of age in a less oppressive, more open society, thanks to American liberalism, the homophile movement, and the counterculture.

With their new media platform, Nichols and Clarke challenged how both gays and straights related to sexuality. They embraced the "hippie ethic" that they said countered the ideal of macho "masculinism." "A truly complete person," they argued, "is neither extremely masculine nor extremely feminine." They believed the sexual revolution would culminate when people embraced all aspects of their sexuality and abandoned the homosexual/heterosexual dichotomy.[9]

Nichols and Clarke understood how the counterculture had altered the American sexual landscape. Not coincidentally, at the same time that the homosexual was emerging into visibility, the white heterosexual masculine ideal was undergoing a metamorphosis. John Lennon, Bob Dylan, Mick Jagger, and Jim Morrison had become male role models and sex symbols who not only defied the traditional John Wayne type; they dismissed him as a flag-waving, uptight, prejudiced square. *You know something is happenin', but you don't know what it is, do you, Mr. Jones?* These new male role models were rail thin, long-haired poets who were clever, sensitive, and sensual. They had money, women, and power. Millions eagerly anticipated their next albums, next tours, next proclamations. They filled stadiums with thousands of screaming young men and women who worshiped them and held their lyrics as maxims for living. *All you need is love* and *It don't take a weatherman to know which way the wind blows.*

This major transformation of heterosexual "masculine" values had a huge impact on how Americans related to stereotypical notions of both masculinity and homosexuality. With the rock singer as sex object so firmly at the center of the culture, one man's passion for another did not seem quite so unnatural as it once did.[10] And if the straight male sex symbol was a strutting longhair covered in eye makeup, how could the stereotype of the effete homosexual carry the same stigma? *Girls will be boys and boys will be girls. It's a mixed up muddled up shook up world.*

Chicago '68 and Woodstock were just two events that generated media coverage dramatically displaying how far white American youth had moved from "straight" society in the 1960s. For the new generation of gays, the Stonewall Riot of 1969 was the event that displayed their own break with the past. Those homosexuals who battled the NYPD were not the passive, effete, vulnerable *Boys in the Band* looking for sympathy or a cure for their "sickness." The Stonewall rioters showed the world that gays too could follow the call of the Rolling Stones' "Street Fighting Man."

Ev'rywhere I hear the sound of marching, charging feet, boy 'cause summer's here and the time is right for fighting in the street, boy.

The Stonewall Inn was located on Christopher Street in two former horse stables that were renovated and merged into one building in 1930. A teahouse called Bonnie's Stone Wall opened on the ground floor and soon attracted a bohemian clientele who gravitated to the teahouses and cafés of Greenwich Village in the wake of the prohibition ban on serving alcohol in bars. By the 1940s the teahouse had evolved into the Stonewall Inn, a popular restaurant that frequently held wedding receptions and banquets. A fire in the 1960s gutted the building, leaving the ground floor vacant until a 420-pound mafioso named Fat Tony Lauria decided to open a "fag bar" in the space under the protection of the Genovese crime family. After covering over the charred walls of the restaurant with black paint, Fat Tony christened his new enterprise the Stonewall Inn, saving himself the further expense of replacing the rusting sign that hung above the entrance.[11]

When the new Stonewall Inn opened in 1967, the City's gay bar business underwent a dramatic change. The New York Appellate Court ruled in two separate cases that the State Liquor Authority could no longer shut down bars because they served homosexuals. The SLA now had to provide "substantial evidence of indecent behavior" to revoke the liquor licenses of gay bars. No longer were bars closed because same-sex customers were caught kissing or propositioning each other. Raids and bar closings became less frequent. Soon non-Mafia investors, who had previously avoided the gay bar scene because it was too risky, began to open legitimate establishments.

The mob sold off their holdings in gay bars to legitimate businessmen and reinvested their money in private clubs—premises that were beyond the regulatory reach of the State Liquor Authority. Private clubs enjoyed the same legal sanctuary from police inspection as did private homes. Judges would only issue warrants for police raids on clubs if the cops could make specific claims to unlawful activity.

Detectives, however, had trouble getting past the clubs' bouncers to gather evidence. Like most gay clubs, the Stonewall's heavy front door had a peephole to screen out investigators from customers. To maintain the ruse that the Stonewall was an actual club, customers paid a dollar admission fee, three dollars on the weekends, and signed a registration book. Few registered their real names. Some popular aliases were Donald Duck, Elizabeth Taylor, and Judy Garland.[12]

To further ensure that the club would not be raided by the authorities, Fat Tony paid about two thousand dollars per month to cops in the Sixth Precinct. To keep up the appearance of propriety, the local police staged occasional raids after forewarning the management. The "raids" would be scheduled early enough so the bar could reopen before crowds arrived. After paying three hundred dollars rent per month for the shabby space and giving a cut of the action to the local Mafia don, Fat Tony and his investors consistently cleared a handsome profit.[13] On an average weekend, the Stonewall raked in $11,000.[14]

The lack of official oversight enabled the Stonewall's owners to cut corners on everything from hygiene to fire safety. Because there was no running water behind the main bar, bar bartenders could not wash the glasses. When a patron was finished with a drink, the bartender would simply dip the glass in a vat of dingy water and then refill it for the next customer.[15] By the end of the night, the collective dregs had transformed the water into a gray murk.[16] Homophile activists who condemned the shabby conditions of the Mafia-run joints blamed the Stonewall's unhygienic practices for an outbreak of hepatitis among its customers.[17] Fat Tony also got away with dangerous fire code violations that made the Stonewall a potential firetrap. The club had no rear exit, so if there had been a fire on a weekend night, hundreds of customers would have had to escape through a single narrow passage leading to the front door.[18]

In addition to violating fire code and public health laws, the Mafia owners dealt drugs: everything from marijuana and LSD to Desbutol, a powerful combo of the upper Desoxyn and the sedative Nembutol; "smooth you out as it helps you up." Patron Vito Russo wrote that at the Stonewall "it was possible to buy any known substance available in capsule form."[19]

The lack of police oversight also freed transvestites from New York State laws against cross-dressing. While many transvestites and lesbians enjoyed the Stonewall's anarchic atmosphere, most of the bar's patrons were men in their upper teens and early twenties. The great attraction was certainly not the decor or the watered-down drinks. Young men came to the Stonewall to dance. The *Homosexual Handbook*, published in 1968, described the Stonewall scene: "The younger, more agile and more sensationally demi-dressed, jerk and bump on the rather large dance area at the end of the room. . . . Spotlights point directly down and they light the dancing youths dramatically." Because the State Liquor Authority still prohibited clubs from allowing people of the same sex to dance together, the bouncers would warn the dancers to desist whenever the cops approached the door by cutting off the music and flooding the dance floor with horribly bright light.

On most nights the Stonewall's door was controlled by Ed "The Skull" Murphy, a closeted Mafia minion who had been involved in the infamous Chickens and Bulls operation in the early 1960s. After Murphy escaped prison time by becoming a secret FBI informant, he found a job at the Stonewall. From his position as doorman, The Skull pushed drugs, leched after teenagers, and earned "tips" by "introducing" underage patrons to middle-aged Chicken Hawks. One night a coworker witnessed a kid handing Murphy a bag full of wallets that were presumably stolen from customers over the course of the evening.[20]

As in most Mafia-run joints, the Stonewall operators exploited the opportunity to blackmail successful older patrons. A staff member would strike up a conversation with a successful-looking man, learning his name and profession. If the mark worked in a law firm or stock brokerage, he was later blackmailed with the threat of being outed to his colleagues. The discovery of this operation led to the famous Stonewall raid on June 28, 1969.

Sometime in early 1969 INTERPOL, the UN-affiliated international police organization, noticed an unusual number of negotiable bonds surfacing in foreign countries and requested that the New York Police Department investigate whether they were counterfeit. Police detectives found that the Mafia had been acquiring large numbers of bonds by blackmailing gay employees of New York banks. From studying police reports on various gay clubs, investigators concluded that the extortion rings were operating in Greenwich Village. The Stonewall, the firetrap that lacked running water behind its bar, quickly became a prime suspect in a multimillion-dollar international criminal enterprise.

Police brass figured that breaking the blackmailing ring would require months of investigation and that in the meantime the extortion would continue. So why not just put the bar out of business? Knowing the relationship between the Sixth Precinct and the neighborhood gay bars, the commander of the NYPD's First Division assigned the task of shutting down the Stonewall to his Morals unit, which was in charge of crimes involving pornography, censorship, and gay bars. Cops from the corrupt Sixth Precinct were not to be directly involved in the raid on the Stonewall.[21]

The infamous Stonewall raid was not a routine shakedown or another one of the cops' "periodic harassment raids." It was part of a strategy to ruin a Mafia dive that was blackmailing gay patrons and defrauding banks out of millions of dollars.[22] Deputy Inspector Seymore Pine and Detective Charles Smythe of the Morals unit were given responsibility for accomplishing the worthy mission of shutting down the Stonewall.

On Tuesday June 24, 1969, Inspector Pine led a raid on the Stonewall, arresting the staff and confiscating the bar's liquor. To the customers and observers on the street outside, the bust seemed to be a routine raid by corrupt cops looking to squeeze the Mafia owners for more money. A twenty-six-year-old Ronnie Di Brienza recalled his feelings watching the Tuesday night bust:

> The establishment and their elite Gestapo, the pigs, have been running things too long. First you had the Negro riots a few years back, which woke up white cats like myself to the fact that, though I am white, I am just as much considered a nigger as the black man is. From those early battles came the more intense militant organizations who, like myself, are sick and tired of being niggers, and want to become real and human. We have reached the bottom of the oppressed minority barrel. . . . Gay people . . . too, have turned the other cheek once too often.[23]

Such frustration was shared by thousands of New York gays who had been harassed by the police over the years. This intense suspicion and anger was bound to explode eventually. Over the next three days according to Di Brienza, Village gays could be heard grumbling about the Tuesday night raid: "Predominantly, the theme was, 'This shit has got to stop!' "[24]

Inspector Pine's campaign against the Stonewall got off to a slow start. The day after the Tuesday night bust, the club was up and running as if nothing had happened. Pine decided that before the next raid, he would get a warrant not only to seize the alcohol but also to confiscate the vending equipment and cut up the bars.

At 1:20 A.M. on the morning of Saturday, June 28, 1969, Pine and Detective Smythe arrived in front of the Stonewall for a second raid with four plainclothes police officers from the Morals squad and two uniformed patrolmen. Only after they entered the bar did they notify the Sixth Precinct of their operation and request backup. Inside they joined two undercover female officers borrowed from the Chinatown Station. The female cops had two responsibilities. After getting past The Skull, they were to inconspicuously note all the violations that could be prosecuted. They were also needed after the bust to perform the odd task of examining the cross-dressers to separate the transvestites from the transsexuals. Transvestites, who had not had a sex change operation, would be arrested under the New York State law against cross-dressing. Transsexuals would be free to go.

The jukeboxes were silent and the lights were up even before Pine announced, "Police! We're taking over the place." Following the routine of a typical bar raid, the staff was quickly hustled into a backroom while customers were separated into two groups. Transvestites were to be "examined" in the bathroom while the other customers were lined up in front of the exit, waiting to be released after showing their IDs. The police also began ripping apart benches that ran along the wall of one of the rooms. Pine wanted to make it as difficult as possible to reopen the Stonewall even if a judge allowed the bar to resume operation. The surprisingly violent smashing of the benches heightened tensions that had hung in the air since the Tuesday night raid. As the customers lined up in the heavy June heat to show their identification, the officers faced an unusual amount of resistance. Usually gays in raided bars were only too happy to flash their identifications, many of them fake, and disappear. But that night was different. "We're not taking this," one patron barked, "I'm not showing you my ID!"

The transvestites were also in a cantankerous mood. Ordinarily they would just admit to the officers that they were cross-dressing and surrender to arrest, knowing they would be released after just a few hours in jail. But on this occasion they refused to play along with the humiliating routine of being "examined" in the bathroom. Pine recalled how "they were very noisy that night. Usually they would just sit there and not say a word, but now they're acting up: 'Get your hands off me! Don't touch me!' They wouldn't go in [to the bathroom], so it was a question of pushing them in, fighting them." Pine decided to avoid further conflict in the bar by just "taking everybody in" and sorting everything out at the precinct house. The officers collected the liquor and began releasing everyone except the bar staff and the troublesome transvestites.

The process of clearing out the customers who were not under arrest did not go smoothly. As the patrons were marched out of the club, the police assumed that as usual, they would disperse into the streets and head home, or to another bar. That night, the ejected customers stood in the street watching what the police would do next and talking to each other about raids that had been launched against Village gay bars over the previous weeks. Morty Manford, a nineteen-year-old from Queens who had been enjoying the night dancing in the Stonewall, also held his ground on the sidewalk. As he stood watching the cops ruin yet another evening, he thought to himself, "Damn, why do we have to put up with this shit?"[25]

As the crowd outside the Stonewall grew to about 150 strong, the scene began to resemble an Academy Award red carpet walk.[26] Patrons exiting the bar were greeted with cheers, some bowed; others threw their arms out in dramatic acceptance of the applause. Several camped it up for the crowd: "Have you seen Maxine? Where *is* my wife—I told her not to go far."[27] One witness recalled how "it became a show. Who's coming out, who's exiting? No one knew it, that it was going to turn to a riot. In everybody's mind all it was, was a bar raid. People were being kicked out of a bar, so there was going to be a little campiness, there's going to be stars coming out onto the street." A reporter from the underground newspaper *Rat* who stumbled across the hubbub recounted how the crowd began shouting for different people who were held inside. "We want Tommy, the blond drag queen!" When Tommy suddenly appeared, he was greeted with uproarious applause and cheers. He smiled and suddenly dashed for the crowd to escape the cops. Two officers gave chase until Tommy ducked into a cab and took off.[28]

The *Village Voice* also happened to have two reporters on the scene. Howard Smith was working late in the *Voice* offices, located down the street from the Stonewall, when he noticed the flashing lights of police cars and a massing crowd. He grabbed his press credentials and ran downstairs to see what was happening. At the same time, Lucian Truscott, a freelance writer who had done some reporting for the *Voice*, was having a drink at the Lion's Head, a straight bar two doors down from the Stonewall. Seeing a potential story, Truscott left the bar and took up position on top of a garbage can to better observe the show. "The stars were in their element," Truscott recounted for *Voice* readers. "Wrists were limp, hair was primped, and reactions to the applause were classic."

When a paddy wagon pulled up partly onto the sidewalk outside the Stonewall, the mood suddenly changed. A quiet descended upon the crowd like "the calm before a storm." Inspector Pine exited the building to ready the wagon for the bar staff and the few obstreperous patrons he had placed under arrest. When Pine surveyed the crowd, he realized something was amiss. The ejected customers had been joined by dozens of curious bystanders including tough street kids who hung out in Christopher Park opposite the Stonewall. "So many showed up immediately," he recalled, "it was as if a signal were given. And that was the unusual thing because usually, when we went to work, every-body disappeared. They were glad to get away. But this night was different. Instead of the homosexuals slinking off, they remained there, and their friends came, and it was a real meeting of homosexuals."[29]

As the police began to pack the bar staff and transvestites into the paddy wagon, the crowd booed and cracked jokes. "Lilly Law's got you now, honey!" But the good humor vanished when a police officer began shoving a transvestite who turned around and slammed the cop with his purse. Another officer rushed over and clubbed him with a nightstick. Moans and furious yells erupted from the crowd. One witness recalled, "People began beating the wagon, booing, trying to see who was being hauled out and off. Several pigs were on guard and periodically threatened the crowd unless they moved back. Impossible to do." One young man roared, "Nobody's going to fuck around with *me*. I ain't going to take this shit!" Pennies pinged against the side of the paddy wagon punctuated by the loud slam of a beer can.

The police next pushed a butch lesbian, kicking and cursing, out the door. Momentarily she broke free, trying to reach the crowd, but a cop grabbed her and threw her into a squad car. She emerged twice again from the car, but each time the police wrestled her back. The whole crowd went berserk. "Police brutality!" "Pigs!" "Up against the wall, faggots!" "Beat it off, pigs!"[30] A young Puerto Rican named Gino picked up a loose cobblestone and hurled it across Christopher Street at a squad car.[31] Bam! The riot had begun.

Pine ordered the paddy wagon to quickly drop off its load of prisoners at the precinct and "hurry back." When bottles began smashing against the front of the club, he ordered the officers on the street to retreat inside the bar and await reinforcements. "Let's get inside. Lock ourselves inside, it's safer." Noticing Howard Smith standing outside the door, Pine asked if the reporter wanted to join them. Smith feared the crowd might mistake him for an undercover detective and saw the opportunity to "be locked in with a few cops, just rapping and reviewing how they work."[32] He gratefully joined the frightened cops behind the Stonewall's heavy bolted doors that were originally designed with peepholes to keep the *police* out.

Once inside, the officers barricaded the doors with tables while the crowd, seeing the retreat, became even more aggressive. Someone grabbed a garbage can and hurled it through one of the Stonewall's windows. At the shattering of the glass, the crowd heaved a collective "Ooooh!" According to Morty Manford, smashing the window was "a dramatic gesture of defiance. . . . We had just been kicked and punched around by the police. They weren't doing this at heterosexual bars. And it's not my fault that the local bar is run by organized crime and is taking payoffs and doesn't have a liquor license." Manford likened the shattering of the glass to "the lancing of the festering wound of anger at this kind of unfair harassment and prejudice."[33] As the besieged police scrambled to board up the windows with plywood, they could

hear the pounding of bottles, bricks, and beer cans and anything else
the crowd could hurl. Someone even tried to rip the trash can out from
underneath *Voice* reporter Lucian Truscott.[34] Pine called the Sixth
Precinct again for reinforcements. Strangely, there was no response.

With a loud boom, the Stonewall's door crashed open followed by a
rain of beer cans and bottles. While Pine and his troops rushed over to
slam it shut, something hit one of the officers below the eye, cutting a
bloody gash. Seeing blood, Pine and three officers charged out to intimidate the crowd. When Pine saw a bearded man throw something, he
leapt into the melee, grabbed the guy around the waist, and dragged
him by the hair into the bar. The door banged shut as the frightened,
angry officers converged on Pine's prisoner, Dave Van Ronk, a well-
known folk singer who happened to be drinking at the Lion's Head
when he noticed the riot and decided to join in. The bleeding cop
started yelling, "So you're the one who hit me." Ignoring Van Ronk's
denials, the officer slapped the musician five or six times and then
punched him in the mouth. As Van Ronk passed out, the other officers
cuffed him. "All right," Pine muttered, "we book him for assault."[35]

Meanwhile, some in the crowd stuffed pieces of paper into cracks
at the bottom of the plywood sheets covering the window, and ignited
them with cigarette lighters. Several men ripped a parking meter from
the sidewalk and used it as a battering ram against the door. A witness
described how "the ramming continues; the boys back up to the park
fence, take a flying start, collide with the door as the crowd cheers
wildly. Cries of *We're the Pink Panthers!* A mad Negro queen whirls
like a dervish with a twisted piece of metal in her hand and breaks the
remaining windows. The doors begin to give." While the parking
meter-turned–battering ram pounded against the Stonewall's heavy
doors, Pine wondered, "Where the hell is the backup?"

Before he could put in another call to the Sixth Precinct, the plywood against one of the windows gave way. As the battering ram
pounded against the heavy door, all the officers reflexively took out
their service revolvers and made sure they were loaded. "We'll shoot
the first motherfucker who comes through the door!" one declared.
Even *Voice* reporter Howard Smith grabbed a weapon; a large wrench
he found behind the bar and jammed into his belt "like a scimitar."
Pine kept his cool, ordering his officers not to shoot. He later recalled:

You're so tense and it's the easiest thing in the world for a shot to go off at that time, and one shot going off will start everybody else off. That's what I feared, because the people were so close to us that there would have been people killed over nothing. The crime that we were arresting anybody for that night didn't warrant anybody losing their life for, and I was afraid that that's what was going to happen. I don't think there was anybody there who wasn't really perspiring—I mean really sweating—because it was touch and go.

Armed with his wrench, Howard Smith noted that "the sound filtering in doesn't suggest dancing faggots any more. It sounds like a powerful rage bent on vendetta."[36]

Adding to the anger, confusion, and cacophony outside was the fact that not all the bricks thrown at the police and their barricades hit the intended targets. One witness recalled, "it was like being in a war. People were crying. People were cut up. I mean people would throw bricks, but you didn't always hit a cop. Sometimes you'd hit another queen. So you didn't know when you saw someone cut, were they cut because the cop hit the guy or were they cut because of running or falling or what?" Just like in war, many of the causalities outside the Stonewall were due to "friendly fire."

The mob became even more frenzied when someone in the crowd lit a trash can full of paper and stuffed it through one of the bar's windows, setting the coatroom ablaze. Morty Manford later noted how "that night, the closet was set on fire both symbolically and literally."[37] A short, scrawny kid poured a can of lighter fluid through another broken window, followed by a match. Flames sprung up ten feet from Inspector Pine, who aimed his pistol point-blank at the frenzied arsonist and was close to pulling the trigger when he heard the sirens of fire trucks and squad cars. Backup was finally arriving.[38]

Cops from the Sixth Precinct cleared the area immediately outside the doors and freed Pine, Smith, and the others from the forty-five-minute siege. Pine ordered the officers to pack the transvestites who had been arrested into a waiting paddy wagon. But when the transvestites were brought out, the crowd, now fully confident in its power, intervened to prevent their departure. Just as it looked like the precinct cops might be overrun, two busloads of riot police arrived.

Equipped with helmets, shields, and billy clubs, the riot police lined up shoulder to shoulder like Roman legions and pushed their way down Christopher Street. Squaring off against one of their flying wedges was a brave, if foolish, group of street kids who formed a Rockette-style kick line while singing,

> We are the Stonewall girls,
> We wear our hair in curls.
> We wear no underwear:
> We show our pubic hairs.

The riot police charged into the kick line, smacking the singing youths with night sticks. Over the next hour, gay rioters dodged cops in the winding streets of the Village, setting fires in trash cans and breaking windows. One participant gleefully recalled his experience battling the police.

> I developed, in that first encounter, a sense of *street fighting* tactics, of how to harass and get away with it; of how to taunt and provoke a response and somehow try to not get hurt. And just years and years of all the resentments and humiliations and things that can come down on the head of a gay person were really—I was really experiencing liberation and radicalization and everything bang!, right then and there.[39] (Italics added.)

The Stonewall Riot was not only an explosion of resentment and frustration; it was a moment of reeducation. After years of being told by the media that gays were passive, vulnerable *Boys in the Band* types, suddenly gays, lesbians, and transvestites were *street fighting* with the NYPD.

While the riot had a huge impact on the several hundred who harassed the cops that night, more significant was the *media trigger* that was pulled, and the resulting reeducation that the media delivered over the subsequent weeks to the millions of homosexuals and straights, who read, saw, and heard news reports of the riot.

When the trouble first began, New York Mattachine Society activist Craig Rodwell, who lived around the corner from the Stonewall, called the *New York Post*, the *Daily News*, and the *New York Times* "because we wanted to make sure this got in the papers. I immediately knew this was the spark we had been awaiting for years." Within two days all the city's dailies ran short stories on the first night's riot, recounting basic facts such as how Pine's officers arrested thirteen people, including Van Ronk, for felonious assault of a police officer.[40] The articles also reported how four of New York's finest were injured in the battle, the worst injury being a broken wrist.[41] The *New York Post* described how homosexuals "shouting 'Gay Power' and 'We Want Freedom' laid siege to the tavern with an improvised battering ram, garbage cans, bottles and beer cans."[42] For the first time, readers were seeing news accounts of homosexuals who were tough and brave enough to intimidate, besiege, and injure the cops.

An hour after the riot police arrived, the turmoil died down. Dick Leitsch, who witnessed the riot, surmised that "after a while, everybody thought, 'Well this is boring. All we're doing is running around the block, here. We've done it ten times now and it's dull. Let's do something else.' So we sort of vanished." Leitsch noticed the streets around the Stonewall suddenly becoming empty, except for the cops. He looked up at the "terrific" full moon and listened to the Village become so eerily quiet, the only sound he heard was the crackling of the smoldering garbage cans.

The next morning as the Village streets were swept of broken glass and the Stonewall's windows were boarded up, word of the riot spread throughout the city and out to the Hamptons and Fire Island. Many who heard the news flocked to Christopher Street on Saturday afternoon to see what had happened. Slogans written in chalk appeared on the black wooden boards that covered up the Stonewall's broken windows: "Support Gay Power—C'mon in girls," "They want us to fight for our country. But they invade our rights," "Gay Prohibition Corrupts Cop$ Feeds Mafia." One witness recalled that many of the curious who surveyed the damage to the Stonewall bore incredulous looks on their faces that said, "I didn't think they/we had it in them/us."[43]

By early Saturday evening, hundreds of gays as well as straights

filled the streets around the Stonewall. Some were political radicals
who saw the previous night's riot as a sign that the gays were ready to
join "the revolution." Others were curious uptowners and "rough
street people who saw a chance for a little action." Everyone was
hoping for a little more of the previous night's excitement.[44]

Lucian Truscott reported in the *Voice* that on Saturday evening a
spontaneous rally formed in the small park opposite the Stonewall.
More interesting to Truscott than the content of the impromptu
speeches was the reaction of the crowd: "Hand-holding, kissing and
posing accented each of the cheers with a homosexual liberation that
had appeared only fleetingly on the street before." Truscott also noted
the older gay onlookers who had just returned from Fire Island standing
with "strained looks on their faces," talking "in concerned whispers as
they watched the up-and-coming generation take being gay and flaunt
it before the masses."[45] Truscott's juxtaposition of the bold new generation reveling in the attention as the older gays cringed at such openness was symptomatic of a major generational divide. Gays who made
their peace with the "conspiracy of silence" and used the stereotypes as
camouflage had long been suspicious and resentful of those who were
openly active in the homophile movement. Now they were seeing
homosexuals hand-holding, kissing, and rioting! Why draw attention
to homosexuality and "gay power" when one could succeed just fine
being in the closet at work and out in the bars? Why let straights in on
the secret that not all gays were passive fops or insane deviates and
blow the cover for those who wanted to remain in the closet?
Truscott's description of the older gays' reaction to the "posing" of the
new generation captured and disseminated the idea that the Stonewall
riot was a revolutionary break with the past.

One of those closeted onlookers in Christopher Park on Saturday
night was Dr. Harold Brown, former chief health officer of New York
City in the Lindsey administration. Brown recalled being drawn to the
loud uproar he heard from his Village apartment and seeing a mob of
mostly "limp wristed, shabby, or gaudy gays that send a shiver of dread
down the spines of homosexuals who hope to pass as straight. I could
not have felt more remote from them. And yet, at the same time, the
scene brought to mind every civil rights struggle I have ever witnessed
or participated in."[46] Brown's initial reaction on viewing the crowd that

hot Saturday night in 1969 was resentment and fear. (Like many who shared his initial feelings, however, he later appreciated the symbolic power of the Stonewall riots. Four years later, Brown would make a well-publicized announcement of his own homosexuality and become openly active in the gay rights movement.)

By eleven o'clock on the evening of Saturday the twenty-eighth, a couple of thousand were milling around chanting "Gay Power," "We Want Freedom Now," "Equality for Homosexuals," "Christopher Street belongs to the Queens!" and "Liberate Christopher Street." The atmosphere around Christopher Park took on the feeling of a political rally, attracting the curious and the angry. As the crowd grew into the thousands, it spilled into the streets. Cars and buses entering Christopher Street were stopped and rocked back and forth. When demonstrators jumped on the hood of one taxi, the driver became so enraged he got out and started swinging. About fifteen protestors jumped him while others hustled the passengers to safety. Another taxi driver was so frightened when his cab was manhandled by the crowd that he went into cardiac arrest. Realizing something was terribly wrong, Craig Rodwell convinced the mob to allow the taxi to escape onto Greenwich Avenue.[47] The cabdriver later died, becoming the only fatality of the Stonewall riots.

Police cars became the targets of the crowd's mounting aggression. A drag queen named Marsha Johnson climbed up a lamppost and dropped a bag containing something heavy onto a squad car's windshield. Three cops standing nearby grabbed a random bystander and dashed into the battered car. A large concrete block smashed the hood of another police car at the corner of Waverly and Christopher. The mob, stunned by the loud thud, at first froze and then surged forward, beating on the car with their fists and dancing on top of it. Dick Leitsch, writing for the *Los Angeles Advocate*, described how a patrol car chauffeuring a high-ranking police officer tried to inch through the crowd. Someone threw a bag of wet garbage through the car window, smacking the official in the face and splattering soggy coffee grounds all over the "pounds of gilt braid" that graced his shoulders.[48]

Like the night before, the local precinct police had once again lost control of the situation, and at 2:15 the riot police arrived. As helmeted officers massed on the corner of Seventh Avenue and

Christopher, their cars and vans were pelted with beer cans and rocks. Two angry cops dashed into the crowd, grabbing a random youth. As they dragged him back to a patrol wagon, they were joined by four officers who pounded the kid with nightsticks. Someone in the crowd yelled "Save our sister!" and a group of what Dick Leitsch described as "nelly" homosexuals surged forward and pulled the boy away from the cops. When the police tried to retrieve their prisoner, the protestors formed a human barricade, "letting the cops hit them with their sticks, rather than let them thru." As had happened the previous night, protestors again squared off against the riot police with a campy Rockettes kick line. Leitsch found it remarkable how, throughout the Stonewall upheaval, it was the more effeminate protestors who were "usually put down as 'sissies' or 'swishes' " who displayed the greatest courage in the face of police violence.[49] Ironically the gays who most resembled the image of the silly, passive fop were the ones who showed the world the fallacy of the stereotype.

The riot police once again began successfully clearing the streets with their flying wedges and nightsticks. In less than an hour, according to Truscott, they "had come and they had conquered."

Back at the station house, a member of the Mattachine Society locked in a holding cell overheard two officers discussing the riots. One officer enjoyed the fracas: "Them queers have a good sense of humor and really had a good time." The other disagreed: "Aw, they're sick. I like nigger riots better because there's more action, but you can't beat up a fairy. They ain't mean like the blacks; they're sick. But you can't hit a sick man."[50] In the subsequent weeks, press coverage of the Stonewall riot challenged the stereotypical notion that homosexuals were fragile, passive, and incapable of being "mean like the blacks."

In comparison to the scale of damage caused by other riots in New York City during the 1960s, the Stonewall riot was mild. One night in 1967, rioters in East Harlem looted an estimated twenty-five stores while snipers on rooftops shot at police and firefighters. The next year, after Martin Luther King was assassinated, hundreds of Harlem stores were sacked or vandalized, 77 people injured, 373 arrested. The Stonewall riot did not become a legendary event because of the amount of the physical damage, one smashed up storefront, or because of the numbers of arrests, less than two dozen. It quickly became legendary because the gay and straight press seized on the surprising fact that the rioters were homosexuals.

Bob Kohler who witnessed the upheaval recalled, "to me the riot was just like a carnival. . . . I didn't see any massive energy. I just saw a riot. I wasn't able to interpret it any further than that." But others did interpret the event. Kohler remembered in the week following the event, "people were running all over the streets with leaflets. Insane people . . . people talking about saving the Stonewall. The Stonewall was a dope drop and should have been bombed three years ago!"

Like the people with the leaflets, the press translated the significance of the riot to their readers. A week after the disturbances, both the *Daily News* and *Post* ran follow-up articles that reflected their political leanings. Under the headline "Homo Nest Raided, Queen Bees Are Stinging Mad," the conservative *Daily News* recounted how "queens" had "turned commandos and stood bra strap to bra strap against an invasion of the helmeted Tactical Patrol Force."[51] The liberal *New York Post* tried to explain the "gay anger behind the riots" by quoting twenty-two-year-old old Dick Kannon on how important the Stonewall was to gays: "It was the best place we ever had. Most gay people were extravagantly paranoid. If there was ever a place that cured that, it was the Stonewall. You felt safe among your own. You could come down around here without fear of being beaten up by some punk out to prove his masculinity to himself. Around here, we outnumber the punks." The *Post* also quoted participants on the significance of the riot. According to "the doorman" at the Stonewall Inn, "People are beginning to realize that no matter how 'nelly' or how 'fem' a homosexual is, you can only push them so far." A "19-year-old blonde with lacquered hair and lavender bellbottoms" told the *Post*, "All my life the cops have sneered and pointed at me and my friends. We've been harassed for doing nothing more than having our fun; not hurting anybody else. Well, the 'gay riots' mean we're not going to take it any more."[52] Less than ten days after the event, the *New York Post* was presenting the Stonewall upheaval as "the gay riots" in which homosexuals demonstrated that they were tough enough to defend the "best place we ever had" against police harassment.

More than any other "straight" publication, the *Village Voice* emphasized the social significance of what Howard Smith called the "gay power riots." The *Voice*'s coverage was criticized as "disdainful" of gays because of the use of demeaning words and phrases—"prancing," "forces of faggotry," "fag follies," "wrists were limp, hair was primped."[53] Although both *Voice* reporters defaulted to the old stereotypes, they also captured the bold aggression of the rioters. Reporting from inside the besieged Stonewall, Smith described the fear of the police officers struggling to maintain the barricades against the onslaught. Lucian Truscott called the Stonewall upheaval an "unprecedented protest . . . to assert presence, possibility, and pride until the early hours of Monday morning. 'I'm a faggot, and I'm proud of it!' 'Gay Power!'" Truscott described how a "show of force by the city's finery met the force of the city's finest. The result was a kind of liberation, as the gay brigade emerged from the bars, back rooms, and bedrooms of the Village and became street people." Truscott summed up his account of the riots by admonishing his readers to "Watch out. The liberation is under way." The *Voice*'s presentation of the riot as a historical turning point was so powerful that the first chronicler of the gay militants of the 1970s, Don Teal, speculated that Truscott's article "may have inadvertently initiated the gay liberation movement."[54]

Truscott's piece contained an anecdote that would become an essential part of the Stonewall lore. On the Sunday after the riot, the reporter bumped into Allen Ginsberg surveying the scene outside the Stonewall. After hearing everything that had happened on the two previous nights, Ginsberg exclaimed, "Gay power! Isn't that great! We're one of the largest minorities in the country—10 percent, you know. It's about time we did something to assert ourselves." Ginsberg went into the Stonewall, which the owners had reopened to display the extent of the damage. After "bouncing and dancing" for a while to the music on the jukebox, the poet headed for his Lower East Side home with Truscott in tow. Along the way, Ginsberg described the difference between gays of his generation and the ones he just saw in the Stonewall: "You know, the guys there were so beautiful—they've lost that wounded look that fags all had 10 years ago." In recounting Ginsberg's comment, Truscott remarked how "it was the first time I have heard that crowd described as beautiful." It was also the first time most *Voice* readers saw gays referred to as "beautiful" in print. Truscott ended his account of the riots with a description of the Beat legend waving from across Cooper Square, yelling "Defend the fairies!"

By the late 1960s Ginsberg had become the preeminent counter-cultural guru, or as Truscott put it, "the prophet of the new age." His comparison of gays in the 1950s to the beautiful men he saw in wake of the riot perfectly captured the idea that the Stonewall upheaval marked a generational divide. The stereotypically effete, passive homosexual of the past was being pushed aside by the tough, "beautiful," proud gay. Thanks to Truscott's report, Ginsberg's comments immediately became part of the Stonewall legend.[55]

The eruption of the Stonewall riot on the streets of the "media capital of the world" was key to the event's transformation into legend. The most detailed and influential accounts of the riots were written by *Voice* reporters who happened to be in the Village on the first night of the upheaval. Local coverage of the event in the city's dailies was followed by national media reports in *Time* and *Newsweek*. Had the first gay riot taken place in any other city, it would not have achieved legendary status so quickly.

Mainstream press coverage of the riot had a huge impact on gays and lesbians who had previously not understood their sexuality in political terms. Sue Sponnoble of Miami recalled:

> We weren't aware of gay activism. I had a sense that I have lived an oppressed life. . . . I had a sense that that was wrong, that it shouldn't have to be like that. I had a sense that there should be a "struggle," but I wasn't sure how to form it. Reading that article with Georgia [her partner], I realized that there were other people like us. The sense of joy we felt when we read that article![56]

Eighteen-year-old college freshman Michael Weyand was electrified by news of the riot. After years of "not owning up to who I was and hoping I would get over it," he suddenly saw "these people were like me" and decided that he too would come out. When Ethan Geto read newspaper accounts of the Stonewall riots, he was a closeted married man working as a political adviser to Bronx borough president Robert Abrams. Geto, who would go on to become one of the most important gay rights activists of the 1970s, had previously regarded his sexual attraction to men as a "personality quirk" rather than as an identity. "Gays" or "homosexuals" to him were effete aesthetes or self-absorbed deviants. He was a street-smart operative in the rough-and-tumble world of New York City politics. As Geto read the articles explaining how the Stonewall riots were a response to the oppression of homosexuals, he realized that gays were a minority just like blacks and Hispanics. Geto was a fervent liberal who believed in defending and expanding the rights of "minorities"; now he suddenly realized: "Wow, I too was a minority, I was 'A Homosexual!' "[57]

The first openly gay writers to publish a reaction to the Stonewall riot were movement veterans Jack Nichols and Lige Clarke, writing in the July 1969 issue of *Screw*:

> A new generation is angered by the raids and harassment of gay bars, and last week's riots in Greenwich Village have set standards for the rest of the nation's homosexuals to follow. . . . The Sheridan Square Riot showed the world that homosexuals will no longer take a beating without a good fight. The police were scared shitless and the massive crowds of angry protestors chased them for blocks screaming, "Catch them! Fuck them!" There was a shrill, righteous indignation in the air. Homosexuals had endured such raids and harassment long enough. It was time to take a stand.

Clarke and Nichols saw the Stonewall riot as marking a new phase in the struggle for gay rights that would "carry the sexual revolt triumphantly into the councils of the U.S. government, into the antihomosexual churches, into the offices of antihomosexual psychiatrists, into the city government and into the state legislatures which make our manner of love-making a crime."[58] The San Francisco-based *Gay Sunshine*, one of the new radical newspapers to emerge in the wake of the riots, agreed that after Stonewall, "It is time to move on and the ground rules and basic assumptions of the gay rights movement are no longer acceptable."[59]

Following the Stonewall riot, young activists in New York "moved on" from the Mattachine Society and the Daughters of Bilitis to form two new gay rights organizations: the Gay Liberation Front and later the Gay Activists Alliance. While the two organizations had major ideological and tactical disagreements, their aggressive style and goals came to characterize what was called the gay liberation movement. Gay liberation sought to surpass the limited goals of the homophile movement, such as securing the right to drink in gay bars or to work for the government. Gay liberationists wanted to transform how homosexuals and straights related to their sexuality. They encouraged all gay people to come out proudly to their families, friends, and co-workers. They refused to negotiate quietly with politicians to secure liberal policies toward gays. Instead they pressured politicians to proclaim open support for gay rights.

Having turned a profit with *Screw*, Al Goldstein exploited the interest in gay politics that Stonewall sparked by launching *GAY*, a newspaper edited by Jack Nichols and Lige Clarke. Lilli Vincenz, who had edited the Washington Mattachine's *Homosexual Citizen*, wrote a lesbian-oriented column for the new publication. According to Vincenz, *GAY* was "the newspaper of the day. If you were gay and you wanted to find out what was going on in the world, you turned to *GAY*." Twenty-thousand people bought the first issue, and within a month, circulation reached twenty-five thousand, surpassing the figure the *Advocate* had taken two years to reach.

GAY reveled in the way the counterculture and the sexual revolution blurred the line between gay and straight and offered new possibilities for the gay rights movement. A photo of Mick Jagger wearing lipstick and eye liner appeared on the cover of the second issue. In an inquiry titled "What Makes Mick Mighty?" *GAY* speculated that both homosexuals and straights were drawn to the rock singer's androgynous sexuality:

> He's not a he-man and he's certainly not a woman, even though he has the propensity for appearing in drag and looks as cheap and tawdry as he possibly can. He is one of the world's great exhibitionists. He likes to flounce about; he likes to capitalize on his pouty brand of good looks, he likes to make the most of his incredibly obvious sexuality. He is a true star, he is Mick Jagger and he is now in New York.

The article concluded that Jagger's popularity was due to his ability "to be all sexes to all people."[60] By transcending strict sexual categories, that is, gay versus straight, male versus female, Jagger not only expanded his audience, he showed them new possibilities for how they related to their own sexuality.

By the end of 1969, *GAY* had the largest readership in the history of the gay and lesbian press. Its high circulation numbers attracted ad revenue from businesses looking to advertise to gay and lesbian readers. Within six months, *GAY* was so profitable that it was released weekly, becoming the first homosexual-run publication to appear with such frequency.[61]

The political significance that the media and activist groups attributed to the Stonewall raid did not sidetrack NYPD inspector Seymore Pine from his quest to shut down illegal gay bars. In March 1970, Pine raided the Zodiac and 17 Barrow Street, followed by the Snake Pit, an after-hours joint that opened at midnight and closed around eight in the morning. When Pine and his detectives arrived at the Snake Pit around five, they found two hundred men packed into a small dark basement that comfortably held fifty. As Pine cleared the bar, he noticed the customers did not disperse but began to gather on the street. Pine had a flashback to the Stonewall riots nine months before: "We can't take gay people for granted any more, we can't assume they're placid and won't rebel."[62] To prevent another riot, Pine ordered the arrest of all 162 of the customers who remained inside and transported them down to the Sixth Precinct.

At the police station, the confused prisoners were all herded into a large room. One of them was Diego Vinales, an attractive twenty-three-year-old Argentinean with an expired visa living in East Orange, New Jersey. Fearing that an arrest in a gay bar would lead to his deportation, Vinales raced up a flight of stairs and tried to leap from a second floor window to the roof of a neighboring building. Vinales fell short and plummeted onto the iron picket fence that surrounded the station house. Six of the fence's fourteen-inch spikes punctured his leg, pelvis, and torso.[63] The cop who discovered him yelled, "Get a doctor!" Another cop on the scene added, "No, it's too late, get a priest."[64]

As word about Vinales's impalement spread throughout the station, the prisoners began defiantly singing "America the Beautiful" and "We

Shall Overcome," followed by a resounding chant of "Gay Power! Gay Power! Gay Power!" While the attention of the police focused on the Argentinean, some of the arrested sneaked into the police captain's office to call the Gay Activists Alliance, the *New York Times*, the *New York Post*, and the *Daily News*. Drawn by the potential lurid photos of Vinales, the *News* dispatched a photographer to the Sixth Precinct.

When the police realized they could not pull Vinales off the spikes, they summoned the fire department, which cut off the portion of the fence stuck in his body and transported both victim and fence to St. Vincent's Hospital. According to a *Daily News* report, the doctors lacked the equipment necessary to remove the spikes and so they requested that the fire department return to the hospital with an electric saw. Firefighters were ordered to scrub and don surgical garments and sterile masks. Using their saw, they cut away the crossbar and managed to ease out the prongs. One firefighter told the *News*, "it's a very tiring and brain wearying job, trying to pull a spike out of a man's interior."[65]

The next morning, members of the Gay Activists Alliance began organizing a protest march for that night against the police. All afternoon, GAA members canvased Manhattan's gay neighborhoods, passing out leaflets announcing a march from the Stonewall to the Sixth Precinct. "Snake Pit raided, 167 arrested," the leaflet read, "One boy near death . . . at St. Vincent's . . . either fell or jumped out precinct window, landed and was impaled on a metal fence! Any way you look at it—that boy was PUSHED! We are ALL being pushed."

That chilly March night in 1970, five hundred protestors gathered at Christopher Park for the largest gay rights demonstration ever. In the crowd were women's libbers, Yippies, GAA, GLF, gays, lesbians, straights. Morty Manford was enjoying dinner with friends in a Village cafeteria when he noticed hundreds of protestors marching toward the Sixth Precinct. Seeing so many people rallying for gay rights, he "felt a tremendous uplift of spirit" and ran out of the cafeteria, yelling to his friends, "I've got to go out and join that march!" The night of the Snake Pit protest was an epiphany for Manford. Ten days later, he joined the Gay Activists Alliance and became, in his words, one of "the new breed of Gay militants."[66]

When the marchers reached the Sixth Precinct, they called for the police captain, "We want Salmeri!" "We want Salmeri!" and chanted,

"Who Gets the Pay—Off? The Police Get the Pay—Off!" and "There's the Mafia in Blue!" The march then moved to St. Vincent's Hospital, where the hundreds of demonstrators joined in a silent candlelight vigil.[67] The ability of the GAA to rally five hundred protestors together in a few hours was testament to the burgeoning influence of the nascent New York group.

The Snake Pit raid and protest brought the issue of homosexuality and gay rights the greatest amount of press coverage it had received since the previous year's Stonewall riots. On Sunday night, two local TV news broadcasts and two radio stations covered the vigil outside St. Vincent's. The following morning, the *Daily News* ran a gruesome five-photo centerfold spread of the impaled victim. The horrific photos had a huge impact. Dick Leitsch, whose Sip-In was the first media event to point out the absurdity of state liquor laws, credited a drop in the number of raids on gay bars after the Snake Pit bust to the published photographs of Diego Vinales's impalement: "The photos of that sickened the public and outraged even the cops. The public attitude was that the cops (and liquor agents) were out of control and being unnecessarily brutal."[68] The *Daily News* photo spread was a media trigger that stirred press interest in the Snake Pit raid, and, consequently, public revulsion at how the liquor laws discriminated against gays.

The *Voice*'s coverage of the raid not only offered the most detailed account, it also presented quite possibly, the most powerful argument for gay liberation ever seen in print:

> While official harassment—police or otherwise—is a continuing frustration and fright to the gay world, the real tyranny is subtler and more pernicious. It is the tyranny of the secret and the lie and the pseudonym, the tyranny of discretion, the tyranny of streets not walked and friends not seen and help not asked. It is the tyranny that drove Alfredo Vinales out of a police station window. It is the tyranny of a shadowy underworld driven into itself for warmth and protection, driven to the extremes of self-caricature to cement a perverted identity. . . . The Snake Pit raid is one more illustration of the ugly games that straights inflict on gays . . . driving them finally into an up-front struggle of liberation to

establish, once and for all, that gay is neither perversion nor sissy nor sick nor faggot nor silly. Gay is good.[69]

Homophile organizations fought oppressive laws, police practices, and employment discrimination. The gay liberation movement went after the "subtler," "more pernicious" tyranny of discretion. Its goals were to challenge the stereotypes that camouflaged many gays who lived double lives and to expose the "shadowy underworld" that offered gays "warmth and protection." The gay liberation movement activists were not satisfied with merely securing employment rights and freedom from harassment in the gay ghetto. They wanted to destroy the image of homosexuals as sick, silly sissies and show both homosexuals and straights that "gay is good." Media attention to the Stonewall riot and Snake Pit protest furthered the process, begun by Frank Kameny and Randy Wicker, of breaking the conspiracy of silence. The Gay Activists Alliance (GAA) and, to a lesser extent, the Gay Liberation Front (GLF), then made sure that the press continued to feed the public with stories about the gay rights movement and about homosexuals who defied the stereotypes. The gay liberationists showed closeted homosexuals that they did not have to live double lives, that others just like them were out. Homosexuality would never return to the "shadowy underworld."

One of the greatest tools for promoting the public expression of gay liberation was an annual march begun in New York City to mark the anniversary of the Stonewall riot. The Gay Pride Parade, as it was later called, was an outgrowth of the Annual Reminder, a yearly silent picket outside Liberty Hall in Philadelphia, first organized in 1965. Just days after the Stonewall Riot, the July 4, 1969, Annual Reminder attracted its largest number of participants ever, about forty-five people, including the deputy mayor of Philadelphia with his wife and son. In previous years, organizers enforced a strict dress code for the protestors— button-down shirts and slacks for men, dresses for women. This year the attire was more relaxed. Some women wore pants, some men blue jeans. Several sported "Gay is Good" buttons. But something else was different about the 1969 picket. The novelty of gays quietly marching seemed to have worn off. The *Ladder* reported that "spectators were amused, or intrigued, or even bored." Reporters asked the usual questions but little or nothing appeared about the protest in the next day's newspapers.[70]

The only remarkable moment of the afternoon came when two women who had joined the silent march suddenly broke the rules and started holding hands. Frank Kameny, fearful that they were breaking the traditional solemnity of the protest, started yelling, "None of that! None of that!" and rushed over to tear them apart. Craig Rodwell, who witnessed the incident, flew into a rage. He found a couple of reporters and ranted about how the gay rights leadership was so out of touch that it was preventing homosexuals from doing what heterosexuals did every day.

On the train ride back to New York, Rodwell, who was the originator of the Annual Reminder, had another idea. Why not maintain and channel the explosive energy of the Stonewall riot by marking its anniversary with an annual march in New York City?[71] The parade would not be a silent appeal for rights similar to the Annual Reminder; it would be a bold demand for equality.

At the 1969 meeting of the Eastern Regional Conference of Homophile Organizations, a resolution was passed to move the Annual Reminder to New York during the last weekend in June. Only Dick Leitsch and the New York Mattachine objected out of a fear that such an open display of "Gay Power" would antagonize their liberal allies in the city's government.[72] In keeping with the tenor of the late 1960s, the Christopher Street Liberation Day march would have no dress or age regulations. To promote a "nationwide show of support" for gay pride and homosexual rights, the ERCHO conference pledged to contact homophile organizations throughout the country to suggest parallel demonstrations on that day.[73] "The Christopher Street Liberation Day" would be a national gay holiday.

In the weeks before the first Christopher Street Liberation march in 1970, the gay press reminded readers of the importance of commemorating the last days of the previous June. "These days mean something special for every lesbian and homosexual," Gay Liberation Front's newspaper *Come Out!* proclaimed. "They mark the first time that gays took to the streets angry, proud, joyous—tearing down the prisons in which the sexist society has chained us. They are days to march, to chant, to dance, to love, to rap, to study—with brothers and sisters coming together to openly affirm the beauty of our lives and throw wide open the closet doors which will no longer be nailed shut."[74] The Stonewall anniversary would not be a solemn "Annual Reminder" of discriminatory laws against homosexuals, it would be a loud celebration and display of "gay liberation."

A *Village Voice* article on the June 1970 march described how, on the day before the parade, Bob Kohler, a salty WWII vet who joined the GLF, gave a talk on gay liberation to a group of students from Tennessee. Speaking to the students in the basement of a Methodist church in Greenwich Village, Kohler explained,

> The reason we're despised as homosexuals is because we're supposed to be effeminate and sissy and weak. We're supposed to be womanish and there's supposed to be something wrong with being womanish. But I've been in the navy three years. I've played football and been a lifeguard. I've done all the John Wayne things society says men are suppose to do and I'm still a fag. Well, Sunday we're going to march up Sixth Avenue and you can stare and take pictures and scream fag all you want, and we'll just say "fuck you." Because we don't care any more. We don't want anybody's acceptance. We've begun to stand up by ourselves.[75]

According to Kohler, one of the main goals of gay liberation was to show both the homosexual and straight public that all gays and lesbians did not fit the unflattering stereotypes. Only after that reality was made clear could homosexuals hope to be accepted and respected by American society. The *Village Voice* described how the shocked students were baffled by the muscular, tough guy talking to them like the sailor he once was:

> The students looked at the man from GLF, and somehow he didn't *look* queer. And they looked around, and there were all these men who really didn't seem to have *anything* in common, except they *must* be queer or else why would they still be there. Still, it was strange, so many different kinds of queers, even some older men in business suits, men who

talked in deep voices, men who looked as tough as anyone
regular.[76]

From the moment gay liberation was first discussed in the press, articles emphasized how the tough, aggressive style of the new activists
like Kohler defied and challenged the stereotypes of the homosexual.

The people who assembled on Waverly Street for the first march on
June 28, 1970, did not know what to expect. The previous Friday
night, four gay men had been jumped on Fourteenth Street because
they were holding hands. One of the men was knocked unconscious to
the ground; another had two teeth smashed in. With such potential for
violence, how many people would actually show up for an openly gay
march? How would the marchers be received on the sixty-block trek
from Greenwich Village to Central Park? Sam Agostino and his friend
brought their dogs to the march so that if the parade were attacked
they could pretend they were just out for a stroll.[77]

Shortly before the parade was to begin, one of the organizers, Craig
Rodwell, noticed some troubling signs. Less than a thousand had gathered at the assembly area and some of them had already been pelted by
eggs thrown from a nearby apartment house. Half of the crowd stood
on the sidewalks debating whether to join the march or remain safely
on the sidelines.[78] Jim Owles of the GAA and GLF's Bob Kohler presented a bold, brave face to the media, explaining the parade's significance to the radio and TV reporters in joyful yet serious tones.[79] But
even the rough-and-tumble Kohler secretly feared the marchers might
be on the verge of a disaster.[80]

When the march started, the participants moved so quickly that
some referred to it as "the first run" rather than "the first march." As
the parade moved block after block, it became apparent that the reaction of the spectators was not abusive or violent but enthusiastic, some
even applauding. Marchers began urging friends watching warily from
the sidewalks to "Come on in, the water's fine!" As the parade pro-
gressed up Sixth Avenue, hundreds of onlookers became marchers.
Foster Gunnison, who helped organize the march, lugged his hefty
frame up and down the parade route calculating the numbers of participants, which he estimated at two thousand. Two FBI agents assigned to
the parade sent J. Edgar Hoover a teletype reporting the same number.[81]

The *Daily News* estimated that ten thousand homosexual men and women participated.

Marchers in the middle of the throng could look in both directions and see neither the head nor the tail of the parade. Hundreds of voices joined together to proclaim: "Say it clear, say it loud; gay is good, gay is proud!" "Two-four-six-eight; gay is just as good as straight!" A GAA-led chant summed up the afternoon perfectly, "Out of the closets and into the streets!" Seeing a crowd of tourists lined up at Radio City Music Hall, several of the marchers paid tribute to the Rockettes with a kick line similar to the one that faced off against the riot police outside the Stonewall a year earlier.[82]

As the marchers reached Central Park many climbed onto a large rock outcropping to view the thousands of happy, proud gays and lesbians flowing up Sixth Avenue in the world's first gay pride parade. A reporter for *GAY* recalled standing on the rock, feeling "on top of the world. It was pure exultation. . . . We got to the rock and threw our arms around our friends and kissed. We were gay and out in the open in Central Park, and by god, we were proud!"[83] Frank Kameny could not believe how many gays and lesbians he saw in the park. Just five years before, he and Jack Nichols were able to get only ten people to join the first gay rights picket outside the White House. The previous year's Annual Reminder attracted forty-five. Now Kameny saw thousands. Jack Nichols and Lige Clarke noted in *GAY* how "our eyes filled to the brim with tears as we stood together in Central Park's sheep meadow, hugging each other, cheering wildly, applauding . . . awestruck by the vast throngs of confident humanity wending their way into a promised land of freedom-to-be."[84] People who were enjoying a quiet afternoon sunbathing and strolling in the park were suddenly joined by masses of gays and lesbians holding hands, kissing, and smoking joints. "The sweet smell of grass was everywhere," *GAY* magazine reported.[85] Clarke and Nichols recalled how "around us couples cuddled, smiling secure, proud . . . we saw incredulity on the faces of bystanders. For the first time in their lives they were face to face with an overpowering reality: homosexuals can be beautiful sensual beings."[86] Television cameras ogled at the bold display of gay affection and solidarity.[87] When a reporter from a radio station opened his newscast with, "Ladies and gentlemen, here we are with the boys and the girls in the band," he was shouted down with a chorus of "Fuck You"s. Someone yelled out, "That's exactly the image we don't want!" The reporter collected himself and assumed a more respectful tone.[88]

A burly-looking straight who was playing football in the Sheep's Meadow when the gay marchers arrived was asked by a *Village Voice* reporter what he thought of the march. The football player responded, "Well, I'm from Alabama and at home you back into 'em everywhere. But it sure is something to see 'em all united. Hell, it sure is something."[89]

As evening descended upon the park, Robert Liechti, writing for *Gay Scene*, likened the moment to "the time when Martin Luther King surveyed that vast flock of blacks [after the 1963 March on Washington]. We, too, had been to the mountain top and we are not turning back; we had tasted the sweet morsel of glory and it was good . . . to sit in the shade with one's friends after it was all over in the evening's glow; it was glory, indeed. And man, it was beautiful!"[90]

In his 1951 *Homosexual in America*, Donald Webster Cory had described how all oppressed minorities experience daily reminders of their inferior status. While, according to Cory, "ethnic groups could take refuge in comfort and pride of their own, in the warmth of family and friends," homosexuals had to experience the discrimination alone.[91] Before the gay liberation movement, gays and lesbians might have been able to commiserate with friends or sympathetic relatives, but they did not have a sense of a gay community that they could identify with and be proud of. On the last Sunday in June 1970, the marchers, reporters, sunbathers, and the football player from Alabama all saw the first massive display of "the gay community."

While seeing and participating in the first march moved thousands, media coverage of the event inspired millions. News of the event was broadcast on television by the French News Agency, Canadian Broadcasting, and all of the New York network affiliates.[92] The *New York Times* ran a front-page article on how "thousands of young men and women homosexuals from all over the Northeast marched from Greenwich Village to the Sheep Meadow in Central Park yesterday, proclaiming the new strength and pride of the gay people." Sounding like a homophile newsletter, the *Times* proclaimed how "from Washington, Boston and Cleveland, from Ivy League colleges, from Harlem, the East Side and the suburbs, they gathered to protest laws that make homosexual acts illegal and social conditions that often make it impossible for them to display affection in public, maintain jobs or rent apartments."

The *Times* characterized the marchers not as sick deviants but as members of a minority group who gathered to protest onerous discriminatory policies and "display the new strength of *the gay people.*" (Italics added.) Ethnic groups that experienced discrimination in New York had long used parades and holidays to generate community consciousness and display their power. For the Irish it was Saint Patrick's Day, for the Italians, Columbus Day, the Puerto Ricans began their own parade in 1958. The Christopher Street Liberation parade displayed a new gay community consciousness and generated news reports that proclaimed the existence of "the gay people."

The *Times* quoted the leaders of the Gay Liberation Front and the Gay Activists Alliance on the importance of the parade. Michael Brown, one of the founders of GLF said, "We're probably the most harassed, persecuted minority group in history, but we'll never have the freedom and civil rights we deserve as human beings unless we stop hiding in closets and in the shelter of anonymity. . . . We have to come out into the open and stop being ashamed or else people will go on treating us as freaks. This march is an affirmation and declaration of our new pride." GAA founder Marty Robinson put his trademark political spin on the event: "We've never had a demonstration like this. . . . It serves notice on every politician in the state and nation that homosexuals are not going to hide any more. We're becoming militant, and we won't be harassed and degraded any more."[93] Through Brown's and Robinson's quotes, the *New York Times* presented thousands of its readers with two of the main principles of gay liberation: gays and lesbians had to "stop hiding in closets and in the shelter of anonymity" and proudly push politicians to put gay rights on their agenda.

A *Times* "Week in Review" article the following Sunday quoted Bob Kohler on the new gay militancy: "This generation of homosexuals knows that the only way to loosen up society and eliminate the fear and disgust we arouse in people is through open confrontation. We're going to get loud and angry and then more loud and angry until we get our rights." According to Brown, Robinson, and Kohler, gay rights could not be achieved through a quiet compromise in which gays remained silent in return for limited reforms like reductions in police harassment. The gay liberation movement would create a media presence that would be a loud, angry force for political and social change.

The *Village Voice* proclaimed the march "the first mass coordinated event of the gay liberation movement":

> One year since the Sixth Precinct raided the Stonewall Inn on Christopher Street, and those insane freaked-out sexed up drag queens went berserk and clawed back, actually fought with police in the streets and rioted, sent cops to the hospital, overturned cars, lit fires, and showed all the closet timmies that enough was enough. . . . And there they were. Out in the streets again. Not the precious birthday party queers of "Boys in the Band," not the limp wrested, pinky-ringed sad eyed faggots of uptown chic, but shouting men and women with locked arms and raised fists.[94]

The Stonewall Riot and its media coverage shook the *Boys in the Band* stereotype and inspired the formation of new gay rights groups who would further promote gay liberation. The Snake Pit Raid protest march displayed the power and attitude of the new generation of gay rights activists. And the Christopher Liberation parade made the massive display of gay liberation and gay community consciousness a yearly event. The media attention given to all three was possible only in New York.

Ed "The Skull" Murphy noticed how the numbers of participants in the New York parade doubled between the first and second marches. In 1972, with the financial support of the Village bar owners, Murphy founded the Christopher Street Festival Committee and in two years' time succeeded in reversing the direction of the march. Instead of beginning in the Village and ending in Central Park, the march started uptown and finished at a Mafia-run street fair in the Village. Marchers no longer whiled away the afternoon cavorting in the sunny park. Now they dispersed into the bars or bought sandwiches from mob controlled street vendors. Responding to news of the change, Craig Rodwell, the originator of the march complained, "We've gone back to supporting our local syndicate bars and we've gone back to the ghetto

again. We've gone the full circle."[95] While the main motive for
reversing the march was commercial, the side effect had great symbolic
value. To proceed downtown from Central Park, the Gay Pride March
had to move down Fifth Avenue, Gotham's premier thouroughfare,
following the same route as the nation's oldest minority march, the
Saint Patrick's Day parade. "The gay people" had indeed arrived.

As the years went by and the Stonewall legend grew, Ed Murphy, the
onetime Chickens and Bulls extortionist, began riding in the parades
in a convertible and billing himself as "The Mayor of Christopher
Street" and "The First Stonewaller" in an attempt to take credit for
making the riots happen in the first place.[96] As one of the Mafia min-
ions responsible for blackmailing bond traders in the Stonewall, in a
way The Skull was right.

San Francisco, Los Angeles, and Chicago held smaller demonstrations on the same day as the first New York parade. News about the
parades appeared in newspapers across the nation. The *Philadelphia
News* detailed the "series of celebrations designed to publicize the new
militant fervor among homosexual organizations," while an Associated
Press story on the parades was carried in newspapers from coast to
coast. Readers of Ohio's *Youngstown Vindicator* learned about the
three-thousand-strong New York march and "gay-in" in Central Park
as well as the Los Angeles parade. Charles Costa reported in a 1970
issue of *GAY* that "Gay Pride Week and the U.S. celebration of the
Stonewall uprising have created new enthusiasm in gay communities
throughout Latin America." In celebration of the new gay holiday, gay
bars in Lima, Managua, and Buenos Aires hosted free brunches and
dances under banners proclaiming "*Liberacion.*" *GAY* reported in
1970 that plans were already being made for gay pride festivities in
Costa Rica, France, Great Britain, and Panama for the following year.[97]
Since its inception, the Christopher Street Liberation Day parade has
marked an international gay holiday, yearly generating worldwide
media coverage and reinforcing the gay community consciousness and
power that exploded in the 1970s.

chapter five

THE NEW HOMOSEXUAL

"Pity: just when Middle Class America finally discovered the homosexual, he died," Tom Burke wrote, in the December 1969 issue of *Esquire*.

> He has expired with a whimper, to make way for the new homosexual of the Seventies, an unfettered, guiltless male child of the new morality in a Zapata moustache and an outlaw hat who couldn't care less for Establishment approval, would as soon sleep with boys as girls, and thinks that "Over the Rainbow" is a place to fly on 200 micrograms of lysergic acid diethylamide.[1]

According to Burke, the general public's conception of what it meant to be gay was hopelessly outdated because journalists and novelists ignored "the new homosexual" while Broadway and Hollywood perpetuated the old stereotypes. Burke offered *Esquire*'s readers a perspective on gays that extended beyond the caricatures in *Boys in the Band* who "eat canapés, drink excessively, do a chorus line dance . . . quote old movies, and imitate Judy, Bette and Kate." The subjects of Burke's article were tough, unashamed, and outwardly "indistinguishable from the heterosexual hippie."

The appearance of Burke's views on "The New Homosexual" in a mainstream national publication was a turning point for the gay rights movement. So called "new homosexuals" like Bob Martin had been advocating gay pride and challenging the moderate politics of the homophiles prior to Stonewall, but after the riots the media suddenly became interested in the gay liberation movement. Newspaper and magazine articles and news broadcasts began delivering images of gays that challenged the stereotypes and brought the "new homosexual" into popular consciousness and into the self-consciousness of many gays. Men who had never thought of themselves as homosexual because they did not fit the effete stereotype suddenly had an image with which they might comfortably identify. The first organization the media recognized as the vanguard of the new generation of homosexuals was New York's Gay Liberation Front, which began with a failed attempt by the Mattachine Society and Dick Leitsch to co-opt the new radicalism.

In the days after Stonewall, Mattachine activists walked around Greenwich Village handing out a position paper written by Leitsch hailing "the Christopher Street Riots" as "The Hairpin Drop Heard Around the World":

> Homosexuals are tired of waiting. . . . If the traditional means of winning reform cannot work in this age—if democracy is so dead that the citizens have no means of gaining redress by honest straightforward means—then possibly the only means of reform is in the streets. Perhaps confrontation politics can win the reforms traditional politics could not for us. . . . If reforms are not made, it could be a long hot summer.[2]

For years Leitsch had advocated quiet reform, but by June 1969 he realized that without threats of social upheaval, concessions from liberals would be limited.[3] His flyer caught the attention of Michael Brown, a twenty-eight-year-old New Left radical who had been a staff member on Hubert Humphrey's 1968 presidential campaign but had become politically radicalized after Nixon's election. Stonewall convinced Brown that the time was right for gays to join with militant blacks, antiwar activists, and other radicals to make a concerted push for a social and political revolution.[4] Brown contacted Leitsch and after lengthy discussions persuaded him to channel the emergent radical energies into MSNY by creating a committee of young activists.[5] The Mattachine Action Committee was a cross section of the new gay militant elite, including Bob Martin, eccentric founder of the Student Homophile League; Martin's former girlfriend Martha Shelly, a charismatic twenty-six-year-old tomboy from the Daughters of Bilitis; Lois Hart, a former nun and associate of Timothy Leary; and Marty Robinson, a tough, speed-addicted carpenter who was brave enough to come out to his fellow construction workers. Even in the radical days of 1969 it would have been difficult to find people less likely to be co-opted by anyone. Almost immediately, the committee began to secretly discuss seceding from Mattachine.[6]

Unlike Leitsch, the young activists on the Action Committee saw gay rights as just one of many struggles in a general crusade for social and political revolution. While posting announcements for a Mattachine town meeting, Brown and Shelly noticed leaflets for a demonstration in support of Black Panthers who were imprisoned at the Women's House of Detention, located in the center of Greenwich Village. The Action Committee saw the jailhouse protest as the perfect opportunity to declare their support for the Black Panthers. Leitsch however feared antagonizing the liberal politicians he had been cultivating since the mid-1960s and prohibited the Mattachine Action Committee from declaring an open alliance with the Panthers. In defiance, the committee members simply made up a new name for themselves, the Gay Liberation Front, and added it to the list of demonstration sponsors.

Leitsch intended to use the Action Committee's July 16, 1969 town meeting to speak out against the demonstration for the Panthers and promote instead a silent candlelight vigil in Washington Square Park. After arriving late, he noticed his short haircut and conservative brown suit stood out in the sea of long hair, beards, beads, and jeans that filled the hot church on Waverly Place. Tom Burke, who recounted the moment for the readers of *Esquire*, thought Leitsch looked like a "dependable, fortyish Cartier salesclerk," a perfect representative of the gay stereotype. The standing-room-only audience was tense after hearing Dr. Leo Louis Martello harangue them on their feelings of self-loathing and their passive acceptance of homosexuality as a sickness. Leitsch then took the podium and read a list of grievances that the homophile movement had been unsuccessfully working on for years. He warned the audience not to antagonize Middle America and "the Establishment" with disruptive behavior but to seek "acceptance" through educating straights about gay rights with grace and good humor.

Before he could continue, a booming voice erupted from the audience. "We don't want acceptance, goddamn it! We want respect! Demand it!" Heads turned toward the sounds of Jim Fouratt standing in his shiny leather pants, lizard boots, and cowboy hat. His blond, shoulder-length hair and mustache gave him the look of a countercultural Billy the Kid. Here stood a "new homosexual" in sharp contrast to Leitsch's southern charm and fresh suit. "We're through hiding in dark bars behind Mafia doormen," Fouratt roared. "We're going to go where straights go and do anything with each other they do and if they don't like it, well, fuck them! And if some of us enjoy a little group sex at the docks or in the subways we're going to have it without apologizing to anybody! Straights don't have to be ashamed of anything sexy they happen to feel like doing in public, and neither do we! We're through cringing and begging like a lot of nervous Nellies at Cherry Grove!"[7] Madolin Cervantes, the New York Mattachine Society's only female member (and as many in the audience knew, the only straight), tried to settle the crowd: "Well, now, I think that what we ought to have is a gay vigil, in a park. Carry candles perhaps. A peaceful vigil. I think we should be firm, but just as amicable and sweet as . . ." "Sweet?!" Fouratt howled from the back of the room, "Sweet bullshit! There's the stereotype homo again, man! Soft, weak, sensitive! Bullshit! That's the role society has been forcing these queens to play and they just sit and accept it. We have got to radicalize, man! Why? Because as long as we accept getting fired from jobs because we are gay, or not being hired at all, or being treated like second class citizens, we're going to remain neurotic and screwed up. No matter what you do in bed, if you're not a man out of it, you're going to get screwed up. Be proud of what you are man! If it takes riots or even guns to show them what we are, well that's the only language the pigs

understand." Leitsch tried to interject but Fouratt kept thundering.
"All the oppressed have got to unite! The system keeps us all weak by
keeping us separate. Do you realize that not one straight radical group
showed up during all those nights of rioting? If it had been a black
demonstration they'd have been there. We've got to work together
with all the New Left." With applause echoing off walls, Fouratt led a
group of several dozen out of the church and up Sixth Avenue. Leitsch
frantically tugged at his white tie, shouting for order, but the energized
crowd kept cheering for Jim Fouratt and the new homosexuality.[8]

Recalling Jim Fouratt three decades later, Dick Leitsch still expresses
anger at "that lunatic" who was, by all accounts, one of the most colorful characters in the gay rights movement. By 1969 Jim Fouratt had
been a Roman Catholic seminarian, an off-Broadway actor, a Yippie
leader, and a consultant on the counterculture at CBS records.[9] Abbie
Hoffman described him as "The original flower child, [who] played
the perfect innocent, constantly popping up in the middle of violent
chaos with a surprised 'what me?' look on his face."[10] Underneath
Fouratt's Marilyn Monroe act however, lurked an intense desire for
attention and revolution. His theatricality became particularly useful
when he, Abbie Hoffman, Jerry Rubin, and others formed the Youth
International Party—the Yippies—a group that tried to attract people
to the antiwar movement and radical politics by a "blending of pot and
politics into a political grass leaves movement." The key to the Yippies'
success was their knack for orchestrating media events that transformed
their leaders into celebrities.

Fouratt came up with the idea for the Yippies' most famous stunt, a
protest at the New York Stock Exchange. Eighteen Yippies joined a tour
of the Exchange and threw dollar bills over the side of the observation
platform onto the trading floor below. Baffled brokers abandoned their
transactions and rushed over to grab the falling cash. Hoffman, Rubin,
and Fouratt cheered the pillars of capitalism scrambling against each other
on the floor until the guards ejected them and the rest of the Yippies. The
stunt continued outside the Exchange where the Yippies gathered the
press together to film and photograph the burning of more bills in symbolic disdain for materialism. Hoffman later called the Stock Exchange
protest "a perfect myth." "A spark had been ignited," he declared in his
autobiography. "The system cracked a little. Not a drop of blood had been

spilled, not a bone broken, but on that day, with that gesture, an image war had begun. In the minds of millions of teenagers the stock market had just crashed."[11]

After several successful media stunts, Yippie leaders were invited onto television talk shows, the barometers of American celebrity. In an attempt to show kids that they did not have to act conventionally, Hoffman and Fouratt appeared on the *David Susskind Show* with a live duck that defecated on the sound stage. Young, impressionable viewers who saw the Yippies' hijinks on TV discovered the antiwar movement was more than boring marches and tedious petitioning. The Yippies made revolution fun. Fouratt's appearance on the Susskind show had further significance. In an attempt to be outrageous, he proclaimed his homosexuality in front of millions of viewers. At the time he did not realize the importance of his declaration, but years later young gays and lesbians who saw the broadcast thanked him for inspiring them to come out.[12]

Fouratt enjoyed the media attention and his friendship with Hoffman, but he was frustrated by the discrimination he experienced among the other Yippies. While Hoffman was not antagonistic toward gays, he frequently referred to enemies of the movement as "faggots" and was obviously uncomfortable with Fouratt's homosexuality. Fouratt finally split with the Yippies after he voiced concern about their plans for a protest at the 1968 Democratic National Convention in Chicago. He foresaw too much potential for violence and suspected Rubin and Hoffman were misleading young people with promises of free rock concerts and a "Festival of Life" in Mayor Daley's parks.[13] After dropping out of the Yippies, Fouratt was free to dedicate himself to a new fight. He did not know it at the time, but the Yippies and the gay liberation movement would both succeed by manipulating the media into disseminating their messages to millions of readers and viewers, particularly young ones. Gay liberation would be won through what Abbie Hoffman called "image war."

Although Dick Leitsch appreciated the power of street actions, he feared the new militants like Fouratt would alienate straight allies with their radical politics and overt homosexuality. Leitsch was particularly uneasy with young activists' rallying call, "Gay Power," which invoked Black Power. He complained that "'Gay Power' would raise the specter of militants proclaiming, 'I am homosexual!' and marching to the slogan 'Power to Homosexuals!' "[14] Leitsch asked in an editorial for *GAY*, "How can one be proud of being gay, any more than one can be proud of being white, or black, or left handed? One should be proud to be a human being! Only by being people and not 'homosexuals,' can we relate to all possibilities and achieve our personal potentials. Staying in the ghettos wearing the labels, and limiting our demands to 'gay power' (as opposed to 'people power'), we're perhaps supporting the Homosexual Revolution, but we're sure as hell copping out of the Sexual Revolution."[15] Leitsch hoped to diminish racial and sexual distinctions so people could deal with each other as equal members of a single, unified community.

Leitsch saw the "Gay Power Movement" as a threat to his ability to deal successfully with liberal politicians like John Lindsay; the young militants viewed it as personal and political progress for all homosexuals. Bob Martin explained the significance of "Gay Power":

> What is Gay Power? . . . It is demanding to be recognized as a powerful minority with just rights which have not been acknowledged; it is an insistence that homosexuality has made its own unique contribution to the building of our civilization and will continue to do so; and it is the realization that homosexuality, while morally and psychologically on a par with heterosexuality, does nonetheless have unique aspects, which demand their own standards of evaluation and their own subculture.[16]

For Martin and most gay militants, homosexuals needed to identify themselves through a gay political bloc, a gay community, and a gay culture in opposition to the "exclusive, uptight heterosexuals."[17] While Leitsch was speaking the language of liberalism, Fouratt, Martin, and the militants were talking identity politics.

The Mattachine Action Committee and Leitsch's monopoly on the New York gay rights movement heaved a last gasp at a July 30, 1969, rally marking the one-month anniversary of the Stonewall Riot. "The Non-violent Vigil to Protest Harassment of Homosexuals" was organized by Martha Shelly and Marty Robinson, who had taken charge of the Action Committee after its founder, Michael Brown, resigned. Robinson, the fiery carpenter from Brooklyn, was a perfect spokesman for the new homosexuality. Underneath his boyish good looks raged a charismatic intensity that charmed and impressed fellow activists and construction workers alike. With rousing speeches and sharp statements like "The greatest cure for guilt is anger," Robinson would become a major voice of gay liberation. "Gay power is here!" he shouted from the edge of the fountain in Washington Square Park. "Gay power is no laugh. There are one million homosexuals in New York City. If we wanted to, we could boycott Bloomingdale's and that store would be closed in two weeks." (Robinson later regretted using a line that reinforced the stereotype of the shopping fop.) "Let me tell you homosexuals, we've got to get organized. We've got to stand up. This is our chance."[18] With the sounds of "We Shall Overcome" ringing down Waverly Place, the vigil moved over to Sheridan Square, opposite the Stonewall Inn. For the first time on the East Coast, homosexuals marched together publicly for gay rights.[19] One participant recalled: "People were getting into a great high: they were singing, had their arms around each other. There was a great feeling." In an article about the march, the *Village Voice* wondered, "maybe it wasn't just a joke. Maybe there really was a gay power."[20] But when the police told organizers they could not proceed to the local precinct house, the Mattachine marshals, dressed in lavender sashes, thanked the demonstrators for showing up and asked everyone to go home.[21] After the Stonewall riot, such polite, orderly vigils generated much more disappointment than enthusiasm. The Mattachine Action Committee lost its street credibility.

A few days before the vigil, a leaflet appeared on the Village streets with the question "DO YOU THINK HOMOSEXUALS ARE REVOLTING? . . . YOU BET YOUR SWEET ASS WE ARE." The flyer announced the formation of a new gay rights group at the Alternate U, an inexpensive evening school in an industrial loft that offered classes on everything from Marxism to self-defense. About forty people including Fouratt, Shelly, and Brown attended.[22] When the discussion turned to what the purpose of the new group should be, the room exploded with plans to reach self-actualization, challenge stereotypes, and overthrow the United States government. A split arose over whether the Front should join the New Left radical movement or focus entirely on gay rights.[23] The political revolutionaries in the room were convinced that if one were radical about one thing such as homosexuality, then he or she had to be radical about everything.[24] Others thought the membership needed to "get our heads together first, then join the rest of the revolution when we knew where we were."[25] After the political radicals lost a close vote on the subject, they walked out and convened their own meeting in a room next door.[26]

Only one decision was made that evening but it was a big one. At the suggestion of Martha Shelly, "the Gay Liberation Front" was adopted as the name for the new group. Each word in the title had significance. No other homosexual rights group had used "gay" in its name before that night; the Mattachine Society and the Daughters of Bilitis had even avoided "homosexual." Instead of "homophile," the euphemism created by the previous generation of activists, or "homosexual," the clinical label given by heterosexuals, "gay" was what homosexuals called each other. No longer would they be known by the labels that had been assigned to them by the straight world.[27] And by echoing the name of the Vietnamese National Liberation Front commonly known as the Viet Cong, the Gay Liberation Front aligned themselves with the image of righteous peasants fighting the most powerful army in the world.[28] The name alone was a powerful symbol that challenged stereotypes every time it appeared in media reports.

During the first few meetings three keynotes of GLF emerged: pride in homosexuality, militancy against oppressors of gays, and an advocacy of the overthrow of capitalism. The issue that remained unresolved was whether the Front would focus solely on gay rights or pursue a greater social and political revolution. Although the GLF proclaimed its allegiance to "all the oppressed: the Vietnamese struggle, the third world, the blacks, the workers," debates over this commitment would tear the group apart within a year.[29]

The founders of the Front rejected the hierarchy and institutional structures of the Mattachine Society and Daughters of Bilitis and attempted to be as democratic and indeed, as "structureless" as possible.[30] There were no officers, and meetings lacked set agendas. In imitation of the "participatory democracy" of the New Left, decisions were made by consensus rather than majority rule. Each month, a new meeting moderator was chosen by pulling his or her name out of a hat. The weekly meetings attracted fifty to a hundred gay and lesbian militants whose politics ran from Marxist to Nixonian Republican. Discussions frequently devolved into intense arguments about how to live openly as homosexuals or whether sexual oppression was rooted in class struggle.[31] Karla Jay, one of the randomly selected moderators, had to call the raucous meetings to order by pounding an iron support column with a baseball bat.[32] All who attended were automatically considered members and were free to talk about any subject they chose, for as long as they wanted or until shouted down by someone with something else to say. Kay Lahusen thought GLF meetings were "the best theater in town," but the participatory democracy of the Front inhibited both participation and democracy.[33] Decisions were made by whoever happened to show up that night and were quickly abandoned at the next meeting, if they were even remembered.[34]

Some GLFers such as Michael Brown and Lois Hart were dedicated to consensus-building, but a few loud voices and strong personalities tended to dominate meetings. Jim Fouratt, who enjoyed raucous, dialectical discussions, often challenged the consensus even when he agreed with it.[35] His frequent disruptions contributed to rumors that he was an FBI provocateur, a baseless charge that has been unfairly repeated in at least two important histories of the gay rights movement.[36] GLF tried to uphold its commitment to consensus-building, but sometimes votes were necessary to end the more contentious debates. Votes often triggered walkouts by the losing side. At GLF meetings "the only absolute was confrontation," John Murphy recalled. "Everyone in the GLF confronted the entire straight world, and often one another as well."[37]

Ideological divisions among the members added to the confusion of the GLF. The counterculture and the New Left radicals in GLF believed in revolution but were divided over how to conduct it. While the countercultural radicals emphasized grassroots growth of self-expression within a supportive liberated community, the New Left wanted to transform the political and economic institutions that were seen as responsible for individual feelings of alienation and personal dissatisfaction. In an article announcing the formation of GLF written for the radical newspaper *Rat*, Michael Brown, Lois Hart, and Ron

Ballard sought convergence of these two paths to revolution. They declared the Front's commitment to overthrow "this rotten, dirty, vile, fucked-up capitalist conspiracy." But instead of condemning particular institutions or announcing a political strategy, they advocated revamping norms of personal behavior. The GLF's plan to attack the existing political and economic institutions by undermining social mores also generated fractious debates.[38]

In addition to the countercultural revolutionaries and political radicals, GLF contained reformers who did not seek a complete reconstruction of America's institutions. Social reformers wanted homosexuals to impress straights by being cooperative neighbors and competent co-workers who also happened to be gay. They believed daily interaction with straight society would leave positive impressions that would eventually result in progressive change. Political reformers such as Marty Robinson and his one-time lover and friend Jim Owles, influenced by the Student Nonviolent Coordinating Committee (SNCC) success in registering southern black voters, wanted to organize gays into a political bloc that would force mainstream politicians to address their concerns.[39] GLF's program was so amorphous and its rhetoric so contradictory, that it served briefly as a big tent for the various types of revolutionaries and reformists.

Because almost everyone had an ideological stake in every decision, debates over trivial issues could dominate GLF's attention for weeks. A visitor once attended a meeting that began and ended with a debate over whether to tolerate the presence of a straight reporter from the *Village Voice*. Three weeks later, he returned and found GLF debating the same issue. Adding to the confusion of the meetings was the presence of people who were high, most commonly on marijuana or speed, which could be purchased from a drug dealer who operated out of the men's room.[40] All of the rambling, incoherent preaching and arguing, however, had its charm. Participation in a GLF meeting offered gays the opportunity to be loud and free in a way they had never been encouraged to be. Before joining GLF, Arthur Evans and Arthur Bell sat through a few Mattachine Society meetings that made them feel like they were in Sunday school. Evans recalled how their first GLF meeting "completely changed our lives for everything. Everything was changed after that. . . . I feel a great sense of gratitude to GLF for that."[41] Karla Jay, who went on to become an important writer on gay and lesbian issues was moved by seeing "loud," "proud," "eloquent," "persuasive" women in GLF. Sitting in the meeting, she envisioned expanded possibilities for her life and realized that, "Maybe there were other women like me who were political, had a feminist consciousness, and wanted to sleep with women."[42]

By the fall of 1970, months of chaos within the motley organization forced the Front to restructure itself into a collection of affinity cells that operated under the GLF banner but pursued actions outside of the control of the general membership.[43] Some cells took over practical responsibilities. The twenty-eighth of June Cell published the newsletter; the Aquarius Cell organized dances. Others had more lofty responsibilities, like the International Cell, dedicated to "uniting all gays throughout the world."[44] Some cells were based on ideology, such as the "Planned Non-Parenthood Cell," an environmentalist group that promoted population control. A clique of Marxist Leninists who saw their sexual "liberation as linked to class struggle" formed The Red Butterfly Cell.[45] Marty Robinson and the "Gay Commandos" worked to reform the American political system through aggressive political protests. A group of intellectuals including Arthur Bell, who later wrote a memoir, *Dancing the Gay Lib Blues*, and Arthur Evans, a Columbia PhD candidate, formed the Radical Study Group, which met weekly to discuss radical critiques of society.[46] Other cells were based on identity. The transvestites created two groups: Transsexuals and Transvestites (TAT) and Street Transvestite Action Revolutionaries (STAR), which provided temporary housing for young, homeless transvestites in an abandoned mobile home, until the owner reclaimed his RV and drove it away with a few drag queens sleeping inside. Lesbians and gays of color spun off to start Third World Gay Revolution and Salsa Soul Sisters, while Hebrew GLFers founded the Jewish Gay Revolutionary Party.[47] Gays who were under twenty-one years old had their own political and social group called Gay Youth.[48]

Eventually GLF's big tent accommodated nineteen cells, twelve consciousness-raising groups, a men's Wednesday night meeting, a women's Sunday night caucus, three communes, a Radical Study Group, and a rifle club.[49] GLFer Ralph Hall feared the proliferation and autonomy of the cells, "One person alone, acting as an individual cell, could bomb the Empire State Building . . . and proclaim he did it under the name of GLF, for the gay liberation cause and humanity as well. All we could do is censure and slap him on the hands and say that was a 'no no.' "[50] The cells limited GLF's ability to "get it together" and coordinate significant political actions, but they enabled the Front to withstand constant splintering and became platforms for future organizations that would have a great impact on the movement.[51]

Despite the chaos, GLF's successes provided organizing models for future gay liberationists. During a discussion about how to raise funds, someone suggested the Front hold a gay dance at Alternate U. Not only would the dances bring in cash needed for bail and food for "street people" but they also would provide an alternative to Mafia-run bars, like the Stonewall.[52] One GLF newsletter issued after a dance declared, "Your presence was proof that gay people will meet outside the tired Mafioso bars in a common effort to improve their own community."[53] The *Village Voice* described one of the dances: "On the third floor, in the not so dark, several hundred bodies pound to the sound of tape-deck rock and twirling light-show slides, 95 percent men and boys, smiling, dancing, hugging, kissing, pinching, all as though no one had ever mentioned another sex." The room reeked of perspiration, marijuana, amyl nitrate, and freedom. The dances were a way to recruit new members, like John Murphy, who became active in GLF after attending a dance where he met homosexuals "who were a far cry from the stereotyped pansies and dykes."[54] Some of the lesbians, like Karla Jay, felt comfortable at GLF dances, but most female GLFers were repulsed by the "sweaty bunch of men packed together, subway rush-hour style . . . groping and dryfucking." True to GLF's tendency to splinter, the lesbians demanded a separate women-only room during the dances and soon began organizing their own social functions.[55]

GLF's greatest success arose when it submitted a classified ad to the *Village Voice* announcing a "Gay Community Dance." A couple of days later someone from the *Voice* called to explain that the advertisement could not be printed because the tabloid's policy of not publishing obscene words in classifieds prevented it from using the word "gay." When asked why the *Voice* considered "gay" obscene, the staffer claimed the weekly equated "gay" with "shit" and other four-letter words and suggested GLF use "homophile" instead.

On the morning of September 12, 1969, GLF began to picket the offices of the *Voice*, located three doors up from the Stonewall Inn. Almost one hundred demonstrators stood chanting outside the offices until late in the afternoon when the publisher, Edwin Fancher, agreed to meet with three GLF representatives. After Fancher accepted most of GLF's demands including freedom to use "gay" and "homosexual" in classified ads, one of the GLF representatives in an upstairs office stepped to a window and flashed a V for Victory sign to the crowd below.[56] A "Gay Power Victory Dance" was held a couple of weeks later to commemorate the protest. The flyer announcing the dance explained the significance of GLF's victory: "Gay is no longer a four-letter word, even at the Village Voice. Friday . . . members of the homosexual community demonstrated the reality of gay power. . . . GLF hopes that all members of the community will take note of this and that they will take appropriate action to bring about the day when the Voice may become truly representative of the people of the Village."[57] The *Voice* protest showed many in the New York gay community that homosexuals were not just victims of discrimination—they could be successful agitators for change.[58]

Over the next few months under the leadership of Marty Robinson and Jim Owles, the Front's Gay Commando cell began to use disruptive demonstrations to pressure politicians. At a campaign stop on a warm September afternoon in Queens, conservative mayoral candidate Mario Procaccino began shaking hands with a crowd that included Owles. The candidate grasped the shaggy militant's hand but before he could move onto the next prospective vote, Owles asked Procaccino what he was "going to do about the oppression of the homosexual?" The politician suddenly dropped his friendly smile and assumed a look of concern. While patting Owles's hand, he said "Young man, I can see that you're very interested in this problem. That is one of the many problems that we must face in New York. It is sick rather than criminal, and we must show understanding and compassion for them." Owles did not expect a bold statement of support for gay rights from Procaccino, and he was not looking for one. Gay liberation scored a victory just by cornering a mayoral candidate into publicly addressing the issue of homosexuality.

Robinson discovered that public confrontations forced politicians to address gay rights. He dubbed these hit-and-run protests "zaps." Jerry

Hoose recalled the political and personal impact of the zaps. "Whoever saw gay oriented questions being thrown at political candidates? It didn't happen, it was totally a new thing. . . . I had been through so much humiliation since the time I came out, and to be able to stand up and be in your face the way we were. It was a very heady time, it was a wonderful time."[59]

Zaps not only accomplished the political feat of forcing politicians to address the issue of homosexuality, they enabled participants to feel a sense of power—gay power. Years later, *Life* magazine reported how gays who participated in zaps "claim that demonstrations offer them the best therapy for the humiliations inflicted by an antihomosexual society. 'One good zap' they say, 'is worth months on a psychiatrist's couch.' "[60]

The Gay Commandos zapped another mayoral candidate, Republican State Senator John Marchi, at a speech before the well-heeled membership of the Gotham Young Republican Club. During a question and answer period, a GLFer rose with a query: "Senator Marchi, are you aware of the emerging militancy within the homosexual community, and how does this relate to your views on law and order? Will homosexuals become targets or will you be responsive to their needs?" The senator attempted to deflect the question by saying that homosexuality was a concern of the state legislature, not the mayor. The Gay Commando, however, would not relent: "Senator, it's not just for the legislature. As mayor you have control of the police force. How will this affect the lives of New York's 800,000 homosexuals?" Marchi countered that he would "enforce the laws and prevailing social mores of society." When asked whether he considered homosexuals an oppressed minority, the Senator answered with a sharp, "No." GLF did not leave it alone. As the candidate walked out of the room someone buttonholed him and exclaimed, "Evidently you feel no social suffering is involved in the issue. You don't seem to feel obligated to address yourself to it." Marchi offered a "Well, yes" and then walked away.[61] While GLF was not able to push Marchi to advocate gay rights, the mere fact that a Republican state senator from Staten Island addressed homosexuals openly without referring to them as perverts or deviants was progress in 1969.

A few weeks before the election, thirteen Gay Commandoes infiltrated a mayoral debate sponsored by the League of Women Voters at Temple Torah in Queens. After being skipped over in the question and answer portion of the discussion, Marty Robinson interjected, "It's 1776, Mr. Procaccino. The homosexual revolution has begun." While Robinson asked the candidate's opinion on gay rights, the police began to move toward him and Jim Owles. But before the two could be ejected, members of the League of Women Voters rose to their defense. After the police backed away, Robinson and Owles launched into the questioning again, provoking their removal in front of the press and TV cameras. The president of the League of Women Voters then took up the inquiry about homosexuality. Marchi said something about not providing room in his platform for homosexuals but was interrupted when Gay Commandos in the audience stormed out of the room.[62] The zap made the *New York Post* and NBC-TV news and became a model for how to use media to challenge stereotypes of the passive, weak, frivolous homosexual. "We had come out," a GLF newsletter proclaimed. "In this temple, people talked to us, met us and many were astounded. In America there are a few token, publicly-known homosexuals. No wonder people think we are weird. They never see us. That night they did. Twisted characterizations of what it meant to be homosexual gave way to the sight of real people, determined self-respecting homosexuals. Hello, world! Dig us."

By all accounts, Marty Robinson did not read much. He may not have even heard of Marshall McLuhan. But he had an intuitive sense of the power of media and how to manipulate it. He knew that news reports on the zaps would show homosexuals and straights alike that gays could be serious and political.[63] Through zaps, Robinson introduced America to "the new homosexual."

Having gotten the attention of the politicians and the press, GLF's Gay Commandos announced that they expected the mayoral candidates to address the concerns of homosexuals at a Greenwich Village Association candidates' night. Rather than appear in person, each of the politicians sent representatives to the gathering, but they all responded more or less favorably to questions on gay rights. Robinson and Owles were especially pleased with the evening after learning that one of the journalists in attendance was a *Time* magazine reporter who was working on a cover story about homosexuality.[64] A national weekly magazine such as *Time* was just the type of media forum that the Front needed to reach closeted or nonpoliticized homosexuals around the country.

Not everyone in GLF favored Robinson's reformist political activities. The revolutionaries believed the Gay Commandos were not politicizing the homosexual community, but making it too comfortable with the system by securing reforms. Some extreme militants did not want to see significant progress toward gay rights; the greater the oppression the more radicalized the population would become. Owles claimed that a few GLFers "wanted the police to shut down the bars so they would see no alternative but to join up with the movement and pick up a gun."[65] GLF's cultural revolutionaries thought the reformers' political activity would distract gays from what was truly important—the liberation of their own consciousnesses. Efforts to gain recognition by politicians and mainstream media just further mired gays within "the system" and promoted "ego tripping," some activists argued, instead of the countercultural ideals of humility, selflessness, and community. Rather than go through the national news media, cultural revolutionaries insisted the only way to raise consciousness was to communicate through alternative newspapers, leaflets, and word of mouth.[66]

GLF did start its own newspaper called *Come Out*, which was hailed as "a paper for us by us." After only eight editions, *Come Out* collapsed when it ran an article, "S&M and the Revolution," which claimed sadomasochism was a revolutionary act. The newspaper's two female staff members thought the article was oppressive to women and quit. The four men who remained could not decide what to do, so they agreed to dissolve the paper.[67]

GLF's failure to fully appreciate how the mainstream media could be used to promote gay liberation is one of the main reasons why its success was so limited. The Front rarely solicited attention from the press and prohibited members from speaking individually to the media, since no one could express the will of the "whole body." After a marathon eight-hour debate, fifteen GLFers produced a muddled memo, titled "Our Relationship to the Media," that called for the "re-definition of media to include alternatives to the attitude that media is *print*, i.e., dances, demonstrations, coffee house, leaflets, cruising."

> We must begin to recognize that we have a gay media and
> we must develop it and break away from "their" narrow
> conception of what media is. This will go hand in hand with
> developing our gay consciousness. . . . We want to expand
> and extend our gay media with "gay soul" and "gay pride."
> . . . This will be revolutionary, this will be our power. Do
> you suppose that the gay bar is gay media?[68]

Perhaps gay bars were "gay media," but like cruising and dances, they contributed little to the success of the movement. GLF's refusal to use the so-called "pig media" to publicize its existence and message was a self-imposed constraint to success. Articles in gay newspapers might contribute to the consciousness-raising of homosexuals who read gay newspapers, but they did *not* reach those who might be afraid to buy such publications or did not live in cities where they were sold. By narrowing their focus to gay media, GLF could not reach enough closeted homosexuals or straights to challenge stereotypes and foster the cultural revolution that so many GLFers advocated.[69]

While most GLFers could not imagine how the mainstream media could be used to promote gay rights, they certainly understood the deleterious effect negative reports had on the movement. In late October 1969, millions of *Time* magazine subscribers read a story titled "The Homosexual: Newly Visible, Newly Understood." The article pleased many homophile stalwarts because rather than ignore the opinions of gays on homosexuality, *Time* legitimized their voices by including the perspectives of Dick Leitsch and Frank Kameny. It also refuted the commonly held fear that homosexuals were created by conversion at a young age, and it challenged some of the old stereotypes: "the catty hairdresser or the lisping, limp-wristed interior decorator" and "his lesbian counterpart" the "butch . . . who is aggressively masculine to the point of trying to look like a man."[70] Despite the generally sympathetic approach to homosexuality, the article referred to GLF dismissively as one of the radical groups that "turgidly call for 'the Revolution of Free and Frequent Polysexuality.'" *Time* also called upon American society to "devise ways of discouraging the condition" (homosexuality) and presented a biography of a homosexual who was supposedly "converted" to heterosexuality. "Women arouse me now," the former homosexual proclaimed, "it's a total reversal."

Enraged by *Time*'s characterization of homosexuality as a curable "condition," the Front began picketing the Time-Life Building in Rockefeller Center.[71] Chanting "ho, ho, Ho Chi Minh," GLFers handed out leaflets while construction workers on a job site across the street pelted them with eggs.[72] Only after GLFer Bob Kohler invited the construction workers to "Come on down and fight it out on the sidewalk, if you're so fucking smart!" did the police intervene—they threatened to arrest Kohler for incitement to riot.[73] The protest failed to pressure *Time* executives into meeting with GLF, but the ABC-TV New York affiliate broadcast footage of the demonstration and of Jerry Hoose railing against the magazine. Hoose recalled how the protest "raised the consciousness of a lot of people who saw that the few of us there were fair prey, game for anything. We were on television, we were exposed, and that helped other people to come out the next time."[74] Even if the intended goal had not been achieved, a more subtle but equally important one had. The "new homosexual" was on TV. The GLF, however, was too idealistic, splintered, and disorganized to strategically and systematically manipulate the mainstream media.

GLF's limited successes convinced its leaders that they were ready to take over the entire gay rights movement. Jim Fouratt later recalled, "We wanted to end the homophile movement. We wanted them to join us."[75] The attempted coup took place at the Eastern Regional Conference of Homophile Organizations (ERCHO), organized by Foster Gunnison in the fall of 1969. New York's GLF and the Student Homophile League delegations from Columbia, Cornell, and NYU pushed a resolution that would have put ERCHO on record as supporting the November 1969 Mobilization Against the Vietnam War, a huge protest in Washington, D.C., that was expected to draw hundreds of thousands.

At earlier homophile conferences, the submission of an antiwar reso-lution would not have caused great turmoil, but the 1969 ERCHO meeting took place at a moment of extreme political tension in the United States. On the right, Nixon was secretly bombing neutral Cam-bodia in an attempt to achieve "peace with honor"; the FBI was waging a covert war against the Black Panthers that culminated in the assassina-tion of Chicago party leader Fred Hampton in his bed. Meanwhile, the left was tearing itself apart. The 1969 Students for a Democratic Society (SDS) convention was its most unruly, and its last. Three weeks prior to the ERCHO conference, the SDS splinter group, the Weathermen, launched its Days of Rage—actually a single night of running through Chicago, smashing car windows, and terrorizing residents in the name of revolution—a tame precursor to the group's subsequent terrorist campaign detonating bombs in public buildings, including the New York City Police Headquarters and the Capitol in Washington. During the 1969 ERCHO conference, the militants, who firmly believed that moderation was "selling out," faced off against the homophile delegates who saw anything beyond moderation as self-destructive Jacobinism.

The conference quickly became a contest for the soul of the gay rights movement. The radicals began by denouncing Madolin Cervantes, treasurer of the New York Mattachine, because she was straight.[76] The homophiles saw straight activists like Cervantes as "adornments to the movement itself" who "thereby bring the crusade for homosexual rights into the mainstream of American life."[77] Jim Fouratt disagreed. At one point he strode up to Cervantes and shouted that she had no right to participate in the conference.[78] He later admitted, "We were a nightmare to them. They were committed to being nice, acceptable, status quo Americans and we were not; we had no interest at all in being acceptable."[79]

The militants convened a "radical caucus" under the chairmanship of Bob Martin and assembled a list of resolutions calling for support of the Black Panthers, striking West Coast grape pickers, and the Chicago Eight. Gunnison and other old-line delegates succeeded in defeating the resolution in support of the antiwar march on Washington but conceded to a number of other radical proposals. ERCHO then voted to dissolve itself before the radicals could offer any more controversial resolutions.[80]

In a letter to *Playboy*, Martin bragged about how the radicals forced ERCHO to become "the first association of homophile organizations to take a position as homosexuals on non-homosexual issues, thus breaching a wall which the homophile liberals had successfully maintained since the beginning of inter-organizational cooperation in 1966."[81] *Playboy* also published Foster Gunnison's version of what happened at the ERCHO conference:

Martin gives a false picture of the young radical contingent bulldozing its platform through the Eastern Regional Conference of Homophile Organizations, leaving the elderly liberals in total defeat. The fact is that, immediately afterward, E.R.C.H.O. voted to suspend itself for one year—a curious move, akin to shooting yourself in the head before the next guy does it for you. In this way, however, we prevented a takeover of our organization by the extremists, and when the dust settles, the homophile cause can be resurrected as a sane and rational movement.[82]

ERCHO, however was not resurrected; and the homophile movement never recovered.

Frank Kameny, Barbara Gittings, and Kay Lahusen were also confronted with the GLFers' arrogance when they showed up at a Front meeting a few weeks after the ERCHO conference to observe the new generation of activists at work. Before they could sit down, Fouratt interrogated them. "What are your credentials?" he demanded. Barbara Gittings replied "I'm gay, that's why I'm here."[83] Fouratt then gave a speech calling them lackeys of the establishment and arguing that their presence compromised GLF's new consciousness. The general assembly voted to let the homophile legends stay but spent an hour and a half debating whether the "pigs" should be allowed to participate.[84] Kameny, Gittings, and Lahusen had once been young rebels who criticized Donald Webster Cory, Del Martin, and the older generation of homophile activists for "being over the hill" and "out of touch." Now they found GLF doing the same to them.[85]

Since the constant bickering, debating, and berating thwarted GLF's ability to engage in focused, concerted political activity, the emphasis of the organization shifted to consciousness-raising sessions where lesbians and gays exchanged stories about the hardships of being homosexual in American society. Borrowed from the women's movement and the criticism-self-criticism sessions of the Communist Party, consciousness-raising was intended to enlighten participants to the ways that a hostile society shaped their identity. Most in GLF thought the sessions would enable gays and lesbians to speak honestly in a protective atmosphere that was not politically charged like the weekly meetings.[86] Some even hoped the participants' "self-realization" and "actualization" would inspire others to join the movement. The weekly sessions would thereby radiate liberation into the greater society beyond GLF. The Front's newsletter boldly proclaimed, "We are going to transform the society at large through the open realization of our own consciousness."[87] While such indirect social impact is impossible to assess, the consciousness-raising sessions did spawn new interpretations of the gay world and straight society and served as an intellectual wellspring of the gay and lesbian movements. Allen Young, a writer and editor of several books on gay history and politics, found the consciousness-raising sessions significantly influenced his work.[88]

The sessions, however, occasionally devolved into collective whining or political indoctrination.[89] People who did not buy into the absolute necessity of revolution were criticized for not being "aware."[90] Some GLFers bashed Marty Robinson for being too reformist, too interested in becoming a political leader, and too promiscuous.[91] Robinson remembered how "They'd turn on you and say 'Well, you're kinda pushy, so if you're an honest person, you might examine yourself to see if you're really interested in self-improvement.' Then they'd get you to a point when you were ineffectual and non-aggressive." He and others thought the encounter groups were a way for the emotionally stronger members to browbeat others into compliance.[92] Ralph Hall recalled, "Weekly, I listen to those politically articulate dogmatists. . . . I watch them shrewdly manipulate and brainwash the membership. Those who do not fall for their bullshit rhetoric are openly criticized and cleverly attacked when they express their disapproval. Persons questioning points of view or dissenting to majority consensus of GLF are openly embarrassed, insulted, and/or humiliated. . . . At times one gets the feeling an uncontrollable few on the floor will rise, lasso a victim, and proceed to hang him."[93] Such pecking parties did a great deal of emotional damage. Ultimately the Front's focus on intramural consciousness-raising and its neglect of the "pig media" greatly curtailed its ability to reach out beyond the GLF membership.

One of GLF's consciousness-raising groups gave birth to Lesbian Feminism, the most significant force to hit both the feminist and gay rights movements. The planning sessions for the lesbian dances gave female GLFers the opportunity to form networks and get to know each other. Following the suggestion of fledgling writer Rita Mae Brown, some of them formed a consciousness-raising group with independent lesbians in the women's liberation movement. Brown had been the founder of the Student Homophile League chapter at NYU but became a member of the National Organization of Women (NOW) after discovering that male homosexuals could be dismissive of lesbian concerns and just as chauvinistic as straights. She also discovered conservative feminists who were openly hostile to lesbians. Betty Friedan warned that the lesbian feminists were a "lavender menace" that might give the women's movement a bad name if feminism were associated with "man-haters" and a "bunch of dykes."[94] When Brown failed to convince NOW to reach out to lesbians, she quit and joined GLF. She and others in the consciousness-raising groups concluded that all men perpetuated values and attitudes that oppressed all women and that the problems of lesbians were central to feminism.[95] In the spring of 1970, several women met in Brown's apartment to craft an essay that would become the founding document of lesbian feminism. "The Woman-Identified Woman" explained the political significance of lesbianism, its role in the women's movement, and the reason lesbians needed to commit themselves to women's liberation before gay liberation.

Brown, Karla Jay, and others decided to publicize the significant presence of lesbians within the feminist movement at the Second Congress to Unite Women on May Day 1970. During one of the conference sessions, the lights went out in the auditorium and then flickered on to reveal seventeen women in the aisles wearing T-shirts emblazoned with "Lavender Menace." The next day the Congress passed a series of resolutions on lesbian rights beginning with the ironic declaration: "Be it resolved that Women's Liberation is a Lesbian plot."[96] Karla Jay recalled the importance of the "Lavender Menace" protest in her autobiography:

> Only weeks earlier, we had been a random group of women associated primarily with gay liberation and women's liberation. For the moment at least, we emerged a victorious organization with a sense of solidarity, common purpose, and sisterhood. We knew we would no longer accept second-class status in the women's movement or the gay movement. We would be equal partners, or we would leave the straight women and gay men behind.[97]

The women's movement had no choice but to begin addressing issues that were important to lesbians. Feminist theorists began defining lesbianism as a Female Nationalism that excluded men. Jill Johnston, the country's first openly lesbian columnist, declared in a 1971 issue of the *Village Voice*, "Until all women are lesbians there will be no true political revolution."[98] Many straight feminists even felt pressured to declare themselves "political lesbians," a label that confirmed the worst fears of not only conservative traditionalists but moderate feminists as well.[99]

The redefinition of lesbianism as Female Nationalism and the feminist acknowledgment of lesbian issues contributed to the breakdown of gay and lesbian collaboration in the gay rights movement. The need to develop a sense of self outside the influence of men drove the women in the Gay Liberation Front to form Radicalesbians, another GLF splinter group that had significant social impact. Radicalesbians and the rise of lesbian feminism also played a major role in drawing away young activists from the Daughters of Bilitis, which dissolved in 1971.[100]

Some men in GLF heeded the radical lesbian critique of manhood and decided to establish the 95th Street Collective, a commune where they could develop nonsexist, nonmale life styles as "effeminists." One of the members of the collective described how the members were "mostly femme males who have the ability to love one another and have stronger emotional bonds than the 'straight' homosexuals." He argued that male homosexuals who were masculine were unliberated. Eventually members of the collective formed their own cell, the Flaming Faggots. They claimed gay liberation was antithetical to woman's liberation and that male homosexuality was counterrevolutionary because it emphasized male bonding, which was by definition oppressive: "Gay Liberation works toward repealing the sodomy laws, assuring jobs and housing for faggots, serving a socially oriented function of holding dances, picnics, boat rides, etc. rather than fighting for the real change that is necessary to free ourselves and all oppressed people; the death of male supremacy."[101] The revolutionary effeminist's goal was to become "unmanly without parodying women" by "learning how to cry," "doing childcare," and "learning to stop hating our mothers and learning to stop bonding with our fathers."[102] Eventually they figured widespread androgyny would undermine the patriarchy and the revolution would ensue.[103]

By late November 1969 all of the consciousness-raising, feuding, and disorganization became too much for several members of GLF, particularly, influential members such as Marty Robinson and Jim Owles. After Robinson failed to convince the Front to organize more zaps against political candidates in the mayoral race, he and Owles concluded that GLF lacked the political focus necessary for success.[104] The two Gay Commandos had been privately discussing the formation of a new organization for weeks when Red Butterfly John O'Brien proposed handing over five hundred dollars in GLF dance revenues to the Black Panther Defense Fund. Robinson and Owles both objected to the allocation, in part, because the Black Panthers often disparaged gays.[105] Panther rhetoric repeatedly employed the term "faggot," and Eldridge Cleaver, the Panther's minister of information, had gone on record saying that "homosexuality is a sickness, just as are baby-rape or wanting to be head of General Motors."[106] In the debate over the donation, Fouratt defended the use of the term "faggot" as a metaphor for "any castrated male made impotent by society" and dismissed Robinson and Owles as "gay power elitists" who had no concern for minorities, women, and transvestites.[107] After the GLF general assembly spent three consecutive meetings trying to reach a consensus on the issue, Owles called for a vote so other matters could be addressed. When the GLF finally voted to donate the money to the Panthers, Owles announced, "I am so frustrated. I can't continue like this. I'm going to have to leave the organization."

He was not the only one who had enough. Robinson continued to attend GLF meetings to secretly recruit members for a new organization that would be dedicated solely to gay rights, the Gay Activists Alliance.[108] Six months later GLF was still debating the donation to the Panthers. According to the minutes of a meeting in May, "Once again the discussion on the Black Panthers changed the atmosphere of the meeting."[109]

The question of whether GLF succeeded or failed is a difficult one. None of its efforts made a particularly significant impact on the political system or the general public. It did, however, create a number of models for future gay rights organizations to challenge stereotypes, attack discrimination, and generate gay pride. GLF's protests against the *Village Voice* and *Time* blazed the trail for future gay rights organizations dedicated to pressuring media to improve the image of gays. Zaps, which were invented by Marty Robinson and GLF's political reformers, would achieve important victories for the Gay Activists Alliance in the early

1970s. It is also worth noting that while the Front was fracturing into manifold splinter groups in New York, Jim Fouratt and other GLFers traveled the country creating other Fronts. "It was like fire, you know, like a prairie fire; let it roar," Fouratt recalled."People were ready. I think we set up about forty chapters, most of them on university campuses."[110] In the early 1970s there were Gay Liberation Fronts in Ann Arbor, Boston, Chicago, Denver, Detroit, Los Angeles, Milwaukee, Philadelphia, San Diego, San Francisco, Seattle, Tallahassee, Tampa, Sydney, Australia, and Cologne, Germany.

Although seminal, the New York City GLF was ultimately destined for failure. The lack of structure and the ideological divisions hamstrung the group's ability to organize and coordinate protests. Neglect of mainstream media restricted the Front from spreading its message far beyond the readership of *Come Out!* GLF also adopted increasingly extreme positions that impeded its success. Its 1970 platform demanded that straights prove their commitment to eliminating sexism by becoming homosexual.[111] "Only Lesbians can be liberated women. Only gay males can escape the sexist role of 'man.' "[112] Such declarations understandably limited the ability of GLF to build coalitions with heterosexual radicals. The GLF platform also called for free birth control, twenty-four-hour child care, full employment for "third world people and gays," elimination of the judicial system and police forces, "free food, free shelter, free transportation, free health care, free utilities, free education, free art," the abolition of the bourgeois nuclear family, and the conversion of heterosexual radicals to homosexuality. A *Come Out!* editorial even proposed burning down the City College because it promoted "establishment thinking."[113] Such radicalism made the GLF appealing to few outside the Front itself and stymied the efforts of more moderate activists to gain the support of straight liberals.

Donald Webster Cory resented how GLF "linked gays with the Panthers and Weatherpeople in the public eye, bomb throwing, irresponsible, antisocial and terrorist."[114] Martha Shelly, Jerry Hoose, and others in GLF, however, did not care about the public eye. They believed their alliances with the Panthers, Weathermen, and other radical groups would eventually coalesce into a massive revolutionary movement. Those alliances and that revolution never materialized.[115]

By the spring of 1971, GLF meetings became increasingly contentious and divided along racial and gender lines. In addition to the lingering resentment about the donation to the Black Panthers, a controversy arose over a group of left-wing GLFers who went to Cuba to cut sugar cane for the Castro regime. Many in the Front objected because they knew Castro had thrown thousands of homosexuals into "re-education" camps.[116] The gay activists' effort to assist Castro's regime was ironic. Back in 1965, stories about Castro's oppression of homosexuals spurred Frank Kameny, Jack Nichols, and Lige Clarke to launch the first public gay rights protest, a brave demonstration in front of the White House. Six years later some in GLF were cutting Castro's sugar.

The ever-present gender conflict had also become an expanding rift after GLF women decided to raid the Front's safety deposit box and expropriate half the money collected at the dances. In the interest of unity, Jerry Hoose, who organized the dances, wanted to support the women's action, but when he started to speak in favor, Karla Jay, the moderator, smacked the support column with her baseball bat and told him he had no right to speak on women's issues. With tears in his eyes Hoose walked out and never returned.[117] As the moderates and consensus builders like Hoose and Kohler left GLF, the zealots took over and drove away other members and newcomers.[118] By the end of 1971, GLF existed in name only.

But the name was important. San Francisco writer Sasha Gregory wrote in June 1972, "Although the Gay Liberation Front has changed dramatically over the first three years of its life, becoming more an idea than an actual group of people, much remains of its spirit. Today GLF means pride in being Gay. GLF means the knowledge of Gay Power. GLF is an awareness of being at the front-line of struggle for gay rights for millions of our brothers and sisters across the country."[119]

The Gay Liberation Front also became an important symbol that brought a toughness and hipness to the popular conception of homosexuals. Donald Webster Cory was not the only person who thought of GLF as the Black Panthers or the Young Lords of the gay rights movement. The struggle for gay rights, however, would not succeed through consciousness-raising sessions, communal living, or manning imaginary ramparts. Fortunately another New York organization had emerged that appreciated the importance of the public eye and knew how to catch it.

chapter six

THE MADE-FOR-TV MOVEMENT

In May 1971, the CBS sitcom *All in the Family* presented its 50 million viewers with a homosexual character who was an earnest, macho former professional football player and one of Archie Bunker's best friends.[1] Years of protests and speeches by liberation activists could not have promoted the idea that gays could be tough and masculine as much as that thirty-minute TV show. Richard Nixon was so shocked by the episode that he discussed it during an Oval Office meeting with Chief of Staff H. R. Haldeman and Domestic Policy Adviser John Ehrlichman:

> **Ehrlichman:** What's it called?
> **Nixon:** Archie's Guys. Archie sitting here with his hippie son-in-law, married to the screwball daughter. The son-in-law apparently goes both ways. This guy. He's obviously queer—wears an ascot—but not offensively so. Very clever. Uses nice language. Shows pictures of his parents. And so Arch goes down to the bar. Sees his best friend, who used to play professional football. Virile, strong, this and that. Then the fairy comes into the bar. I don't mind homosexuality. I understand it. Nevertheless, goddamn, I don't think you glorify it on public television, homosexuality, even more

than you glorify whores. We all know we have weaknesses. But goddammit, what do you think that does to kids? You know what happened to the Greeks! Homosexuality destroyed them. Sure, Aristotle was a homo. We all know that. So was Socrates.

Ehrlichman: But he never had the influence television had.[2]

The President and his men were not the only ones who understood the power of television to shape public perceptions of homosexuality. Many gay liberationists knew they had to capture the attention of the media to attack stereotypes. Only through positive characterizations of homosexuals in articles, newscasts, movies, and TV shows could the liberation movement gain the sympathy of straights, encourage closeted gays to come out, and build an imagined gay community. Among all of the gay liberationist groups, the Gay Activists Alliance (GAA) in New York City was the most successful at triggering the power of mass media to disseminate what it called "gay propaganda."[3] The key to their success was the zap.

On a cold December night in 1969, Jim Owles, Marty Robinson, Arthur Evans, Arthur Bell, and other dissidents from the Gay Liberation Front met in Bell's Upper East Side apartment to found GAA.[4] Their experience in the chaotic GLF had a great impact on the new organization. One of the Front's greatest weaknesses was that a few individual members had too much power. Because decisions were reached by consensus, the members who could speak the longest, the loudest, and most effectively would win the day. Having seen how GLF's participatory democracy generated "more talk than action," GAA's founders chose to run their meetings according to Robert's Rules of Order.[5] Decisions were made by majority votes rather than by consensus, and annual elections filled leadership positions with set responsibilities. While the president moderated the meetings, disputes over the rules of order could be referred to the official parliamentarian.[6] Before anyone could join, he or she had to participate in an orientation session and attend at least three meetings within a period of six consecutive weeks. Members were required to pay fees and to be present at three meetings every six months.[7]

Originally the founders envisioned GAA as a small cadre who would collectively plan and stage zaps. But as the membership grew to an unexpected size and meetings of the entire organization became unwieldy, members were divided into a dozen committees of eight to ten people who were responsible for a single activity. An Orientation Committee ran information sessions for prospective members to learn the rules of the Alliance, a Pleasure Committee coordinated dances, and an Agitprop Committee sent representatives to high schools and colleges to discuss gay liberation with students and teachers. A Committee on Committees was soon needed to coordinate all the committees. The Alliance's constitution endowed the president and the executive committee with substantial power. The executives could veto any application for membership unless overridden by a two-thirds majority of the general membership and could recommend expulsion of a disruptive member, which would have to be confirmed by two-thirds of the members.[8] One GLFer found GAA meetings boring and uninspiring, another found the Activists and their constitutional strictures uptight and stifling: "You can't open your mouth at GAA meetings. You interrupt them and—zing! You're stigmatized!"[9]

GAA's founders, whose politics ranged from "mildly liberal to wildly radical," declared the Alliance to be a "one issue organization," focused solely on the struggle for gay rights rather than a crusade for leftist revolution or the myriad other causes supported by the GLF.[10] Members were obligated to assign first priority to gay rights; GAA explicitly disassociated itself from other movements such as women's liberation or black nationalism so there would be no entangling alliances with groups uncommitted to gay liberation. The single focus also enabled GAA to create a wide constituency that cut across the political spectrum.

One of the Activists' main crusades was challenging antigay messages in the media. When the GAA found gay slurs in the columns of a few *New York Post* writers, including Pete Hamill, they decided to act, even though the *Post* was New York's most liberal newspaper. Activist Marty Robinson explained the reasoning behind the focus on the liberal press: "Homosexuals were fighting their way with liberals. The press, by keeping homosexuals out of the news, by keeping them something unusual instead of everyday circumstance, had also been guilty of participating in our oppression."[11] Robinson knew that all editors and publishers were complicit of the conspiracy of silence. The liberals in the publishing industry, however, were on record in support of the rights of all minority groups and had made a great effort to present the public with sympathetic depictions of other minorities. Zaps would embarrass liberal publishers into recognizing and defending the homosexual minority. The strategy worked very well on the liberal *New York Post*. One morning GAA stormed the *Post*'s headquarters and demanded to speak with the publisher. After an hour of jawboning, the editor appeased the Activists by promising to print more sensitive and balanced reporting on homosexuality. The *Post* soon began giving substantial attention to GAA, and by 1971 Jim Owles praised it for being "the only New York newspaper that is interested in the equality of civil rights for the vast homosexual community of New York."[12]

Shortly after the GAA zapped their offices, the *Post* published a very supportive article on the Alliance's first major street action, a march on City Hall. The article recounted the reactions of two bystanders. A conservatively dressed businessman told the reporter, "It's their own life. They're entitled to their own lives. I'm no activist in this but I think it requires a lot of nerve to march out there." A passerby in a sport jacket and wool cap then interjected, "Well they have no morals." In response the businessman asked, "What are morals? Isn't that morals, too, not to discriminate against people?"[13] *Gay Power* newspaper described the impact of the City Hall demonstration on reporters and spectators:

> The press felt the vibe too. The cameras continued shooting as we circled the area outside City Hall, they photographed us and asked us questions, so many questions. "How did it get started, What about the Stonewall raid, How do the sodomy laws [oppress] homosexuals, What do our parents know, How would we feel if our parents knew, Are we proud of what we're doing, What are we?" The sideliners got an education too. Any concept of namby-pamby homosexuality went by the wayside as they saw and met and witnessed honest-to-God, flesh-and-blood, gorgeous, gorgeous, gorgeous gays. Stereotypes? Did they learn![14]

GAA discovered that the demonstration generated media images that challenged the old negative stereotypes. An ABC-TV reporter bluntly opened his report on the City Hall demonstration with the line, "Limp wrists stiffened today!"[15]

While TV viewers absorbed a new image of homosexuals, the mindset of those who participated in the protest also changed. Arthur Bell recalled the Activists watching themselves on the evening news after the City Hall action and "gloating over the sight of their own happy faces, proud that our march on City Hall was successful, and ready and eager for another full-scale attack on the forces that oppressed us."[16] GAA believed homosexuals were one of the most oppressed minority groups because they were able to hide. Instead of fighting their oppression, most American gays chose to avoid the pain of discrimination by becoming their own police and evading any public revelations. The City Hall march showed participants and onlookers that the heterosexual world was not as dangerous or threatening as they thought. All of a sudden they realized they could proudly assert their rights.[17] If a demonstration could trigger media attention, as in the case of the City Hall march, then a sense of empowerment and pride could be generated in homosexual television viewers and newspaper readers who silently cheered on their fellow members of an imagined gay community.

GAA began to ensure that their zaps generated media attention by inviting reporters along for the show. The liberal *Harper*'s magazine became a target of a GAA media spectacle in the fall of 1970 after it ran a particularly offensive essay on homosexuality. The author of the essay, Joseph Epstein, wrote:

> I do think homosexuality is an anathema, and hence homosexuals cursed. . . . If I had the power to do so, I would wish homosexuality off the face of this earth. . . . There is much my four sons can do in their lives that might cause me anguish, might outrage me, that might make me ashamed of them and of myself as their father. But nothing they could ever do would make me sadder than if any of them were to become homosexual. For then I should know them condemned to a state of permanent niggerdom among men, their lives, whatever adjustment they might make to their condition, to be lived out as part of the pain of the earth.[18]

GAA politely requested *Harper*'s publish a rebuttal article. But after receiving no reply, Pete Fisher, chairman of the Ad Hoc *Harper*'s Action Committee, began planning the zap. Fisher, a sharp Columbia undergraduate with a mop of curly brown hair, invited TV news outfits and instructed the protestors to assume a tone that would appeal to television viewers: "civilized, intelligent, educated, consciousness raising, hospitable—no demands, no threat, no damage to offices or files." A press release invited reporters to "have a cup of coffee and talk to a real live human homosexual as opposed to the ugly, cardboard myth depicted by Epstein."[19]

After a rehearsal at Arthur Bell's apartment, the show began on a Tuesday morning at nine when forty Activists, trailed by a WOR-TV news crew, entered the headquarters of *Harper*'s. They immediately set up a table with coffee and doughnuts and began placing leaflets on every desk in the office. As workers filtered out of the elevators, the protestors politely shook their hands and introduced themselves, "Good morning, I'm a homosexual. We're here to protest the Epstein article. Would you like some coffee? Cream and sugar? Pamphlet?"[20] On the sidewalk outside the office, Activists provided passersby with flyers that read,

> What are homosexuals like? As a service to the people of New York and the readers of *Harper*'s magazine, Gay Activists Alliance has arranged to make a group of homosexuals available to meet with the public, to meet with those who would like to test the truth of the remarks, which appeared in *Harper*'s. All those who are interested in rapping with us are encouraged to drop in and join us in our Surprise Visit to *Harper*'s offices on the 18th floor of the Park Avenue Building, 2 Park Ave., any time today. Coffee will be served: stop by on your coffee break. Bring a sandwich on your lunch hour—have lunch with a homosexual at *Harper*'s.

To enhance the entertainment value of the protest, Fisher and Tom Doerr played guitars and sang songs for the cameras. GAA left at the end of the workday after the editor promised to search actively for an article favorable to homosexuals. The most important result of the protest, however, was the media attention.

A news producer at WOR-TV saw his station's coverage of the *Harper*'s zap and decided to run a three-part news special on GAA and the gay rights movement. The first installment featured an interview with Arthur Bell, an older Activist who worked in public relations for Random House. Bell recalled at one point in the televised interview being asked, "Will you ever be completely happy?" His response was, "I'm happy when my work is going good, when my love life is going good, when I'm attuned to the world. With me, being attuned is never a constant; therefore I can never be completely happy. Can you?" The interview went so well the station later sent cameras to a GAA meeting and videotaped Bell at work, "a sort of day in the life of a living, breathing homosexual." Footage of Bell walking down the street was augmented with a voice-over that intoned: "*Sometimes when the weather is nice, Mr. Bell walks to work. There is nothing to distinguish him from other New Yorkers, except he is an admitted homosexual.*"[21] The producers told Bell they purposely promoted gay rights by giving the series "a direction: the human aspect of the homosexual (as opposed to political, angry, etc.)." A few days after the series aired, Lem Tucker, head of WOR News called Bell to say that thanks to the gay rights feature his program went up five Nielsen points. "Hooray for gay," Bell later reminisced, "we're box office!"[22]

GAA's TV appearances were not always so warmly welcomed by studio executives. On the same day as the *Harper*'s demonstration, Activists armed with whistles attempted to disrupt a taping of the *Dick Cavett Show* in response to antigay remarks and jokes that comedian Mort Sahl had made during his guest appearance. GAA sympathizers who worked for the station served the cause by providing GAA with the tickets to the live studio audience. "We always had friends who worked inside," Arthur Evans recalled.[23] But the plans were discovered and Dick Cavett, who had seen the WOR-TV news report on the *Harper*'s demonstration, agreed to arrange a scheduled appearance on his nationally televised show in exchange for a truce.[24] Activists Marty Robinson and Arthur Evans were chosen to be interviewed along with Dick Leitsch. Evans had decided to use his network television debut to come out to his parents in rural Pennsylvania. Not knowing why their son was to be interviewed, they told their extended family and friends to watch the Thanksgiving night broadcast.[25]

The usually smooth and charming Cavett opened the questioning with: "What are you really after?" For the next forty minutes Robinson, Evans, and Leitsch answered that question for Cavett and much of America, including Evans's shocked parents. Robinson, a tough, clean-cut carpenter, was a perfect spokesman for GAA. Sporting a new haircut that enhanced his boy-next-door look, Robinson explained how "heterosexuals live in this society without scorn—they live openly, their affection is idolized in movies, theater. Homosexuals want the same thing: to be open in this society. To live a life without fear of reprisal from anybody for being homosexual—to live a life of respect." Arthur Evans described one of the greatest dilemmas for gays:

> We're faced with a kind of cruel alternative: if we deny our emotions, don't show them in public, and appear to be straight, then we can have a career; but if we're open, and show our affections the way heterosexuals do, and lead an open sexual life, then our careers are ended. We feel that it is repressive and unjust that we have to face that alternative. There is no reason why we can't be full people, both economically and in terms of our feelings! . . . This is a matter of political rights, our Constitutional rights, which we have under the Declaration of Independence: "Life, liberty, and the pursuit of happiness."

Evans then asked Cavett, "We should have that, too, don't you think?" When talk turned to the Epstein article in *Harper*'s, Evans said that "a point that was really offensive, to my mind, was the statement by Joseph Epstein that homosexuality is a curse, which should be wiped off the face of the earth. . . . If someone had said that about the Jews or the blacks, *Harper*'s magazine would have been burned to the ground. The fact that they said it about homosexuals was left unnoticed by the press, or by any politician or spokesman for society. . . . People sit back and say, 'oh, how 'bout that.' " Robinson declared, "I can say, to Mr. Epstein, that my own personal experience as a homosexual is that of a happy human being. My homosexuality is one of the assets of my life: I like my lifestyle, I love my lover, I'm happy being what I am." During the interview Dick Cavett offered little comment except: "I don't know what we can learn from this, exactly," but afterward he adopted a policy of avoiding jokes that might offend homosexuals.[26] John Murphy, a member of the GLF and a harsh critic of the Alliance, wrote in his memoir that the GAA appearance on the Cavett show was the first occasion that the oppression of homosexuals was discussed on TV at length and with intelligence.[27] About a week after the program, Evans received a letter from his parents asking him, "Why do it on television and embarrass the neighbors?"[28]

Not to be outdone by Cavett, fellow cosmopolitan liberal David Susskind hosted a show featuring a debate between GAA and four Aesthetic Realists, a group dedicated to converting gays to heterosexuality. Foster Gunnison, the homophile leader, commented on GAA's performance: "It was truly ironic. Here were four fellows (the other side) who anyone could pick out of a crowd as being gay so pronouncedly stereotyped were their mannerisms, speech, and train of thought (if it could be called that), and then our four—none of whom (save a tiny bit in Battcock) reflected any of the stereotype. Surely this must have been well-noticed."[29] The talk show appearances enabled GAA to put a new face on homosexuality and gay rights. Television images of smart, articulate, respectable gay men carried the message of gay liberation into millions of American homes.[30]

Bruce Voeller, a gay father of two and professor of biology at Rockefeller University, saw the GAA appearance on the Susskind Show and was particularly impressed with how "normal-looking" they were—a stark contrast to the flamboyant type that made straights uncomfortable.[31] Voeller soon joined GAA and later became its president and the founder of the National Gay Task Force. GAA's media presence had a bandwagon effect on membership.[32] After the Activists' many TV appearances, attendance at the weekly GAA meetings soared above three hundred people.[33]

The response to the television appearances showed GAA the value of media manipulation. An internal GAA memo stated:

> As important as it is to change the laws, that alone is not going to change social attitudes. If the Gay images presented on these shows and films are good, we have a chance to educate millions of people while they're held captive by a

screen offering ostensibly escapist material. There are gay movies and gay books and gay papers but who uses them except for a small percentage of gays? Through the popular commercial media we have a chance to reach both straight and gay people who would otherwise never be even remotely touched by Gay Power.[34]

Another GAA memo boldly stated, "Media may be indirectly responsible for liberating the homosexual."[35] The liberation movement had few legislative or legal successes, but it was effective in using, and sometimes pushing, the media to reshape what it meant to be gay for both straights and homosexuals.

The Alliance was always interested in countering gay stereotypes in the media, specifically the myth that gays were all effeminate. An internal GAA memo complained that TV presented "the typical society view of gay people, mincing faggots short on brains and intelligence and long on sentiment, frills and swishes."[36] "A limp wrist. Flamboyant attire," a GAA press statement declared. "A love for the theater and the arts. These don't necessarily make a homosexual. The tough looking cop on the corner, doctors, lawyers, the married guy in the office with a couple of kids—nobody's gay proof. Too many people can't get this through their heads."[37] GAA tried to reduce anxieties about homosexuality by pushing the idea that gays could be "ordinary." A New York columnist drew a parallel between the Alliance's attempt to downplay the disparity between gays and straights and the Civil Rights movement's emphasis on the similarity between blacks and whites: "The Gays, like the blacks a decade ago, are pushing for integration; they are not yet secure enough to make a virtue of their difference from the mass of society."[38]

GAA set up a media committee to monitor the depictions of gays in TV shows, publications, movies, and books. The media committee's mission statement declared, "Gay rights have suddenly become big news. We can't let this opportunity slip right through our fingers. We have to keep watch. We have to watch *carefully*. We have to advise, suggest and then holler like hell when something goes wrong." The media committee was particularly concerned with depictions of the "colorful" homosexual. GAA claimed that they did not want to deny the existence of effeminate or "obvious" homosexuals, but they feared the "constant repetition of stereotyped gay images, whether real or faked for the movie cameras, prevents people from realizing that we gays come in many different sizes, shapes and colors. Besides, the media rarely humanizes those stereotyped gay characters, but uses them for laugh getters instead."[39] The Alliance sent letters of complaint regarding negative stereotypes to various publications and television producers including CBS, *The Tonight Show*, the *New York Times*, *Life*, and *Mad Magazine*, and wrote Bantam Books to condemn the demeaning presentation of homosexuals in the book *Shaft Has a Ball*.[40] Media insiders who were angered by negative portrayals of homosexuals began assisting GAA. Someone at ABC-TV sent the Alliance a script for an upcoming episode of *Marcus Welby, M.D.* in which a gay man was advised to get help for his "sickness." Seventeen Activists raided ABC's headquarters and commenced a sit-in.[41]

Legendary entertainer Bob Hope admitted in an interview that the Alliance also "worked on me. They gave me a terrible time." Hope angered GAA when he camped his way through a skit on a network television special and joked about how the Gay Liberation Parade was the first time a cop rode side-saddle at the head of a parade. "I said they were holding the parade in Queens," Hope recalled. "They [GAA] wrote NBC and demanded equal time."[42] Johnny Carson was also threatened with a zap after he delivered a monologue that the Alliance deemed offensive. Jack Paar made the mistake of telling his viewers, "If your child loses a tooth tell him to put it under his pillow and a member of the Gay Activists Alliance will come and leave a quarter." When the *Paar Show* failed to respond to GAA's demands for an apology, the Alliance acquired thirty tickets for a taping from a supporter who worked for ABC. Paar himself learned about the Activists' plans and personally called GAA to invite some members to be interviewed. In front of an audience of seven million people, Bruce Voeller, Arnie Kantrowitz, and Nath Rockhill invited lonely, closeted gays to come out and recognize that there are many healthy, happy homosexuals throughout the country. "In short, persuaded them that they are not alone," according to the GAA newsletter. The Activists tailored their appearance to Parr's audience, "humane and appealing, not very angry." When Paar asked "If Jean Genet writes about having sex with a goat, shouldn't we be offended?" Kantrowitz popped back, "If anyone should be offended it is the goat." "The audience laughed," Kantrowitz recalled, "and I knew I had them." At the end of the interview, Paar told the Activists, "All right, the camera is yours. What is it you want to say?" In a rational tone, Kantrowitz told viewers that the people sitting next to them may be gay, members of their own families perhaps. "Why not let them be who they are?"[43] Many of the calls and notes ABC and GAA received regarding the show came from people in middle America who found the discussion uplifting.[44]

Not all homosexuals supported the Alliance's attempt to shape the media image of gays to the tastes of middle America. A Queens College student voiced frustration with GAA's tendency to use only spokesmen who were "beautiful, clean-cut, movie-TV star type figures." Ironically, he felt the Activists discriminated against him as an effeminate homosexual. "If I were to speak, they'd peg me as a cumbersome artifact that doesn't fit into their décor. They want to accommodate straight looking gays—we must all look straight and act straight and not fit into their stereotyped image. The whole thing makes me sick."[45]

One way the GAA triggered media images of tough and serious gays was through nonviolent, confrontational political activity. During the Cavett interview, Arthur Evans described the way GAA and the liberation movement connected personal development and political struggle:

> We've a phrase called "coming out"—gay people, when they
> first realize that they're gay, have a process of "coming out,"
> that is, coming out sexually. We've extended that to the
> political field. We feel that we have to come out politically,
> as a community which is aware that it is oppressed and
> which is a political power bloc feared by the government.
> Until the government is afraid of us—afraid of our power—
> we will never have our rights.

GAA began to generate some fear among New York politicians in the winter of 1970 after the Alliance decided to launch a campaign to pass a municipal bill that would prohibit discrimination based on sexual orientation in employment, in public accommodation, and in housing.[46] While most GAA leaders knew the legislation, known as Intro 475, had little chance of passage, they saw it as the perfect launch initiative for their new organization. An effort to pass the bill would define GAA publicly as a gay liberation group willing to work within the system, while petition drives and demonstrations would generate media images that would challenge stereotypes of the frivolous, silly homosexual and encourage closeted or politically inactive gays to join the cause. GAA envisioned the Intro 475 crusade, which Marty Robinson called "an anti-closet drive," as "an activist approach to consciousness raising."[47] Members hit the bars and streets of Greenwich Village and Times Square to collect signatures on petitions that called upon liberal councilwoman Carol Greitzer to introduce the bill. Greitzer was a perfect target, for not only did she represent Greenwich Village, the neighborhood with America's most politically strident gay community, she also had a reputation for insensitivity to the concerns of homosexuals.[48] In a few months GAA collected six thousand signatures.

Greitzer probably dismissed the shaggy-haired, pale young man who walked into City Hall to deliver the petitions as just another hippie radical. Jim Owles, GAA's first president, was actually an experienced political activist who was discharged from the Air Force for engaging in antiwar activities. Although Owles was not a dynamic presence during meetings, he displayed a fearless dedication during demonstrations. During the march on City Hall, he jumped into a line of police officers guarding the doorway. The police caught him and threw the slight young man down the steps. Owles popped up and ran back to the doorway, where he was dragged inside the building by the neck and arrested.[49] After seeing that display of either bravery or foolishness, Marty Robinson dubbed Owles, "the scrappiest little faggot in New York."[50] When Owles presented the petitions to Greitzer, her cold look and countenance gave him the "impression she was taking bad medicine." The councilwoman declared she "didn't relate to the homosexual cause" and rejected the petitions.[51] After Owles reported her reaction to the GAA, planning began for a more forceful delivery of the petitions.

One evening, three dozen Activists infiltrated a meeting of Greitzer's Village Independent Democrats Club. As soon as Greitzer entered the room, Marty Robinson shouted, "Listen, Carol, baby, you're antihomosexual, antihomosexual!" Arthur Evans then yelled, "Carol Geitzer refused to accept our petitions. . . . If she doesn't relate to the homosexual cause, the Village Independent Democrats don't relate, and we are prepared to sit in." Other Activists began to chime in until Robinson demanded, "Will you co-sponsor a bill?" After Greitzer offered the weak excuse that she had been unable to accept the petitions from Owles because she already had too many other papers to bring home, she reluctantly promised to submit the bill.[52] Greitzer became the first politician to succumb to the zap.

Had Intro 475 been passed, it would have been the first law in the nation to prohibit discrimination against homosexuals. As GAA hoped, its mere submission to the City Council's Committee on General Welfare garnered attention from the local newspapers and the UPI, which distributed the story to papers everywhere from Dallas, Texas, to Naples, Italy.[53]

The Carol Greitzer protest became a model for zaps against politicians. GAA ignored conservatives for the most part because in the 1970s accusing right-wing politicians of discriminating against gays would have increased their popularity. Liberals were particularly vulnerable to zaps because they publicly committed themselves to equal rights for minorities and therefore could be shamed into supporting gay rights. Marty Robinson called the strategy, "climbing up the liberals." When confronting a zap, liberals faced a dilemma. "Either the liberal starts dealing with us," Arthur Evans excitedly recounted thirty years later, "or he calls the police in and has us roughed up. Ok Mr. Liberal, what are you going to do? You can't live the contradiction any more—you are going to have to choose. Whatever you choose, the TV cameras are rolling."[54] When election day arrived, most Activists voted for the same liberals they had zapped repeatedly.[55]

GAA knew zaps were largely dependent on the mass media to be effective. Pete Fisher recalled, "It is through the media that we reach the public in order to embarrass a politician, and it is through the media that we reach the gay population and those straights who may be sympathetic to our goals."[56] For GAA, television was the most important medium and they conducted their zaps as if they were TV shows. Arthur Evans described a typical zap:

The set was already in place. The aim was to use television to reach peoples' feelings to create a drama to enact a drama where people could see with their own eyes. "Ok the government is acting this way. The corporation is responding this way, the police are responding this way, and the lesbians and gays are responding this way—ok who looks the best? Who has the best sense of humor? Who is the most theatrical? Who has the best lines? Who's putting on the best show here? And it was always us. And the times we got beat up we came out looking heroic, which we were. . . . The aim was to reach the existential and emotional life of gay men who were not interested in politics who did not connect their sexuality with political issue. Who just had a tight little shell of internalized sexual feelings and maybe some guilt and just wanted to get through the day and not deal with things. We wanted to reach their anger and some inspiration with something exciting. So they would be sitting in their living rooms and they would see us and say My God! What's going on here? We were interesting. We were the most interesting show on TV.[57]

Like television shows, good zaps had obvious heroes, villains, and fools. Arthur Evans had a way of also adding a bit of drama to a zap. With a long, shaggy mane that gave him the look of a biblical prophet, he would stick his face inches away from editors and politicians and scream, "Answer the homosexuals! Answer the homosexuals!"[58]

The zap was an important tool for consciousness-raising because participants experienced a new sense of self-confidence while everyone else saw a "new model of gayness."[59] According to Evans, who was regarded as GAA's theoretician:

Gays who have as yet no sense of gay pride see a zap on television or read about it in the press. First they are vaguely disturbed at the demonstrators for "rocking the boat"; eventually when they see how the straight establishment responds, they feel anger. This anger gradually focuses on the heterosexual oppressors, and the gays develop a sense of class-consciousness. And the no-longer closeted gays realize that assimilation into the heterosexual mainstream is no answer; gays must unite among themselves, organize their common resources for collective action and resist.[60]

Evans understood the importance of media to the gay rights movement. Words that are merely spoken in a speech or conversation do not possess the same power as those that are published or broadcast, even by a small press or local television station. In the mid-1950s the gay press gave credibility to the ideas of the early gay rights movement by putting them in print. Evans grasped intellectually what Marty Robinson grasped instinctively: in the TV age a social movement needed television coverage not only to spread its message but to give its message credibility. Appearing on television meant that the powers-that-be recognized a person or cause as worthy of the attention of millions of people. Gays and straights who had previously dismissed the importance of the gay rights movement suddenly realized that it was important because it was discussed on TV. The main goal of every GAA protest and zap was media coverage, particularly television; the stated goal of the protest was secondary.[61]

Media coverage of zaps on Mayor John Lindsay made the GAA famous. For years Lindsay had quietly worked with the New York Mattachine to reduce harassment of gays by the police. GAA wanted the mayor to take a public stand in favor of gay rights.[62] A public endorsement of gay rights by a nationally known politician like Lindsay would bring instant credibility to the movement and the cause. The great liberal mayor however had his eye on the presidency and was very reluctant to make such a controversial move. Unfortunately for Lindsay and his presidential ambitions, he lived in the same city as the GAA.

After Lindsay refused to meet with GAA to discuss Intro 475, the Activists decided, in Arthur Evans's words, "to make him feel in his personal life the same consequences we feel in our personal lives as a result of his politics." When John and Mary Lindsay attended the opening night gala at the Metropolitan Opera, Activists dressed in tuxedos and suits surrounded them in the grand lobby and shouted, "End police harassment, support civil rights for gay people!" Later,

GAA swarmed around the Lindsays at the opening of a Broadway play and chanted, "Homosexuals need your help, end police harassment." The mayor remained cool as always, but to his embarrassment, his wife Mary kicked and punched her way through the mob. When he scolded her and she barked back, Arthur Evans thought, "Good, this has become a marital issue with them!"[63]

The first time GAA made the pages of the *New York Times* was in April 1970 when they zapped Lindsay on the steps of the Metropolitan Museum of Art. Lindsay was in the middle of a speech marking the museum's hundredth anniversary when Marty Robinson walked up to the podium and introduced himself to a shocked audience: "Mr. Mayor, I'm a member of Gay Activists Alliance and I want to know when you intend to speak out on homosexual rights. . . ." Before the young Activist was able to mention Intro 475, police in crash helmets quickly bundled him away from the podium and down the stairs. Later Robinson vowed that he would never again start a zap with an introduction.[64] Some GAA protestors moved into the Museum's Great Hall and chanted "Gay Power," according to a *New York Times* report. Meanwhile, Lindsay kept his cool and shook hands with the crowd. One of the Activists who remained outside the museum grabbed the Mayor's hand and refused to let go until police pried his hands away.[65] A GAA press release later celebrated this image of tough homosexuals wrestling with the cops: "It takes three straights to dislodge one gay!"[66] Lindsay continued shaking hands but was soon caught in the grip of yet another Activist. Arnie Kantrowitz was terrified as he stood waiting to take his turn squeezing the mayor's hand but was emboldened by the brazenness of his fellow Activists: "We made each other feel powerful."[67]

Although *GAY* magazine was the only publication to share GAA's enthusiasm for the zap, all of the major New York papers covered it. GAA often hijacked media events like the mayor's museum speech. Events that were originally organized to generate publicity for politicians or institutions were suddenly transformed by zaps into advertisements for GAA and gay power.

A week later, GAA zapped Lindsay's weekly Sunday evening TV show, *With Mayor Lindsay*. In preparation for the show, about twenty Activists met in an apartment near the studio and rehearsed their demonstration. The Political Action Committee had prepared lines the protestors would deliver during the question-and-answer segment of the show. After receiving the script, the Activists conducted a run-through during which they rehearsed when and how to chant, applaud, boo, and stomp their feet collectively. About ten minutes into the video-taping of Lindsay's discussion with a conservationist about Earth Day, an Activist ran up to the mayor and shouted, "Homosexuals want an end to job discrimination!" Another then bounded forward, yelling, "Let that man speak!" GAA members, who made up about a third of the audience, started chanting, "Answer homosexuals!" Security guards momentarily restored order by removing a few of the rabble-rousers. But when Lindsay mentioned the benefits of one-way nonreturnable bottles, Owles shouted, "What about a one-way nonreturnable mayor?" and raised an indignant finger as security hustled him out the door. When the conversation moved to the topic of noise pollution, Lindsay warned, "If you are stuck in a traffic jam, it's illegal to blow your horn." An Activist added, "It's illegal to blow anything!" When the mayor spoke of aban-doned cars, someone yelled, "What about the abandonment of homo-sexuals?" Kay Tobin demanded, "What good is environmental freedom if we don't have personal freedom?" The remaining Activists then began to roar: "Answer the homosexuals! . . . What about the laws against sodomy? . . . We want free speech! . . . Lindsay, you need our votes. . . . Homosexuals account for 10 percent of the vote. . . . We want an end to harassment of homosexuals." Other audience members chimed in, "Answer the questions! . . . Lindsay's a phony."[68] The mayor, smiling and rubbing his hands, tried to ignore the abuse, but after twenty minutes he promised that the Activists could meet with his counsel outside the studio. GAA and the mayor's office soon began negotiations that would lead to Lindsay's endorsement of Intro 475 a year later.[69]

Most of GAA's disruptions of Lindsay's television show were cut out of the broadcast tape, but the station invited Jim Owles and Marty Robinson to appear on a newscast the next night to explain the reasons for the zap. In a calm, reasonable manner the two Activists asserted that "homosexuals were a substantial part of the voting constituency in New York and that it was time for politicians to recognize the needs of their gay constituents."[70] Owles and Robinson explained that zaps were needed to force politicians to address the needs of their gay constituents and to mobilize a "gay con-stituency" capable of asserting itself on the political stage.

Politicians always had gay constituents, and some were concerned about offending homosexuals partly because they were never certain how many gay voters there were. In the 1960s, the Mattachine Society mobilized gay support for sympathetic liberals, such as Lindsay, and appealed to them for protection after elections. But prior to GAA, there was no organized, mobilized, and visible gay constituency with the power to force national politicians to address its concerns. GAA knew that in America's two-party system, minority groups based on common race, sexual orientation, ideology, or religion have little opportunity to affect public policy by forming their own political parties. They must influence the Democratic or Republican parties, which depend on the support of the majority. For minority constituencies to be effective, they must convince politicians that even if their demands are unpopular with the majority, ignoring them would be too costly. To achieve such power, a significant number of the minority members must be well-informed about the political issues, unified on the importance of their particular concerns, and able to command a substantial number of votes or dollars. In short, the minority constituents must become a minority constituency.

During the 1970 election campaign, GAA combined zaps and media stunts with grassroots organizing to generate a gay constituency. The Election Committee sent numerous candidates questionnaires about their views on gay rights and received strong statements of support from Congressional representatives Ed Koch, Stephen Solarz, and Shirley Chisholm. State assembly candidate Tony Olivieri earned GAA's praise after he declared that if elected he would always include homosexuals in his references to minority groups, along with blacks and Puerto Ricans. "Some of the politicians," however, "needed prodding and got it," as Activist Arthur Bell wrote in his *Village Voice* column. When Arthur Goldberg, the former Supreme Court Justice and Democratic gubernatorial candidate, failed to respond to the GAA questionnaire, he became a key mark. One morning, Activists infiltrated an Upper West Side crowd waiting for a Goldberg campaign rally. As soon as the candidate emerged from his white limousine, the protestors (with cameras rolling), surrounded the distinguished jurist and asked if he supported protection of gays against police harassment and the repeal of state laws against sodomy. Goldberg said he thought

"there are more important things to talk about." The Activists
responded with their stock "Answer homosexuals!" chant. Goldberg,
surrounded and outnumbered, cut short the glad-handing and
retreated into the limo. GAA then encircled the car and treated the
candidate to a final chant "Crime of Silence, Crime of Silence!" Jim
Owles found a state assemblyman who supported Goldberg in the
crowd and bragged that "we showed Arthur Goldberg that wherever
he appears here in this city, he can expect to be asked questions by
homosexual constituents."[71] Shortly before the election Goldberg
issued a press statement in which he proclaimed:

> I believe that all issues concerning consenting relations
> between adults in private are mishandled when they are dealt
> with adversely in the legal area. Questions of fair employ-
> ment, bonding, police harassment, and other related matters
> should not be answered negatively for a man or woman just
> because his or her private life involves homosexuality. Pre-
> sent laws and attitudes are wrong. The law must change and
> social attitudes must change. I will work to these ends if I
> am elected.[72]

Arthur Goldberg, former U.S. Supreme Court Justice, became the first
statewide candidate to bow to the power of a gay constituency.

U.S. Senate candidates, Democratic Congressman Richard Ottinger
and Republican incumbent Charles Goodell, also announced support
for gay rights after Activists confronted them about their silence on the
issue during the 1970 election.[73] The *New York Times* ran a front-page
article on how Goldberg, Ottinger, and Goodell all called for an end
to discriminatory laws and practices against homosexuals. The *Times*
reported it was the first time any political candidate had taken an official position on homosexual rights.[74] A *Daily News* story on the
emerging power of GAA concluded with a quote from Jim Owles:
"We're going to pressure and browbeat and take over offices and anything else that needs to be done to educate the straight community.
We're not going to allow our demands to be watered down." Although
the GAA constitution prohibited the endorsement of any candidates,
Activists descended upon New York's gay neighborhoods and handed

out over fifty thousand leaflets advertising the candidates' positions on gay rights. The Alliance also forwarded the candidates' views to gay publications that stridently endorsed sympathetic politicians.[75] State Senate candidate George Spitz attended a GAA meeting and thanked the Activists for publicizing his support for gay rights: "Thank you for making me look good."[76]

In terms of immediate political results, GAA's efforts were not entirely successful. The statewide candidates who supported gay rights, Goldberg, Ottinger, and Goodell, all lost. But according to the *New York Post*, the election marked a "recognition of the gay community as a political entity to be taken seriously."[77] State assembly candidate Tony Olivieri, who responded to GAA's questionnaire and supported gay rights, unlike his opponent, became the first Democrat since 1919 to represent the Silk Stocking district on the Upper East Side. In a *Post* article that called him the "Gays' Advocate," Olivieri admitted that since he had won by five hundred votes out of a total of 86,402, the gay vote "may well have made the difference."[78] A *Times* article on the rising political influence of GAA reported that the Activists' success in 1970 convinced politicians that "a homosexual vote" existed and had a direct impact on legislation.[79] Democratic officials including Manhattan borough president Percy Sutton, Councilwoman Greitzer, Congressman Ed Koch, and Assemblyman Olivieri publicly endorsed Intro 475, and Consumer Affairs commissioner Bess Myerson eliminated prohibitions against homosexuals in public dance halls, cabarets, and catering establishments.[80]

As Marty Robinson had hoped, GAA had begun successfully "climbing up the liberals." News reports appeared about liberal politicians publicly defending the rights of homosexuals. Straights, who had previously regarded homosexuality as a social problem or a source of comedic fodder, suddenly heard politicians respectfully discussing gay rights. Gays who had been told for decades that they were sick and morally suspect saw mainstream politicians seriously discussing, and in some cases defending, their rights. Many gays discovered they no longer had to suffer quietly through their oppression. They could assert their rights through an emerging gay constituency. By the end of 1970, GAA had become a unique organization. Like the Black Panther Party, it presented a militant image that excited and inspired young people, but it also acquired influence within the political system that surpassed the Mattachine Society. In a *Village Voice* article, Marty Robinson aptly characterized GAA as a "critic-liaison to the establishment."[81]

Activist Ethan Geto provided GAA with key advice on how to manipulate New York's politicians. Geto, a closeted, married father of two, spent his days working as a political adviser to Bronx borough president Robert Abrams and his evenings at GAA headquarters plotting how to press politicians into supporting gay rights legislation. After listening to an impassioned plea by Geto, Robert Abrams became the first New York public official to testify in favor of Intro 475. When GAA members decided to infiltrate City Hall posing as journalism students on a class trip, Geto sketched out the floor plan and instructed them to stand over the secret security buttons embedded in the floor so that the guards could not set off the alarm.[82] The impostors successfully made their way to Mayor Lindsay's office, thanks to Geto's map, and used chains and handcuffs borrowed from one of the leather enthusiasts to shackle themselves to a railing. Nathalie Rockhill, GAA's vice president, even entered Lindsay's office and chained herself to a leg of his desk. Rockhill jangled her chains in front of the TV news cameras and announced a declaration of war against the mayor.[83] In the wake of the zap, extra police were detailed to City Hall and the number of officers deployed outside the mayor's office was doubled. In a newspaper article titled, "Gay People's Shenanigans Give Mayor New Headache" a police officer complained that because of GAA, "we have to make sure he's always watched."[84]

Politicians and journalists were not the only targets of GAA's zaps. Fidelifacts, a New York private investigation agency, was zapped in early 1971 after its president, Vincent Gillen, told the *New York Times* how his investigations provided employers with information on the personal background of job applicants. Gillen complained that "the problem of homosexuality seems to be increasing," but he claimed he could distinguish homosexuals from straights by going on "the rule of thumb: that if one looks like a duck, walks like a duck, associates only with ducks and quacks like a duck, he is probably a duck."[85] The quote raised an irresistible opportunity for a show. The next day, two dozen members of GAA and the Daughters of Bilitis picketed outside Fidelifacts' Times

Square headquarters led by Marty Robinson, dressed in a puffy duck costume covered in white down. Even in Times Square, the sight of dozens of gay protestors marching behind a giant duck attracted attention. The scene grew even more bizarre when a film crew showed up to shoot the opening credit sequence for the movie *Shaft*. Director Gordon Parks must have thought the GAA protest made for a perfect "only in New York" moment. He had Shaft, played by Richard Roundtree, walk through the middle of the protestors who were carrying signs reading "Gay Activists Alliance" and "I got my job through the NY Times, I lost my job through Fidelifacts." Accustomed to cameras at their protests, the Activists paid Shaft no mind as he sauntered by giving them a "What the hell!?" look. Only the GAA could rattle "the cat who won't cop out when there's danger all about."

After making their major motion picture debut, a delegation of about fifteen Activists along with a big duck and a news crew entered the Fidelifacts offices for a high-camp sit-in. The performance, including a physical assault on one of the Activists by an employee, gave the TV cameras great footage. Jim Owles was on the scene to connect a message to the images: "The important thing is to draw the public's attention to the existence of Fidelifacts and other companies like it."[86] The Activists also intended to draw attention to GAA itself.

To supplement its mainstream media coverage, GAA shot video of its own zaps and broadcast them on a weekly public access TV program and later produced a weekly prime time show, "The Gay Activist," on cable.[87] *Crawdaddy*, the widely-read rock and roll magazine, celebrated GAA's innovative use of video: "Portable, street television can serve any community action group, which depends for its growth and development on internal communication and on bridges to the 'outside' community. What GAA has put together can serve as a tangible, non-abstract prototype for other groups to learn from."[88] A report by the Videotape Committee explained why broadcasting zaps became as important as conducting them:

> No other medium in the history of the world is capable of reaching as many people at once as television. While a book might be considered a best seller when one million copies have been sold, a film or play is a hit when the same number

of people have paid to see it; yet television programs viewed
by one million people are considered a failure. A program on
nation-wide television may reach as many as thirty million
people at one showing. . . . Television has shaped more
thoughts and made more objects, people and ideas house-
hold words than any other medium in man's history. Cur-
rently the medium is presenting the typical society view of
gay people, mincing faggots short on brains and intelligence
and long on sentiment, frills and swishes. The fact that
people have this view of gays reinforced steadily by the
medium points up both the realization of the power of television as well as the need for change.[89]

As twenty- and thirty-year-olds who grew up watching television daily,
GAA members knew how much TV shaped their own perceptions of
reality and how powerful it would be in their campaign to change popular sentiment and secure equal rights.

GAA also found video useful for their own consciousness-raising.
The Alliance decided to zap the city clerk after he made disparaging
remarks about gay marriage. Although most Activists saw gay marriage
as a sell-out to the bourgeois, heterosexual ideal, they could not resist a
great opportunity for a spectacular zap.[90] Activists with video cameras
strode into the city clerk's office and staged a wedding reception for
two gay grooms and two lesbian brides. While being serenaded by a
wedding singer, guests ate a cake adorned with plastic lesbian and gay
couples. When the video recording of the wedding was shown at GAA
headquarters, the crowded room cheered for themselves and laughed at
scenes of their friends answering the clerk's phones and inviting callers
to the ceremony. Although viewing their own zaps did not publicize
GAA to the outside world; it enhanced their perceptions of their own
power. After growing up with negative images of homosexuals on mainstream TV, GAA created positive images on their own television shows.[91]

Zaps and TV appearances caught the attention of many college and
high school administrators and teachers, who invited Activists to speak
to their students about homosexuality and gay rights. A fifteen-year-
old girl who learned about the GAA on the *David Susskind Show*
worked with her teacher to bring Activists into her high school to

speak to the students.[92] In response to the speaking requests, GAA formed an Agitprop Committee to "politicize high school students who are gay and to motivate them to assert their rights and dignity by coming out and joining the struggle for gay liberation."[93] The principal of a Manhattan high school praised the GAA presentation, "Our students and teachers experienced an excellent learning situation. The content of the discussions helps eliminate erroneous stereotypes and contributed to increased tolerance and understanding among our students. We are looking forward to future visits by your group."[94] By 1974, GAA had spoken to more than eighty-five thousand high school students and thousands of others, including cadets at the New York Police Academy and GIs at Fort Dix.[95]

As news about GAA spread throughout the country, requests for information and advice began to pour in from Nebraska, Kansas, Tennessee, Seattle, Milwaukee, Minneapolis, St. Louis, and France. One anonymous Bostonian pleaded with the New York Activists for help: "SOS: Gay people in Boston lack guts. The law is kicking them around. GAA please come to Boston. Help us out. Save your brothers and sisters. The laws here in Boston fear you people. GAA is needed in Boston." The University of Maryland Student Homophile Association reported launching a GAA-inspired zap on the Students for a Democratic Society chapter because the radical group had avoided the issue of gay rights.[96] The Gainesville (FL) Gay Liberation Front requested films of zaps for instructional purposes while the Gay Liberation Front of Hawaii asked to become affiliated with GAA.[97] When homophile legend Frank Kameny formed a GAA in Washington, D.C., he needed advice from New Yorkers on how to employ chains during zaps:

> How do you get them? Could you send a sample link or two? What length of chain is needed for a desk-chaining? How do you attach the chains to the desk? I would think that putting them around a leg, for example, would be useless, since the desk could always be lifted up an inch to two and the chain removed. Do you use locks? How do you attach the chains to the GAA member? Do you use manacles or shackles of some kind? Details please. Are they attached to arms, legs, bodies, or what? Do you attach the chains to

each other as well? Why doesn't GAA publish a Manual on Desk-Chaining? While this may, perhaps be somewhat humorous, I am serious in requesting this information.[98]

Activists did not want to create a national organization, but they toured the Midwest and the South to organize autonomous GAA groups in Pittsburgh, Columbus, Cleveland, Detroit, Kalamazoo, Indianapolis, Minneapolis, Des Moines, Milwaukee, Louisville, Memphis, Nashville, and Baton Rouge. In some cites, GAA convinced established gay rights groups to adopt the Alliance's structure and tactics, but in cities that lacked any political organization, Activists began organizing by working the crowds in the local gay bars.[99] Gay rights groups based on the GAA model were formed in New Haven, Philadelphia, Cleveland, Indianapolis, Syracuse, Vancouver, Morris County (NJ), Suffolk County (NY), Los Angeles, San Francisco, Baltimore, Miami, Bangor, Omaha, and at the University of Notre Dame.[100]

Few of the GAAs outside New York survived more than two years, but wherever they arose they generated new media images of homosexuals. *The Bergen Record* in New Jersey reported on a meeting of the local GAA: "They look like what they are: two dozen serious people, mostly young, mostly hip. There is quite a lot of long hair and faded, patched blue jeans. They might be almost anyone this side of a borough council or PTA. They are homosexuals and they have decided to stand up and be counted . . . they've declared themselves. It's called coming out."[101] A *Daily News* article about a meeting of a Brooklyn-based GAA observed, "Few at the meeting resembled a straight person's image of a homosexual and they were lost in the crowd. There were no bizarre clothes or hair, most of the group wore open collar shirts or sweaters and plain slacks."[102]

National magazines began to recognize GAA's growing influence. A special *Newsweek* report, "The Militant Homosexual," identified the GAA and San Francisco's Society for Individual Rights as the "largest most important gay groups."[103] A *Life* magazine article, titled "Homosexuals in Revolt," pronounced 1971 "the year that one liberation movement turned militant" and called GAA "homosexual liberation's most effective organization." *Life* offered its middle-American readership a photo spread that included pictures of GAA's wedding party in the city clerk's office, of Activists with fists clenched shouting a "football style 'gay power' cheer at police" and of a police officer grabbing Jim Owles by the back of the neck.[104]

Many of the country's gay liberation organizations adopted GAA's symbol, the Lambda, the eleventh letter of the Greek alphabet. GAA came up with a couple of explanations for adopting the Lambda as its symbol. Pamphlets and letters issued by the group claimed the Lambda sign "stands for total exchange of energy and activity, as such it means political activism." In actuality its most common usage is as a symbol for wavelength photophysics. GAA's third president, Bruce Voeller, claimed the Lambda was the "first letter of Love, Lesbos and Lacadaemon, the capital of ancient Sparta famed for warriors and homosexual relationships between them." According to Voeller the Spartans decorated their shields with the Lambda as a "symbol of brothers fighting together."[105] The real story behind the Lambda was that activist Tom Doerr, a graphics designer, chose it because it was pretty.[106] The sign soon caught on as a symbol for gay liberation and the GAA made thousands of dollars selling Lambda-decorated buttons, patches, gold and silver pendants, T-shirts, and sweatshirts.[107] In December 1974, the first International Gay Rights Congress, held in Edinburgh, Scotland, adopted the Lambda as the international gay rights symbol.[108]

Another prominent symbol of GAA's power and dynamism was its headquarters.[109] After outgrowing their space in the Church of the Holy Apostles, the Activists rented an abandoned four-story turn-of-the-century Victorian firehouse in Soho, a rundown manufacturing neighborhood before galleries and boutiques replaced the artists and addicts. Every Thursday night, members would meet in the high-ceilinged main hall, which was wide enough to park two fire engines, to discuss organizational business and plan zaps. Committee meetings and small social gatherings were also held on the two other floors and in the basement. When Jim Owles spoke at the opening of "the Firehouse" he promised it would be a gay cultural center that would show straights and homosexuals "that being gay means more than the baths and the bars."[110] The Firehouse presented classical concerts, cabaret nights featuring folk singers and comedians, potluck dinners, fashion shows, art exhibitions, plays, self-defense lessons, and figure drawing classes featuring nude models. During Gay Pride Week, Wooster Street outside the Firehouse became the site of the first gay street fair, featuring a kissing booth, various games, prizes, crafts, strolling minstrels, and fortune-tellers.[111] Pete Fisher recalled the importance of the Firehouse as a symbol. "It was *our* space. To have your own gay home and political center is very empowering."[112]

The most popular activity at the Firehouse occurred every Saturday night, when hundreds lined up to get into the Firehouse to experience the largest gay dance club in New York. Once the party got started a thousand people, mostly gay men, would jam together, getting high on the various readily available drugs, drinking the free beer, and dancing under strobe lights. The dances, organized by the appropriately named Pleasure Committee, were "heaven's cross between Woodstock and Dante's Inferno." Those who had enough of the dance floor could retreat to the second floor for a cup of tea or coffee in a quiet room with a piano and television.[113] Arnie Kantrowitz enjoyed climbing the Firehouse's spiral staircase and looking down at the crowd splashed with strobe lights: "It felt like power. These are our people, our troops!"[114] While GAA's televised zaps made political activity glamorous, the dances made it fun. The Gay Liberation Front's Alternate U provided an alternative to the "mafia-run joints" but could not match the size and symbolism of the Firehouse. *GAY* ran a story about the GAA dances under the headline "Gay Power Challenges Syndicate Bars: Dances Draw Large Crowds." As gay bars throughout the city suddenly saw a striking drop in attendance on Saturday night, the dances became the organization's main source of income. The dances brought in $4,300 in the first three weeks, and in 1971 grossed over $39,000 with only $9,000 in expenses.[115]

The success of the dances raised fears among some Activists that their group might lose its political focus. An exasperated Marty Robinson asked the GAA membership, "What are you going to do, dance your way to liberation?" An attempt was made to better combine politics with pleasure by giving dances political themes and by decorating the main hall with a forty-foot-long collage containing images of zaps, famous homosexuals (Walt Whitman, Gertrude Stein, and Allen Ginsberg) and a poster of a smiling John Lindsay. During the dances, videotapes of zaps were shown on the third floor in an attempt to raise the political consciousness of partygoers. Although the main hall was too dark to see the mural during the dances and few visitors ventured to the third floor to watch the zaps, even Marty Robinson began to see the political value of the Saturday night parties. "We can have people come in here at 9 o'clock for a dance and leave with their fists clenched," Robinson raved. "This place is no less political than love beads or a be-in in the park. It's different than a Panther breakfast program. People can touch it. This is a bombshell. This is the Promised Land maybe." When a bomb threat brought one Saturday night dance to a halt, the crowd of nearly a thousand gays emptied out onto Wooster Street, chanting, "Gay Power! Gay Power!" Robinson related the impact of a night at the Firehouse for a closeted homosexual to the presence of minorities on television: "The dances shatter isolation, the very heart of what kept gays apolitical for years, no reinforcement. It's not unlike getting blacks on TV."[116] Whether closeted homosexuals made contact with other gays at Firehouse dances or on television, their isolation was broken. NBC even brought the Firehouse dances into the nation's living rooms when the network filmed one for a documentary on gay liberation.[117] One night, GAA was able to transform a dance into a demonstration by stopping the music early and inviting everyone in the Firehouse to join an early-morning march to the apartment building of a city councilman who opposed Intro 475.[118] Arnie Kantrowitz recalled feeling "powerful" on that march to the councilman's apartment house: "I could kiss my friends and hold hands on city streets with only a minimum of self-consciousness, and that was my 'gay liberation.' "[119]

Not everyone felt included in the fun at the Firehouse. A group of black lesbians in GAA who did not feel completely comfortable in the "white boy's playhouse" formed a Black Lesbian Caucus, which met every Sunday to discuss racism in the gay community.

The Alliance displayed its power and influence most effectively during the 1972 presidential campaign. The numerous fund-raising dinners and cocktail parties held in New York City offered GAA ample opportunities to push gay rights into the national political scene. The Alliance submitted to each presidential candidate a series of demands that included a public pledge to end discrimination in the armed forces, in civilian jobs, and in housing. Eugene McCarthy, George McGovern, John Lindsay, Shirley Chisholm, and Hubert Humphrey responded with declarations of support for the GAA program. Republican longshot Paul McCloskey and People's Party candidate Benjamin Spock also declared their backing. When Senator Edmund Muskie of Maine refused to endorse gay rights, fifty Activists confronted him before a fund-raiser at the Park Avenue Regency Hotel and distributed leaflets declaring, "a contribution to Muskie's campaign is a contribution to our oppression." As the police shouldered the Activists aside, a Pittsburgh newspaper reported that the candidate, "looking grim, went inside."[120] Later Muskie erupted to his staff, "Goddamn it, if I've got to be nice to a bunch of sodomites to be elected President, then fuck it!"[121] He remained the only major Democratic candidate not to endorse gay rights.

A nationally syndicated columnist described how Ted Kennedy, a potential candidate, ran into thirty Activists in front of the St. Regis Hotel before a political event. Bruce Voeller followed the Senator into the hotel but was quickly intercepted by a squad of plainclothes and uniformed police who were about to spin him out the revolving door, when Kennedy murmured, "Let him through. He's with me."[122] During a brief tête-à-tête in the lobby, Kennedy promised to "endorse and support civil rights for homosexuals. It's time that discrimination on the basis of security grounds ended and I can see no reason for keeping people from having jobs solely because of their homosexuality."[123] Most Activists did not think a major political shift would result from the liberals' public declarations of support for gay rights, and they even knew liberal politicians might suffer a loss of support after publicly defending homosexuals. According to Pete Fisher, the Alliance wanted to "get in the press and in the paper and reach closeted gays all across the country and help bring our message out to other gays . . . 'Be like us. Stand up, say you're gay, be proud, be happy in your gayness and *organize!*'" Presidential politics offered another opportunity for GAA to mount the national stage.

John Lindsay was particularly vulnerable to zaps during his 1972 presidential run. The GAA decided to use the spotlight of his campaign to maintain public attention on gay rights. As the mayor of New York, he could not duck the question of gay rights and skip town like Muskie, nor could he quickly endorse GAA's program and then neglect the subject like most other Democrats. In the fall of 1971, Lindsay supported Intro 475, but when the General Welfare Committee refused to move the bill to the rest of the City Council, the Activists blamed the mayor for not testifying personally in a show of support or challenging the leaders of the police and fire department unions who opposed passage.[124] Councilman Ted Weiss, who sponsored Intro 475, said there was nothing Lindsay could have done to save it, and a spokesman for the mayor labeled its defeat a "disappointment to the administration."[125]

GAA and other groups may even have been partly responsible for the defeat. One councilman said he decided to oppose the bill because of the Activists' disruptions of the public hearings. He may have been referring to the time when two cops teased a transvestite named Bebe by refusing to allow him to use either the men's or ladies' rooms. Bebe decided the only way to deal with them was to urinate on the staircase. In GAA there was a saying, "you don't fuck with a drag queen."[126] Council members also complained that the transvestites who attended the hearing were using the women's room. In response, drag queens in the balcony rushed to the council floor in protest. One councilman, who opposed the measure, remarked, "That's the nub of the problem—transvestitism."[127] Whatever the reasons for the General Welfare Committee's decision, John Lindsay was not at fault. Yet GAA pledged to harass "Hizzoner" wherever he campaigned in the presidential race.

The Alliance's most famous zap occurred at a $300,000 fund-raiser at Radio City Music Hall where the mayor was supposed to perform a song-and-dance routine before the premiere of the film *Hot Rocks*. Immediately after comedian Alan King introduced Lindsay, Activists Cora Perrotta and twenty-year-old Morty Manford handcuffed themselves to the railing at the front of the mezzanine and put the hall's world-famous acoustics to use: "Lindsay lies to homosexuals! . . . He's an actor! . . . Gays demand action on civil rights." Other Activists in the balcony threw bags of leaflets onto the seats below. Rich Wandel, disguised in a suit and fake Abe Lincoln beard, set off an air horn while Steve Askinazy yelled from the mezzanine, "Gays have been second-class citizens too long. Lindsay has given us nothing but lies. Lindsay's a phony!" Other air horns soon started to blow. As the plainclothes police cut loose Manford and Perrotta's handcuffs and ushered them out of the hall, Lindsay tried to control the situation: "If I may remind the gentlemen of the Gay

Liberation Front [sic] you are in the wrong forum. All you are doing is damaging your chances of getting the bill I'm supporting through the City Council." Alan King paced restlessly on the stage, begging Lindsay for the opportunity to confront the Activists, but after Wandel and Marty Robinson began chanting "Lies, Lies, Lies!" the comedian and the mayor retreated behind the curtain.[128]

Outside the hall, Activists handed out a leaflet that read, "Since Lindsay has not lived up to his promises, we will destroy his political career." The GAA knew they could not single-handedly destroy the mayor's career, but they were also aware that Lindsay could not afford to have his fund-raisers repeatedly ruined. Rich Wandel promised that "we are going to trash his campaign every time he makes an appearance in California or elsewhere in the nation. All we have to do is send a few letters or make a few phone calls." The GAA sent liberation organizations in Boston, Miami, San Francisco, and Los Angeles a presumptuous "Declaration of War by the Entire Gay Community of the United States on John V. Lindsay."

On the day the General Welfare Committee voted against passing Intro 475 onto the council, seven Activists again sneaked into City Hall and chained themselves to a brass railing leading to the mayor's office. A few hours later twenty-five members of GAA stormed into the Lindsay campaign headquarters.[129] Activists also disrupted the opening of Lindsay's Long Island presidential campaign office by chanting so loudly that the candidate cut short his speech to 250 enthusiastic young supporters after only five minutes and retreated to his limousine. When asked how he felt about the Alliance's latest disruption, the mayor deadpanned, "Routine, strictly routine."[130]

Lindsay quickly responded to the council's rejection of Intro 475 by declaring in a letter to Activist Bruce Voeller that "the discriminatory and often cruel and abusive treatment of this minority [homosexuals] is a serious problem which cries out for solutions." The mayor also issued an executive order that a person's "private sexual orientation" could not be a factor in making hiring decisions in any city agency, but a GAA spokesman called the mayor's action "about the weakest thing Lindsay could do."[131] The Alliance had a problem with the word "private" because they thought it would inhibit gay municipal employees from holding hands in public or other displays of affection. Although the mayor's office denied it intended to inhibit public affection, GAA refused to give Lindsay a break.[132] The moderate editorial board of *GAY*, which had often criticized GAA for its zaps on sympathetic liberals such as Lindsay, now praised its efforts:

> No matter what the more conservative elements in the gay community may think of the militants in their midst, one fact will stand out clearly: The militants will prove themselves effective in eliciting gay rights promises from major Democratic candidates for president. The letter to the Gay Activists Alliance from Mayor John V. Lindsay proves that the Mayor, far from being angered by GAA zappers at Radio City Music Hall, City Hall and at his campaign headquarters, is in fact, anxious to stay on the good side of the gay community.[133]

Given the frequency and intensity of the zaps on Lindsay, however, it is likely the mayor was both angered and anxious. The Alliance knew the value of the zaps against Lindsay and the other presidential candidates. Zaps not only elicited public declarations of support and policy changes in New York City, the numerous news reports also maintained GAA's public exposure and generated media images of tough, political, serious gays.

The Alliance's greatest political victory was its contribution to George McGovern's decision to endorse gay rights during the 1972 general election campaign. During the primaries, McGovern ordered his staff to issue a statement of support for civil rights for homosexuals after he noticed his name was not on a GAA list of acceptable presidential candidates.[134] When he further tried to ingratiate himself with gay voters by sending an assistant to City Hall to read a statement backing Intro 475, the applause of supporters in the hearing room was so loud and continuous that the chairman had to call a recess.[135] *GAY* endorsed McGovern and a group of two-dozen prominent homosexuals formed the Gay Citizens for McGovern Committee.

As the 1972 Democratic Party convention approached, gay activists had reason to hope that the Democrats would adopt a gay rights plank in their party platform. In the wake of the 1968 fiasco in Chicago, the Democratic Party changed the rules governing the presidential convention and the selection of its delegates. Instead of excluding radicals from the hall, the 1972 Democratic national convention in Miami welcomed many as delegates.[136] Gay rights advocates were one of many special interests that planned to petition the Democratic Platform Committee to approve unconventional planks.[137]

The national committee refused to endorse gay rights, however, because they feared Nixon would exploit the issue in the general election.[138] Not only did McGovern support this decision, his people selected Kathleen Wilch, a delegate from Ohio, to speak before the convention against the plank. In front of television cameras, Wilch claimed a declaration of support for gay rights would "commit the Democratic party to seek repeal of all laws involving the protection of children from sexual approaches by adults" and force the "repeal of all laws relating to prostitution, pandering [and] pimping. . . . It is ill-considered because it would commit this party to repeal many laws designed to protect the young, the innocent and the weak."

Activist Ethan Geto had taken a leave of absence from the Bronx Borough President's office to become the northeastern press secretary for the McGovern campaign. As he sat in a Miami hotel room watching Wilch's speech on TV, he was overcome with disgust and embarrassment.[139] In front of a national television audience, a McGovern delegate was dredging up all the horrible stereotypes that GAA and other groups had spent years fighting against. Geto was caught between two allegiances. The politico in him understood the practical considerations that went into the decision to distance McGovern from gay rights. Throughout the campaign the liberal McGovern would be criticized for being out of the mainstream, or as Vice President Spiro Agnew put it, "the Triple-A Candidate: abortion, amnesty and acid."[140] As an Activist however, Geto knew the dangers of allowing Wilch's nationally televised remarks to go unchallenged. The liberation movement had made great progress in challenging stereotypes about gays and in forcing liberals to take unambiguous stands against sexual discrimination. To allow such a well-publicized snub to pass would be a major setback.[141] Geto decided that one way or another the McGovern campaign was going to make a public statement of support for gay rights, and as McGovern's press spokesman in New York he would make sure it happened. All he needed was a little help from his friends at GAA.

The Alliance first politely requested that McGovern publicly renounce Wilch. In response, the candidate or someone writing on his behalf sent back two private letters of apology. While the letters repudiated Wilch's speech and reiterated support for gay rights, McGovern's name was signed in two different hands, leaving the Activists suspicious of his true sentiments.[142] In any case, the Alliance wanted a public statement and Geto knew how to get it. In front of the Activists, Geto sketched out the floor plans of the McGovern for President headquarters in New York, detailing the positions of offices, doors, elevators, and desks. He selected the time of the zap to maximize television coverage and distributed phone numbers of the media organizations to be called once the zap erupted.[143] The GAA press release announcing the zap proclaimed "the only way of obtaining a meaningful response is to create a meaningful nuisance."[144] For GAA meaningful meant well-publicized.

About thirty Activists showed up at McGovern's Fifth Avenue headquarters shortly before lunch on a hot August morning. Bruce Voeller and two others immediately walked to the telephone switchboard and chained themselves to the telephone equipment. A campaign official emerged from one of the offices and tried to stop them, but Voeller wrestled him to the floor. With a secretary asking "What's going on here?" the enchained Activists used the phones to call every major media outlet in the city to deliver the line dictated by the director of the show, Ethan Geto: "I am chained to a desk in George McGovern headquarters."

To protect the protestors from being forcibly ejected, two Activists who were also journalists, Randy Wicker, a reporter for the *Advocate* and Arthur Bell, who wrote a *Village Voice* column, announced they were members of the media and were there to observe the demonstration. Frantic campaign staffers rushed into Geto's office. "Ethan, this is a disaster! Gay protestors are in the office and they're answering the phones! What are we going to do?" Geto reassured them, "Let me handle it." He emerged from his office pretending to be a shocked press secretary and warned other McGovern campaign workers to avoid a confrontation while "the press is here." When the police arrived, Geto claimed the McGovern campaign could control the situation and asked them to leave. In a worried tone, he explained to a TV news reporter, "It's just not McGovern's style to call in the police and remove people forcibly. We're going to let them sit here until they get tired and go away." In front of the cameras, Geto explained that the demonstration was "not an appropriate thing to do because George McGovern is pro gay rights! . . . George McGovern thinks that gay rights is an important thing to accomplish in American politics." GAA got its public statement.

With the threat of ejection removed, the Activists demanded that McGovern himself publicly reaffirm his commitment to gay rights and denounce Kathleen Wilch's comments. Geto retreated to a back office to update the chairman of the McGovern campaign in New York, former mayor Robert Wagner. At first Wagner was confused, "Gay rights? What's that?" After Geto explained, the devout Catholic Wagner immediately refused to support any compromise with the Activists. As Geto and Wagner locked into a heated debate over the response, the mayor's closeted son Bobby sat to the side squirming with discomfort.[145] Meanwhile the Activists who were chained to the phones continued to answer incoming calls and proclaim that gay liberationists had taken over the McGovern for President headquarters. Someone removed the McGovern banner outside the office and replaced it with a GAA sweatshirt. Finally by midafternoon Frank Mankiewicz, a senior adviser to the campaign suggested a practical way to defuse the situation: "Say something to show we're sympathetic and get them out of the office."

With a defiant look, Activist Allen Roskoff stood next to Geto before the assembled TV cameras as Geto, the press secretary, somberly read the statement:

> Senator George McGovern has repeatedly affirmed his commitment to civil rights and civil liberties for all Americans. He has specifically addressed himself to discrimination directed against men and women based on sexual orientation, and has pledged to alleviate such discrimination in the federal government and in other areas of public life. Senator McGovern believes that discrimination based on sexual orientation should be eliminated.

When Activist Hal Offen saw the newscast later that day he burst out laughing as he watched Geto and Roskoff standing stiffly, pretending to be adversaries. He knew they were actually close friends who spent many late nights together making the rounds of the city's gay bars and bathhouses.[146]

On October 7, 1972, McGovern sent a white paper on civil liberties to all national media, in which he pledged to use "the full moral and legal power of the presidency" to end all forms of government and private discrimination against gay people. He also criticized the Nixon administration for not "protect[ing] the basic rights of persons of differing sexual orientation in the United States" and accused it of:

> carry[ing] out a policy of harassment and discrimination. The evidence over the last four years is overwhelming. Sexual orientation has been a criterion for employment by public and government agencies, in work under federal contracts, for service in the armed forces and for licensing in government-regulated occupations and professions. Between three and four thousand military personnel under Nixon have been given less than honorable discharges solely for allegations relating to sexual orientation and for relations between consenting adults. Homosexuals have a difficult time obtaining housing insurance or surety bonding. Data on sexual orientation of individuals has been collected by government and private investigator agencies, and sexual orientation is a standard for immigration into this country.[147]

McGovern was the first presidential candidate of a major party to issue a public statement on the subject of homosexuality and gay rights. But two weeks later, GAA radicals who wanted an even stronger declaration infiltrated a union rally for the candidate and questioned him on his commitment to gay rights. The Senator tried to ignore the disruption and read his speech, but Morty Manford, a feisty Columbia College student, repeatedly interrupted. A union official who was presiding over the rally reprimanded the young man, "Homosexuality—that is not an issue at this meeting. The Senator is here with limited time. You will not be recognized, sir." The *New York Post* reported that "as Manford was escorted out, Mr. McGovern declared he did not believe in discrimination against people on grounds of sex or for any other reason and added 'I think that answers it all.' "[148]

Moderates in the gay rights movement quickly criticized the notion of harassing liberals like McGovern, while giving Nixon a pass. Jack Nichols and Lige Clarke of *GAY* complained, "It seems they're going after the wrong man. Doesn't anybody want to get rid of Richard Nixon any more?" Manford and most members of GAA certainly wanted to see Nixon ousted, but they had another campaign to wage. Like the zaps on the city clerk's office or Fidelifacts, the demonstrations against Lindsay and McGovern were primarily intended to generate media images. News reports of aggressive gays intimidating mayors and senators made lasting impressions on homosexuals and straights alike. "The big issue," according to Arthur Evans, "is the liberals moved and the media saw them move."[149]

The 1972 election marked an important change in American politics and in the meaning of liberalism. In his 1951 book, The *Homosexual in America*, Donald Webster Cory had called upon liberals to embrace the cause of equal rights for homosexuals just as they had begun to join the fight for the rights of racial and ethnic minorities. While liberals of the 1960s, such as Hubert Humphrey, Lyndon Johnson, and Robert Kennedy, never had to address the issue of gay rights, Lindsay and McGovern had no choice thanks to zaps and media triggers that pushed gay rights onto the front pages and TV screens.

Almost two decades before the founding of GAA, Donald Webster Cory also surmised that the majority of homosexuals would not be comfortable enough to come out until newspapers, magazines, and broadcast media presented the public with serious and sympathetic discussions of homosexuality.[150] Only the mass media could carry the issue of homosexuality into America's living rooms and spur "the interchange of opinion, the conflict and the controversy, which alone can establish truth."[151] Once the mass media started presenting serious discussions of homosexuality and gay rights, Cory hoped the American public would begin to consider the legitimacy of rights for homosexuals. More than any other gay rights group, the GAA reshaped the image of homosexuals in the mass media. Their zaps forced editors and broadcasters to tamp down on a long practice of mocking and demonizing the stereotypical homosexual and pushed America's liberals to initiate a national debate over gay rights.

GAA had also become the most watched gay rights group in the country. The appearances of GAA members on television talk shows and news broadcasts presented the American public with the image of the new homosexual who was tough, serious, and sane. Their zaps transformed the GAA leaders into what Cory called "gay heroes" who counteracted the common perception that all gays had mincing gaits and limp wrists. For the first time, the stereotypes that had long camouflaged closeted homosexuals and made straights uncomfortable were being challenged through the mass media. GAA's "Made-for-TV Movement" was a revolutionary hit.

chapter seven

THE INNER CIRCLE AFFAIR

The most famous fistfight in the history of the gay liberation movement was a terrible mismatch.[1] One April night in 1972, Michael
Maye, a 215-pound former Golden Gloves champion and president of
the New York City fireman's union, squared off against Morty Manford, a scrappy five-nine, 145-pound Columbia College student and
member of the Gay Activist Alliance. The immediate outcome was pre-
dictable. Manford quickly collapsed in a bloody, dazed heap on the
street and joined the legions of homosexuals who were victims of an
irrational antigay rage. But Manford did not allow his beating to go
unpunished and unnoted. Despite police hostility, he filed charges
against Maye; in doing so he triggered media attention that publicized
gay bashing, police harassment, and governmental indifference to discrimination against homosexuals. Liberal politicians, who had previously ignored these problems, rallied to the charismatic victim's
well-publicized cause. The trial and attendant media attention also
enabled Manford to introduce the public to a new word for the irrational fear and rage against homosexuals: homophobia.

The term "homophobia" was coined by George Weinberg, a
straight psychologist who worked with Frank Kameny as a spokesman
for the homophile movement and later became a friend and adviser to
many of GAA's leaders. The origins of the concept of homophobia can

be traced to an evening in the mid-1960s after Weinberg discussed homosexuality on a television talk show.[2] As he sat in the green room alone with a young female producer, he noticed she began to tremble. After wondering, "What the fuck is this? I'm charming, why would a woman act like this?" he realized she thought he was gay. Weinberg noted that other people experienced intense anxiety and rage toward homosexuals. He surmised their nervousness and anger might be attributed to repressed homosexuality or jealousy over the assumed promiscuity of gays. Weinberg had his eureka moment in 1966 while sitting in a bathtub after smoking half a joint: "This is a fucking phobia!" He began lecturing and writing about "homophobia" and in 1971 published *Society and the Healthy Homosexual*, which defined the condition as "the dread of being in close quarters with homosexuals" due to repressed homosexual feelings or other insecurities.[3]

The creation of the word "homophobia" represents a significant shift in the history of the gay rights movement. In his book, Weinberg claimed he "would never consider a patient healthy unless he has over-come his prejudice against homosexuality."[4] He knew the symbolic value of the word "homophobia," which "suddenly says wait a minute, you're the one who has the problem. It isn't just me . . . I don't have to explain myself. You're the fucking nut. You're the one up all night worrying about my having a good time. That's what the movement liked." Weinberg knew that characterizing people with antigay senti-ments as "homophobic" completely delegitimizes their position by "diagnosing" them not as unjust or cruel but as abnormal and sick. He felt so strongly about the importance of the concept that he spent the entire advance he received for the publication of his book on pub-licity for it.[5]

Weinberg introduced the concept of homophobia to his friends at GAA, Morty Manford and Ethan Geto. The two savvy Activists imme-diately saw the potential political value of the word. The label of homo-phobe had a different and perhaps greater power than "racist," "male chauvinist," or "anti-Semite." "Homophobia" inverted the typical objection to homosexuality as a psychologically perverted illness by designating those who objected to gay rights as the sick ones. Geto and Manford decided that GAA needed to wage a public information cam-paign that would push "homophobia" into the lexicon.[6] The opportunity for such a public information campaign arose a few months later during what became know as the Inner Circle affair.

The Inner Circle is an organization of municipal political reporters who gather annually with Manhattan's political elite at the New York Hilton to eat, drink, and lampoon each other in musical numbers and skits. In 1972, membership in the fifty-year-old organization was still restricted to men and held for life, so the Inner Circle was very much an old boys' club. Even the seating arrangement at its annual gathering was archaic. Except for the few women who held the title of commissioner in the city government, female guests were seated on the balcony overlooking their dates at tables on the ballroom floor.[7] One reporter said it reminded him of *shul*.[8]

Enhancing the odd sexual dynamic was the rule that all freshmen members had to attend the gathering in drag. As Eddie O'Neil of the *Daily News* remarked, "We've got a saying, the first year, you've got to be a whore."[9] On stage, members played women and acted "swish" in a variety show. One of the skits on the night of April 15, 1972, even featured a lisping male reporter in drag who pestered a politician about Intro 475, the gay rights bill that stood before the city council.

In statements to the press and the authorities after the event, GAA spokespeople claimed the decision to zap the Inner Circle was made when one of the guests became offended by the performance and telephoned GAA headquarters.[10] According to the story, the Activists had been relaxing over hot dogs and beer after a long day of demonstrating in Albany when the call mobilized them back into action. They immediately mimeographed leaflets about antigay bias in the media and twenty-five protestors rushed uptown to the Hilton. Although historians have perpetuated this myth,[11] the truth is that days before the Inner Circle affair the GAA voted to zap the event at Ethan Geto's suggestion after a *Daily News* editorial referred to gays as "fairies, nances, swishes, fags, lezzes—call 'em what you please."[12] Geto figured that disrupting a gathering of New York political journalists and editors would get GAA onto the pages of every newspaper in the city. How could all those reporters in the ballroom not cover it?[13]

As an adviser to Bronx borough president, Geto was an invited guest of the Inner Circle. After stopping at the Firehouse in his tuxedo to make sure the plans for the zap were set, Geto went uptown to the Hilton, took his seat next to Robert Abrams in the ballroom, and anxiously awaited the protest. The Activists arrived at the Hilton during the intermission, shortly after the curtain came down on a drag performance about feminists.[14] Uniformed Firefighters Association Vice President Frank Palumbo recalled how he and the other guests "had just been served our steaks when 20 or 30 people burst into the ballroom and began throwing leaflets all over the tables." He claimed one of the protestors had an electronic bullhorn and started calling guests "closet queens" and "bastards." John O'Sullivan, a fireman and officer in Michael Maye's union, also described the GAA activists "shouting these names, 'bastards,' 'closet queers.' They were saying, 'We're not queer, it's you people here that's queer.' "[15] A rage mounted in Maye's chest as he watched the Activists snake their way between the tables shouting slogans, throwing leaflets, and accidentally bumping guests.[16]

Activists Bobby Rome and Bruce Voeller snuck behind the curtain and seized the microphone. After Rome launched into a speech about how "the media opposes homosexuals," sixty to seventy guests stood up and began hooting, jeering, and applauding to drown them out.[17] A huge employee of the hotel silenced Rome by pushing him against a wall and landing a punch that knocked him to the ground. A couple of tuxedo-clad guests also attacked Voeller. One wrapped a wrestler's armlock around his neck while another punched him in the chin. Rome and Voeller escaped further harm after a man in a tuxedo intervened, exclaiming, "I'm a friend of yours. Get out of here."[18]

At first Michael Maye's friends were able to restrain him, but when Bruce Voeller began his speech over the microphone, a wild-eyed Maye suddenly jumped up, snatched the nearest gay activist by the collar, and lifted him off the ground with one arm.[19] He continued to hold the youth in the air as he shook him and yelled, "What the fuck are you doing here? You don't belong here. If you don't get the fuck out of here, I am going to kill you."[20] State Senator Bob Garcia, who grew up with Maye in the South Bronx, quickly intervened, shouting "'Take it easy Mike. That is what they want. Take it easy.' "[21] Maye released the protestor but soon grabbed another whom he described as, "a tall, blond, golden-haired fellow wearing a gaudy type of shirt."[22] Environmental Protection administrator Jerome Kretchmer remembered, "I saw Mike get up. I saw him kind of reach out and grab one of the kids, hold onto him for a minute, and myself and some others got in the way. I went over and talked to Mike for a minute or two and I said 'Mike! Calm down, there is no sense in doing that.' "[23] This time Maye did not listen.

While Maye led the blond protestor by the collar out of the ballroom, firefighter Frank Palumbo and a friend grabbed the arms of another Activist and followed Maye into the lobby.[24] Maye testified that the GAA member he escorted "reached back with his right hand and grabbed me by the groin." Maye then threw an "overhead right onto his head," which knocked the young man to the ground. As the blond protestor fell, he held on to the front part of Maye's pants and ripped out a sizable hole.[25] Judge Orest V. Maresca testified that if Maye "didn't have his shorts on, his private parts would have been exposed."[26] While Maye tussled with the blond protestor, Palumbo claimed someone pulled his hair and he responded with a punch that sent the young man to the floor. Bedlam broke out as tuxedo-clad gentlemen fought with the Activists and everyone began shoving and pulling each other down the escalator.[27]

After Morty Manford heard a commotion in the lobby, he left the ballroom and saw Maye and Palumbo punching protestors. He rushed to the melee and kicked Maye in the groin.[28] Maye then punched Manford in the face, knocking him to the ground, and repeatedly kicked the cowering young man until other guests intervened.[29] As Manford got up, he pointed his fingers at the man he reckoned was his attacker and demanded his arrest,[30] but neither the police in attendance nor the gawking hotel security guard attempted to interfere.[31] As Manford screamed for a police officer, Maye said, "You're not demanding anything" and pushed him onto the escalator, which the young man rode down on his back.[32] During his trial, Maye admitted, "Tuxedo-clad gentlemen were throwing the demonstrators—not throwing them, pushing them down the escalator."[33] One of his friends recalled, "All hell broke loose and fists were flying and these guys were going down the escalator with a lot of blood on them—nobody in tuxedos, just the gay ones."[34]

While lying on the escalator Manford recalled how a bald man stood over him and "beat at me in the stomach with all his strength." According to a witness, Maye "flew down the escalator" to join in and stomp on Manford, grinding his heel into the student's groin four or five times until they reached the bottom.[35] Manford and the Activists were not powerless victims of "gay bashing" but they certainly took more punches and kicks than they threw.

As the pile of bodies on the escalator reached the floor below, two witnesses saw Maye bound back up the escalator. When he reached the top, he straightened out his jacket and returned to the ballroom, announcing, "We won't have any more trouble from him tonight."[36] A friend pointed out his ripped pants and went backstage to retrieve a pair of dark blue costume pants that were worn in the show. Maye changed, watched the remainder of the show, and attended a reception after the event.[37]

Although Manford was buckled over in pain when he reached the bottom of the escalator, a bald man picked him up to take another swing. "Please stop!" Manford cried. But the bald guy landed one final punch. Friends picked Manford up and led him out of the building, where he crumpled onto the sidewalk with glazed eyes, "moaning and trembling."[38]

Jim Owles was standing at the bottom of the escalator when the Activists and guests began pushing each other down the steps. Before he could join the melee, someone knocked him to the floor with one punch. "I got up again," Owles recalled, "and he hit me in the face again with his closed fist."[39] Owles blacked out for a while and consequently could not identify his assailant. A police officer, standing near Owles, refused to intervene or arrest anyone despite the pleadings of at least one witness.[40]

After Leonard Cohen, a Manhattan deputy borough president, witnessed the cop's refusal to become involved, he went back inside the ballroom and told Bronx borough president Robert Abrams and his aide Ethan Geto what he had seen. As Cohen left the dinner in disgust, Geto was filled with panic.[41] After all, the zap had been his idea. He quickly left the hotel and discovered Manford, his best friend, lying on the sidewalk swollen and bloody. Geto had recently separated from his wife and had been spending almost every evening with Manford talking about politics and the movement. Frantic with concern, Geto rushed over to a police sergeant and asked if an ambulance had been called. When he got no response, Geto declared, "I am a city official and I would like to know if there is an ambulance on call." The sergeant snapped, "We are taking care of it, just mind your own business." When Geto heard the officer's response, he prudently decided not to wait for an ambulance and took Manford by cab to St. Luke's Hospital, where the young militant was x-rayed, treated for multiple contusions, and given painkillers.[42]

Back at the Hilton, both guests and Activists continued to demand that the police intervene. Bruce Voeller and Bobby Rome, who were beaten behind the stage curtain, pleaded with the police to escort them into the ballroom so that they could identify their assailants and press charges. When they specifically accused Michael Maye, a sergeant responded, "I'm not going in after Mickey Maye on the say-so of the likes of you." A patrolman chimed in, "I wouldn't arrest Mickey Maye for you creeps."[43]

George Douris of the *Long Island Press* and a member of the executive committee of the Inner Circle was one of many guests who seem to have been caught up very easily in the violence. Douris was sitting with his twelve-year-old son when Rome commandeered the public address system. Douris recalled telling Rome, "Please don't do it this way. . . . I was talking, I swung my right arm which was bitten. As a Greek I talk with my arms. I didn't swing to hit." He claimed that when a fight broke out around him he "started swinging to protect" himself.

Why did so many guests at the Hilton participate in the violence that night? One reason is that they greatly resented the disturbance of what they considered a very special occasion. Raymond Gimmler, president of the Uniformed Fire Officers' Association, said, "It was like your wedding or something and these guys came breaking in."[44] "I am a professional firefighter," Maye declared, "and it does annoy me when something like this out of the ordinary—I very, very seldom get out with my wife and it does annoy me."[45] The Inner Circle gathering was more than just a party for many guests, it was a rare opportunity to dress up in tuxedos and hobnob with the mayor in a fancy midtown hotel.

Another reason for the violent reaction to the protest involved hostility over the political and social conflicts of the early 1970s. Joseph Famm, a reporter for WABC radio and president of the Inner Circle, considered the demonstration an invasion of his space and a violation of his right to enjoy a dinner and performance without disturbance: "We were running a private affair, and they had no business coming in. . . . No one should invade our privacy. . . . I saw these long-haired people shouting obscenities. I asked them to leave. We thought this was outrageous. We felt our civil rights were violated."[46] Maye told the *Post* that "if anyone's civil rights had been violated, it was the rights of those gathered together in peaceful assembly to enjoy an evening together without harassment or abuse."[47] Famm and Maye's complaints of civil rights violations were typical of many in the "Silent Majority" who felt the longhairs and radicals were threatening their right to law and order. This resentment was a powder keg that many guests carried into the ballroom that night. The insults, obscenities, and accidental bumps of protestors were the sparks that set off the violent explosion.

The contrast between Maye and Manford mirrored the generational and political conflicts that erupted the night of the Inner Circle gathering. Michael Maye was a married father of five who had served in the Korean conflict as part of an Army Ranger intelligence and reconnaissance team. He became the Golden Gloves heavyweight champion in 1951 and subsequently won nineteen professional fights.[48] The son of an Irish rebel who fought in the 1916 rebellion, Maye joined the fire department in 1957 because, as he said, "in my neighborhood you either became a cop, a fireman or a priest."[49] He distinguished himself as a firefighter, winning six commendations for bravery. After he became president of the 11,300 member Uniformed Firefighters Association, the intensely patriotic, conservative Maye honored Richard Nixon with a New York City fireman's helmet.

Maye often resorted to physical intimidation and violence to assert his control over the union. "He's a union leader of the old school," said one union leader, "You had to use your hands—and anything else—in those days, and Mickey believes you still do." A fireman recalled one time "when a union trustee—I think he was from Brooklyn—disagreed with Mickey at a meeting. I forget what it was about, but it doesn't matter. Well, Mickey is a great parliamentarian, so he took the microphone away from this guy and punched him in the face. Knocked some teeth out, I think." The *Post* photographed the trustee outside the meeting hall and printed it with the caption: "A fireman who said he was punched by UFA president Michael Maye leaves the meeting." One fireman said, "you either hate Mickey or you love him. Nobody's neutral."

Morty Manford was one of the more radical members of the Gay Activists Alliance. In September 1970, on his twentieth birthday, Manford zapped John Lindsay during an antiwar speech at New York University. While the mayor stood on a stage boldly condemning the Vietnam War as "the largest source contributing to . . . recession, frightfully growing unemployment and galloping inflation," Manford, wearing a Columbia University sweatshirt, marched down the center aisle and up the stairs onto the speaker's platform. "Pardon me for interrupting, Mr. Mayor," Morty offered, "but this is the only way that we can get to you since you refuse to see us through regular channels." Security guards immediately rushed over to the Columbia sophomore and hustled him off the stage. Lindsay then resumed his place at the microphone and invited anyone wishing to speak to come forward. Laughter erupted from some audience members who were tickled by the incongruity of Manford's swift removal and the mayor's subsequent invitation. A bit flummoxed, Lindsay soldiered on with his complaints about how the peace movement tended "to expand the gap between the young and the old, the black and the white, and the hard hat and the long-hair, rather than to unify them in such an effort" against the war.

At that point, Manford, who had been released by the security force, strode back down the aisle and rejoined the mayor on the stage. After Lindsay stepped aside and surrendered the platform, the determined youngster launched into a diatribe about police harassment against homosexuals: "The Gay Activists Alliance has no other way to deal with police harassment in New York City. We must confront the mayor in public. This past month over three hundred gays were arrested in the downtown area by Lindsay's police force. How do you plan to control your police, Mayor Lindsay? Why don't you listen to your homosexual constituents? . . . If Lindsay can't control the police force then he's not capable of handling this city of ours. . . . I ask the Mayor what he intends to do."[50] Taking their cue, the audience began to jeer Lindsay as he stood stoically behind the student. Before stomping off the stage, Manford took one more shot, "He doesn't listen to the people—don't try!" Lindsay did not even attempt to resume the speech. After he suggested that the protestors address their grievances to one of his aides, he made a beeline for the exit. Outside, dozens of gay rights demonstrators chanted, "Answer the question! Answer the question!" followed by "End police harassment!" and "Ho, Ho, Homosexual!"[51] Before he could escape into his car, Lindsay heard someone yell, "John Lindsay, you're a good man." Turning to the crowd, the mayor exclaimed, "Whoa! A friendly voice? I'll die of shock."

Mayors traditionally performed comedic routines at the annual gatherings of the Inner Circle. On the night Manford was beaten, Lindsay, half joking, complained to the audience, "I've had more trouble with queens than any politician since Henry VIII."[52] The mayor was right.

Although on the surface, the firefighter and the gay activist seemed very different, they had more in common than they imagined. Like Maye, Morty was known to throw a punch. During a protest at Columbia, Manford scuffled with a couple of security guards and a college dean. And Michael Maye was no stranger to the New York's gay bar scene.[53] One of his relatives, who was involved with organized crime, hired Maye in 1962 as a bouncer at Dirty Dick's, a gay bar near the docks in the West Village. In those days, Dirty Dick's was the only place in town that was both a "gay dancing bar and a costume bar with everything from transvestites to leather." Ironically, given the Inner Circle Affair, Maye's main responsibility had been to *protect* the gay customers. Joey, who managed the bar, recalled the night "four Italian kids from New Jersey came by. . . . When the punks finally tried to get in, Mickey started swinging. He knocked down two. I knocked down one, and one of them ran away." Maye was friendly with the clientele he was paid to protect. He often exchanged quips with a young man called Gypsy and sometimes entertained friends from the fire and police departments at the bar.[54] During his trial, Maye denied working as a bouncer at Dirty Dicks, but he did admit to having drinks there "five or ten times."[55] By the summer of 1972, Maye and Manford would have much more in common than the occasional scuffle and visit to West Village. They would both be involved in a historic criminal trial.

The day after the attack at the Inner Circle gathering, Manford could not identify Maye by name, so he filed a "John Doe" complaint. After witnesses and news accounts alleged Maye was one of the attackers, Manford examined photographs and positively identified him.[56] Manford later admitted the positive identification of Maye might not have been based solely on his own recollection: "After speaking to witnesses, I felt I had enough evidence to make the charge."[57] He also went to the civilian complaint review board and filed a malfeasance complaint against the police for their inaction on the night of the protest.[58] Despite the criminal complaint, the police did not investigate the case, nor did District Attorney Frank Hogan's office issue a warrant for Maye's arrest. A criminal court judge did not understand the delay in the Maye case: "We get thousands of these cases a year. A complaint is made, then the police bring in the defendant for a preliminary hearing. If the facts are ascertained, the defendant is held on bail for a hearing. It's that simple." Michael Kramer of *New York* magazine interviewed "five respected criminal lawyers all familiar with police and judicial procedures, [who] could not remember the last time a complaint was deemed insufficient even for a defendant to be picked up by the police for a preliminary hearing."[59] When the *Post* called the NYPD public relations office for information on the case, an officer belittled the situation. "It stinks," he shouted. "I would get off it if I were you, they can't identify Maye. They should have been arrested for trespassing."[60]

The apathetic response of the police to the criminal complaints of homosexuals was not unusual. On two separate occasions the previous August, officers on Long Island clubbed and maced demonstrators who had been peacefully protesting police brutality against homosexuals. No officers in either incident were arrested or charged. The previous fall, a New York City police officer punched a GAA activist during a protest against presidential candidate Edmund Muskie.[61] The NYPD was infamous for looking the other way when a crime victim was gay. A week before the Inner Circle incident, police looked on while a pack of high school students jumped and beat a member of the GAA during a protest outside the offices of the *Daily News*. After the cops separated the victim from his assailants, they refused to arrest anyone.[62] In a letter to the *New York Post* regarding its coverage of the Inner Circle attack, GAA Activist Pete Fisher complained that

> muggers in Greenwich Village know that police will not arrest them for beating and robbing gays even if they remain at the scene of the crime and the victim tries to press charges. Just last week I was beaten by four teenagers right

in front of several police. When will this stop? The police
encourage attacks on gay people by refusing them protection of the law all the time.

The police department's refusal to address violent crimes against homosexuals was part of the city's matrix of homosexual oppression. When it
came to antigay violence, the police did not intervene, the DA did not
prosecute, and the press did not report. The Inner Circle beatings also
could have been just another "unreported incident" of gay bashing.
"The only difference is that this time," Fisher wrote to the *Post*, "for
once—it was mentioned in the straight press thanks to Mr. Hamill."[63]

If not for Pete Hamill, the liberal *New York Post* columnist, the
Inner Circle beatings would also have gone unnoticed by the public.
The day after the incident, the *Daily News* carried a brief item about
how the Inner Circle club "played to a glittering, laughing-room-only
audience." There was no mention of the incident despite the fact that
several *Daily News* editors had attended the dinner and Manhattan
deputy borough president Leonard Cohen telephoned the newspaper
about the Maye attack. Under the headline "Politicians Spoofed in
Song and Story at Writer's Gambol," the *New York Times* described the
evening as pleasant and fun-filled but uneventful. An FBI agent who
attended the dinner found it significant enough to submit a report on
it to headquarters, but none of the New York newspapers seemed to
find the story "fit to print."[64] In reality the old boy club that was the
New York journalistic community did not want to taint their festivity
with reports of violence.

Ethan Geto was outraged at the lack of coverage in the papers. Here
was a story that was certainly more important than the one he and GAA
tried to trigger with the zap itself; yet the entire New York press corps
took a pass on it. Geto contacted his friend Pete Hamill, whom he had
taken, along with Hamill's girlfriend, Shirley Maclaine, on a few tours
of the New York gay scene. After Geto told Hamill about the Saturday
night beatings, the reporter discussed the incident with another witness,
John Scanlon, over drinks at Elaine's.[65] Enraged at the injustice, Hamill
wrote a blistering column for the Monday edition of the *Post*, which
pursued the story in a long article printed on Tuesday. Not until
Wednesday did the *New York Times* and the *Daily News* carry their first

reports on the violence at the Inner Circle, undoubtedly in response to the *Post*'s coverage.[66] Hamill's column was a media trigger that set off a chain reaction of coverage in the city's newspapers. Had he chosen to disregard the story, the Inner Circle beatings would have continued to be ignored by the press and unknown to the public.[67]

The *Post* continued to provide the most extensive coverage of the incident. Gale McGovern wrote the editor, "And if the Post hadn't covered the story so thoroughly, it's a sure bet the *Times* and the *News* wouldn't have covered it at all. This is what the gay activists call media oppression, and this is why they were leafleting at the Inner Circle."[68] Author Merle Miller commended the *Post* "for its extensive coverage of the beatings of the members of the Gay Activists Alliance . . . and for its editorial demands for an investigation into the bestial frenzy. . . . But it is a measure of the bleakness of the press in New York that the two other newspapers in the city have covered the event reluctantly and sparsely, and that neither has expressed shame and indignation at what happened."

Calvin Trillin in the *New Yorker* and Michael Kramer of *New York* magazine also praised the *Post* for its thorough coverage. But not everyone celebrated the *Post*'s tenacity. Mickey Maye complained about the paper's "almost daily campaign of pressure, distortion and harassment."[69]

With media coverage of the incident and editorials condemning the lack of an arrest or indictment, liberal politicians became involved in the cause. City Council Minority Leader Eldon Clingan declared that if the police commissioner didn't "get off his backside," he would call upon the Public Safety Committee of the Council to investigate.[70] Councilwoman Carol Greitzer, once a favorite target of the GAA, demanded the police commissioner investigate the failure of the police officers to intervene in the fray.[71] In a public statement, Congresswoman Bella Abzug urged the police commissioner to investigate whether the protestors "were reportedly stomped and beaten in public view while police refused to intervene or to let the victims identify their assailants." Abzug went on to describe homosexuals as "human beings, citizens, and taxpayers who are entitled to the full protection of the law."[72] Congressman Ed Koch joined the GAA cause when he criticized District Attorney Frank Hogan from the well of the House of

Representatives, while Mayor Lindsay ordered the police department to investigate and report on "the deplorable incident."[73] From the brutal beatings to official indifference, the Inner Circle affair generated powerful symbols that forced liberal politicians and the media to respond publicly in favor of civil rights for homosexuals.

GAA spurred on the media attention with a press conference, featuring Manford theatrically sporting an eye patch, followed by an anti-Michael Maye rally that included an address by Gore Vidal. In a letter to supporters, the GAA celebrated how the Inner Circle affair "generated the best news coverage by far the gay liberation movement has ever received. . . . The glaring light of publicity drew the gay community and to some extent, the straight, liberal establishment, into the fray at last. Better late than never." Even Maye had a grudging appreciation for the success of GAA's media campaign. In an interview with the *Post*, he complained that the whole episode was "obviously and deliberately contrived to bring maximum publicity and judging by the treatment accorded the incident by some portions of the press media the goal of these individuals was achieved."[74]

Not all supporters of gay rights relished the effect of the Inner Circle affair on the movement. Sandy Reichman wrote in the *Post*:

> Mr. Hamill built a case for the gay liberation movement, a case that they actually don't need. For he well knows as does anyone watching Intro 475 that the lunatic fringe caused the disruption at the Inner Circle show. People who seriously want to see Intro 475 pass the City Council are aware of the activists working quietly behind the scenes in an orderly fashion.[75]

Reichman had a point. Intro 475, the bill guaranteeing rights for homosexuals, ran into fresh opposition during the Inner Circle controversy. Zaps were useful in attracting the media attention that could disseminate a message, but they also antagonized some less militant supporters of the GAA agenda.

GAA lawyers, including William Kunstler, filed a petition with the New York State supreme court to require John Lindsay and Hogan to arrest and prosecute Maye and other identifiable assailants. The supreme court quickly responded by directing Lindsay and Hogan to show cause why they would not arrest and prosecute Maye.[76] Hogan convened a grand jury, and after questioning seventeen witnesses, including Maye and Manford, the jury charged that "with intent to harass, annoy, and alarm another person, Maye struck, shoved, kicked and otherwise subjected Morty Manford to physical contact."[77] Rather than charge Maye with assault, the grand jury charged him with harassment—a violation, like speeding or disorderly conduct, that carried a possible sentence of fifteen days in jail and a $250 fine.[78]

Under the dismissive headline, "Maye Hit with a Rap in Gay Tiff," the *Daily News* quoted GAA president Richard Wandel's reaction to the decision: "A simple harassment charge, in view of the assault which took place at the Hilton, is ludicrous. It's another example of how gay women and men have no rights in our society and how justice does not apply for political figures."[79] Emily Goodman, lawyer for GAA, told the *New York Times*, "If an ordinary person committed these acts he'd have been arrested forthwith, indicted for several serious crimes of assault and be in jail." Instead, Maye received "nothing more than a traffic ticket."[80] The slap on the wrist, however, fed the media frenzy. The level of media attention given to the Inner Circle affair can be seen in the headlines on the front page of the May 22, 1972, edition of the *Post*. Two headlines announced, "Nixon in Moscow and Talks Begin" and "Arrest Maye in Gay Beating."

In the interest of balance, Frank Hogan also brought up one of the protestors, Allen Roskoff, on a fourth-degree trespassing charge. City councilmen Eldon Clingan, Carter Burden, and Charles Taylor all viewed the indictment of Roskoff as an attempt to balance the Maye charge with another against a gay rights activist. In a public statement, the liberal councilmen used Roskoff's indictment to raise "the underlying issue here, namely Civil Rights for homosexuals, by recognizing that all people are entitled to equal rights and equal treatment regardless of their sexual preferences expressed in private."[81] Roskoff refused to surrender at the DA's office as requested by Hogan. Instead, he awaited arrest in Clingan's city hall office accompanied by the city council minority leader and Councilman Burden.[82] The Assistant DA assigned to Roskoff's case later dropped the charges, as he said, "in the interest of justice" and because "the court's time could be put to better use."[83]

Similar to how the media's reporting of Emmett Till's murder in 1955 raised consciousness about the plight of blacks in the South, the Inner Circle affair, though on a much smaller scale, generated sympathy for gays. The mounting media coverage of Manford's beating, and later Maye's trial, presented the public with the image of a righteous young Ivy League student who was brutally beaten because of his sexual orientation. News reports routinely contrasted the slight Manford with Maye, "the 210-pound union leader and former Golden Gloves heavyweight champion." Manford knew how to exploit the publicity. As he recounted in a letter to his supporters:

> More than any event in the history of our city, the Inner Circle beatings can be the vehicle to educate the large masses about Homosexuality and the double standard by which Homosexuals are judged. These issues must be promoted for discussion so that meaningful change can be realized.[84]

One of the issues that the media raised was the continued harassment of the GAA following the incident. The *New York Times* reported on the beating of Doug Sorace, a GAA activist who brought a camera to the Inner Circle protest. One night, two men followed Sorace from Fifty-fourth Street and Lexington Avenue to Eightieth Street and Fifth Avenue, where the pursuers confronted him and demanded, "Give us that film of the Inner Circle. It would be better for you if you did." After Sorace told them he had no film, one held him while the other punched his stomach and groin. The police later found Sorace so badly beaten, they had to take him to the hospital.[85] The *Village Voice* described the attack as a "professional beating" and reported, "The same day, another GAA member was also followed presumably because he had also been seen with a camera."[86] In *New York*, Michael Kramer also wrote about the mysterious beating of the "gay-libber" who had allegedly taken pictures of the Inner Circle incident.[87]

The *Voice* reported that the week after Sorace's beating, another Alliance member was discussing the case on the telephone at the GAA Firehouse when a third party broke into his conversation to inform him sarcastically that the phone was being tapped. The next day another taunting voice interrupted a conversation. The telephone company confirmed to a *Village Voice* reporter that there were two lines where there should have been one. Michael Kramer reported in *New York* that after he began to investigate the affair, he awoke one morning and found an index card slipped under his door. The card read, "Lay off Mickey." Such harassment so infuriated Congressman Ed Koch that he went to the House floor and denounced the "nightmare" that he likened to the movie "*Z*," about the Greek right-wing dictatorship of the 1960s in which "there are beatings of dissidents which the government, because of complicity of public officials, sought to cover up."[88] The ominous news reports and speeches about the late-night beatings of witnesses, wiretaps, and threatening notes gave readers a wider view of the widespread, sometimes physically violent, oppression of homosexuals that Manford and the GAA had long wanted to expose and publicize.

Manford also used the media attention that the Inner Circle affair triggered to introduce the general public to the concept of "homophobia."[89] At a press conference two days after the attack, Manford lectured reporters from the New York newspapers, the local television stations, the UPI, and NBC on homophobia:

> When homophobes want to have same-sex love, they are unable to do so in a civil manner. Their hatred for and fear of it is so acute, they cannot behave rationally. They cannot accept their own homosexual proclivities, and so must resort to violent rape—the violent violation of the body of a member of the same sex. On Saturday night I was so raped by a number of men at the Inner Circle affair, I have reason to believe one of these men was Michael Maye, President of the United Firefighters Union.[90]

Manford made extensive use of the term "homophobia" during his testimony in Maye's trial. "At this point just as I had my hands on this man to pull him back, I was quickly grabbed from behind by some homophobic savage."[91] Rich Wandel, president of the Gay Activists Alliance, released a press statement during Maye's trial that illustrates the power of the term "homophobia" and its importance in GAA's media campaign. "A mental disease is rampaging throughout this country. The

Homophile "militants" gathered at 1965 ECHO conference. Standing: Jack Nichols (fifth from left), Frank Kameny (second from right). Seated: Julian Hodges (first on left), Dick Leitsch (second from right). (courtesy of the New York Public Library)

Barbara Gittings. (courtesy of Bettye Lane)

Bob Martin, aka Stephen Donaldson, founder of the Student Homophile League at Columbia University, in 1966. (courtesy of the New York Public Library)

Ed "the Skull" Murphy, mob henchman and bouncer at the Stonewall Inn. Before working at the Stonewall, the Skull was involved in a Mafia blackmailing scheme that extorted more than $1 million from nearly 700 closeted homosexuals, including a U.S. Congressman, an admiral, two generals, and a "much admired television personality." (courtesy of Bettye Lane)

Boarded-up window of the Stonewall Inn after the riot in June 1969. The police raid that precipitated the riot was part of an operation to break a Mafia blackmailing scheme. (courtesy of Bettye Lane)

Thousands rally in Central Park at the end of the gay pride march in June 1970, marking the first anniversary of the Stonewall riot. (courtesy of Rich Wandel)

Gay Activists Alliance leadership: Arthur Evans (right), known as GAA's theoretician. (courtesy of Bettye Lane)

GAA's Marty Robinson embodied the aggressive style of the so-called "New Homosexual." (courtesy of Bettye Lane)

Jim Owles, GAA's first president. Robinson dubbed Owles "the scrappiest little faggot in New York." (courtesy of Bettye lane)

"Answer the homosexuals! Answer the homosexuals!" Arthur Evans confronts New York City municipal official during a "zap." (courtesy of Rich Wandel)

Marty Robinson in a duck costume during a protest against Fidelifacts, a New York–based private investigation firm that provided employers with information on the personal background of job applicants. (courtesy of Rich Wandel)

Police try to restrain a GAA member at a 1973 City Hall protest in New York. (courtesy of Bettye Lane)

Jim Owles during a mock gay marriage ceremony at the City Clerk's Office. (courtesy of Rich Wandel)

The Gay Activists Alliance "zaps" the ABC television network's office in protest over a homophobic episode of their show *Marcus Welby, M.D.* (courtesy of Bettye Lane)

Gay and lesbian couples speak to millions on *The David Susskind Show* in 1973. (courtesy of Bettye Lane)

GAA headquarters in a Victorian-era firehouse located on Wooster Street in what is now Soho. (courtesy of Bettye Lane)

Carol Greitzer, the first politician to succumb to a GAA zap, addresses an audience in the GAA Firehouse in 1973. Notice the famous GAA mural on the wall behind her. (courtesy of Bettye Lane)

Liberal New York City mayor John Lindsay, GAA's favorite political target. Lindsay once joked, "I've had more trouble with queens than any politician since Henry VIII." (courtesy of Bettye Lane)

Ethan Geto, GAA's political strategist and expert on New York City politics. (courtesy of Bettye Lane)

Bruce Voeller displays his arm chained to a phone at George McGovern's presidential campaign headquarters in New York City. (courtesy of Bettye Lane)

In 1972, George McGovern was forced by a GAA zap to become the first presidential candidate of a major party to endorse gay rights. (courtesy of Bettye Lane)

Morty Manford at a press conference after the Inner Circle beatings in 1972. Manford used the controversy over the beatings to publicize the concept of homophobia. (courtesy of Bettye Lane)

Gore Vidal speaks out against homophobia and one of the assailants in the Inner Circle beatings, Michael Maye. (courtesy of Bettye Lane)

Morty Manford (second from left) with his mother, Jeanne (center), and father, Jules (second from right), at the 1973 gay pride march. Jeanne and Jules founded PFLAG, Parents and Friends of Lesbians and Gays, in the wake of the Inner Circle Affair. (courtesy of Bettye Lane)

Wreckage from fire bombs that gutted GAA headquarters in 1974. (courtesy of Bettye Lane)

Manford displays unexploded cans of lighter fluid for an ABC News reporter. (courtesy of Bettye Lane)

National Gay Task Force ceremony in 1978 honoring Midge Costanza, aide to President Jimmy Carter. From left to right: Jean O'Leary, Gloria Steinem, Midge Costanza, Arthur Laurent, Bella Abzug, and Bruce Voeller. The previous year, Costanza arranged a historic meeting between Carter administration officials and NGTF at the White House. (courtesy of Bettye Lane)

Carter's tacit embrace of gay rights during his administration cost him support among evangelicals during his bid for reelection in 1980. (courtesy of Bettye Lane)

Anita Bryant and family in 1977. The former Miss Oklahoma became a spokesperson for an anti-gay rights movement. Her ability to wrap God, family, and patriotism around the anti-gay rights crusade posed a great challenge to the gay power movement. (courtesy of Bettye Lane)

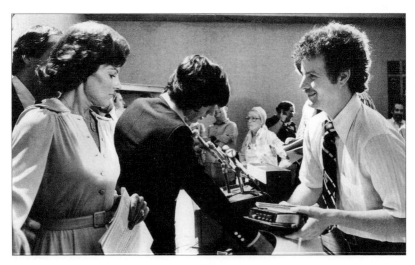

Bryant refuses to be interviewed by San Francisco reporter Randy Shilts after he introduced himself as gay. A few years later, Shilts's reporting on the AIDS crisis would break the media silence on the epidemic. (courtesy of Bettye Lane)

Gay activists countered Bryant's patriotic appeal with a little flag waving of their own. (courtesy of Bettye Lane)

Questions about Ed Koch's sexuality arose during his successful run for mayor of New York City in 1977. As mayor, Koch was slow to react during the early days of the AIDS crisis. (courtesy of Bettye Lane)

ACT-UP banner at AIDS awareness protest. ACT-UP used zaps to force the federal government and drug companies to increase access to experimental AIDS drugs. (courtesy of Rich Wandel)

name of the disease is 'homophobia.' A homophobic believes that homosexuals must be forbidden to enjoy the freedoms and the responsibilities of a free society. We must be forbidden to hold responsible jobs, to possess social status and to even have suitable living quarters."[92] The trial and the attendant publicity gave the GAA a powerful forum to publicize the concept of homophobia.

The significance of Manford's and GAA's usage of the word is highlighted by the way it was reported in the press. The *New York Post* quoted Manford's testimony about how he "was grabbed from behind by 'a homophobic savage.'" The *Post* then explained to its readers, "'Homophobic' as used by Manford is defined as one who has an irrational fear of homosexuals."[93] According to the *New York Times* "Mr. Manford testified that he had not recognized his 'assailant' as the union leader when the whole episode began. All he knew then, he said, was that he was being attacked by 'a homophobic savage.'"[94] The *Long Island Press* also reported that Maye "was described by the complaint yesterday as a "homophobic savage."[95] The *Village Voice* ran an article by Arthur Bell, a GAA member, under the headline "Morty Manford and the Flaming Homophobe." Bell wrote, "The one good thing that came from the trial is that it opened a new line of tactics for the gay liberation movement." 'We're embarking on a course of aggressive defense tactics,' Manford declared. 'We're now putting the homophobes on the line.'" Even the readership of the *Voice* needed a definition: "Homophobes are those women and men who are frightened of homosexuals, without trying to evaluate why. Their fear, says Morty, is often manifested in their hatred of a lifestyle contrary to their own."[96] Michael Blaine of the *Voice* incorporated the word in his piece on the delay in prosecuting Maye:

> It is not known what triggered Maye's rage, but Michael McPherson, a GAA member says he overheard Maye muttering "God I hate those bastards!" while digging the knuckles of one hand into the palm of the other. . . . It is still unclear why Maye was not arrested. It is still unclear why "investigations" have to be conducted. It is still unclear why Maye made that quick trip up to Albany. But through the haze of confusion a tentative diagnosis can be offered. Acute Homophobia.[97]

Maye facilitated his characterization as a homophobe by his own remarks to the press. Manford wrote to a supporter, "When Maye was interviewed on TV after the last court appearance, he said something to the effect of: 'I don't know what I am doing here. Homosexuals, Queers and every degenerate in the country is here.' The interview on TV was fantastic. He fully demonstrated by his words and actions and mannerisms, the sick, dangerous homophobe he is."[98] But it was the coining of the word by Weinberg, its use by Manford, and its dissemination to the general public through the media that enabled people to even think of Maye as a "homophobe" and not just as someone who hated homosexuals. (By 1974, even *TV Guide* was using the word "homophobic" when it called an episode of *Police Woman* that centered around three murderous lesbians "the single most homophobic show to date.")[99]

Maye's trial was great theater. On the night of the Inner Circle dinner, Manford was a loud tough who fought back by kicking Maye in the groin. But in the courtroom he was a soft-spoken innocent victim who did nothing to provoke the irrational behavior of the "homophobe." In the weeks leading up to the trial, Ethan Geto coached Manford on how to play the press. But when Geto provided key eyewitness testimony against Maye, he claimed he had met Manford and the Activists only a few times prior to the Inner Circle affair as part of community outreach for the borough president's office.[100]

Although the case against Maye looked very solid in the press coverage of the trial, on July 5, 1972, Manhattan supreme court justice Shirley Levittan dismissed the case on grounds of insufficient evidence.[101] After Levittan rendered the decision, Maye told reporters, "I don't know what to say. It's pretty sad: it's been such a waste of time."

Later that year, Maye lost his reelection bid as the fireman's union president. The Inner Circle affair undoubtedly contributed to turning the election against him. As one fireman said to a reporter, "We don't pay him to go around beating up kids. We pay him to get us a good contract. This homo thing is making us all look bad. We could use some more money instead."[102]

The Inner Circle affair transformed Manford into a celebrity of the gay rights movement. A few months after the verdict, *Michael's Thing*, a gay-oriented magazine, ran an article entitled "Morty Manford's National Ambitions."

The case also clearly established for the first time the principle that gays are entitled to equal protection under the law and that homo-phobic bigots like Maye will not be able to attack us with impunity. Manford's courageous insistence that Maye be brought to justice remains to this day one of the sterling accomplishments of the gay movement and provides an example that no gay activist or gay-bashing prizefighter should—or will—ever forget.[103]

When Manford won an unopposed election to the GAA presidency in 1973, a sustained standing ovation shook the Firehouse. One Activist called it "election by acclamation."

One of the enduring legacies of the Inner Circle affair was the creation of Parents of Gays, the forerunner to Parents and Friends of Lesbians and Gays (PFLAG). A few years prior to the Inner Circle affair, Morty came out to his parents, Jeanne and Jules, after he attempted suicide. His parents were terribly worried. Several years before, their eldest son Charles had been so tormented over his own homosexuality that he committed suicide. Jeanne and Jules were not going to allow that to happen to Morty. Jeanne told her son "that he was still the same person I had always loved and been proud of. How could my feelings change because of this added knowledge."[104] Coming out was a great relief to Manford, who described how it removed a barrier between him and his parents "because I don't have to watch my every word, deed, action and motion any more. And I don't have to make up a story when I want to go out to a gay bar."[105] At first Jeanne, an elementary school teacher, worried about her son's homosexuality: "Would my son be able to finish college? Would he get into law school if he chose law as his profession? Would he be admitted to the bar? Would he have trouble with police?"[106] But she began to read about homosexuality and was particularly impressed by George Weinberg's book *Society and the Healthy Homosexual.* She also began to meet Morty's friends and "found them to be intelligent lovely people, to whom I enjoyed talking."

Manford's parents became gay rights activists after they saw a television news broadcast about the beating of their son and the refusal of the police to intervene. Jeanne was enraged:[107] "How dare they touch my son! The nerve of them! Who are they! I pay taxes and the policemen stand by and let him get beaten by those thugs."[108] She fired off a letter to the *New York Post*.

> I would like to commend The Post for its coverage last week of the tragic incident that took place at the Inner Circle dinner, when hoodlums who work for our city were allowed to beat up the young men of the Gay Activist Alliance and walk away while our police stood by watching. It might be that these "men" have themselves some deep rooted sexual problems or they would not have become so enraged as to commit violence in beatings.

Like her son, Jeanne attributed the violence to "deep rooted sexual problems," which became known as homophobia. She also noted the significance of the *Post*'s coverage for the gay rights movement:

> I hope that your honest and forthright coverage of the incident has made many of the gays who have been fearful, gain courage to come out and join the bandwagon. They are working for a fair chance at employment and dignity and to become a vocal and respected minority. It is a fight for recognition such as all minority groups must wage and needs support from outsiders as well as participants in the movement.

Jeanne understood how important it was for the mainstream media to acknowledge and defend the minority rights of homosexuals.

Perhaps the most significant part of Jeanne's letter to the *Post* was her declaration, "I am proud of my son, Morty Manford, and the hard work he has been doing in urging homosexuals to accept their feelings and not let the bigots and sick people take advantage of them in the way they have done in the past and are continuing to do." This declaration of pride resonated with parents of homosexuals who were ashamed not only about their children but also about themselves and how they may have fostered their children's homosexuality. At the time, many psychologists attributed homosexuality to an overbearing mother and a detached father. In response to her letter to the *Post*,

Jeanne began receiving notes from grateful parents and children, and television talk shows asked her and Morty's father, Jules, to present their views on homosexuality to millions of viewers.

Ethan Geto and Morty understood how to leverage Jeanne's and Jules's public acceptance of their son's homosexuality. Jeanne was a sweet, kindhearted schoolteacher; Jules was a concerned, upstanding dentist. Geto and Morty coached Jeanne and Jules on how to perform for the cameras, but both were naturals. "They felt the issue deeply," Geto recalled. "They had lost one son, and they almost lost Morty."[109]

Geto used his experience in public relations to help line up fifty television appearances including one on the *Phil Donahue Show*. Over the television airwaves, the Manfords reassured millions of parents that they were not to blame for their children's homosexuality. Jeanne explained how she "did not conform to the Freudian image of the mother of a homosexual. I am not and never was a nagging or domineering woman. My husband was not and is not a passive father." She had a simple, unadorned, nonthreatening way of explaining her acceptance of homosexuality: "I don't know anything about being gay, but if my son was gay, it had to be all right." The appearances of a middle-aged, middle-class, married couple who supported gay rights showed the audience that radicals and homosexuals were not the only supporters of the movement. As Jeanne once said, "I, who never crosses a street against a traffic light, have been called a revolutionist! If it means doing what one believes to be right, I have no quarrel with the appellation."

Jeanne became a celebrity within the movement after Morty invited her to march in the 1972 Gay Pride parade. As she and her son walked up Fifth Avenue, she carried a homemade sign that read, "Parents of Gays Unite in Support of our Children." When spectators on the sidewalk began cheering as she approached, she assumed the applause was for Dr. Benjamin Spock, who was marching just ahead of her with the Gay Veterans of Vietnam. But all along the parade route people thanked and kissed her. They talked about their parents and how they wished their mothers were at the parade. Jeanne "had not realized until then that I was doing anything unusual. I refuse to care about what my neighbor or associates think about me. I am not a closet parent."[110] In its article about the 1972 parade, the *New York Times* mentioned Morty and his mother, who was quoted proclaiming, "I'm proud of my son,

I'm not ashamed of him."[111] During the parade, someone snapped a photograph of Mrs. Manford and her sign, which became one of the images chosen to adorn a 1973 calendar featuring revolutionaries. Two decades later, Anna Quindlen celebrated Jeanne's march in her *Times* column which began, "It was 20 years ago next month that an elementary school teacher named Jeanne Manford made history."[112]

Inspired by the reaction of the people at the parade, Jeanne, Morty, and Ethan Geto talked about the possibility of starting a group for parents to meet, discuss their children, and learn that homosexuality was "normal."[113] In early 1973, they placed an advertisement in the *Village Voice* that invited parents of gays and lesbians to meet in a Greenwich Village church. At the meetings, parents described how it was more difficult for them to "come out" to their friends and relatives about the sexual orientation of their children than it was for their sons and daughters to reveal their own sexuality. One mother told the group, "You worry that it's going to affect your social life and your husband's business life. Many people tend to blame you when they hear you have a gay child. They think you must be some kind of monster."[114] In the summer of 1974, on a visit to Southern California, Jeanne and Jules were introduced to Adele and Larry Star, who had tried unsuccessfully to form a support group for parents after their son came out. One night over dinner, the Stars and the Manfords decided to create a West Coast counterpart to the New York Parents of Gays. Since then, hundreds of affiliated chapters have been formed. Under its new name, Parents and Friends of Lesbians and Gays (PFLAG), the Manford's organization is an international institution with over 80,000 members and 460 chapters in almost every state in the nation and in Britain, France, and the Netherlands.

In his 1951 *The Homosexual in America*, Donald Webster Cory described how the repression of the homosexual minority had a unique bitterness because often it was faced alone. While ethnic groups could take refuge "in the warmth of family and friends," gays and lesbians found that those who were "closest to us, whose love we are in extreme need of, accept us for what we are not."[115] For the past three decades, PFLAG has quietly helped tens of thousands of homosexuals and their families vanquish such feelings of isolation and estrangement.

chapter eight

THE GAY LOUNGE

At the same time that Morty Manford was waging battle against Michael Maye and homophobia, he founded the nation's first gay student lounge at Columbia University. Manford's effort to emulate black and Latino students who created "minority lounges" quickly evolved into a battle to push the liberal Columbia administration to officially recognize homosexuals as a minority group worthy of its own lounge. Columbia University's official recognition of a gay student lounge marked the first time a major American institution publicly and officially acknowledged the minority status of homosexuals.

Manford became involved with the Student Homophile League shortly after enrolling at Columbia in 1968. Two years later SHL changed its name to Gay People at Columbia (GPC) and announced that it was turning its attention from political action to social activities that would encourage students to come out.[1] GPC abandoned its political focus, in part, because Manford and other leaders reasoned that members could join the fight for legal equality through the Gay Activists Alliance or other liberation organizations that were formed in the city after the Stonewall riots. Gay People at Columbia could focus on another goal of the gay liberation movement: the creation of a community in which closeted homosexuals would feel free to come out.

When SHL, under founder Bob Martin, applied for university

recognition in 1967, the administration insisted that the group never
organize social events that might promote sexual activity. SHL quickly
abandoned that pledge and became the nexus for gay social life on
campus. Gay People at Columbia continued SHL's effort to help closeted students become more comfortable with their sexuality by organizing meetings on each floor of every dorm. One junior attested to the
significance of the GPC gatherings:

> I really think that GPC was indispensable. It is the only way
> someone is going to come out on campus. I don't think
> anyone is going to come out on their floor unless they feel
> they have support. They are not going to do it by them-
> selves. I came out on my floor when I went to a floor
> meeting as a member of GPC and that was a good feeling.[2]

Morty Manford thought a gay student lounge would provide a refuge
on campus for closeted students looking to come out. He also knew
that the university's establishment of a minority lounge for gays and
lesbians would stand as a permanent symbol of the minority status and
rights of homosexuals.[3]

The creation of the gay lounge was part of a larger student-driven
movement to reserve spaces for minorities. The first minority lounge
was established in an office formerly occupied by the university's Naval
Reserve Officers Training Corps program. The university dissolved its
NROTC chapter in 1969 in response to antiwar sentiment on campus
and, to a lesser extent, SHL's complaints about the Navy's discrimination against homosexuals. Two years later, an African-American student group that espoused black nationalism took over the NROTC's
vacated office and christened it the Malcolm X Lounge, reserved
exclusively for "the sons and daughters of Africa."[4] In a 1971
announcement of the new lounge, the Student Afro-American Society
(SAS) declared:

> The idea of integration seems as ridiculous as the people who
> propose it as a solution to the problems of black people in this
> country. It should be very clear to europeans [sic] that black
> people are no longer concerned with being the same as they

are; that is to possess the same values and standards as white people.[5]

The liberal Columbia administration endorsed the Malcolm X lounge because it understood that black students were marginalized on campus socially, and it sympathized with their need for a space where they would feel completely accepted.[6]

Shortly after SAS acquired its meeting place, a group of Latino students "occupied" a space in another dormitory and demanded their own ethnic lounge. The president of the university, William McGill responded immediately by having the police clear them from the room but then began negotiations that ended with the official recognition of a Latino lounge.[7] The Asian student organization then decided they deserved their own gathering place. Rather than capture some cubical, they submitted a formal request for space to one of the Undergraduate Dormitory Councils (UDC). Soon after the UDC granted them a rarely used TV room, the administration acknowledged the Asian lounge.

The liberal Dean of Columbia College, Carl Hovde, had some difficulty reconciling his support for ethnic lounges with his commitment to the melting pot concept. Like most liberals he hoped to see a society in which there was no segregation or differentiation based on race or ethnicity. Dean Hovde, however, justified his approval of the minority lounges in a 1971 public statement:

> These minorities in varying measures live in a society which has denied them opportunities equal to those enjoyed by the majority of the population. . . . It is for many reasons understandable that there is a felt need for a facility where social and cultural cohesion is more easily obtainable than in other lounges.[8]

The liberal student editors of the *Columbia Spectator* also conceded that "setting aside rooms for the primary use of minority students is perhaps not logically consistent with the 'melting pot' ideal of racial brotherhood, but it is a means that leads to a desirable necessary end."[9]

While liberals at the university grudgingly embraced the ethnic lounges, a conservative student group charged that allocating exclusive

space for minority groups was "segregationist, racist and morally rep-
rehensible." Echoing the liberals of the 1950s, the leader of the conservatives, Fred Lowell, declared that "integration is the only solution
to racial problems."[10] To underscore their point, he also claimed that
at Columbia conservatives were an "oppressed minority" and therefore
they deserved a lounge too.

Given Gay People at Columbia's transformation into a social organization and its interest in providing students with a comfortable
atmosphere in which they could come out, GPC naturally wanted a
"gay lounge." Manford reasoned that homosexuals like the ethnic
minorities needed a lounge because "whether we are oppressed
because of our ethnic or racial background or because of our sexual
orientation, our oppression is nonetheless onerous."[11] Rather than
seize a space, GPC followed the lead of the Asian group and submitted
a formal request.

In April 1971 representatives of GPC addressed the student-run
Undergraduate Dormitory Council (UDC) of Furnald Hall on the
need for a gay lounge. Manford and other GPC members complained
that campus homosexuals were forced to find social activity in New
York's gay bars, which exposed students to potential police harassment
and the organized crime syndicates that ran many gay establishments.[12]
Because no official gay meeting place existed at Columbia, Manford
claimed that homosexual students feigned heterosexuality on campus
and "then went to the West Village and the Upper East Side to be gay":

> When one exists in a heterosexual milieu, the brief moments
> in a gay bar become precious time for cruising. Little human
> (and I use that word in a total sense) interaction can take
> place. What gay people at Columbia need is a gay lounge, a
> place where gay people can congregate openly as gays
> amidst the heterosexual towers of ivy on Morningside
> Heights.[13]

After a discussion between GPC and the Undergraduate Dormitory
Council about the proposed lounge, Harold Sackheim, the UDC president and one of Manford's straight friends, proposed that the council
give the gay student group a space in the basement of the Furnald

dormitory. The council decided to gauge the sentiment of the dorm residents toward the lounge by conducting a poll and by organizing "rap sessions." The poll results overwhelmingly approved the lounge by a margin of two to one. During the rap sessions a few straight students said a lounge would enhance their own social development by offering a place to get to know gays in a relaxed atmosphere.[14] Manford envisioned a gay lounge that would welcome heterosexuals and relieve their antigay anxieties. He predicted, "at first the lounge will have a great impact on the University but people will become used to gays holding hands on College Walk just as they got used to long hair or interracial couples."[15] Manford's charismatic presence at the rap sessions reassured uneasy students, one of whom recalled, "when people heard he was coming they thought he'll either be a flit and try to make a pass at someone, or be really creepy. He's a likeable guy. He's so middle America, the way he talks and looks and everything else you can't help but respect and like him."[16] Manford embodied the GAA ideal; a tough yet respectable homosexual who countered the old stereotypes.

While the dormitory council conducted its polls and rap sessions, members of the administration went on record about the prospective gay lounge. According to the *Columbia Spectator*, Philip Benson, the Director of Student Interests, opposed the gay lounge because the main criteria for granting space to a student group was "the presence of alienation and identification problems," and the only groups meeting this criteria were blacks, Latinos, and Asians. President McGill expressed a similar sentiment less diplomatically: "It is not a question of why one gets a lounge but where to draw a line."[17] Manford and fellow GAA radical Arthur Evans, who was a PhD candidate in philosophy at Columbia, jumped on the "draw a line" comment in a leaflet that argued that indeed "gay people in general are an oppressed class in the United States."

We have had enough. We have had enough of the perpetuation of a heterosexualist milieu by officials of the Columbia University administration. WE HAVE HAD ENOUGH OF BEING "BEYOND THE LINE." GAY PEOPLE AT COLUMBIA, UNITE! ORGANIZE! RESIST![18]

McGill's language also angered members of the Furnald Hall dormitory council, which voted on April 28, 1971, to establish the lounge. Sackheim later claimed the vote "came about as a direct result of McGill's statement about gays in the *Spectator*."[19] McGill's statement also raised fears among dormitory council members that he would overrule their decision. They demanded Dean Hovde confirm their right to decide how space would be utilized in their dormitories.[20] Hovde responded with a letter to Manford and Sackheim in which he informed them that he had vetoed the UDC decision to create the gay lounge.

Before 1968, the word of a dean was final in undergraduate housing matters, but that policy changed in the wake of the spring student riots and police crackdown. In an attempt to restore student confidence, Hovde broadened the powers of the student run dormitory councils to allocate space. Three years later, the Furnald dormitory council voted unanimously to use Hovde's 1968 promise to form the basis of an appeal to the university trustees to overturn his gay lounge veto.[21]

Among the administrators, President William McGill, a trained psychologist, harbored the strongest resistance to the gay lounge. His opposition derived from his belief that young men became gay after being exposed to homosexuality during a period of adolescent sexual ambiguity. If young people avoided exposure to gay activity, McGill concluded, they would develop "normally." At the time, McGill's concerns about the spread of homosexuality mirrored the opinion of much of the psychiatric community, which was just beginning to reevaluate its diagnosis of homosexuality as a sickness. He therefore did "not think it proper to provide under University auspices a center that might have a profound effect on the sexual orientation of young people who are essentially innocent in this dispute."[22] Officially, however, the decision to allow the GPC to establish a lounge rested with Hovde, a member of the ACLU, who was much more comfortable with the emergence of gay rights activism on campus than the president. In his view:

> It's a healthy and proper thing that the gay movement has arisen on campus. . . . I intend to be as helpful as I can to the gay students here, who indeed have obvious problems which the rise of the gay movement will certainly improve.

I do not regret the development of this movement but
rather think it a good thing, one long overdue indeed.[23]

Hovde supported "the gay movement" as a force that would improve
the lot of an oppressed people, but he also shared the common belief
that gays converted young heterosexuals to homosexuality and so
refused to officially recognize the lounge.[24] Since Hovde acknowledged that, like the ethnic minorities, homosexuals experienced discrimination, he needed to justify the obvious double standard implicit
in his refusal to support the lounge. Hovde argued that homosexuals
were not minorities like blacks or Latinos. "One is born Black or
Latin," Hovde wrote, "and the identifying characteristics are permanent, while sexuality is a shifting and subtle set of drives."[25] He also
claimed that since sexual activity was a private concern, the university
should not get involved.[26]

When the institutional resistance became clear, GPC decided to
follow the aggressive tactics of the black and Latino groups. In May
1971, ten members of GPC occupied the proposed site of the gay
lounge, a storeroom in the basement of Furnald Hall. Upon entering
the room, Manford announced, "This is not a demonstration or a sit-
in. This is our lounge."[27] On the wall outside the room someone hung
a banner that read "Welcome to the Alan Ginsberg Center for the
Rehabilitation of Straight People." Although the banner writer mis-
spelled Allen Ginsberg's name, it was an appropriate choice for the
lounge. In 1944, the legendary beat poet was suspended from
Columbia in part because he was caught sleeping with Jack Kerouac.

A little over a quarter of a century later, seven GPC members
camped out together on the floor of a newly inaugurated gay lounge.
The next day forty more students joined them and they drew the attention of the *New York Post*, which described the events in an article entitled "Defying Ban, Gay Group Grabs Room at Columbia."[28] Like the
formation of the Student Homophile League, the gay lounge controversy triggered media coverage that characterized gays as students
rather than as lunatics, deviants, or criminals. On Tuesday morning
Dean Hovde denounced the lounge and told the occupiers to leave,
but the students voted to defy the dean and remain in the "Alan Ginsberg Center."[29]

The de facto establishment of the lounge and the attendant publicity necessitated a meeting among members of GPC, Hovde, Benson, and Coleman. An account of the discussion reveals much about conflict between the gay right activists and liberals like Hovde who recognized the need to protect the rights of homosexuals but saw sexuality as a personal matter that went beyond the purview of the university. Hovde opened the debate over whether gay students should have a lounge by explaining that he refused to support it because he believed the university had to maintain "institutional neutrality" regarding the sexual orientation of the students. Arthur Evans challenged Hovde's claim that Columbia was institutionally neutral: "The university established heterosexuality as a way of life. It is not value-free. It has committed an act of aggression against gays and it has an obligation not to unthinkingly reflect the prejudices of the surrounding society." Student Vincent Bencivenga exclaimed, "the University has significantly failed me. We should be able to take the strength that is gleaned from open recognition of our sexuality. Why can't the university see its way to helping me realize my full human potentiality?" Hovde responded, "Isn't that situation improving informally? I mean all of you are here." Bencivenga challenged Hovde's contention that sexuality was a private matter that the university did not have the responsibility to protect: "A homosexual's sexuality is as big an unchosen disadvantage to him in society as a black person's blackness. I can see someone sitting in your chair forty years ago saying, 'Well your color is an intensely personal issue and an informal one, and we can't get involved formally.' " In response to a student's question about the criteria for the college's support for a minority lounge, Hovde agreed that "many of them apply to homosexuals. It is GPC's focus on a private matter which is the one disqualifying difference between it and ethnic minorities' request for lounges." Manford jumped on that distinction: "It's as if you're saying that you can see color or the slant of someone's eyes so you deal with it, but you won't deal with sexuality because you can't see it. We're arguing in vain. You're trying to humor us." The *Spectator* reported that after the students announced their intention to hold the lounge indefinitely, the meeting broke up in bitterness with the students "crying out in anger and the Dean frequently murmuring inaudibly."[30]

The administration and conservative students were not the only opponents to the idea that homosexuals constituted a legitimate minority and therefore deserved a lounge. The strongest resistance came from the black student organization. The *Spectator* published a statement from Student Afro-American Society (SAS) expressing resentment with

> the classification of itself and other Third world groups into 1) make believe groupings of oppressed minorities along with social misfits such as local camps and homosexual groups. SAS can find nothing whatsoever that serves to adjoin itself with this group of misplaced persons. SAS understands that homosexuals play an important part in the european [sic] culture and that they have a number of mentors among the founders of western society to mold themselves after; yet it feels that in a time when black people are working to create a nation of men and women, they don't have time to wallow in the mud with people who cannot decide if they are men or women.

SAS opposed the recognition of homosexuals as fellow minorities because they did not want to be grouped with people they regarded as "social misfits." Manford countered with his own editorial in *Spectator* claiming that the black opponents to the gay lounge "discredited themselves in attacking gays. . . . It is incumbent upon oppressed minorities to recognize other oppressed minorities and not use them as scapegoats the way society does."

After the *Spectator* printed Manford's response to SAS's statement, he was physically attacked by a black student. Never one to hold grudges, Manford nonchalantly recounted the incident for the student newspaper, "he started choking me and I threw him off. That was it."[31] On campus there were several instances of verbal conflicts between the black and gay student groups. A few students conducted a "fag hunt" in one dormitory and a gay student was told to leave his room by his black roommate.[32] Manford lay most of the blame on President McGill for playing one minority group against another: "I charge McGill with full responsibility for the current reaction crisis."[33]

That spring, Henry Coleman attended a meeting of university deans from around the country who asked him what was new on Columbia's campus. He responded, "You are not going to believe this. The blacks and the gays are fighting." "Oh no!" a dean from another school exclaimed, "What happens at Columbia will happen to us in two years."[34]

President McGill was uncertain about how to handle the gay lounge controversy. He felt very uneasy with the rise of gay militancy on campus. He told an audience at the College of the Holy Cross in 1971, "We are surely ear-marked for agitation and confrontation by organized homosexuals at Columbia next year." McGill characterized his situation as president as "walking the narrow line between genuine concern for the civil rights of homosexual and alumni outrage over the thought of organized homosexual activity on the Columbia's Campus . . . an art that I have not yet quite mastered."[35] After the university recognized SHL in 1967, the administration received dozens of letters from alumni who expressed a strong fear of the organization spreading homosexuality on the campus. McGill anticipated even greater alumni opposition to a gay lounge space where students might engage in "recruitment." Therefore he chose to pursue a benign neglect policy toward the gay lounge. The administration did not try to evict the students but it also refused to officially recognize, and therefore sanction, their meeting place.[36]

On any given afternoon, one would walk into the officially nonexistent lounge and find four or five students sitting on dormitory-issued chairs or on a well-worn red rug. A free cup of coffee could be poured from a large urn that sat on the lone table. The room was steaming. The exposed water pipes and radiator gave off so much heat that even in the middle of the winter an air conditioner hummed in the background.[37] Along with regular meetings of the GPC, the lounge held poetry readings and lunches every Friday afternoon. The legendary poet W. H. Auden stopped by to attend one of GPC's many wine and cheese parties. While relaxing in the lounge, students discussed common problems such as their families' reactions to their homosexuality or plans to zap the university-sponsored Christmas Ball.[38] One patron of the lounge said, "The lounge gives us a focal point, it creates a sense of community, of identity and generates a refusal to be cowed."[39]

In the fall of 1971, Manford looked outside the university for allies in the struggle for recognition. He registered a complaint with the New

York ACLU which sent Dean Hovde a letter demanding the university recognize the lounge.[40] Manford also took GPC's case to the New York City Council's General Welfare Committee, which was holding hearings on Intro 475. A section of the bill prohibited an "educational corporation" from "deny[ing] the use of its facilitates to any person otherwise qualified by reason of his race, color, religion, or sexual orientation." On November 14, 1971, Manford sat before the city council and described the history of the lounge, citing the ACLU's conclusion that the lounge controversy was an "instance of blatant discrimination against a large portion of the Columbia community and an unjustifiable discrimination directed at a group of people solely on the basis of sexual orientation." The next day's edition of the *New York Times* ran a front-page article about the bill and cited Manford's testimony.[41]

Back on campus, the president of the Furnald dormitory council, Harold Sackheim, appealed Hovde's denial of recognition of the gay lounge to the university trustees. For the first time in Columbia's history, the decision of a dean was being appealed to the university's trustees. In his announcement of the appeal, Sackheim lashed out at the administration, "What they are saying to the gay people, in effect, is 'you're not good enough for us but come in through the back door'— separate bathrooms for niggers."[42] The next day, under the title "Paternalism," the *Spectator* printed an editorial that condemned the idea of loco parentis: "The University should worry about the quality, cost and relevance of the education it offers and not whether students are walking the straight and narrow." The student newspaper demanded that the administration abandon its paternalistic restriction of the sexual freedom of students and recognize the gay lounge.

While Sackheim worked within the channels of the university power structure, Manford adopted the direct action tactics he learned in the Gay Activist Alliance. He decided that the university would provide the lounge with new furniture, one way or another. One morning in early December 1971, Manford and a fellow member of GPC, Alex Jimenez, each picked up broken chairs from the lounge and marched across the campus to the dean's office. The chair-bearing students entered the office and attempted to swap the old lounge chairs, one with a broken rung and the other with a missing arm, for a couple of the dean's leather-backed chairs. Their defiant heist was thwarted, however, by four security guards who showed up and demanded that they drop the furniture. The students refused and a scuffle ensued. Dean Coleman intervened, exchanging a couple of shoves with Manford and yelling above the fray, "Morty, this is not the way to get furniture!"[43] After the security guards restored order, Manford asked the assistant dean, Peter Pouncey, if he could call his mother. Pouncey, who considered the request rather "effete," consented.[44] Morty picked up the phone and called ABC News, which soon set up its arc lights outside the dean's office. He then rushed out and read a prepared statement in front of the cameras:

> The guilty liberals in the Administration have not only denied official recognition to the gay lounge, but they have refused to provide safe and comfortable facilities for those who use the gay lounge. Since the administration cannot be trusted to provide for our safety and comfort, we are taking these matters into our own hands. For the past eight months we have tolerated the inequalities thrust upon us, but no longer! We are tired of sitting on broken chairs! We are tired of all the inequalities! We are tired of being "beyond the line!"[45]

Coleman quickly organized a meeting with Manford, Jimenez, Associate Dean Pouncey, two assistant deans, a student senator, and Harold Sackheim. From eleven that morning until well into the evening, the dean's office was closed to visitors, the door was locked, and two security guards were stationed at the entrance. Manford and Jimenez assured Coleman that they would not run away with the chairs if the office were unlocked, but the seasoned dean was not worried about Manford and Jimenez. He feared that campus radicals might suddenly rally to the gay rights cause and storm the building. Coleman was understandably concerned about security. Less than three years before, in the spring of 1968, students held him hostage in that same office. A bit shaken by Manford's action, Coleman averred, "I am past the year of '68. I am not going to deal on the level of sit-ins, threats or taking furniture."[46]

During the meeting, Sackheim proposed that his dormitory council just quietly allocate money for the lounge, but Manford and Jimenez rejected the idea because their real goal was to gain the university's formal recognition. By the end of the evening, the assembled group reached a settlement whereby a committee would be selected to choose furniture for the lounge from university storage. The administrators also agreed not to take disciplinary action against the students. In the next day's *New York Times*, a front-page article described the incident under the headline "Columbia Agrees to Equip 'Gay' Area."[47] The fall 1971 semester ended with new furniture and a victory for the gay lounge, but the university still had not given formal recognition to the lounge and, by extension, public acknowledgment of the minority status of homosexuals.

After the publicity of the chair incident, Manford began to get dozens of letters, some supportive, while others resembled the following anonymous note: "Dear Morty. If you want a chair for your lounge. We have a good slightly used electric chair that we would be glad to have you sit in. (signed) Warden Bert Jones Sing Sing."[48]

The spring semester opened with Hovde's resignation as dean. The *Spectator* theorized that the strains of campus upheaval, including the activity of the GPC, might have accelerated his resignation, but fellow administrators Henry Coleman and Peter Pouncey both claim Hovde just wanted to return to teaching.[49] Fortunately for the gay lounge, Pouncey, a more sympathetic administrator, took over the dean's office.

President McGill and the trustees continued to seek a way to avoid giving the lounge the recognition the GPC demanded. The administrators knew they could not escape confronting the dormitory council's appeal, but they were looking for a legal reason to deny recognition. Back in 1967, Columbia asked Henry Proffitt, a partner in the law firm of Thatcher, Proffitt, Prizer, Crawley & Wood, to investigate whether the university could use New York State's antisodomy law to justify withholding recognition of the Student Homophile League. Proffitt concluded that the state penal code did not apply, because there was no direct connection between the stated nonsocial mission of SHL and acts of sodomy.

Four years later, the university again turned to Proffitt's firm to investigate the possibility of using the sodomy law to justify closing the gay lounge. Omer S. J. Williams, another partner in the firm, informed the trustees that "while homosexuality as such, is not sought to be proscribed by the legislature, certain activities of homosexuals constitute violations of the Penal Law and, if permitted by the University on its property, may involve University responsibility for permitting such activities."[50] The lawyer concluded that because the gay lounge might facilitate sodomy, the university had the right to prohibit its existence and veto the decision of the Furnald Dormitory Council. However, Williams further recommended that the trustees refrain from any confrontational moves and just permit the gay lounge to exist without officially recognizing its existence. The trustees seem to have taken Williams's advice. They politely heard the dormitory council's appeal on April 13, 1972, and allowed the semester to end without responding. McGill and the trustees thought Dean Hovde's veto of the gay lounge was secure. What they did not know was that his replacement, the new dean of Columbia College, Peter Pouncey, had decided to overturn the veto even before he assumed office.

The thirty-four-year-old Peter Pouncey was the youngest dean since Columbia's founding in 1754. Unlike his predecessors, he was open to the political and social changes that had rocked American universities in the 1960s.[51] He told the *New York Times*, "I am not of a temperament to think that I am sort of permanently poised on a time bomb. I fundamentally believe in the rationality of all constituencies of the college—even though that is hard to maintain."[52] Pouncey did not fear the lounge would contribute to the conversion of Columbia boys to homosexuality. He insisted the de facto existence of the lounge made recognition or nonrecognition "a rather academic point" and that by recognizing the lounge, "we are not advertising something, but simply recognizing it."[53] Pouncey did anticipate an intense reaction from opponents of the lounge, especially anxious alumni. The dean might have the authority to recognize the lounge, but the alumni had the power to make his job very difficult.

In an attempt to end the lounge controversy at the beginning of the academic year, on September 18, 1972, Dean Pouncey wrote a statement in which he maintained that he refused to recognize the lounge as "good" but he nevertheless recognized parity between the gay lounge and the ethnic lounges because the gay students were also minorities who experienced discrimination.[54] Before releasing the statement, the dean showed it to McGill, who, Pouncey later recalled, "sure as hell didn't agree." But the young dean assured the president, "live with it and you will not have a problem on this campus again."

That night Pouncey and McGill attended a gathering of well-heeled alumni at the Plaza Hotel. Pouncey, perhaps the youngest man in the room, was scheduled to address the tuxedo-attired Columbians. He had decided to use the forum to announce his gay lounge decision. He began his speech by celebrating the college's tradition of teaching students to question commonly held opinions, and then he shrewdly mentioned his recognition of the gay lounge. To his great surprise, the assembled alums accepted the news without protest. Much had changed since 1967, when the founding of SHL provoked intense opposition from the alumni.

After the event, Pouncey and McGill climbed into the president's limousine. While cruising up Central Park's West Drive, McGill turned to his young colleague and said, "You certainly talked your way out of that."[55] The controversy was over. The next day's *Times* ran another front-page article, which announced, "For the first time a college administration has recognized a facility for homosexuals."[56]

Columbia University's recognition of the right of gay students to have a minority lounge marked the first time a major American institution officially acknowledged that homosexuals were a minority group. Twenty years earlier, Donald Webster Cory, in his *The Homosexual in America,* had argued that homosexuals should be seen not as sinners or psychological deviants but as members of a minority group. Cory hoped that once homosexuals were seen as a minority, American liberals would have no choice but to defend their rights.[57] By the early 1970s, the gay rights movement had achieved that goal. Liberal politicians and powerful liberal institutions, such as media organizations and Columbia University, were publicly compelled to acknowledge the minority rights of homosexuals. The general acknowledgment of the minority status of American homosexuals, however, still faced tremendous resistance from two powerful sectors that had long competed over the American mind: religion and science.

Many religious leaders and institutions continued to regard homosexuality as a sinful state that an individual chose, while the American psychiatric community diagnosed homosexuality as a psychological sickness that needed to be "cured." As long as most of the general public saw gays and lesbians as sinful or sick, there was little hope that homosexuals would be recognized as a minority group worthy of equal rights. The tactics and arguments of the gay rights movement could do little to counter the religious condemnation of homosexuality. The American psychiatric establishment, however, proved much more vulnerable to the power of the zap.

chapter nine

"IT'S OFFICIAL NOW: WE'RE NOT SICK"

The following written exchange appeared on one of the graffiti-covered walls of the New York City subway system in early 1971. In large black letters:

My mother made me a homosexual.

Beneath it, in a different hand:

If I get her the wool, will she make me one, too?[1]

This campy dialogue gave straphangers a glimpse at questions that divided gays and straights alike: Was homosexuality a sickness? And if so, what caused it? Just three years later, a campaign waged by both psychiatrists and activists radicalized the debate by pushing the American Psychiatric Association (APA) to reconsider its labeling of homosexuality as a mental disorder. Although some observers of the psychiatrists' battle over the sickness label likened it to medieval scholasticism, it triggered media coverage that altered the way millions of gays and straights viewed homosexuality.

After centuries of criminal prosecution, homosexuals in the first half of the twentieth century actually welcomed psychiatrists' efforts to convince the public that homosexuality was a sickness. Anglo-American criminal codes had severely punished sodomy ever since Henry VIII transferred prosecution of the "detestable and abominable vice of buggery" from the ecclesial courts to the civil authorities and declared it a felony punishable by death. The criminal prosecution of acts of sodomy continued in both Great Britain and the United States into the mid-twentieth century.

In the mid-nineteenth century, scientists and physicians began to propose an alternative to viewing sodomites as criminals or sinners. K. M. Kertbeny, an Austrian-Hungarian advocate for sexual rights, invented the word "homosexual" in 1869 to designate people with a "healthy love for their own sex." Shortly thereafter, Carl Westphal, a professor of psychiatry in Berlin used the word "homosexual" in a published case history of a female whom he diagnosed as having a congenital disease of "contrary sexual feeling." His contemporaries, Frenchmen Paul Moreau and Richard Kraft-Ebing, attributed homosexuality to environmental forces combined with a "hereditary taint." For the next hundred years, Kertbeny's term, "homosexual," would be associated with the words "disease" and "sickness."

The designation of homosexuality as a sickness or a defect offered some positive protection to homosexuals. Magnus Hirshfeld, the pioneering advocate for homosexual rights in Germany, asserted in 1896 that since homosexuality was a defect, criminal persecution of sodomy was immoral and illogical. Throughout the first half of the twentieth century, homosexual rights advocates in Europe and the United States would return to this argument when challenging their countries' draconian sodomy laws.[2]

In the early twentieth century, Sigmund Freud offered a highly influential view of homosexuality. In his *Three Essays on the Theory of Sexuality,* he argued that homosexuals should be diagnosed as mentally ill only if they exhibited serious deviations from "normal" behavior and if their capacities for survival and "efficient functioning" were severely limited. Freud's observations led him to conclude that many homosexuals were high functioning and even "distinguished by especially high intellectual development and ethical development."[3] In an unpublished 1935 letter, Freud reassured an anxious American mother of a homosexual that "many highly respectable individuals of ancient and modern times have been homosexuals, several of the greatest men among them (Plato, Michelangelo, Leonardo da Vinci, etc.). It is a great injustice to persecute homosexuality as a crime and cruelly too." The Father of Psychoanalysis saw no reason to classify homosexuals as mentally ill and rejected the suggestion of one of his collaborators, Ernst Jones, that homosexuals be barred from becoming analysts.[4]

Freud made a great contribution to the future gay rights movement by claiming that all children passed into a homosexual phase during their sexual development. Some remained fixated in the homosexual phase while most moved through it on their way to heterosexuality. Even heterosexuals retained some homosexual desires within their libidinal drives: "Those who call themselves homosexuals are only the conscious and manifest inverts, whose number is nothing compared to that of the latent homosexuals."[5] The revolutionary idea that homosexuality was an element in the sexuality of heterosexuals would be revived during the debate over gay rights and the sickness model. Gay rights activists argued that straights who condemned homosexuals were denying a bit of themselves, or as the Gay Liberation Front put it, "We are your greatest nightmare and your deepest desire!"[6]

Freud was pessimistic about the ability of psychoanalysts to "cure" homosexuals by transforming them into heterosexuals. In this respect, his views resembled those of his contemporaries who believed homosexuality was an irreversible congenital trait. Such pessimism toward "treating" homosexuals pervaded the psychiatric profession in the decade after Freud's death in 1939. In the United States, the Freudian dogma was so dominant that homosexuals were rarely accepted as patients because they were considered "too difficult" to cure.[7]

In the late 1940s a new generation of heretical psychoanalysts led by Sandor Rado revised the way American psychiatry approached homosexuality. Rado, head of the Columbia University Psychoanalytic Clinic for Training and Research, contradicted Freud by arguing that there was no common homosexual phase of development. Everyone had a heterosexual drive. For some men, satisfaction of the heterosexual impulse was too painful because the female organ reminded them of castration. Men with such a phobic response to sex with women resorted to homosexual sex.[8] Because Rado thought homosexuality was

just a phobic response and not a fixation, he and his followers concluded it could be more easily cured than Freud thought. The prestigious Columbia Psychoanalytic Clinic adopted this optimistic approach
to treating homosexuality and became a leading proponent of using
psychoanalytic conversion therapy on homosexuals. Analysts soon
enjoyed a new boom industry in the treatment of homosexuals.

Prior to 1952, American psychiatrists lacked standardized terms and
diagnoses. Without official definitions of mental illnesses, therapists
had great difficulty communicating with each other, and perhaps more
pressing, collecting reimbursement from insurance companies for
treating aliments that were not officially diagnosed as sicknesses. The
American Psychiatric Association solved the problem by adopting the
American Medical Association's practice of listing and categorizing
maladies. Although many psychiatrists were uncomfortable with
applying the medical model of diagnosis to mental illness, the APA in
1952 issued a forty-page Diagnostic and Statistical Manual (DSM),
which listed homosexuality as a mental disorder.

The official listing of homosexuality as a sickness in the DSM gave
legitimacy to discrimination. The federal government and private businesses could point to the DSM to justify exclusion of homosexuals
from jobs. Even those who sympathized with gays might have trouble
accepting certifiably insane people as equals, especially when the psychiatric community grouped their condition with fetishism, pedophilia,
transvestitism, exhibitionism, voyeurism, sadism, and masochism.

Listing homosexuality in the DSM also spurred efforts to discover its
"cure." American psychoanalysts grew optimistic in the 1960s about
converting homosexuals to heterosexuality after Irving Bieber, president
of the American Academy of Psychoanalysis, claimed he had confirmed
Sandor Rado's theory that homosexuality stemmed from the family
dynamic by comparing the family patterns of 106 homosexual men and
100 male heterosexual controls. He attributed homosexuality to the
combination of an overbearing mother and a distant father. Without
interference from the father, the son impedes his own Oedipal desires by
turning toward homosexuality. According to Bieber all male homosexuals experienced sexual arousal from women, but because of their early
childhood experiences, their attraction to women generated fear and
forced them to seek sexual gratification from men.[9] Bieber reversed

Freud's idea that heterosexuals passed through homosexuality and retained latent homosexual drives: "We assume that heterosexuality is the biologic norm and that unless interfered with, all individuals are heterosexual. . . . In our view every homosexual is, in reality, a latent heterosexual."[10] Bieber's alteration of Freud is significant. According to Bieber, heterosexuals did not have homosexual phases and latent desires, as Freud had argued. Homosexuals deviated from the normal heterosexual development.

Since Bieber and his followers considered homosexuality to be a deviation rather than a fixation, conversion to heterosexuality was just a matter of getting the patient back on track, or as he put it: "What you have in a homosexual adult is a person whose heterosexual function is crippled like the legs of a polio victim."[11] Bieber argued that like some polio victims, a significant percentage of homosexuals could be rehabilitated. His study claimed that thanks to him and his colleagues "29 of the 106 homosexuals under their care had become exclusively heterosexual during the course of psychoanalytic treatment." Bieber proclaimed his 27 percent conversion rate the "most optimistic and promising results thus far reported."[12] (Twenty-five years later Bieber admitted to a former patient and friend that he had never conducted a follow-up survey to make sure his conversions remained "exclusively heterosexual."[13])

New York psychoanalyst Charles Socarides also published reports of his successes in "curing" homosexuality in the 1960s. Socarides graduated from the Columbia University Psychoanalytic clinic, where he had come under the sway of Sandor Rado. Like Bieber, Socarides believed homosexuality resulted from a weak father and overbearing mother, although his language was much more strident: "The family of the homosexual is usually a female-dominated environment wherein the father was absent, weak, detached or sadistic." Socarides, who blamed himself bitterly when his son came out a decade later, argued that a homosexual needed sex to get a " 'shot' of masculinity" and "like an addict he must have his 'fix' or experience severe emotional reactions." When renegade psychiatrists began calling for the elimination of homosexuality from the DSM, Socarides warned that removing the sickness stigma would allow "the homosexual to overlook the deep psychological disturbance that is the basis of the homosexual

existence." Society needed to recognize that like addicts and alco-
holics, homosexuals did not need to be ignored or punished, they
needed to be helped.[14] Socarides claimed a 35 percent success rate in
converting his patients to heterosexuality.[15]

Bieber and Socarides were not bigoted quacks. Although both were
wrong about the nature of homosexuality, they exhibited genuine concern for the welfare of homosexuals and even called for the repeal of
criminal penalties for homosexuality. When Bieber was an Army psychiatrist, he had led a campaign to eliminate the punishment of homosexuality in the military justice system.[16] Bieber believed that wiping out
negative attitudes toward homosexuality would contribute to healing
homosexuality rather than encouraging it. Bieber told the *New York
Times* in 1963 that "public acceptance, if based on the concept of homosexuality as an illness, could be useful. If by a magic wand one could eliminate overnight all manifestations of hostility I think there would be a
gradual important reduction in the incidence of homosexuality."

Socarides became interested in studying homosexuality after the
police arrested one of his first patients and stamped his record with the
label "DEGENERATE." That label devastated his patient and convinced
Socarides that "this kind of punishment and humiliation benefits neither
the individual nor society." From that moment on, Socarides later wrote,
"it became my aim to do my utmost to correct the inequities against
homosexuals and to document homosexuality as a psychiatric condition
which needed investigation, research and medical personnel trained to
help the individual and enlighten the community."[17]

Although Bieber and Socarides opposed the criminal punishment of
homosexuals they did not want homosexuals to be recognized as a
socially acceptable minority group. As Socarides told the *Times,* "The
homosexual is ill, and anything that tends to hide that fact reduces his
chances of seeking and obtaining treatment. If they were to achieve
social acceptance it would increase this difficulty."[18] After Bieber and
Socarides became noted psychiatric experts on homosexuality, they
were quoted by newspapers and appeared on talk shows as representatives of the scientific perspective on homosexuality. While their social
views on homosexuality may have been "sympathetic," articles quoting
their scientific opinions reinforced the view that homosexuality was a
curable sickness.

It would be naïve to view Bieber's and Socarides's enthusiastic involvement in public discussions about homosexuality as purely an altruistic commitment to public information and science. Their fame and supposedly high success rates enabled both men to carve out a lucrative niche market in the treatment of homosexuals. According to a 1971 *New York Times* report, a homosexual patient who underwent therapy to eliminate his so-called phobia toward heterosexual activity would undergo treatment in excess of 350 hours.[19] On average, Bieber's patients underwent treatment three times a week for two to five years.[20] When questions arose in the early 1970s over whether or not homosexuality was a sickness, Bieber and Socarides had various motives for charging into the debate.

In the 1960s, Pavlov-influenced behaviorists joined the psychoanalysts in offering conversion therapies for homosexuals. Behaviorists viewed a neurosis as a persistent habit acquired by learning.[21] Therefore, a neurosis such as homosexuality could be "unlearned." In scenes straight from the Stanley Kubrick movie *A Clockwork Orange,* behaviorists administered emetics to their homosexual patients while showing them pictures of nude males. As the patients vomited in front of the gay porn, they theoretically "learned" to associate physical sickness with homosexual desire. Behaviorists who preferred positive reinforcement had their patients masturbate in dark rooms. Shortly before climax, the patient would signal the therapist, who would flick a switch to illuminate pictures of nude women.[22] In theory the patient would eventually associate sexual pleasure with the female nude form. Dr. Joseph Wolpe, of Temple University's Behavior Therapy Institute, claimed "about 75 percent of patients became heterosexually oriented after just six months of [aversion] therapy."[23] In 1966 the behaviorist therapists formed their own national organization, the Association for the Advancement of Behavior Therapy.

All of the therapeutic treatments of the psychoanalysts and behaviorists were based on the assumption that homosexuality was a sickness. Every book and magazine article that proclaimed the success of sexual conversion reinforced the stereotype of the sick homosexual who needed help. At the same time the sickness diagnosis of homosexuality and its cures began to be reported as "scientific fact," however, a few bold scientists published important dissents.

Alfred Kinsey's monumental 1948 study of the sexual behavior of American males irrevocably challenged the idea that homosexuals were a small number of sick individuals. Based on surveys and thousands of interviews, Kinsey concluded that 37 percent of all men had physical contact to the point of orgasm with other men. His findings buttressed his contention that there was no link between homosexuality and psychopathy and provided statistical support for Freud's ideas on the homosexual desires of heterosexuals.[24] Kinsey's book triggered media reports that publicized his idea that "the majority of persons who engage in abnormal behavior were emotionally disturbed . . . however, that such disturbances were primarily the result of the individual's fear of society's reaction to his behavior because of existing taboos."[25]

The medical and psychiatric establishment largely dismissed Kinsey's study, but the assertion that such a high percentage of males engaged in sexual acts with other men sparked widespread debates over homosexuality and deviance within the general population.[26] Could 37 percent of the American male population be considered truly "deviant"? Could so many millions all be psychopaths?

Evelyn Hooker, a psychology professor at UCLA, presented another important challenge to the sickness model in 1957 when she published an article reporting no differences in the psychological adjustment of groups of homosexual and heterosexual men.[27] After becoming friendly with a former student who was gay and meeting his friends, Hooker began questioning the conventional thinking that the "homosexual personality type" was distinguished by femininity, fear of women, narcissism, sexual compulsiveness, and paranoia."[28] Her former student and his friends convinced Hooker to do something that had never been done—conduct a psychological study of homosexuals who were not under psychiatric treatment or "found in mental hospitals, disciplinary barracks in the Armed Services, or in prison populations." Thirty gay men were matched in pairs with thirty straight men on the basis of age, education, and IQ. The subjects' responses to Rorschach tests were recorded and shown to three psychiatrists who were asked to pick the homosexuals from each of the pairs. Hooker found that many of the heterosexuals gave what would be deemed homosexual responses to the inkblots, while many of the homosexuals were labeled straight by the expert judges.[29] Hooker's methodology was weak. Her research sample was too small and she used Rorschach tests, which are now dismissed by researchers as too subjective. Her conclusions however were instrumental in breaking the consensus view of homosexuality as a sickness.

Hooker had a great influence on Judd Marmor, a psychiatrist who began his career trying to convert homosexuals through psycho-analysis. "I wasn't too successful," he later admitted. Eventually his social interactions with homosexuals revealed that "psychoanalysts didn't know enough gay people outside the treatment community who were happy with their lives, who were satisfied and well-adjusted." Marmor included Hooker's work in his 1965 *Sexual Inversion*, a groundbreaking collection of studies showing that sexual deviance did not necessarily mean social maladjustment.

Hooker's and Marmor's prominence on the issue of homosexuality came to the attention of Stanley Yolles, director of the National Institute of Mental Health (NIMH). During liberalism's bright shining moment under the Kennedy and Johnson administrations, the NIMH instituted numerous reform programs to promote deinstitutionalization of the mentally ill and access to mental health services. Yolles invited Hooker to chair a commission to advise the NIMH on how to "sweep it [homo-sexuality] out from beneath the rug." Judd Marmor also joined the com-mission, which notably excluded Bieber and Socarides. The final report called for the decriminalization of homosexual acts between consenting adults and challenged the practice of labeling all homosexuals as patho-logical. The report however was not completed until power was handed over to the Nixon administration, which buried it until 1972.[30] Never-theless, when the gay liberation movement in the early 1970s prompted the media to look for opinions on homosexuality that dissented from the Socarides-Bieber line, reporters looked to Hooker and Marmor.

The academic discussion among the mental health professionals about the origins of homosexuality had great significance for doctors and thousands of homosexual patients, but it had little impact on the general public until homophile legend Frank Kameny and the gay rights movement entered the discussion. While the rest of the homophile leadership accepted scientific opinion on homosexuality or refused to wage a public fight against it, the Washington Mattachine in 1965 issued a revolutionary statement declaring that "homosexuality is not a sickness, disturbance, or other pathology in any sense, but is merely a reference, orientation, or propensity, on par with, and not different in kind from, heterosexuality."[31] Kameny criticized the research methods of the psychiatrists who claimed they proved homosexuality was a pathology and called upon homophile activists to proclaim their sanity and demand it be recognized. Kameny knew removal of the sickness designation would have great symbolic value for the gay rights movement, more significant than elections or legislation.[32]

When the flowering of gay liberation caught the media's eye after Stonewall, magazines and newspapers began covering the debate over homosexuality and mental illness. Much to Kameny's frustration, reporters sought the opinions of the best known experts on homosexuality at the time, Bieber and Socarides.[33] A 1969 *Time* magazine article, "The Homosexual: Newly Visible, Newly Understood," cited Bieber in describing the origins of homosexuality. "In the case of homosexuality," *Time* intoned, "parents with emotional problems can be a powerful cause, leaving their child with a solid identification with the parent of the same sex and with deeply divided feelings for a parent of the opposite sex. . . . Most experts agree that a child will not become a homosexual unless he undergoes many emotionally disturbing experiences during the course of several years."[34]

Alongside the main article, *Time* inserted a transcript of a panel discussion about homosexuality featuring Charles Socarides; Wardell Pomeroy, who was one of Kinsey's collaborators; Dick Leitsch; Frank Kameny, an anthropologist; and an Episcopal priest. Socarides was the only one on the panel who saw homosexuality as a mental disorder. Everyone else attacked the sickness model for its inaccuracy and injustice. At one point the priest spoke of two homosexuals he knew who had been "married" for fifteen years: "Both of them are very happy and very much in love. They asked me to bless their marriage and I am going to do it." Pomeroy then chimed in. "I think they are beautiful. I don't think they are sick at all."[35] Probably for the first time, millions of *Time* magazine readers discovered a priest and a scientist who agreed that homosexuals could be "happy" and "beautiful."

Kameny's call to arms against the sickness model resonated powerfully with the gay liberation activists. One of the ideas often repeated in the slogans and rhetoric of the gay liberation movement was that homosexuality was healthy. For decades, magazine articles and books had pushed the idea that homosexuality was a sickness. In the early 1970s, gay liberation activists were suddenly appearing on television talk shows to denounce the psychiatric establishment's views on homosexuality. One New York psychologist told the *New York Times* that "the Gay liberation movement is the best therapy the homosexual has had in years."[36]

The most effective political tactic of the gay liberation movement, the zap, was also the perfect weapon against the medical establishment. Scientific debates over questions like whether homosexuality was a phobia or a neurosis were traditionally settled over years of experimentation, research, and rational debate at conferences. Because nonexperts were excluded from such debates, political activists had little influence on "expert opinion." The American Psychiatric Association however was an institution that could be zapped. Just as political candidates were forced to embrace gay rights after having their fundraisers and offices disrupted; psychiatrists were also vulnerable to the power of the zap when it was turned on their conferences.

After the Student Homophile League at Columbia University launched the first public demonstration against the American psychiatric community in 1968, gay and lesbian militants around the country targeted meetings of mental health professionals. Later that year at the annual meeting of the American Medical Association in San Francisco, activists held a press conference to condemn Charles Socarides's proposal for a government-financed center for the cure of "sexual deviants," a plan that the activists likened to "the final solution."[37] The rise of Gay Liberation Fronts from coast to coast brought a more confrontational spirit to the campaign against the sickness model. In San Francisco, the local GLF interrupted and taunted Irving Bieber during an address to the 1970 APA convention. At one point a rattled Bieber addressed the protestors: "I never said homosexuals were sick—what I said was that they had displaced sexual adjustment." Amid hoots from the audience someone yelled, "That's the same thing motherfucker!"[38] When an Australian expert on aversion therapy described his use of electric shocks to make "unhappy homosexuals" responsive to women, a heckler asked, "Where did you do your residency? Auschwitz?"[39] Not content with shouting from the gallery, the San Francisco demonstrators called for an official voice at the conference: "We've listened to you, now listen to us." Most of the psychiatrists in the audience were annoyed. Some demanded their money back from the APA. One asked the police to shoot the protestors. But Kent Robinson, a liberal psychiatrist, approached veteran gay activist Larry Littlejohn and volunteered to lead an effort from within the APA to organize a panel of homosexuals at the next convention. Later in 1970, Charles Socarides fell victim to the wrath of the Chicago GLF during an American Medical Association workshop in the Windy City. The protestors won so much sympathy from the audience that they were invited to send two representatives to join the panel on the stage.

Citing the disruptions of both the American Psychiatric Association and American Medical Association conventions, psychiatrist Kent Robinson convinced the APA to include a panel of gay men and women who rejected the sickness diagnosis for its 1971 annual convention at the Shoreham Hotel in Washington, D.C. Although Frank Kameny was an invited speaker, he and members of his Washington Gay Activists Alliance decided to zap the convention anyway, "just to keep the heat on," and, naturally, to attract media attention. At the opening ceremony, Kameny sat in the audience as an honored guest while dozens of protestors burst into the hall from a door behind the stage.[40] In the confusion Kameny seized the microphone and declared, "Psychiatry is the enemy incarnate. Psychiatry has waged a relentless war of extermination against us. You may take this as a declaration against you!"[41] Flashing forged credentials, Kameny's commandos infiltrated an exhibition area where they discovered a booth marketing aversive conditioning techniques for treating homosexuals. The demonstrators immediately lifted their cover and demanded the removal of the booth or they would tear it down. To avoid further disruption to the conference, the booth was dismantled. After the conference, Kameny put aside his declaration of war on the APA and, along with Robinson, began quietly persuading sympathetic psychiatrists to support a resolution to remove the sickness designation from the DSM.[42]

Robinson also influenced the APA to hold a panel discussion called "Psychiatry, Friend or Foe to Homosexuals? A Dialogue" at the 1972 Dallas convention. Only people who were friendly to gay rights and sympathetic to the removal of the sickness designation were invited to speak. Frank Kameny and Barbara Gittings were joined on the panel by Robert Seidenberg and Judd Marmor, who represented sympathetic psychiatrists. Gittings and Kay Lahusen convinced Marmor, the moderator, to also include a homosexual psychiatrist on the panel. Gittings phoned psychiatrists around the country trying to find one willing to discuss his homosexuality openly in front of his fellow analysts.[43] Because homosexuals were thought to suffer from pathology, a disorder that affects the whole personality, the APA officially barred them from careers in psychiatry. As in most professions however, gays were able to quietly enter the psychiatric field and flourish. Every year, dozens of closeted psychiatrists gathered together in gay bars during the annual APA conventions to convene what they jokingly referred to as the GAY-PA. When Gittings telephoned the gay psychiatrists looking for a recruit to join the panel, however, the reception was cool. In phone call after phone call, Gittings heard how public declaration of homosexuality was professional suicide for psychiatrists. Every closeted psychiatrist had too much at stake to risk being blackballed by the APA—everyone except John Fryer.

In 1972 John Fryer's career was in crisis. Recently dismissed from his residency at the University of Pennsylvania because of his homosexuality, Fryer could not land another position because of the rumors that followed him. With little to lose, he reluctantly agreed to join the panel on the condition that he could wear a disguise and use a microphone that distorted his voice. At first Frank Kameny refused to accept the conditions. Gay liberation, after all, was about removing masks.[44] Kameny did not appreciate the symbolic impact of the disguise. An article in the gay magazine *Vector* later claimed Fryer "wore the mask because he said he spoke for all gay psychiatrists who have to hide their sexual identity."[45]

Fryer was interested in anonymity, not symbolism. He bought an extra-large tuxedo to make his frame look smaller and a rubber Richard Nixon mask that he distorted so his presentation did not look like a joke.[46] The hideous result made him appear deformed. Wearing a bushy wig, Dr. H. Anonymous (H for "homosexual") sneaked into the convention space as if he were an FBI informant at a Mafia trial. While his fellow APA members digested his obviously profound fear of exposure, he announced that there were more than two hundred homosexual psychiatrists attending the convention: "As psychiatrists who are homosexual, we must know our place and what we must do to be successful. If our goal is high academic achievement, a level of earning capacity equal to our fellows, or admission to a psychoanalytic institute, we must make sure that we behave ourselves, and that no one in a position of power is aware of our sexual preference." As he spoke, Fryer glared through his mask at a man in the front row who had recently fired him because of his homosexuality. One conference participant recalled, "It was a very dramatic session with this fellow speaking with a grotesque mask on."[47] When Dr. H. Anonymous finished, the audience honored his brave presentation with a standing ovation. "I felt very empowered," Fryer recalled. But still fearful. Dr. Anonymous's fear of exposure endured for another twenty-two years, until he revealed his identity at the 1994 APA convention.[48]

Frank Kameny noted that the Dallas conference was the first conference in which only positive views on homosexuality were voiced in the public forums. Whether the APA's new consideration for homosexuals resulted from education, sympathy, or intimidation, it marked a turning point in the relationship between psychiatry and the gay community. The intellectual tide seemed to be turning against the sickness model by 1972. The wider sexual revolution had spawned a societal reevaluation of sexual stigmas and categorization. "Do your own thing" had become the catchphrase of the day, while in the mental health field a new generation of therapists like George Weinberg openly rejected the dogmatism of psychoanalysis and Sandor Rado's views on homosexuality. In 1971 American psychologists officially removed homosexuality from their "abnormal psychology" category, the American Medical Association trustees urged legalization of all private acts between consenting adults, and the APA's Task Force on Social Issues suggested that homosexual behavior in certain settings, such as prisons, might not be pathological.[49] In response Dr. Henry Brill, chairman of the APA Committee on Nomenclature, (which was responsible for updating the DSM), concluded that "homosexual behavior was not necessarily a sign of psychiatric disorder: and that the Diagnostic Manual should reflect that understanding."[50]

Changes in APA's leadership also made elimination of the sickness diagnosis for homosexuality more likely. In the early 1970s, a group of young psychiatrists formed the Committee for Concerned Psychiatry, which worked to get liberals elected to APA offices so that they could alter the profession's positions on social issues such as feminism and homosexuality. These reformers met to hatch their plots in the home of John Spiegel, whose wife dubbed them the "Young Turks." At least two of the Young Turks were gay, including Spiegel, who came out to his fiancé six weeks before their wedding. In the fall of 1972, Spiegel was elected to the APA Board of Trustees; Judd Marmor, longtime gay rights advocate and one of Spiegel's best friends, was elected vice president; and another liberal, Alfred Freedman, was elected APA president. When the closeted John Spiegel succeeded Freedman as APA president in 1973, the forces behind changing the listing of homosexuality in the DSM had a committed ally at the top. With a fifth column at the ready, the time was ripe for a final assault from outside the medical community.

Over the previous few years, the New York Gay Activists Alliance had been too focused on politics and media to devote much attention to the psychiatric community. But in the early fall of 1972, GAA member Charles Silverstein, a PhD candidate in psychology, discovered that the Association for the Advancement of Behavior Therapy (AABT) planned to hold a conference in October at the New York Hilton, site of the Inner Circle affair five months prior. Silverstein had the idea to zap the AABT when he read that the association promoted a bizarre aversion therapy in which a patient's fingers were hooked up to wires while his penis was inserted into an erection meter. Pictures of attractive male nudes were projected in front of the patient. If the meter detected arousal, the patient's fingers would receive painful electric shocks.[51] After Silverstein described this procedure, the GAA membership enthusiastically voted to make a return visit to the Hilton to protest the behaviorist therapy and the sickness model. Activist Ron Gold, who was also a *Vanity Fair* reporter, invited the *New York Times* and WNBC-TV along for the show.[52]

About one hundred protestors descended upon the Hilton distributing pamphlets and yelling, "Aversion therapy is *Clockwork Orange!*" The media-savvy GAA knew the power of connecting their protest to a pop-cultural reference, especially one as visually compelling as the Kubrick movie. The *Times* reporter picked up on the reference and repeated it in his article, along with an explanation that the central figure in the film "is forcibly made to watch scenes of rape and violence, so that he will learn to abhor and thus be cured of his propensity for violence."

While GAA members outside the Hilton entertained pedestrians with darkly comical reenactments of aversion therapy sessions, Silverstein and Gold led a group into the hotel to confront the therapists. After the Inner Circle beatings earlier that year, the GAA had concerns about being roughed up by the hotel security. Silverstein decided to preempt the guards by warning the heads of AABT about the bad publicity if violence broke out at their conference. None of the therapists wanted their organization tarnished by negative media coverage such as occurred in the wake of the Inner Circle affair, so Hilton security guards were asked not to interfere with the demonstration.

During one of the behaviorists' presentations, Ron Gold, who had a long history of undergoing torturous psychiatric treatment, stood up and unleashed a blistering attack: "It is brainwashing. You can't deal with an individual homosexual's problem without also dealing with the antiquated mores of society. Change must come at a broader, society wide level." Charles Silverstein, officially representing the Institute for Human Identity, a counseling center for gays, also addressed the conference: "We must refuse to use aversion techniques. We must refuse to change homosexuals. It is a technique of violence and I don't believe it works."[53] The *Times* did not know Silverstein was a member of GAA and the catalyst for the zap, so it reported his remarks as an objective, professional confirmation of Ron Gold's statement. (While Gold was very pleased with the newspaper coverage, he was furious with NBC for not broadcasting any of the footage its cameramen had shot at the demonstration. In typical GAA fashion, he later wrote a letter of complaint to NBC for not putting the zap on TV.)[54]

Aside from the media attention, the GAA zap might have had little significance if a Columbia University psychoanalyst named Robert Spitzer had not been in attendance at the conference. Spitzer was a member of the APA Committee on Nomenclature—the committee in charge of editing the Diagnostic and Statistical Manual. He happened to be at the AABT conference because he was disenchanted with psychoanalysis and wanted to explore other methods of treating patients. Until the GAA protest, Spitzer had never thought much about gay rights and he had accepted the official designation of homosexuality as pathology. When Ron Gold disrupted the AABT conference, Spitzer was so angry that he asked a friend who happened to know Gold to introduce them so he could deliver a scolding. The confrontation quickly mellowed and the two men began discussing homosexuality and psychiatry. After Gold learned Spitzer was on the DSM Nomenclature Committee, he persuaded the analyst to arrange for GAA to present its case against the sickness model to the committee. Much to Gold's surprise he also convinced Spitzer to help organize a panel on the diagnosis of homosexuality at the next APA convention. Spitzer still believed homosexuality was a sickness, but he enjoyed intellectual controversy. "And anyway," he thought, "what harm could come from a little discussion?"[55]

At the February 8, 1973, meeting between representatives from GAA and the Nomenclature Committee, Ron Gold delivered a scathing presentation that bashed the psychiatric profession's approach to homosexuality like "a bull in a china shop":

> We are told, from the time that we first recognize our homosexual feelings, that our love for other human beings is sick, childish and subject to "cure." We are told that we are emotional cripples forever condemned to an emotional status below that of the whole people who run the world. The result of this in many cases is to contribute to a self-image that often lowers the sights we set for ourselves in life, and many of us asked ourselves, "How could anybody love me?" or "How can I love somebody who must be just as sick as I am?"[56]

Although there were no plans to revise the Diagnostic and Statistical Manual until 1978, Gold implored the panel to revise it immediately and thereby bring "to pass a more enlightened medical and social climate."[57] Jean O'Leary, chairwoman of GAA's Lesbian Liberation committee, next provided vivid examples of how the APA's diagnosis reinforced discriminatory attitudes and policies, such as the Defense

Department's refusal to grant security clearances to homosexuals because they suffered from mental illness; a New York City Taxi Commission requirement that all gay cabbies had to receive psychiatric evaluations twice a year to assure their "fitness" to drive; and the refusal of a university to grant a charter to a gay liberation group because of fears of "homosexual conversion." The committee members were liberals who were moved by Gold's and O'Leary's appeals to social justice, but as medical experts they needed a scientific basis to justify changing the DSM.[58]

As an aspiring psychologist, Charles Silverstein knew that to convince the committee to revise the diagnosis of homosexuality, he needed to make a lucid presentation that displayed an understanding of systems and classifications—"Exactly the opposite of a gay liberation presentation."[59] Silverstein read the committee a long statement that surveyed the work of Kinsey, Hooker, and Marmor and quoted Freud's sympathetic letter to an American mother about her son's homosexuality. Although the committee members were moved by Gold's and O'Leary's passionate descriptions of the social impact of the sickness diagnosis, nothing impressed them more than Silverstein's calm, professional appeal.[60] After years of zaps, disruptions, and threats, Silverstein delivered the message in a way the doctors could analyze and discuss as scientists. Since no one on the Committee was an expert on homosexuality, his numerous references to scientific research were both informative and convincing. When the Activists left, committee chairman Henry Brill turned to Robert Spitzer, the psychiatrist who opened the door to GAA, and said, "Okay Bob, you've gotten us into this mess. Now what do we do?"[61]

The *New York Times*, alerted to the meeting by Ron Gold, ran a story under the headline "Psychiatrists Review Stand on Homosexuals." The article quoted Chairman Brill as saying, "There's no doubt this label has been used in a discriminatory way. We were all agreed on that." The *Times* also noted at length Brill's liberal attitude toward homosexuality: "Dr. Brill said the committee also agreed that whether a person prefers to have sexual relations with a member of the same or of the opposite sex was in itself not an indicator of a mental disorder. 'This term has been misused by the public at large,' Dr. Brill said. 'The public assumes that all homosexuals are dangerous or sex fiends or untrustworthy or some other part of a stereotype. This, of course, isn't so. We know of many successful, well-adjusted people in various professions who are homosexual.' "[62] Written in the *Times*'s impartial style, the article was not obviously promoting revision of the DSM. But with quotes from Sliverstein's presentation, Brill's positive response, and even Freud's letter on homosexuality, the "paper of record" drew its readers to the commonsense conclusion: the sickness diagnosis of homosexuality was unjust. In gratitude, GAA president Bruce Voeller wrote a note to the *Times* praising their "quick and excellent follow up on several newsworthy topics we brought to your attention."[63]

As promised to Ron Gold at the Hilton zap, Spitzer organized a debate on the sickness designation at the 1973 APA convention in Hawaii. The panel discussion, titled "Should Homosexuality Be in the APA Nomenclature?" featured the celebrities of the sickness model debate: Judd Marmor, Charles Socarides, Irving Bieber, and Ron Gold. Marmor claimed the sickness designation was a product not of scientific knowledge but of a social value system. Socarides asserted that homosexuality was indeed a sickness that stemmed from "a pathological family constellation . . . a domineering mother who will not let her child achieve autonomy and an absent, weak or rejecting father." *Newsweek* recorded Ron Gold's response in a paper he titled "Stop, You're Making Me Sick": "Ron Gold, a member of the Gay Activists Alliance, countered that a number of other psychological surveys have found no significant differences between homosexuals and heterosexuals with regard to neuroses or deep-seated psychopathology. 'The illness theory of homosexuality,' he charged, 'is a pack of lies, concocted out of the myths of a patriarchal society for political purpose.' "[64]

Newsweek's presentation of the panel discussion reveals an interesting dynamic involving gay rights activists, their opponents, and the media. While the debate in Hawaii was officially about the DSM, the magazine ran a story about it under the headline "Are Homosexuals Sick?" After Kameny, Gold, and other activists pushed the APA to address the sickness designation, the media brought the discourse into the public forum. News reports on the zaps at psychiatric conferences triggered articles about the sickness debate. Both the activists and their opponents were given media platforms to showcase their ideas. Several radio and TV talk shows invited George Weinberg and Charles

Socarides to debate each other on the subject. Press coverage raised the stakes for all sides by scrutinizing the APA's internal review process over whether or not to revise the DSM's characterization of homosexuality as a sickness. Removal of the sickness nomenclature would effectively place the APA on the side of the gay rights movement. After all the media attention, failure to do so, would confirm Bieber's and Socarides's ideas for millions of Americans.

The evening after the debate about homosexuality at the Hawaii conference, Frank Kameny and Ron Gold were invited to a gathering of the GAY-PA in a Waikiki Beach gay bar. Gold decided to take Spitzer along so he could see for himself how many of his colleagues were homosexual. Spitzer was shocked when he walked into the bar and saw men he had known for years. Although Gold told him to keep quiet, Spitzer could not resist asking his fellow psychiatrists the kind of questions "only a straight guy would ask," like "When did you realize you were homosexual?"[65] Some of the psychiatrists in the bar became upset when they realized Spitzer was not gay. Like most closeted professionals they had much to lose by disclosing their homosexuality. Some even wanted to avoid all discussion of revising the classification of homosexuality in the DSM. Gold later reported to GAA that the gay psychiatrists were the most oppressive group at the conference.[66] When one of the psychiatrists in the bar, whom Gold called "the Grand Dragon of the Gay PA," realized Spitzer was straight, he demanded Spitzer leave immediately. Gold shot back, "He's doing more for homosexuals than anyone in the room, including you!" Just as Gold and the Grand Dragon were about to come to blows, a soldier in full uniform entered the bar. As soon as he saw Gold, he rushed over, threw his arms around him, and burst into tears. Between sobs, the man in uniform explained that he was a closeted Army psychiatrist attending the conference. Gold's speech earlier that day inspired him to visit a gay bar for the first time in his life and Gold happened to be in the bar he chose. As Spitzer and Gold tried to console the weeping officer, Spitzer decided to join the fight against the sickness diagnosis.[67]

Prior to confronting Ron Gold in the New York Hilton, Spitzer did not know anybody openly gay. Over subsequent months he met several gay activists who were comfortable with their sexuality. After "seeing their humanity and identifying with their suffering," Spitzer's liberal social views began to include opposition to antihomosexual discrimination.[68] He surmised that if homosexuals were going to achieve civil rights, the sickness designation had to be eliminated. Spitzer operated from compassion and social conscience, but he knew he had to find a scientific justification for changing the DSM.

In considering how to frame the argument against the sickness label, Spitzer first decided to survey the DSM to uncover something common to pathologies that did not apply to homosexuality. He found that people who suffered from most disorders listed in the DSM typically experienced serious distress or their conditions interfered with their overall functioning. Spitzer reasoned that while "it used to be thought that every homosexual must be dissatisfied with their condition, if you accepted what the activists said, clearly there were homosexuals who were not distressed by being homosexual. Instead they might be distressed by how people reacted to their being gay." Spitzer submitted a report to the Nomenclature Committee arguing that while homosexuality may not fall within the "normal" range of sexual behavior, it did not impair social effectiveness.[69] He argued that for behavior to be listed as a psychiatric disorder, it had to be accompanied by subjective distress and/or "some generalized impairment in social effectiveness or functioning."[70] Spitzer referred to Evelyn Hooker's study comparing functioning levels of gays and straights and concluded that since general functioning was not necessarily impaired, homosexuals could not be diagnosed as having a disorder.

Spitzer knew the psychiatric community would not accept a complete removal of homosexuality from the diagnostic manual. Since many psychiatrists made a living out of treating homosexuals, he had to devise a new category of "sexual orientation disturbance" for homosexuals who were unhappy with their orientation and wanted treatment.[71] He would later label this condition "homodysphilia."

The question remains whether the removal of homosexuality from the DSM was based on science or politics. The answer is both. Spitzer wanted to help fight the social problem of antihomosexual discrimination by finding a scientific argument for the revision. Although he succeeded in constructing a scientific argument, it was flawed. If, as he argued, a condition had to impair general functioning or cause great distress to be considered a disorder, then pedophilia for example would not be considered a mental illness. Decades later, Spitzer recalled how he simply ignored this sticking point: "I believed in my argument because believing it enabled me to do something."[72]

Spitzer offered the APA a quintessentially liberal compromise that had something for everyone. "Gay was good" to the extent that it was not inherently bad. A new category, "sexual orientation disturbance," allowed for the possibility that homosexuality may work for an individual, or it might not. Removal of homosexuality from the list of disorders would appease most gay rights activists and keep the peace at the next conference, while the addition of sexual orientation disturbance to the DSM permitted APA members to continue treating homosexual clients. Ron Gold complained that Spitzer's new category reinforced the idea that homosexuality was less than healthy, but Frank Kameny reassured Spitzer, "I don't mind saying that 'gays who are distressed have a mental disorder' because any gay who wants to be straight is crazy."[73]

The Nomenclature Committee unanimously approved Spitzer's statement of support for equal rights for homosexuals, but it was bitterly divided on revision of the DSM. To avoid further debate, the committee simply passed the issue over to the Council on Research and Development, which advised the APA on matters of policy. The Council of Research and Development approved Spitzer's proposal because its policy was to accept the advice of the experts on the subcommittees. It is possible the council failed to notice that neither were there experts on homosexuality on the Nomenclature Committee nor did the Nomenclature Committee actually approve the revision. But the council certainly realized that rejecting Spitzer's proposal at such a late stage would be explosive.[74] The question of revising the DSM moved to the Assembly of District Branches, and then to the Reference Committee, chaired by John Spiegel, one of the closeted Young Turks. After Spiegel's committee lent its support, the resolution finally reached the APA board of trustees.

Some in the gay rights movement demanded that homosexuals be part of the board of trustees' deliberations on the revision and threatened to demonstrate at the APA headquarters if a "gay presence" was not welcomed. Cooler heads voiced concern that overt participation of gays in the proceedings or aggressive protests might make the decision look political, and could detract from the legitimacy of the "scientific" reevaluation of homosexuality. An important new gay rights organization, the National Gay Task Force (NGTF), took the latter approach.

Before founding NGTF in 1973, Bruce Voeller was the third president of the New York Gay Activists Alliance. "Voeller was always different," George Weinberg recalled. While most Activists were twentysomething bohemians, Voeller was a thirty-eight-year-old divorced father of two, with a professorship at Rockefeller University. He enjoyed hobnobbing at Upper East Side cocktail parties as much as dancing late into the night at the Firehouse. His blond hair and movie star looks heightened his "slick style" and humorless chill that so annoyed many in GAA.[75] Voeller thought the resentment toward him stemmed from "blue jean elitism," a reverse snobbery that dismissed the radical credentials of anyone who did not dress like a Yippie. His frustration exploded when the famous composer Stephen Sondheim made the brave gesture of visiting the GAA's Firehouse. As Sondheim walked around dressed in a button-down shirt and natty sports jacket, an Activist bellowed, "Get the faggot in the slacks!" Enraged and embarrassed, Voeller yelled back, "If this movement isn't open to all gays, there is no movement!"

Conflicts between the Alliance and their president arose over other issues as well, ranging from Voeller's suggestion that they hire someone to clean up after the dances, to his plan to give GAA a corporate structure with a board of directors in charge of decision making. The membership felt Voeller was betraying the fundamental democratic vision of the Alliance; Voeller thought the meetings had become "tedious, unfair and unproductive."[76] Soon Voeller was calling his young, disheveled opponents like Morty Manford and John O'Brien "trolls," while they referred to him as a "homofascist."

John O'Brien was the Gay Liberation Front member whose proposal in 1969 to donate five hundred dollars to the Black Panthers had led to the schism from which the GAA emerged. After leaving the disintegrating GLF, O'Brien continued in his role as a disruptive element within GAA and was an aggressive opponent of Voeller. On October 4, 1973, tensions erupted after Voeller gave a speech appealing to the membership to stop the infighting and get down to serious activism.

In response O'Brien called for Voeller's censure. Utterly frustrated and exhausted, Voeller resigned from GAA on the spot after having served less than ten months as president.[77]

Prior to his resignation Voeller had been thinking of creating a new organization. Like Marty Robinson and Jim Owles when they split from the GLF, he thought GAA had become too disorganized to be successful. He wanted to form a new group that would be less democratic and more corporate. The day after he resigned, he began calling Alliance members who might be interested in advancing the gay rights movement to its next phase. The initial organizational meeting was held in Voeller's Soho apartment, a block away from the Firehouse. In attendance were Ron Gold, Nathalie Rockhill, Gregory Dawson, and Tom Smith, one of GAA's few black members. The five decided that their group would synthesize the reformist homophile approach with the aggressiveness of gay liberation into a hybrid with broader appeal.[78] Like GAA it would challenge corporations to adopt antidiscrimination policies and urge media organizations to eliminate stereotypical characterizations of gays. But like a homosexual version of the NAACP or ACLU, the nascent organization would lobby, not zap.

Its name even echoed those organizations: the National Gay Task Force, NGTF. *The Advocate*, which praised the creation of the new group, found its name "horrible . . . it just sits there like a clunk."[79] By design NGTF's name had none of the revolutionary romance of the Gay Liberation Front. Revolution, intimidation, and consciousness raising were not part of its program. The road to gay rights would be paved with policy change, negotiation, and public relations.

NGTF believed zaps had outlived their purpose: to get "the establishment" talking about gay rights.[80] By 1973, activists did not have to force gay rights into American political discourse. Thanks to GAA it was there to stay. Now, journalists were doing the job: pressing candidates to articulate positions on security clearances, homosexuals in the military, housing rights, and immigration. Unlike the homophile groups of the 1950s and 1960s, NGTF did not need to push candidates to take public positions in favor of gay rights; it could work to elect candidates who denounced discrimination based on sexual orientation. As Martin Duberman, charter board member of NGTF, noted in his diary, the new organization would operate in "the liberal reform mode: 'let us in,' rather than 'let us show you new possibilities.' "[81]

Duberman, the author of numerous books and a distinguished professor, was an ideal NGTF board member, as was Father Robert Carter, a gay Jesuit priest. Voeller hoped that just as GAA's tough politicos successfully challenged the public stereotype of the ineffective homosexual, NGTF would be comprised of well-spoken professionals like Duberman and Carter who would show society that the gay rights movement was more than a bunch of confrontational "blue-jean elitists." In the 1950s and early 1960s, only those on the margins of society proclaimed their sexuality to the media. Gay professionals were forced to remain in the closet to protect their careers. Thanks to the liberation movement, homosexual professionals had greater confidence to come out, especially if they worked in fields dominated by liberals, such as architecture, the arts, and academics. The bravery of gays who came out in the 1960s and early 1970s made it possible for Voeller to assemble a distinguished board, thereby conferring the NGTF with instant credibility and fund-raising clout.

Voeller nominated Howard Brown, former director of the New York City Health Services Administration and a member of Lindsay's cabinet, to head NGTF. Brown had resigned his municipal post when he heard that Drew Pearson, a *Washington Post* columnist who previously outed two closeted members of California governor Ronald Reagan's staff, planned to write an exposé on homosexuals in the Lindsay administration. The article was never published; Brown quietly assumed a professorship at NYU. In 1972, Brown suffered a serious heart attack. "And for two days, there was a possibility I would die. I thought a great deal about what I would leave behind me if I died."[82] Inspired by GAA's fight for Intro 475, Brown felt a responsibility to serve as a role model for fellow gay professionals and young people. He asked Martin Duberman, Ron Gold, and Bruce Voeller for advice on publicly announcing his homosexuality.[83] The four men planned Brown's public revelation to maximize its impact.

Gold and Voeller asked everyone they knew in the media to cover Brown's announcement, which was picked up and featured in all of the evening news broadcasts. The *New York Times* ran a front-page article titled, "Ex-City Official Says He's Homosexual."[84] The next

day, the *Times* ran a story on a speech Brown gave to a medical sym-
posium on human sexuality in which he declared, "I have been invited
here not as a medical expert but as a street homosexual." The *Times*
noted, "Dr. Brown's statement drew sympathetic and favorable reaction
and when he finished, Dr. Robert Cross, chairman of the conference,
turned to Brown and said 'that was a moving and courageous statement
which will make all of us think a little more about homosexuality.' "
Although Brown told the *Times* that he intended to become "a militant
homosexual" who "would march in demonstrations and, if necessary,
be arrested," Voeller had more strategic objectives in mind.[85] He
wanted Brown to leverage his relationships and friendships with the
mayor and other public officials to influence policy.[86] Like others on the
NGTF board, Brown would be an insider who was "out."

NGTF's challenge to the sickness designation became a model for
the gay rights movement in the postliberation era of the mid-1970s.
Instead of demanding a presence at the deliberations of the American
Psychiatric Association trustees, the NGTF trusted that John Spiegel
and the liberal Young Turks on the board would ratify the recommen-
dations of its subcommittees. A zap or a public demand for a voice at
the meeting would only jeopardize what seemed to be the inevitable
removal of homosexuality from the diagnostic manual.

In November 1973 an APA insider informed the NGTF that the
trustees would vote in favor of removing homosexuality from the diagnostic manual the following month. The Task Force was concerned,
however, that the APA would change the listing without publicity.[87]
Ron Gold, who had been a reporter for *Vanity Fair*, knew "the whole
thing was about public perceptions," not medical diagnosis. Without a
public announcement and extensive media coverage, little attention
would be paid to the official proclamation of the sanity of homosexuals.[88] After a brief negotiation, the APA agreed to hold a press conference to announce the decision, while the NGTF held a separate
press conference at the APA headquarters.[89] The trustees would make
the decision; the Task Force would explain its significance to the press.

On December 15, 1973, the APA board of trustees voted unanimously to remove homosexuality from the diagnostic manual. The
APA trustees also asked forty-two states and the District of Columbia
to repeal their "irrational" laws against sodomy but stopped short of

acceding to NGTF's request that they declare homosexuality "normal." During the press conference, APA president Alfred Freedman deplored "all public and private discrimination against homosexuals in such areas as employment, housing, public accommodation and licensing" and urged "that homosexuals be given all protections now guaranteed other citizens."[90]

At the gay activist press conference in APA headquarters, the movement was represented exclusively by the National Gay Task Force leadership: Howard Brown, Bruce Voeller, Barbara Gittings, and Frank Kameny. GAA's absence from the podium marked a shift in the power and philosophy of the gay rights movement. Ron Gold sent a memo to each of the press conference participants instructing them to underscore the impact the APA's decision would have on discriminatory immigration restrictions, sodomy laws, and custody cases.[91] The *Washington Post* quoted Frank Kameny as saying the decision "represents the culmination of a decade-long battle. . . . A hundred years ago people called homosexuality a sin. The high priests became the psychiatrists and if they didn't clear you, you were sick."[92] The *New York Times* quoted from Ron Gold's press release, which claimed that linking homosexuality to mental illness "has forced many gay women and men to think of themselves as freaks. . . . It has been used as a tool of discrimination in the private sector, and in the civil service, military, Immigration and Naturalization Service, health services, adoption and child custody courts." In front of the assembled reporters Ron Gold summed up the APA decision simply, "We've won!"

The day after millions were "cured" with a stroke of the pen, the American public awoke to front-page headlines such as the *New York Times*'s "Psychiatrists in a Shift. Declare Homosexuality no Mental Illness." *Washington Post* readers read, "Doctors Rule Homosexuals Not Abnormal" and "Twenty Million Homosexuals Gain Instant Cure." While the *Washington Star* announced, "Victory for Homosexuals,"[93] *The Advocate* declared, "Gays Leave Sick List" and "Sick No More." In mock relief, the *Gay Community News* proclaimed, "It's Official Now: We're Not Sick." While the revision of the APA diagnostic manual did not launch an unimpeded march toward social acceptance of homosexuality, it did move the power of "the experts" to the side of the gay rights movement. According to psychologist George Weinberg, "The really naïve, conventional homosexuals could feel liberated, and parents who thought the experts really had the rulebook, changed their minds: 'Maybe my son can come home for Thanksgiving after all.' "[94]

The immediate social impact of the revision is difficult to assess. After the APA's announcement, the *New York Post* polled a sampling of heterosexuals and found that most had heard about the APA decision and agreed with it. But when asked how they would react if their children told them they were homosexual, nearly all said they would try to get them to see a psychiatrist. A thirty-one-year old sheet-metal worker from Queens told the *Post* he "wouldn't like it" if his son came out. "I guess I'd feel it was my fault. I wouldn't beat him up, but I'd try to find out what happened. I'd ask him to go to a doctor."[95] Despite the revised "expert opinion," the gay rights movement still had to overcome nearly a century of classifying homosexuality as a sickness.

The first challenge to the revision of DSM arose from within the psychiatric profession. At the press conference announcing the APA trustees' decision, reporters raised the important question of whether the change resulted from political pressure, rather than scientific inquiry.[96] The APA president fed into this concern at the press conference when he paid tribute to "the organized homosexual community," which he said "fanned" the debate over the sickness model and "vigorously protested the prejudice that derives from classifying their condition as a mental illness." Conservatives within the psychiatric profession, led by Charles Socarides and Irving Bieber, seized on the question of political intimidation and insisted the general membership of the APA have a chance to overturn the decision through a referendum.

Some opponents of the decision feared it would convince confused young men and women that it did not matter whether they chose to be homosexual or straight. An irate psychiatrist wrote a letter to the APA's newspaper, *Psychiatric News*, claiming the trustees' "decision will give young homosexuals an easy way out and make the job of practitioners like myself much more difficult."[97] In a ludicrous misapplication of Freudian theory, one psychoanalyst complained that "the Board of Trustees did not have the strength and guts to resist superficial social pressure from homosexuals who, having a collective Oedipal complex, wish to destroy the American Psychiatric Association. It is a bad day for psychiatry." Many psychiatrists worried about the impact of politics on what they believed to be a scientific question. One letter writer to the APA newsletter characterized the trustees' decision as a cowardly capitulation to the mobs that disrupted their conferences and wondered whether schizophrenics might be the next "special interest" group "to march and raise enough hell that they can change anything in time."

Abram Kardiner, a former professor of psychiatry at Columbia who taught Robert Spitzer, raised an argument that would later come to have a significant political impact. In a letter to *Psychiatric News*, Kardiner claimed that homosexuality was a symptom of social disintegration: "The family becomes the ultimate victim of homosexuality, a result which any society can tolerate only within certain limits." If Spitzer's proposal for revising of the DSM reflected the liberal "live and let live" ethos, Kardiner's letter presaged the conservative "family values" crusade against gay rights.

On December 16, 1973, a day after the trustees announced the removal of homosexuality from the DSM, the annual conference of the APA opened in New York. Bieber and Socarides took advantage of a provision in the APA bylaws that allowed for referenda on the trustees' administrative decisions. The APA leadership was caught in a conundrum. Opposing the referendum might precipitate a schism within the psychiatric profession with both sides claiming scientific certainty, while holding the vote would call into question the credibility of the APA as a scientific organization: how could a true matter of science be decided by a vote? After Socarides and Bieber quickly collected two hundred signatures on a petition calling for a referendum, the trustees had no choice but to permit a vote on whether or not homosexuality was a sickness.

The referendum made the battle over the diagnostic model overtly political. Socarides called the vote "a wonderful, democratic vital tool." John Spiegel, the closeted president-elect of the APA, complained that the referendum would reduce a major question of clinical science to a "popularity contest."[98] According to Robert Spitzer, "each side thought they were on the side of science and each one thought the other guy was playing politics."[99] In fact, each side had no choice but to play politics.

The vote posed another threat to the gay rights movement. Over the years, the sickness model debate attracted enough media attention that a loss would mean an all too public reaffirmation of the old stereotype of the mentally ill homosexual. The movement had to act. But how? NGTF realized that a zap or a protest would only confirm the appearance of political pressure. Many psychiatrists did not really care whether or not homosexuality was listed as a sickness, but they were very concerned with the scientific credibility of their professional association. The Task Force feared the uncommitted voters might side with Bieber and Socarides just to show that their profession could not be swayed by social changes and political pressure. What was needed in this instance was a behind-the-scenes appeal.

Once again a closeted insider came to the assistance of the movement. Someone at APA headquarters informed Voeller that the list of APA members and their addresses was available for purchase through the APA business office. NGTF decided to send every APA member a letter urging the reaffirmation of the trustees' decision.[100] NGTF's first move was to ask a longtime ally in the psychiatric profession, Judd Marmor, to sign the letter drafted by Robert Spitzer and Ron Gold. Marmor, who was running for the presidency of the APA, wanted the opposing candidates to sign as well. The Task Force contacted them and convinced them to sign the appeal, along with the APA's two vice presidents. One of the signatories had warned that acknowledgment of the organizational role of homosexual activists in the letter would have been the "kiss of death," so Spitzer and Gold avoided any reference to the conflict over homosexuality or gay rights. To win the swing vote, the appeal focused solely on the need to preserve organizational consistency.

> The undersigned recognize the complexity of the many issues involved in this decision and the diversity of views within our Association. Nonetheless, we feel that it would be a serious and potentially embarrassing step for our profession to vote down a decision which was taken after serious and extended consideration by the bodies within our organization designated to consider such matter.

To raise money for their massive direct-mail marketing campaign, NGTF instructed donors to make their checks out to an ally in the effort, St. Mary's Episcopal Church in Harlem, so the contributions would be tax deductible.[101] Although the NGTF bought the APA membership list and paid $3,000 to send the letter to 17,910 voters, its name appeared nowhere in the appeal.[102]

The restrained strategy of the Task Force combined with Spitzer's compromise category of "sexual orientation disturbance" carried the day. In a vote held in April 1974, 58 percent supported the original decision to remove homosexuality from the list of disorders. About half the membership did not vote.[103] Had the NGTF sent the psychiatrists an overtly political appeal, or had the referendum been restricted to whether homosexuality should be in or out of the DSM, those promoting the sickness model, represented by Bieber and Socarides, probably would have won.[104] After witnessing the political machinations behind the APA's momentous decision on homosexuality, Ron Gold concluded that the "science of psychiatry is a joke."[105]

The following year, Bieber and Socarides tried to demand yet another vote, claiming the NGTF's letter improperly influenced the referendum. The referendum had so severely damaged the psychiatric organization's credibility, however, that the trustees refused to allow another vote and prohibited the future use of referenda to decide scientific issues.[106]

The demise of the sickness model is a monumental event in the history of the gay rights movement. In the mid-1960s Frank Kameny began his battle to convince homophile activists to recognize and publicize their sanity. Just nine years later, key figures in the APA embraced that crusade, triggering news coverage that prompted a widespread reevaluation of homosexuality.[107] Removing homosexuality from the DSM also temporarily thwarted the use of science to justify antigay discrimination. Kay Lahusen recalled how "people who wanted to discriminate against homosexuals could no longer say, 'Look, the psychiatrists call it an illness. It's considered a sexual perversion. And we can't have people who are sick working for us. We're entitled to stop them from being schoolteachers or from hiring them.' . . . They said we are sick. Now they just say we're immoral."[108] An argument based on immorality was less troublesome to gay rights activists like Kay Lahusen because morality was *relative*, while science was *fact*. It was a short-lived reprieve; activists would soon discover that the scientific and moral arguments against gay rights were far from silenced.

Bruce Voeller hoped the revision of the DSM would mark a new era of cooperation between the APA and the gay rights movement. Just six weeks after the trustee's announcement, he wrote a letter to the APA's medical director proposing a joint campaign to repeal sodomy laws, to pass fair employment and housing legislation, and to reform custody rules that limited visitation rights of homosexual parents in divorce cases. He also wanted the APA to help challenge federal policies that prohibited homosexuals from immigration and naturalization, military service, and jobs that required security clearances. Voeller believed that since secondary schools and universities used the fears of "conversion" to homosexuality to justify prohibitions on gay student organizations, the APA and NGTF could use the new medical view of homosexuality to argue in favor of gay student organizations.[109]

Although the APA rejected Voeller's call for concerted collaborative action with NGTF, over the subsequent years the psychiatric community proved to be a valuable ally in the struggle to expand and defend gay rights. In 1975, outgoing APA president John Spiegel condemned the refusal of many school boards to hire gay teachers, and his successor Jack Weinberg publicly criticized discrimination against homosexuals in the military. Two years later Weinberg protested the refusal of the federal government to naturalize homosexuals, and later he condemned Anita Bryant's crusade to repeal legislation that protected homosexuals from discrimination in Dade County, Florida.

While the country's political climate turned increasingly conservative in the 1980s, the APA remained a bastion of liberalism. It granted a formal vote to gay and lesbian psychiatrists as a "minority group" in 1982 and a few years later formed a task force on homosexuality to study, among other issues, "homophobia." Under the chairmanship of Robert Spitzer, the Nomenclature Committee published the most recent version of the DSM in 1986. This manual, which is still used today, contains no designations that link sexual orientation with psychopathology.

Despite its profound impact, the legacy of the battle over the sickness model was not entirely positive for the gay rights movement. Media coverage of the APA's decision promoted the idea that homosexuals were not insane, but the publicity created a media marketplace for dissenting opinions. In a 1975 book, *Beyond Sexual Freedom*,

Charles Socarides predicted that since homosexuality was no longer labeled a sickness "it will henceforth be touted as simply an acceptable variation on the norm," a "lifestyle." Socarides quoted a letter from Columbia professor of psychiatry Abram Kardiner, whose work bridged the fields of sociology and psychiatry:

> Supporting the claims of the homosexuals and regarding homosexuality as a normal variant of sexual activity is to deny the social significance of homosexuality. To do this is to give support to the divisive elements in the community. . . . Above all it *militates against the family* and destroys the function of the latter as the last place in our society where affectivity can still be cultivated [italics added]. Homosexuals cannot make a society nor keep ours going for very long. It operates against the cohesive elements in society in the name of a fictitious freedom. It drives the opposite sex into a similar direction. And no society can long endure when either the child is neglected or when the sexes war upon each other.

According to Socarides and Kardiner, tolerance for homosexuality threatened family life because it opened up a path that negated its value. Soon men and women would turn toward homosexuality and society would devolve into a giant battle of the sexes.[110] Also in 1975, another Columbia University psychiatrist, Herbert Hendin, warned against tolerating homosexuality in both a *New York Times* editorial and his book, *The Age of Sensation*: "It is no accident that the increasing acceptance of homosexuality parallels increasing *attacks on the family* [italics added]. . . . Homosexuality is a sign of the family's failure to be what society needs it to be: a force for stability, the locus of affection, the place where children learn love, trust and belief."[111]

Hendin, Socarides, and Kardiner offered analyses that were more subtle and in retrospect more powerful than the old fears of gays and lesbians converting young people to "homosexualism." Linking homosexuality with the breakdown of the family was, and remains, a particularly effective weapon to use against the gay rights movement. Opponents of discrimination against gays and lesbians might ask,

"Why should anyone care how homosexuals conduct their personal lives?" In the voice of scientific objectivity, Hendin, Socarides, and Kardiner gave a simple answer: Tolerance for homosexuality undermined society. As Hendin wrote:

> While oppression and intolerance of the individual homosexual is both cruel and foolish, the notion that social approval is a way of dealing with the question is equally destructive and mindless. . . . The more we approve of or institutionalize symptoms of disruption, the more we distract ourselves from the individual tragedies involved and the less chance we have to reverse the forces that tear the sexes apart and encourage homosexuality.

None of the three psychiatrists were religious men who saw homosexuality as a sin. They all opposed criminalization of homosexual activity between consenting adults and condemned discrimination based on sexual orientation. Socarides thought homosexuals in the military should be allowed to be open about their sexuality without fear of punishment or discharge, and Hendin had "nothing but contempt" for Anita Bryant and her Save Our Children campaign. But in the mid-1970s these New York liberal psychiatrists gave scientific authority to the religious right's apocalyptic predictions about the deleterious effect of homosexuality on the family.[112]

Decades later Herbert Hendin renounced his portrayal of homosexuality as a threat to the family and the social order. New studies, he said, have shown that sexual orientation is far less open to choice than he previously believed; people do not subconsciously or consciously choose the "gay lifestyle" to avoid family life. Hendin admitted that in the 1970s he could not have predicted how many gays and lesbians would form lasting relationships and stable families. Today adoption rights, civil unions, and gay marriages offer homosexuals possibilities for family life that they only dreamed of thirty years ago. According to Hendin, the ever-increasing number of homosexuals who form stable families indicates that gays and lesbians might even be *more* "pro-family" than large segments of the heterosexual population.[113]

chapter ten

MISS OKLAHOMA VS. MACHO MAN

"It was not just another Texas-style party," *Time* magazine reported in a September 1975 cover story. "At a lavish ranch outside Austin last spring, some 300 ranchers, bankers, oilmen and politicians drank, ate barbecue, smoked pot and paired off for lovemaking. The only unusual aspect of the weekend long party was that the guests were homosexuals." Back in 1969, *Esquire* heralded the young, tough, militant "New Homosexual." Six years later, *Time* was introducing millions of Americans to an ubiquitous homosexual "who could be anybody's neighbor—a Maryland teacher, a Texas minister, a Minnesota state senator, an Ohio professor, an Air Force sergeant. Your husband may be a homosexual."[1] According to *Time*, the number of homosexuals coming out of the closet in all walks of life was "evidence of the spread of unabashed homosexuality once thought to be confined to the worlds of theater, dance, fashion, etc."

The spread of "unabashed" homosexuality nationwide was the driving goal of the gay liberation movement. In the 1950s and 1960s the stereotypical media images of homosexuals as effeminate fops and insane deviants were so pervasive that few successful gays and lesbians openly associated themselves with homosexuality or gay rights. Many closeted homosexuals even exploited the stereotypes for camouflage. By avoiding stereotypical behaviors, gays and lesbians could appear straight in the eyes of co-workers and family members, while continuing to enjoy the gay lifestyle in underground bars and exclusive parties. Some gays did not even acknowledge their own sexuality simply because, unlike the stereotypical gays they saw in plays and on television, they saw themselves as tough and aggressive. Campaigns in the 1970s to trigger news reports that challenged the stereotypes, to insinuate gay rights into mainstream politics, and to remove homosexuality from the official list of psychological sicknesses were all part of a general effort to encourage closeted people to come out, and straights to become more comfortable with homosexuals who revealed their sexuality. *Time* magazine's 1975 cover story on homosexuality claimed that successful homosexuals who might have chosen to live double lives in previous generations had begun to come out in great numbers to their families, friends, and co-workers in the mid-1970s. One of the most famous closeted homosexuals to come out in this atmosphere was veteran NFL running back Dave Kopay, who published a best-selling memoir about his experiences as a gay professional football player. Arthur Bell, a founding member of the Gay Activists Alliance whose media campaign helped spawn the new openness, could confidently proclaim in the mid-1970s: "We're everywhere and we're everything."[2]

At the same time, network television shows with millions of viewers reinforced the idea that homosexuals could be tough and rugged through imagery and plotline. *The Washington Post* ran a 1976 op-ed piece about the ubiquitous presence of gays on TV titled "And Now the Year of the Gay." "You can hardly dial around on prime time without clicking on to some actor explaining to a disappointed, would-be girlfriend that he's gay," columnist Nicholas Von Hoffman complained. Every show, according to the commentator, seemed to offer a requisite episode with a gay protagonist who was "big, hairy, courageous and an ex-football quarterback." "Is a new stereotype being born?" Von Hoffman wondered. "Is network television about to kill off the bitchy, old-time, outrageous gay and replace him with a new type of homosexual?"

Von Hoffman was particularly troubled by an episode of the prime time network sitcom *Alice* in which the waitresses on the show are "dumbfounded at being told that this large, hirsute, disguised double X chromosome doesn't crook his finger." Alice displays her liberal open-mindedness by allowing the gay character to take her adolescent son off for a weekend of fishing. Like the episode of *All in the Family* that featured a gay ex-football player, the *Alice* episode concludes with the tough guy revealing his homosexuality to his young fishing buddy. Instead of expressing shock and discomfort like Archie, however, Alice's boy thinks it's cool. The message was clear to Von Hoffman and millions of others: "American kids are brighter, wiser and more liberal than their elders."[3] While such a message upset Von Hoffman, who seems to have preferred the days of the stereotypical sitcom fop, American homosexuals in the 1970s were gratified by the prospect of a future when straights like Alice and her son would be comfortable with the sexuality of their gay co-workers, neighbors, and friends.

The tough homosexual made his major motion picture debut in 1975 with the film *Dog Day Afternoon*, starring Al Pacino. The movie was based on the true-life story of John Wojtowicz, a Gay Activists Alliance member who, in 1972, attempted to rob a Brooklyn bank to finance a sex change operation for his transvestite lover. After the police thwarted the robbery and surrounded the bank, Wojtowicz took the bank tellers hostage and offered to exchange them for money and a flight out of the country. News footage of Wojtowicz taunting the police from the door of the bank was broadcast worldwide throughout the afternoon. Hours later the police foiled Wojtowicz's plan, and he was subsequently sentenced to twenty-six years in prison. From prison, Wojtowicz paid for his lover's sex change operation with the seventy-five hundred dollars Warner Brothers gave him for the rights to his story. The resulting Academy Award-nominated film presented Wojtowicz as a gun-toting hero of the downtrodden while Al Pacino's riveting performance challenged all the stereotypes of the effete, passive homosexual.

The media's embrace of nonstereotypical characterizations was partly due to a greater acceptance of homosexuality among a younger generation of media executives and screenwriters who matured in a more tolerant, sexually relaxed society. But the more positive presentations of homosexuals were also the achievements of organizations like the Gay Activists Alliance and the National Gay Task Force, which monitored portrayals of homosexuals in the media. TV executives discovered they could avoid zaps and bad publicity by having gay activists review scripts that dealt with homosexuality before they were aired. In

1974, ABC sent the National Gay Task Force a script for an episode of
Marcus Welby, M.D. that centered on a boy who was molested by a
teacher. NGTF objected to the episode on the grounds that since
"homosexuals were just emerging from media invisibility, greater caution was needed at present to avoid giving offence." After threatening
boycotts, some of the ABC affiliates refused to air the episode. Eventually the network removed a few offensive lines. A *New York Times* TV
critic complained that "in attempting to replace the old and frequently
abusive stereotypes of homosexuals with only positive non-abusive
stereotypes—even if only until the 'prejudice balance' is redressed—the
homosexual groups are veering toward an unreality of their own."[4] A
Washington Post television commentator described how the image of
homosexuals projected by television had become

> as squeaky clean and wholesome as was the image of blacks
> during the most sensitive years of the civil rights struggle. In
> those days stereotypes were avoided so scrupulously that
> from TV you got the impression blacks were just like whites,
> except they didn't have any flaws. From TV today, the
> impression given of homosexuals is that they're just like het-
> erosexuals except they have no hang-ups.[5]

One of the great achievements of the gay liberation movement was the
display of the nonstereotypical, well-adjusted homosexual on the tele-
visions in millions of American living rooms. More than any other
medium, TV had the power to shape and manipulate the conscious and
subconscious prejudices of the American public. The stereotypical
image of the effeminate homosexual had long repelled a public that
viewed the ideal man as rugged and tough. The brawny guy who just
happened to be gay was a more acceptable image to many Americans.
(By the 1990s the image of brawny gay guy had so pervaded the American mind that *muscular guys* were stereotyped as gay.)

While the new TV image of a masculine gay man supplanted the
effeminate stereotype for straight Americans, it also, at the same time,
became the ideal in gay fashion. The lithe, hairless youths who graced
the pages of gay magazines in the 1960s were replaced in the mid-
1970s by mustached men with bulging biceps and hairy chests.

Close-fitting European couture and the mod Carnaby Street style were out, all-American work clothes were in: Levis, lumberjack shirts, work boots, and bomber jackets. Surveying gay fashion in 1976, one gay magazine remarked how "it is getting exceedingly difficult to tell a homosexual from a longshoreman."[6]

One night in 1977, French record producer Jacques Morali noticed the preponderance of macho male stereotypes among partygoers at a gay disco in the East Village. As he surveyed the scene of macho men dancing with each other to the pounding music, it occurred to him to create a musical troupe of singers and dancers, each dressed as different American male archetypes that would double as gay sex symbols. The group would be campy and fun but also empowering and appealing to a gay audience. That night, Morali enlisted the band's first member, Felipe Rose, a professional dancer who showed up at the disco dressed as an American Indian. After signing a singer/dancer to play a sailor and another to dress as a policeman, Morali noticed they all lived in Greenwich Village and decided to call the group the Village People. The group soon expanded to include a construction worker, a leather-clad biker, and, of course, a cowboy. After releasing hits like "Macho Man" and "YMCA," the Village People became "heroes to an audience that encompassed a wide and madcap spectrum" of gays and straights.[7] Although Morali packaged the Village People with what the *New York Times* called "plenty of non-threatening good cheer to middle America," he also wrote songs that contained a subtle but empowering political message.[8] The hit "Macho Man" reflected the new fashion and attitude of the ideal gay hero of the 1970s.

> *You can tell a macho, he has a funky walk*
> *his western shirts and leather, always look so boss*

The song goes on to implore "everyman" to be a macho man—"live a life of freedom . . . make a stand . . . have your own lifestyles and ideals." Such a macho man is a "special godson in anybody's land." The anthemic "Macho Man" captured the metamorphosis of the image of gay men from dandies interested in opera and fashion to the 1970s "machos" clad in "western shirts and leather." Ironically, the Village People and "Macho Man" fed a new stereotype—a "special godson" who mirrored the American tough guy archetype while unabashedly celebrating his "own lifestyle." This stereotype, however, was positive because it associated the homosexual with the American masculine ideal.

The Village People's hit song "In the Navy" not only challenged the old stereotypes, its seemingly patriotic enthusiasm flew in the face of the antimilitary chic of the post-Vietnam era. The song encourages all who "like adventure . . . to enter the recruiting office fast" and promises "no need to wait, they're signing up new seamen fast." The United States Navy was so impressed with the popularity of the hit that it considered using the song in a recruitment advertising campaign on television and radio.

> *They want you, they want you*
> *They want you as a new recruit*

Morali gave the U.S. Navy the rights to the song for free in return for access to a naval base to shoot a music video. Less than a month later, the Village People showed up at a San Diego naval base where, they were provided with a battleship, several airplanes, and hundreds of sailors. After the video appeared on television and the Navy started planning the ad campaign, some newspapers objected to the use of taxpayer money to fund music videos. Although the Navy ultimately canceled the campaign, the publicity further boosted the popularity of the song. The Navy's eagerness to co-opt a Village People hit for recruitment was particularly ironic, given its policy of discharging homosexual servicemen.

In the mid-1970s, several outed military servicemen fought their discharges and became causes célèbres to a gay rights movement eager to demonstrate that anybody could be gay, regardless of profession or degree of "masculinity." A well-publicized campaign to secure the rights of "gays in the military" began in 1971 after Bob Martin, the founder of the Student Homophile League at Columbia University, was ousted from the Navy. After graduating in 1970, Martin, who often cruised the city in a sailor uniform when he was a civilian, fulfilled his lifelong dream of enlisting and served in Italy as a radioman on a NATO base. Less than a year later, he was discharged on grounds of "suspected homosexual activity." Rather than accept the administrative discharge quietly like hundreds of other servicemen every year, the founder of the gay liberation movement demanded a court-martial. Martin mounted a bold defense, arguing that his constitutional rights had been violated by an unfair policy that did not punish outwardly heterosexual sailors who engaged in homosexual acts. While his lawyers gathered evidence from retired sailors who recounted their experiences with "straight trade" in the Navy, Frank Kameny and Foster Gunnison, who had both assisted Martin with the creation of SHL, joined the young man's new cause.[9] Kameny advised Martin on how to appeal to politicians while Gunnison set up a defense fund.[10]

Martin sent press releases about his case to all three TV networks, all the New York and Chicago newspapers, the *Los Angeles Times*, *Newsweek*, Reuters, *Time*, *Life*, *US News and World Report*, UPI, the *Washington Post*, and the Columbia University alumni newsletter.[11] He received public declarations of support from the president of the American Psychiatric Association, Judd Marmor; six U.S. Congressional representatives including Ed Koch and Bella Abzug of New York; the Chief of Naval Operations Admiral Zumwalt; and U.S. senators Richard Schweiker of Pennsylvania and Sam Ervin of North Carolina.[12] Senator Ervin wrote a letter to Secretary of the Navy John Chafee expressing his support for Martin while Congressman Abzug called the case a "witch-hunt" and demanded that Secretary Chafee intervene on the sailor's behalf.[13] Even the dean of Columbia College, Carl Hovde, sent the Navy a letter praising Martin as "a man for whom I have great respect" and making the questionable claim that the young man "never sought controversy."

Martin's case generated headlines in publications ranging from *The Advocate* to *Stars and Stripes* and acquired what Foster Gunnison called "a national status with movement-wide impact."[14] Although Martin lost his fight and the Navy released him in June 1972, five years later a review program set up by Jimmy Carter raised the status of his discharge to honorable. It was the first time a discharge on the basis of homosexual involvement had ever been upgraded. Martin told *Gay Week*, "what an honorable discharge means to me is that it is the nation's way of saying that it is proud of gay veterans and by extension that it is proud of millions of gay veterans and current service people. We've come a long way."[15]

Martin's groundbreaking public battle against the Navy kicked off a series of well-publicized challenges to military discharges that harnessed and directed the energy of the gay rights movement in the 1970s.[16] As Martin wrote in one of his many press statements, "This challenge to the glaring injustices of the military discharge system and to the armed forces' medieval attitude toward homosexuality is only the beginning."[17]

The most famous challenge to the military's discharge policies arose in 1975, four years after Martin began his campaign against the Navy. After conferring with Frank Kameny and ACLU attorneys, Air Force officer Lenny Matlovich, a highly decorated veteran of three tours in Vietnam, decided to purposely reveal his homosexuality to test the military's ban on homosexuals. Two months after he wrote a letter to his supervising officer stating that he was gay, he received a general discharge. When he challenged the ruling, the gay rights movement enthusiastically embraced his cause, which triggered dozens of articles about the patriotic, tough, seemingly "normal" Matlovich. On September 8, 1975, Matlovich became the first openly gay man to appear on the cover of *Time* under the headline " 'I Am a Homosexual': The Gay Drive for Acceptance." Three years later the U.S. Court of Appeals ruled that Sergeant Matlovich's discharge had been illegal and sent the case to a lower court to decide if he should be reinstated. After a federal judge ordered the Air Force to reinstate Sergeant Matlovich with back pay, the Air Force, fearing the precedent that would be set by such a reinstatement, offered a $160,000 tax-free payment in exchange for dropping the case. Many gay activists were outraged when Matlovich accepted, but he later explained that he settled because he would have been unlikely to win in an appeal to the increasingly conservative U.S. Supreme Court.[18] Publicity surrounding Matlovich's case generated widespread debate over the military's longstanding policy of discharging homosexuals. A Gallup poll found that, by 1977, a slim majority of Americans thought gays should be allowed to serve in the military.

The fight against the military's ban on homosexuals marked a major change in the character of the gay rights movement. In 1969, the vanguard of the gay rights movement, the Gay Liberation Front, called for the overthrow of the federal government. By the mid-1970s, the gay rights movement rallied around a decorated Vietnam vet who simply wanted to defend his country. The grandiose vision that the gay rights movement was part of a larger social revolution that would transform the politics of the United States was succeeded, in the mid-1970s, by a more limited focus on securing the rights of open homosexuals to contribute to society.

Along with ideological changes, the gay rights movement adopted major tactical changes in the mid-1970s. Tactics that had helped define and advance the gay liberation movement, such as aggressive protests and zaps, were abandoned as a result of changes in America's political and social landscape. After Watergate and the withdrawal from Vietnam, Americans behaved politically like wounded animals retreating into their dens. Aggression, regardless of the cause, struck many as more exhausting than inspiring. The media, too, began to lose interest in the liberation movement. Scenes of homosexuals shouting down politicians no longer had the novelty needed to attract reporters and cameras. Without press coverage of zaps and protests, many homosexuals lost interest in the gay rights movement. In the mid-1970s, Arthur Evans, a founder of the Gay Activists Alliance, complained, "All across the country, there are signs that the gay movement is beginning to fizzle out. Average gays are bored by demonstrations and rhetoric. When I recently visited New York, an old movement friend told me, you couldn't pay people to take a leaflet on Christopher Street. . . . Name any movement and you'll hear the same lament; 'We're slowing down and our people are growing apathetic.' "[19]

Arthur Evans's former lover Arthur Bell attributed the political apathy to the flourishing gay sex scene that was liberated by legal reforms of the post-Stonewall years and yet to be inhibited by the approaching AIDS crisis. "The movement made it possible to 'be gay,' " Bell wrote, while the gay sex scene "made it possible to be gay with impunity, to drop your inhibitions along with your pants."

Not only did changes in New York State liquor laws permit gays to

dance freely in the city's bars in the mid-1970s, but the easing of official regulation allowed gay bar proprietors to set aside back rooms so
that customers did not even have to leave the premises for sex. In an
article for the *Village Voice*, Bell described the "dimly lit or pitch black
chambers" in bars with names like the Anvil, the Mineshaft, the Stud,
and the Toilet "where whips crack and urine and Schlitz are often
served in the same container . . . TV dinners for young men in a
hurry." The city's gay sex scene was so unrestrained that many felt nos-
talgic for the years when gay New Yorkers had to dodge undercover
cops while cruising subway men's rooms. A new bathhouse, the
Broadway Arms, exploited this nostalgia by featuring the "IRTearoom,"
a back room designed to look like a subway bathroom lined with graf-
fiti and urine-covered tiles. The atmosphere was enhanced by a sound
system that played a recording of screeching subway cars. Another
bathhouse featured an eighteen-wheeler for those who wanted to enjoy
the excitement of having sex in a tractor-trailer on the desolate West
Side docks without its various attendant dangers.[20] The old days of
official repression of gay sex in New York gave purpose and energy to
many gay rights militants in the 1960s and early 1970s. As the repression dissipated in the mid-1970s so did much of the political fervor of
the New York gay community.

No group suffered more from the declining interest in gay activism
than the Gay Activists Alliance. The beginning of the end of the
Alliance began shortly after three o'clock on the morning of October
15, 1974, when a fire broke out in the upper stories of GAA's Firehouse headquarters. Within minutes half the building was engulfed in
flames. After the inferno was extinguished, firefighters discovered three
uncapped, half-full cans of charcoal lighter fluid and a book of matches
with a cigarette "fuse" that had failed to burn completely. Investigators
estimated that fires were set in at least six places on the upper floors.
Someone who lived across the street told police that around two-thirty
two cars, each occupied by one man, took off from the building at high
speed. Morty Manford, the president of GAA, announced to the press
that the act of arson was part of "a wave of harassment against gays that
included fire bombings of [gay community] churches."[21] The Firehouse arsonists, however, had another motive. A day after the blaze,
GAA reported missing $4,000 worth of electronic equipment,

including the stereo system that kept the Firehouse rocking during the Saturday night dances and the video equipment that recorded the zaps for GAA's public access TV show. A firefighter reported that "the building was wide open and the front door was unlocked when they arrived."[22] The arsonists had keys to the building and knew their way around. The Firehouse was probably not torched by antigay sociopaths; the fire was most likely set by insiders who wanted to cover up a theft. No one was ever arrested for the crime.[23]

Even before the loss of its headquarters, the Alliance had been lurching toward factionalism, schism, and irrelevance. Almost all of its founders had left by 1974. Marty Robinson and Arthur Evans both moved to San Francisco. Others simply began to grow out of the radical activist lifestyle. The new generation of Activists was not as disciplined or as unified as the founding members had been. Tensions between the men and women that had always existed in GAA exploded in 1973 when the lesbians left to form their own organization, Lesbian Feminist Liberation. Months later Bruce Voeller led some of the most gifted and level-headed Activists out of the Alliance to form the National Gay Task force. GAA's membership plummeted from well over two hundred in 1972 to about fifty by 1974. When the Alliance tried to organize a picket at ABC's studios in 1974 it attracted eight protestors. One Activist lamented, "It is a sad but inescapable fact but the days when we could snap our fingers and have a couple hundred people on a picket line are gone forever." The loss of members paralleled a diminishing media presence. Between 1970 and 1974 the *New York Times* mentioned GAA in 140 articles, between 1975 and 1981 the Alliance was cited just 20 times.

The Alliance's finances were also in a shambles. Runaway inflation of the mid-1970s hit GAA at the same time its revenue declined. As police harassment of gay nightlife slackened, the Saturday night dances had serious competition from new bars and gay discos. The week before the fire, the membership voted to save money by cutting Morty Manford's seventy-five-dollar-a-week salary as president.[24] When Manford resigned in protest and was followed by his good friend Ethan Geto, the Alliance simultaneously lost its most famous member and its shrewdest political adviser. GAA found itself caught in a downward spiral of declining membership, influence, press coverage, revenue, and talent.

As the organization fractured, radicals of various stripes began to fill the gaps. By the end of the 1970s GAA was split into factions of the Revolutionary Socialist League, North American Man/Boy Love Association, and the Gay Atheists League. Meetings were bogged down with motions to expel members for making threats against each others' lives.[25] A 1980 press release on GAA's principles included the statement, "we not only believe, we know through our active historical experience, that a massive upheaval, a revolution, will be necessary to abolish anti-Lesbian and gay bigotry and make it possible for us to shape our own lives."[26] By 1980 GAA had begun to sound like the Gay Liberation Front in 1969. After Activists met to officially disband the Alliance a year later, Arnie Kantrowitz published a piece on the closing ceremony of GAA titled "The Day Gay Lib Died." In reality the gay liberation movement had been dead since the mid-1970s.

The political conditions that fostered the gay liberation movement in the early 1970s had all but dissipated by the mid-1970s. The Gay Activists Alliance made national news in the early 1970s by attacking liberals who refused to endorse gay rights. By the mid-1970s there were not many liberals left to "climb up." Activists no longer had to force the subject of gay rights into the national political dialogue, now mainstream news reporters routinely asked politicians to comment on the issue. When politicians disparaged homosexuals, liberal commentators in the mainstream media quickly jumped on the hypocrisy.[27] Politicians and their advisers also caught up with the media-savvy gay activists. Most liberal politicians found they could preempt zaps by voicing "opposition to discrimination based on sexual orientation" rather than specifically supporting "gay rights." The political debate over gay rights suddenly became less theatrical, less impassioned. A sense of purposelessness quickly pervaded the movement.

Politicians in urban communities even began to exploit the issue of gay rights to get elected. New York State assemblyman Mark Alan Siegel campaigned in gay bars in his Upper East Side district, and Bella Abzug visited the Continental Baths during her Congressional campaign. The *Wall Street Journal* described how "Abzug addressed hundreds of enthusiastically cheering patrons, most of whom wore nothing but white towels wrapped around their waists." By the late 1970s, virtually every serious contender for the mayor's office in San Francisco had to openly court the gay community. Homosexual voters in San Francisco joined with other minority groups and liberal activists to form a political machine that challenged the bastions of business and finance and upper-middle-class families.[28] Gay voters even made their presence known in Texas, where State representative Ronald Walters of Houston admitted in 1976 that he "could not have been elected without gay support."[29]

In another sign of the changing times, open homosexuals were gaining political influence not by zapping politicians but by running for office themselves. GAA founder Jim Owles became the first open homosexual to seek a New York City Council seat in a failed 1973 campaign against his old nemesis Carol Greitzer. That same year in San Francisco, Castro street businessman Harvey Milk made his first unsuccessful bid for the board of supervisors. Allan Spear, a closeted Minnesota state senator, was so sick of enduring gossip behind his back that he came out and was reelected in 1974. Elaine Nobel became the first major party candidate to run openly as a lesbian in a successful 1974 campaign for the Massachusetts state legislature.

Gay rights was also on the legislative march in American cities. By 1978 nineteen cities and four counties in the United States had adopted gay rights legislation. Another thirteen cities including New York, San Francisco, Boston, and Portland protected homosexuals from discrimination when applying for municipal jobs. Even Wichita, Kansas, and Columbus, Ohio, passed municipal gay rights laws.

The repression and "conspiracy of silence" that fired up gay activists in the movement's early years seemed to have lifted by the mid-1970s. Gay liberation groups lost their targets, and their energy.

Ethan Geto, Jim Owles, and a few other former GAA members exploited the new political legitimacy of gay rights when they abandoned the declining Alliance to form a new organization, the Gay Political Union, a group founded specifically to lobby liberals. During the 1976 presidential election, Geto, who was Indiana senator Birch Bayh's presidential campaign manager in New York, arranged for the

Senator to attend a Gay Political Union reception.[30] Accompanied by
the Secret Service, Bayh became the first serious contender for a major
party's presidential nomination to campaign in a gay bar. Whereas only
just a few years before, the Gay Activists Alliance "climbed up the liberals" by zapping their fund-raisers and campaign rallies: now, the Gay
Political Union won the allegiance of liberal politicians by donating
money to their campaigns.

Ethan Geto also organized a small group of closeted and openly gay
and lesbian New York politicians and high-placed government officials
who secretly met in Geto's apartment to discuss gay rights: "We called
it the Study Group because there were people who just did not want
to belong to anything that had the word 'gay' in it." Study Group
meetings attempted to convince closeted public officials to support gay
rights openly and come out publicly. During one of the strategy sessions about the New York City gay rights bill, someone in the Study
Group suggested that antihomosexual discrimination would be less
acceptable if it were seen as a human rights violation. To connect gay
rights to the larger cause for human rights, the movement to pass the
municipal gay rights bill adopted a new symbol: a pink triangle,
evoking the patch placed on homosexual inmates of Nazi concentration camps.[31]

Another sign that the gay liberation movement had achieved success
in making homosexuality more politically and socially acceptable arose
during the 1977 New York City mayoral race when questions emerged
about the sexual orientation of Congressman Ed Koch, the Democratic Party nominee. During the primary race, Koch's advisers tried to
dispel the rumors by enlisting Bess Myerson, former commissioner of
consumer affairs and the 1945 Miss America, to escort the candidate
to various public functions. Koch's media adviser David Garth recalled
how, on the campaign trail, "All the mommas would say, 'You make
such a nice couple' and Ed would look at the ground and paw it quietly."[32] As "the first Jewish Miss America," Myerson was beloved
among older Jewish New Yorkers. Not only did she help counter
rumors about Koch's sexuality, but she also helped win votes in that
key Democratic constituency.

After Koch won the Democratic Party nomination, partisans of
Mario Cuomo, the Liberal Party candidate, tried to revive the gossip

about Koch's sexuality. Sound trucks cruised around the outer bor-
oughs blaring "Vote for Cuomo, not the homo!"[33] When reporters
asked about the tactic, Koch denied he was homosexual but claimed
that if he were, he would not be ashamed because, "God makes you
what you are." After Koch won the election, Cuomo claimed he and
his campaign had rejected any effort to "get us involved in digging up
information" on Koch's sexuality. "Aside from anything else," Cuomo
said, "I knew it would backfire and wind up hurting me. It looks as
though that's just what's happened." Cuomo told *Times* reporters that
a pollster said that Koch's popularity actually increased in the days after
the press reported the rumors.[34]

Once elected mayor, Koch fulfilled his pledge to ban discrimination
in city employment practices, including within the police and fire
departments, which had long opposed hiring homosexuals. Later
Koch also defied pressure from the Catholic Church and Jewish
orthodox communities, extending John Lindsay's ban on discrimination against homosexuals to all businesses contracting with the city.[35]
The political success of a mayor who was both a trusted ally and a suspected homosexual confirmed the false impression that the liberation
movement had irreversibly secured social tolerance for homosexuality
in New York.

The increasing tolerance and acceptance of homosexuality encouraged a greater openness among gay New Yorkers. When H. Gerald
Schiff, a gay accountant, returned to Gotham in the late 1970s after a
five-year absence, he found "an entirely different city . . . much more
openly gay, more willing to seek out gay professional people, gay
clients, gay customers, more conducive to 'coming out.' "[36] What
Gerald Schiff had discovered was a new gay community.

One great achievement of the gay liberation movement was the
development of a "gay community" consciousness. In the 1960s the
idea of "gay pride" appealed to only a small number of bold homosexuals with little to lose, like Frank Kameny. The gay liberation movement orchestrated media events and media triggers to counter the
stereotypical effeminate images with more attractive, more respectable
images of the new homosexual. Unlike the gay American professionals
in the mid-twentieth century, large numbers of gay doctors, lawyers,
and businessmen in the 1970s proudly identified themselves with "the

new homosexual" and conceived of themselves as members of a homosexual minority and a national gay and lesbian community.

The identification of large numbers of wealthy homosexuals with a
gay community enabled new gay rights organizations to garner large,
tax-deductible donations that could be used to build institutions that
served the gay community. Morty Manford took advantage of the new
climate when he founded the Lambda Club, a popular community
center in New York City that offered psychological counseling and
medical programs for homosexuals. In 1973 Manford organized the
National New Orleans Memorial Fund, which raised millions of dollars
for the victims of a fire in a French Quarter gay bar that killed thirty-
two patrons. Previous generations of American homosexuals who
lacked a gay community consciousness would not have rushed to the
assistance of other homosexuals with such generosity. Gay liberation
had generated a national community consciousness that would be critical during several crises that American homosexuals would face over
subsequent decades.

The move away from shaping public opinion through the media and
the political system made sense given the increasingly conservative
social and political climate of the late 1970s and 1980s. After Morty
Manford earned a law degree, he directed the Lambda Legal Defense
Education Fund, which took the struggle out of the streets and into
the courts. The Lambda Legal Defense Education Fund did not
orchestrate zaps to push politicians and journalists to support gay
rights; instead it worked to transform the law by challenging antigay
legislation in the courts. The other major American social rights movements, civil rights and the women's movements, had also moved their
struggles away from the increasingly conservative state and national
legislatures in favor of working through the courts, which were seen
as more likely to buck public opinion in favor of minority rights. The
retreat of the minority rights movements from the battle for public
opinion made tactical sense at the time and resulted in stunning successes over the subsequent decades.

But success in the courts fed the conservative backlash to the
social changes of the 1960s and 1970s. Every legal decision that
favored gays, abortion rights, and affirmative action provided a rallying cry and a fund-raising tool for conservative groups. While lib-

erals were winning in the courts, the conservative right cobbled together a vast army of politicians, voters, and think tanks into a grassroots movement that has continued to be a dominant force in American electoral politics.

As the opponents of gay rights coalesced quietly, the gay community and its defenders seemed be seduced by the great achievements of the gay liberation movement. Positive depictions of gays in popular culture and the introduction of gay rights into mainstream political discourse contributed to the false sense that the movement was no longer neces-sary. In reality, American homosexuals continued to face an array of penalties more severe than in any Western nation outside the Commu-nist bloc. Sodomy between consenting adults was still illegal in thirty-eight states, carrying prison sentences of up to twenty-one years and in some cases life. In some parts of the country, the presence of gays and lesbians in the media awakened politicians and their constituents to push for tougher prohibitions on homosexuality. The Georgia state legislature suddenly thought it necessary in the mid-1970s to rewrite the state sodomy law to also apply to sex between lesbians.[37] In addi-tion to achieving significant success, the gay liberation movement also incited a backlash that would become a major political force by the end of the decade.

Hints of the looming backlash could be seen in the 1975 *Time* mag-azine cover story on the ubiquitous homosexual. Five years earlier when *Time* published a feature on homosexuality, it sought expert advice from psychiatrists Charles Socarides and Irving Bieber. Although both thought homosexuals were sick, they also advocated full civil rights for them. In the wake of the 1973 American Psychiatric Association decision to remove homosexuality from its diagnostic manual of psychiatric disorders, psychiatrists such as Herbert Hendin voiced concerns that the decision would legitimize homosexuality as a "lifestyle" and encourage young people to choose it over family life. When *Time* needed an expert on homosexuality for its 1975 article, it consulted Hendin, "the expert." No longer were homosexuals said to be created by overbearing mothers, weak fathers, and childhood seduc-tion, as Bieber and Socarides had argued. Hendin informed *Time* that "homosexuality will spread especially among the young, if social sanc-tions are removed."

> Says psychoanalysist Herbert Hendin: "anything goes" is a
> legitimate attitude for consenting adults toward each other,
> but for a culture to declare it as a credo is to miss entirely
> the stake all of us have in the harmony between the sexes
> and in the family as the irreplaceable necessity of society.
> This is a society that is increasingly denying its importance
> by calling it tolerance, preaching resignation and naming all
> this progress.[38]

According to Hendin, homosexuals were not a threat in themselves,
but their media presence and laws specifically protecting them from
discrimination promoted homosexuality as another "acceptable"
lifestyle choice. If homosexuality were free of traditional social stigma,
more young people might choose to be gay and lesbian, rather than
raise families. Therefore, Hendin concluded, the sacred foundation of
society itself, the family, was threatened by gay rights. Throughout the
rest of the 1970s and beyond, this argument became the ideological
underpinning of an anti–gay rights backlash.

   Time noted in 1975 that as in previous years many straight Americans remained "viscerally hostile" toward homosexuals while others
"advocated full acceptance and equality." A growing third category of
heterosexuals, however, were "more tolerant, want to be fair and
avoid injustice and yet cannot approve behavior that they believe
harmful to the very fabric of society. They are especially concerned by
the new contention that homosexuality is in every way as desirable as
heterosexuality." More people seemed to feel that the gay liberation
movement had gone beyond securing equal protections of the law and
had begun actively promoting the acceptance of homosexuality.
According to *Time*,

> It is the goal of full acceptance, which no known society past
> or present has granted to homosexuals that makes many
> Americans apprehensive. So much so that it sometimes
> skews debates about basic American rights. Many fear the
> demands that seem to flow logically from the assertion that
> "gay is good." For instance the legal right to marry; homo-
> sexual instruction in the school sex courses; affirmative

action or quotas in hiring; and gay love stories to go with heterosexual puppy-love stories in libraries and schools.[39]

In the minds of an increasing number of Americans, the public presence of homosexuality was both annoying and threatening. In response to the *Time* article, one reader wrote, "Homosexuality was once called 'the love that dare not speak its name.' Now it won't shut up."

Conservative religious leaders in the mid-1970s turned their attention from the "evils" of homosexuality or sodomy and began railing against gay rights activists and the media presence of homosexuality. Monsignor George A. Kelly, Professor at St. John's University warned readers of *The Catholic News* of the increasing power and prominence of "politicized homosexuals . . . a special breed of men and women on a crusade to sell the homosexual life style to as many people as they can. . . . And there should be no doubt that legal equality of homosexuality with heterosexuality (hopefully leading to social equality) is precisely the long range goal of the self-styled gay activists." Kelly accurately explained how the gay liberation movement had succeeded: "The strength of gay activism derives from its political base on the campuses of our more distinguished American universities. Gays have come out of the college closet with a vengeance. . . . Realizing the educative power of the media, they have persuaded both NBC and CBS to allow 'gay input' to programs dealing with homosexuality."[40] Kelly understood that the gay rights movement had begun to succeed by breaking the conspiracy of silence and manipulating the media.

Anxiety about the public presence of homosexuality on the campuses and airwaves was different than the old concerns about gays converting young people through seduction or working in sensitive government positions. In the eyes of the new opponents to gay rights, homosexuals themselves were a lesser threat than laws that banned discrimination based on sexual orientation or TV shows that encouraged the social acceptance of homosexuals. To their way of thinking, every law and television program that promoted greater tolerance for homosexuals undermined the American family. A new movement was needed to target gay rights laws and media corporations that seemed sympathetic to homosexuals. By the mid-1970s the gay liberation movement had precipitated its own dialectical opposite: an anti–gay rights movement.

Fittingly, the first major political manifestation of the anti–gay rights backlash emerged in New York City, home of the "greatest homosexual population in the world" and the media capital of the world. Between 1971 and 1973, Intro 475, the first legislation in the United States to ban discrimination based on sexual orientation, failed to move out of the city council's General Welfare Committee despite coming up for a vote three times. During debates on the bill, opponents complained that the legislation would allow transvestites to become firemen, police officers, and teachers.[41] When the bill reappeared in 1974 as Intro 2, the city council sponsors tried to diffuse the "transvestite issue," by amending the bill to state that nothing in it "should be construed to bear upon standards of attire or dress codes." The amendment reassured enough swing voters on the general welfare committee to move the bill to the whole city council.

The so-called "transvestite amendment" divided the gay activist community. Always a firebrand, GAA president Morty Manford promised to fight for the rights of cross-dressers, while Bruce Voeller, National Gay Task Force president, claimed the transvestite amendment "doesn't dilute or affect the bill; it's just a clarification."[42] Neither Manford nor Voeller nor any other New York activists anticipated how insignificant the issue of "transvestites becoming firemen" had become to opponents of gay rights by 1974.

Once the General Welfare committee passed the measure on to the city council, it seemed certain to become law until the Catholic Church launched a last-ditch grassroots campaign to defeat it. In letters to parishioners and editorials in the New York archdiocese's official newspaper, church leaders pronounced the bill as "contrary to the best interests of society" and a "menace to family life."[43] The church's commentaries did not dredge up the old fears of transvestites in the police force or gay teachers seducing and converting students. The Church Committee for the Protection of Family Life in New York City issued a statement that "religious opposition has never been based on the idea that many homosexuals are child-abusers or that most homosexuals are seducers of young people. Nor have religious representatives recommended the firing of all persons of homosexual tendencies from sensitive positions."[44] The church argued that officially banning discrimination would remove the social stigma from homosexuality and threaten the family. *Catholic News* asserted, "Passage of Intro 2 will be interpreted by many as public license to uninhibited manifestations of sexual preference or sexual relationships and the absence of any moral norm in human sexuality." *The Tablet*, the Brooklyn diocesan newspaper, claimed:

> In its present form Intro 2 appears: 1) to admit homosexual orientation as a proper and equal alternative to heterosexual orientation. 2) To coerce public acceptance of overt homosexual activity. 3) To propose conditions in employment, housing, and the use of public accommodations which would amount to an atmosphere favorable to engaging in and promoting overt homosexual activity. 4) To coerce the general public into unwanted contact with homosexual subculture. 5) To deny parents, educators and persons responsible for child care and youth guidance the right to protect children and teenagers from a powerful immoral influence. The general public has the right to live in an environment which excludes daily exposure to a deviant life-style where they live and work.[45]

Opponents of the discrimination ban acknowledged the right of homosexuals to live without harassment and have equal access to housing and most jobs; they argued however, that legal protections for homosexuals would threaten the family and violate the rights of heterosexuals. There was great power in the argument that granting rights to homosexuals conflicted with the right of heterosexuals to protect the sanctity and stability of "the family."

In the days leading up to the vote on Intro 2, council members were flooded with mail opposing the measure. Suddenly opponents to the bill were no longer talking about transvestites; they were repeating the arguments of the church. "This is not a civil rights issue," said Republican minority leader Angelo Arculeo. "It is an attempt to give legal identity to the homosexual's orientation and thereby mandate public acceptance."[46] Councilman Monroe Cohen, who was one of the bill's sponsors, changed his position after the public uproar. In explaining the switch, Cohen said publicly, "I cannot accept the homosexual lifestyle for my three children." Councilman Samuel Wright, D-Brooklyn, said he "could not find it in my heart to vote no," but he abstained because his Bedford-Stuyvesant constituents were "afraid the homosexual lifestyle might influence the young and the uninitiated, make homosexuality seem normal." In a twenty-two to nineteen vote, the council rejected Intro 2 largely due to the Catholic church's campaign.[47] Over the next decade, the claim that homosexuals were a threat to the family, to society, and to the rights of parents would become conservatives' principle argument against legally protecting homosexuals from discrimination.

Popular discomfort with the gay rights movement had a profound impact on how the Democratic presidential candidates in 1976 approached the topic of homosexuality. The gay rights movement was just one of the social movements that pushed the 1972 Democratic nominee George McGovern and the other liberal Democratic candidates to support positions that were mostly unpopular with the majority of the electorate. At the time, all of the Democratic presidential hopefuls except Edmund Muskie endorsed gay rights. Four years later, Democratic candidates desperate to retake the White House after eight years of exile were determined to resist being maumaued into taking unpopular positions on social issues. Democratic candidate, Senator Henry Jackson, declared that homosexuality was "wrong" and "bad" and that he would "not be a party to acquiescing and promoting it. I am not about to give in to the gay liberation and codify into law the practice of homosexuality. . . . It is the first beginning of a breakdown of a society."[48] When Jackson was heckled by gay rights demonstrators at a campaign rally in Queens, he snapped back: "Go on and have your own rally. Our people want hard work. We don't want gay work. We don't want gay jobs. You have your gay jobs. You just do your own thing and stay away."[49] Four years earlier a similar public statement by a major Democratic candidate would have been unlikely. By 1976 the political winds had begun to shift against the gay rights movement.

The Democratic Party nominee, Georgia governor Jimmy Carter, actually called homosexuality a "sin." Carter ran as a born-again Christian and aggressively courted the evangelical vote, particularly during the early primaries in the South. But once the primary race moved to the North and West, Carter was forced to address the issue of gay rights and gave surprisingly liberal support. In a letter to a gay group in Philadelphia, Carter declared, "I oppose all forms of discrimination on the basis of sexual orientation. As president I can assure you that all policies of the federal government would reflect this commitment." Carter even promised to sign a national gay rights bill that Bella Abzug had submitted to the House of Representatives.

In early 1976, Jean O'Leary joined the National Gay Task Force staff after leaving GAA. O'Leary won a seat as a delegate to the 1976 Democratic National Convention and attended the party platform hearings on behalf of NGTF. O'Leary lobbied for a statement of support for gay rights in the presidential platform, but Carter's people resisted, sensing that after McGovern's landslide loss in 1972, the Democrats needed to move closer to the political center. While lobbying for the gay rights plank, O'Leary met one of Carter's key aides, Midge Costanza, and they soon became lovers.[50] Costanza put the gay rights language before a vote of the platform committee, but it was tabled by a vote of fifty-seven to twenty-seven.

After his inauguration, Carter appointed Midge Costanza the first female assistant to the president. The gay rights movement now had an agent in the West Wing. Costanza made a historic contribution to the cause by arranging a meeting at the White House with the National Gay Task Force. Wearing ties and dresses reminiscent of the homophile demonstrators of the mid-1960s, the Task Force delegates, including Jean O'Leary, Bruce Voeller, and Elaine Noble, met with Costanza and other administration officials to discuss various issues, including the military's policies on the discharge of homosexuals, the denial of security clearances based on sexual orientation, and income tax provisions for same-sex households. As a result of NGTF's follow-up meeting with Immigration and Naturalization Service officials, the INS declared its intention to review an immigration policy that barred gay aliens from the United States.[51]

The White House meeting had two major effects. As the NGTF had hoped, media reports on the visit marked the normalization and political legitimacy of the gay rights struggle in the eyes of many Americans.[52] But those same reports also contributed to the rising anxiety of people who had been watching the gay rights movement on TV for years and feared perverts and radicals had hijacked their country, from the streets of the nation's cities to the offices of the West Wing. One of these anxious Americans was Anita Bryant, a television personality and former Miss Oklahoma who had recently begun fronting a campaign against a Miami law that banned discrimination based on sexual orientation.

While standing on the White House driveway, journalists asked NGTF leaders for their reactions to Anita Bryant's crusade against a Dade County homosexual rights ordinance. Some in the delegation were annoyed. How could Anita Bryant's local movement possibly compare with a White House visit?[53] Neither the NGTF nor any political commentators foresaw how this local grassroots campaign was symptomatic of a national conservative reaction to gay liberation's success in carving out a positive presence for homosexuality in America's media and political sphere.

Bryant told the press after the NGTF's White House visit, "I protest the action of the White House staff in dignifying these activists for special privileges with a serious discussion of their alleged human rights." Bryant complained that the campaign for gay rights legislation was intended to do more than outlaw discrimination: "Behind the high sounding appeal against discrimination in jobs and housing, which is not a problem to the 'closet' homosexual, they are really asking to be blessed in their abnormal life style by the office of the President of the United States. What these people really want hidden behind obscure legal phrases, is the legal right to propose to our children that there is an acceptable alternate way of life—that being a homosexual or lesbian is not really wrong or illegal."[54]

Bryant accurately deduced the ulterior motive behind the White House visit and the gay rights bills that had been passed by dozens of municipal legislatures in the mid-1970s. Gay rights activists from Donald Webster Cory to Ethan Geto had worked to challenge the image of homosexuals as psychological deviants and criminals by replacing it with the view that gays and lesbians were minorities worthy of rights, just like other minority groups. When the Gay Activists Alliance first pushed for a municipal gay rights bill in New York City, the Activists thought a gay rights law would not only limit antihomosexual discrimination in housing and jobs but would also signify official recognition of homosexuals as minorities. As more people perceived homosexuality to be a minority status rather than a sickness or a sin, more homosexuals would feel free to abandon the closet and live openly. Gay rights activists celebrated the increasing acceptance of homosexuals as a legitimate minority; Bryant saw it as a threat to the social order. Unfortunately for the gay rights movement, Bryant's views were shared by a growing portion of the population who were anxious about gay liberation's great success in making homosexuality socially acceptable.

In 1977 when religious conservatives in Dade County, Florida, decided to fight to overturn a municipal ban on sexual orientation discrimination, they enlisted Anita Bryant, celebrity singer and the second runner-up in the 1959 Miss America contest. Bryant combined glamour with a wholesomeness that was enhanced by her position as a spokesperson for the Florida Citrus Growers. Every day, the former Miss Oklahoma appeared on TV in juice commercials reminding Americans that "a day without orange juice is like a day without sunshine." Leaders of the movement to pass the Miami gay rights law initially dismissed Bryant as "a joke; a cracker from Oklahoma who still lived in the pre-disco age."[55] They did not see that her square persona actually made her appealing to a citizenry increasingly anxious about the previous two decades of dramatic social upheaval.

Like the campaign against gay rights legislation in New York City in 1975, the Save Our Children Campaign attempted to convince voters that tolerance of homosexuality threatened society. In an announcement of her support for the Save Our Children Campaign, Bryant declared:

> I don't hate homosexuals! But as a mother I must protect my children from their evil influence. Defending the rights of my children and yours. Militant homosexuals want their sexual behavior and preference to be considered respectable and accepted by society. They want to recruit your children and teach them the virtue of becoming a homosexual. . . . I don't hate homosexuals. I love them enough to tell them the truth. . . . [We] must not give them the legal right to destroy the moral fiber of our families and our nation.

Bryant's "I don't hate homosexuals" refrain was a significant departure from the previous generation of antihomosexual rhetoric that
evoked sick deviants looking to seduce young people. Instead, she
employed the argument that a ban on discrimination would signify
the social acceptance of homosexuality, which would encourage
young people to eschew family life in favor of the "homosexual
lifestyle." Although the Save Our Children campaign constantly
evoked the image of the gay sexual predator in its advertisements, ultimately its most effective line of argument was that the gay rights law
threatened "the family."

To petition the Dade County metro commission to put the gay
rights legislation up for popular referendum, the Save Our Children
Campaign only had to collect ten thousand names; sixty-four thousand
signatures were collected just six weeks after its inception. The metro
commission accordingly voted to put the referendum on the ballot in
a special election on June 7, 1977. Bryant understood the significance
of the looming vote:

> By its action today, the commission, for better or worse, has
> made Dade County a national battleground in the fight for
> civil rights of parents and their children. Homosexual acts
> are not only illegal, they are immoral. And through the
> power of the ballot box, I believe the parents and straight-
> thinking normal majority will soundly reject the attempt to
> legitimize homosexuals and their recruitment plans for our
> children. We shall not let the nation down.[56]

The involvement of the telegenic orange juice queen in the anti–gay
rights campaign triggered a national media frenzy. The *St. Louis Globe-
Democrat* published glowing editorials: "Bravo for Anita Bryant," and
"Let's Hear It for Anita Bryant." The *St. Joseph (MO) Gazetteer* asked,
"Whose moral values will prevail? Society's or those of homosexual
activists?" Nationally syndicated columnists like Gary Wills and Russell
Baker commented on the Miami law, while *Who's Who,* an NBC-TV
show, aired an account of the Save Our Children campaign.[57]

Around the country, people who had become increasingly uneasy
with gay rights thrilled to news clips of Bryant bashing the Miami law

and then belting out "The Battle Hymn of the Republic." One evening the Miami bureau editor of the Associated Press received a phone call from a few diners in a Kansas City restaurant who wanted to chat about Bryant: "Apparently they got to talking about the ordinance and were opposed to it and so they phoned to give us their view. That kind of grassroots interest is what happened with the Dade County bill." Bryant's involvement triggered such media interest that on the night of the referendum Walter Cronkite told his millions of viewers that the fight in Dade County was "an internationally watched campaign that had become a symbolic battleground for the gay rights movement everywhere."[58]

Bryant's participation posed a particular problem for the gay rights movement. In her television appearances and comments to the press, she wrapped the American flag around the anti–gay rights movement by claiming that tolerance for homosexuality presented a threat to the family, and by extension, to American society. *People* magazine even quoted Bryant's claim that "heaven is on her side" and "there's no sympathy up there for gays."[59] On NBC's *Today Show*, host Tom Brokaw asked Bryant if she favored a federal law outlawing homosexuality. "I believe," she intoned, "in God's laws and the law of the land should be in alignment with it." Brokaw pushed her further, asking if she wanted "a federal law against gays." She replied, "yes I do." The former beauty queen's ability to weave celebrity, motherhood, patriotism, and God together with antigay discrimination posed a serious threat to the gay rights movement. The made-for-TV movement had met the made-for-TV backlash.

The leaders of the campaign to pass the Miami gay rights law soon realized they were outmatched by the Save Our Children media campaign and hired two gay public relations consultants, Jim Foster of San Francisco and Ethan Geto of New York. Geto reorganized the loose coalition that had formed to defend the gay rights law into a more professional organization and reformulated its message. He decided to avoid getting bogged down trying to counter Bryant's demonization of homosexuals and instead to present the gay rights ordinance simply as a human rights issue: "No matter what you think about homosexuality, don't homosexuals deserve a job? A roof over his or her head? To be able to eat?"[60] Geto also advised the Miami coalition not to waste time and energy reaching out to the socially conservative Cuban and African-American communities. The campaign to defend the Miami gay rights law would shoot to win just enough votes operating under a simple formula: "Beach + Liberals + Condos + Gays = Victory."[61]

Geto also launched a campaign to counteract the national media attention triggered by Bryant and Save Our Children. The GAA veteran realized that even if the gay rights movement lost in Dade County, it could score a greater victory though a media campaign of its own. Geto hoped media reports on the referendum would "show the nation that there were talented, skilled professionals"—like himself—"in politics who would come in and give their services to gay people."[62] To counter Bryant's flag waving, the campaign to defend the gay rights ordinance enlisted Vietnam vet Leonard Matlovich and former NFL running back Dave Kopay as spokesmen. What could be more all-American than representatives of the U.S. military and NFL football?

As more and more news reports about the Miami fight reached the homes of millions of Americans, Anita Bryant simultaneously became the greatest threat to the gay rights movement and its greatest inadvertent ally. A 1977 NGTF mailing to its members stated that Bryant's "national prominence . . . insures national news coverage for developments in the Dade County struggle, while the feebleness of her arguments and the embarrassing backwardness of the stance both made her attacks easier to counteract and tends to generate a liberal backlash in our favor." The gay rights movement hoped to turn Bryant into a symbol of bigotry similar to Bull Connor, the Birmingham, Alabama, sheriff who generated unprecedented attention for the civil rights movement when he opened fire hoses and unleashed German shepherds on civil rights marchers in 1963. Throughout the nation, gay rights groups held anti-Anita Bryant fund-raisers. Tens of thousands of dollars were raised at an "Anita-thon" in Cleveland, an "Anita Bryant Look-A-Like" contest in San Francisco, an "Orange Ball" in Chicago, a "Squeeze Anita Weekend" in New Orleans, and a "Disco for Democracy" party at New York's Waldorf Astoria. At an "Anita Roast" in Washington, D.C., City Council member and civil rights veteran Marion Barry told the audience, "I've tried in my public career to be as supportive of gay rights as possible." All around the country in the summer of 1977, thousands of people sported T-shirts that read "Squeeze this Fruit for Anita" and decorated their cars with bumper stickers that declared "A Day Without Equal Rights Is Like A Day Without Sunshine."[63] Donations from all around the country flooded Ethan Geto's operation, finally totaling $300,000. Geto was able to spend $43,000 on advertising space in the *Miami Herald* alone.[64]

The San Francisco-based writer Armistead Maupin noted how the anti-Anita Bryant campaign stirred the political fervor of the gay community in his hometown: "There was never anything for them to identify with before," Maupin wrote. When Bryant appeared at a banquet in Houston, four thousand protestors joined a candlelight march through the downtown and held a massive rally, singing favorites from Bryant's repertory, including "We Shall Overcome," "America the Beautiful," and "Jesus Loves Me." Gazing out over the massive crowd, a beaming Houston gay community activist told a *New York Times* reporter, "I've been trying to organize gays in Houston for three years, and all I can say is, 'Thank You, Anita.' "[65] Bryant's personal appearances in Dallas, New Orleans, and Chicago also touched off demonstrations.[66] One gay newspaper's headline read, "Homosexuality is Hot . . . Thanks to Anita."

> Our parades and marches were greeted with boredom, condescending nods until Anita. Media people love us because we are news and can help fill that huge appetite for volume reporting that is necessary to fill up so many hours of TV time and newspaper editions. . . . Pick up the National Enquirer or turn on your TV. We may be being given a so called negative connotation. . . . That is irrelevant. Children now know that there are millions of homosexuals and that they lead every kind of lifestyle.[67]

One of the leaders of the fight to preserve the gay rights ordinance in Miami told the *New York Times*, "I've traveled almost constantly around the nation. . . . I've detected the politicization of people, both gays and straights, reacting to what happened here in Dade County. Individuals who had never been involved publicly in gay rights, business and professional people, came out of the closet on this issue because of the bigotry and discrimination expressed by our opponents."[68] The gay

rights movement that had suffered from apathy and a sense of purposelessness in the mid-1970s was suddenly revived by a national gay
community that felt itself under attack by Anita Bryant.

Within a few weeks of initiating her crusade, Anita Bryant became an
object not only of scorn and fear but also of ridicule, thanks to Johnny
Carson and other comedians who turned her into a laughingstock.[69]
One television commentator wrote, "Anita Bryant has become the
female Archie Bunker; a living caricature of abrasive bigotry." Night
after night, Carson elicited the cheers and laughter from his largely heterosexual studio audience with jokes about the prudish, self-righteous
orange juice huckster. Was the New York blackout an "act of God"? No,
explained Carson, because "Anita Bryant would never have given him
time off." In a routine about mock predictions for the future, Carson
prophesized that in 1978, "at the insistence of Anita Bryant, the Mup-
pets will undergo a sex test." One night, the King of Late Night promised his audience, "a little later on, Anita Bryant will be out here and try
to knock off Truman Capote's hat with a Florida orange." Other television shows also mined Bryant's laugh factor. When *Laugh-In* producer
George Schlatter discussed possible lightning-rod topics for a new version of the show to be seen on NBC, he conceded that "you don't have
the war anymore—but you do have Anita Bryant."[70]

One television commentator noted that "thanks to the speed with
which television affects social attitudes" Johnny Carson and other
comedians had undermined the forces of "homophobia" more effectively and "more quickly than any amount of homosexually generated
propaganda could have done."[71] For decades, comedians, particularly
those on late-night network television shows, had exploited and perpetuated the stereotype of the effeminate silly dandy, a caricature that
was perhaps the greatest impediment to the credibility of a gay rights
movement. In its campaign to counter the gay stereotypes, the Gay
Activists Alliance in the early 1970s targeted several famous talk show
hosts including Johnny Carson. Just a few years later, Carson and other
television comedians turned their ample wit and unrivaled media presence on the movement's greatest enemy.

In the months after the Miami referendum, Bryant became synony-
mous with bigotry in the minds of so many Americans, that when *Ladies
Home Journal* asked eight hundred American high school students

"Who has done the most damage to the world?" an equal number responded with Adolf Hitler and Anita Bryant.[72]

Back in Miami, however, opposition to the gay rights ordinance proved too strong. On the eve of the election, Leonard Matlovich watched a local news broadcast in horror as a Miami mother told the TV camera: "I don't want my son taught by homosexuals. I don't want him to become a homosexual." Feeling depressed, he immediately called his boyfriend in Washington: "I think we're asking too much, David, in 1977." Matlovich was right. The next day Miami voters chose to repeal the ordinance 208,000 to 92,000: a two-to-one landslide. Assessing the election, *New York Times* columnist William Safire concluded that the vote in Dade County, ordinarily a liberal bastion in Florida, was not the result of Bryant's evangelical, patriotic appeal or her demonization of homosexuals. Instead he pointed out that voters rejected Ethan Geto's framing of the referendum as "civil rights versus outright bigotry" and saw the vote as a question of "tacit toleration versus outright approval of homosexuality." By the late 1970s most Americans were inclined to let consenting adults do what they liked in private. However, according to Safire, they also feared that gay rights laws might signify social approval of homosexuality. Miami voters simply accepted the argument that such public approval might encourage young people to choose the "gay lifestyle" over "family life."[73]

After hearing the dispiriting referendum returns, Matlovich again called his boyfriend: "Better believe the Republicans and the right wing are going to pick up on this, and they are going to use it to gain their political strength . . . you better be scared."[74] Once again Matlovich's words would prove prophetic.

The loss in Dade County was not a total setback for the gay rights movement. In fact, it revitalized the political fervor of the national gay and lesbian community. As news of the referendum returns reached the rest of the nation, spontaneous rallies arose in gay communities throughout the United States. At two in the morning, one thousand people marched through Greenwich Village from the Stonewall Inn to the Bank Street home of mayoral candidate and former Congresswoman Bella Abzug. Awaking to the calls of "Bella! Bella!" outside her window, Abzug threw on her bathrobe and slippers and delivered a sympathetic address to the marchers from her front stoop. After reassuring the masses on her usually tranquil, tree-lined street that the Bryant campaign had revitalized the gay rights movement, she gently concluded with "and now it's time to go to bed." At a late-night rally in San Francisco's Castro district, Harvey Milk thrilled a massive crowd with a stirring address: "This is the power of the gay community. Anita's going to create a national gay force!" Six months later Milk became a symbol of the revitalized "gay force" when he defeated a field of seventeen candidates to become the first openly gay person to be elected to the San Francisco Board of Supervisors.[75] The day after the Miami referendum, gay rights marches were held in Los Angeles, Indianapolis, New Orleans, Boston, and Houston.[76] The intense, countrywide reaction was the manifestation of a cohesive national gay community. The gay liberation movement had transformed America's gay communities from atomized pockets interested in local issues like police harassment into a national community with a fervent interest in the fate of fellow homosexuals in other parts of the country.

The gay and lesbian press began to develop a higher degree of professionalism in the wake of the Anita Bryant campaign. The news editor for the San Francisco's *Bay Area Reporter*, George Mendehall, recalled how in the late 1970s, "the gay press had matured. We took gay journalism a lot more serious than in the beginning of the decade. We had to. Marching in the streets wasn't going to get us liberated. The battlefront was the ballot box—and that called for a new kind of journalism." Gay entertainment and pornographic magazines that had previously eschewed politics began to print political articles and opinion pieces. The leading gay entertainment magazine in the south, *Cruise*, surmised that Save Our Children actually may have saved the languishing gay political movement. The National Gay Task Force was a major benefactor of the gay community's new political interest. In the four months after the Dade county battle, its dues-paying membership doubled. Even the moribund Gay Activists Alliance saw a brief revival of its active support during the summer of 1977.

The gay community's revitalized political fervor culminated in a boycott of Florida orange juice.[77] Gay bars around the country began to serve Tang in their screwdrivers. The Florida orange juice producers immediately felt the impact of the national boycott. Edward Taylor, the executive director of the Florida Department of Citrus, cited evidence that the anti-Bryant "campaign hurt sales. . . . That's no way to sell orange juice." To distance their products from the Miami referendum, Kraft, Minute Maid, and the Florida Citrus growers appealed a Florida law requiring them to stamp the state's name on their products. One of the food processors' lawyers explained, "I have nothing against [Bryant]. But it affects the sale of our products when people boycott it."[78] The Florida citrus growers briefly considered dropping Bryant from their ad campaign until they were pressured by conservative groups to stand by her. Art Darling, director of publicity for the Florida citrus growers, admitted to the *New York Times*, "the whole Anita thing is a mess. No matter what we decided, we're only going to lose. I wish she would just resign."[79] In 1978, NBC dropped Bryant from her regular spot on its Orange Bowl telecast, and the Singer sewing machine company decided not to hire her to host a new daytime television sewing program because of "the extensive national publicity arising from the controversial political activities [she had] been engaged in Dade County."[80] Bryant moaned that the cancellation of her TV show "destroys a dream that I have had since I was a child—a dream to have a television series of my own. . . . The blacklisting of Anita Bryant has begun."[81] Her problem was that while a majority of Americans opposed laws that would signal social acceptance of homosexuality, a significant number also had come to see homosexuality as a private matter worthy of tolerance, if not respect. Many Americans viewed Bryant's campaign not as a defense of the family or the nation but as a manifestation of extremism and bigotry.

The public distaste for Anita Bryant was a sign of how much had changed since the gay rights movement began establishing a prominent presence for homosexuality in American media and politics. A new generation of Americans had grown up in a society in which homosexuality was no longer shrouded in stereotypes. They regularly saw appealing gay characters on sitcoms and respectable gay activists on talk shows. They listened to politicians and journalists seriously discuss "gay rights," a concept that would have been absurd in the previous era when homosexuals were depicted in the old stereotypical ways. They were told by the American Psychiatric Association that homosexuals were not sick. And they boogied by the millions to the sounds of the Village People. Like all revolutions, Gay Power irreversibly altered the entire society.

American homosexuals also changed. They were no longer ghettoized in underground urban subcultures or in lives of secrecy and shame. The gay rights movement created a national gay community that offered American homosexuals a new sense of connectedness to those who openly shared their identity. As a community they could be proud and powerful. No longer could public figures explicitly attack homosexuals without generating antipathy not just throughout the gay community but also among a great number of straights.

The success of the Gay Power, however, came at a steep price. Like all revolutions it was followed by a conservative reaction. The Save Our Children campaign was just one manifestation of a national anti–gay rights movement that fed off popular anxieties about the political and media presence of homosexuality. Voters, uneasy with the new tolerance of homosexuality, rallied to politicians and crusaders who targeted laws that banned discrimination against homosexuals. Not only did gay rights legislation continue to face stiff resistance in many localities; gay rights laws that were passed in the mid-1970s were repealed in Wichita, St. Paul, and Eugene in the wake of the Miami vote.

California state senator John Briggs brought the antigay rights backlash to the nation's largest state in 1978 when he initiated a referendum to fire any schoolteacher, school administrator, or counselor for "advocating, soliciting, imposing, encouraging or promoting private or public sexual acts . . . between persons of the same sex in a manner likely to come to the attention of other employees or students." Much to his surprise, Briggs found almost no public officials willing to support his referendum, and he was openly opposed by all of the Democratic and Republican candidates for governor and all of California's major newspapers. Even former Republican governor Ronald Reagan opposed the Briggs initiative, explaining that while he opposed teaching "a so-called gay life-style in our school . . . Proposition 6 has the potential of infringing on basic rights of privacy and perhaps even constitutional rights."[82] Pollster Mervin Field explained the wide-ranging opposition to the Briggs initative: "The public will tolerate homosexuality, but will not accept it. The ordinances in Dade County and Eugene and Wichita basically said you've got to give homosexuals their rights; you've got to accept them. The ordinances were seen as sanctifying the activities of homosexuals. [The Briggs referendum] is different. It says you've been tolerating this for some time and now you've got to stop tolerating it."[83] Californians voted against the Briggs measure by more than a million votes. Even a majority of the voters in ultraconservative Orange County, Briggs's home district, rejected it.

The defeat of the Briggs initiative signified a stalemate between the gay rights movement and its backlash. The passage of municipal gay rights ordinances that had seemed so frequent and inexorable in the mid-1970s slowed to a trickle in the late 1970s and 1980s. At the same time, campaigns to openly restrict the rights of homosexuals foundered on a few legacies of the gay power revolution: a vital national gay community, a liberal commitment to homosexual minority rights, and a libertarian acknowledgment of sexual orienta-tion as a private matter. Americans may not have wanted to see the passage of new gay rights laws, but they also tended to oppose anti–gay rights laws. By 1980, even Anita Bryant embraced this com-promise. "I'm more inclined to say live and let live," she told the *New York Times*, "just don't flaunt it or try to legalize it."[84] In such a polit-ical environment, the gay rights movement failed to win much polit-ical success over the subsequent two decades, but it also did not suffer a reversal of its revolutionary accomplishments.

Although the anti–gay rights backlash did not pass much new legis-lation in the 1970s, it did become a very powerful force in American electoral politics. In the years before the gay rights movement pushed American liberals to defend the minority rights of homosexuals, there was almost no discussion about gay rights during presidential elections. That all changed during the 1980 presidential campaign. During the 1976 presidential campaign, Jimmy Carter, a born-again Christian, enjoyed heavy evangelical support that helped him sweep the South. Over the next four years, many evangelical and fundamentalist leaders and organizations, including Jerry Falwell's powerful anti–gay rights Moral Majority, became disaffected with Carter in large part because of his limited support for gay rights. Throughout his political career, Ronald Reagan, the 1980 Republican presidential nominee, had never publicly expressed opposition to gay rights and in fact opposed the

Briggs initiative. But Reagan suddenly changed his public position during the 1980 presidential election. The former California governor told the *Los Angeles Times* that the gay rights movement sought "a recognition and acceptance of an alternative lifestyle which I do not believe society can condone, nor can I." When a reporter asked why not, he said, "Well, you could find that in the Bible. It says that in the eyes of the lord, it is an abomination." Carter, who won the southern evangelical vote and every southern state in 1976, lost all but Georgia and West Virginia to Reagan four years later.[85] While a variety of factors caused Southern evangelicals to vote Republican in 1980, the perception that Carter supported gay rights certainly played a major role. Reagan's victory taught Republicans that they could win the support of many traditionally Democratic voters by attacking gay rights, a lesson that they would employ for decades to come. This anti–gay rights backlash, however, was insignificant in comparison to a far graver crisis that hit the American gay community in the 1980s.

THE CONSPIRACY
OF SILENCE REDUX

In December 1981, *Newsweek* ran a story about a mysterious outbreak of "Diseases that Plague Gays." "The promiscuous homosexual male has long been vulnerable to hepatitis and venereal diseases like syphilis and gonorrhea," *Newsweek* reported.

> But an unusual assortment of disorders—some of them deadly—has recently broken out in the homosexual community. . . . The epidemic does not affect homosexual women; it seems closely linked to the life-style of gay men with many sexual contacts. It coincides with the burgeoning of bathhouses, gay bars and bookstores in major cities where homosexual men meet.[1]

By the early 1980s the gay rights movement had achieved revolutionary success combating the idea that homosexuals were sinful, criminal, and sick. At a time when the American public could accept that homosexuals were doctors, lawyers, and soldiers, the initial media coverage of "the gay plague" dredged up the old notion that homosexuals were pernicious threats to society. As Charles Krauthammer wrote in *The New Republic*, "Now just as homosexuality was prepared to take the last step and free itself from the medical mantle . . . comes the 'gay plague.' Just as society was ready to grant that homosexuality is not ill-ness, it is seized with the idea that homosexuality breeds illness."[2]

The first mainstream news report about the disease, later known as AIDS, was a July 1981 *New York Times* article, "Rare Cancer Seen in 41 Homosexuals: 'Doctors in New York and California have diagnosed among homosexual men 41 cases of a rare and often rapidly fatal form of cancer. Eight of the victims died less than 24 months after the diag-nosis was made.' " Doctors identified the cancer as Kaposi's Sarcoma (KS), which usually appeared as spots on the victim's legs and took a slow course of up to ten years. The young gays who had KS however, displayed violet-colored spots on all parts of their bodies and died shortly after being diagnosed. The article noted ominously that "the patients had serious malfunctions of two types of cells called T and B cell lym-phocytes, which have important roles in fighting infections and cancer."[3]

The new disease soon became officially designated as Gay Related Immune Deficiency. Bruce Voeller and the National Gay Task Force saw how the name of the disease placed a stigma on the gay commu-nity and successfully lobbied the Centers for Disease Control to change the designation to something less specific.[4] "Acquired Immune Defi-ciency Syndrome," or AIDS, was chosen to separate the condition from a congenital defect or a chemically induced immune problem.[5]

The outbreak of AIDS came at a particularly rough time. Shortly after Ronald Reagan entered office in 1981, his administration pro-posed a cut of nearly 50 percent in funding for the Centers for Disease Control and Prevention, along with a reduction of $127 million from the budget of the National Institutes of Health.[6] While the National Institutes of Health had spent $36,100 per toxic shock death in 1982 and $34,841 per fatal case of Legionnaires' disease, it spent just $8,991 per AIDS death.

Given the paucity of federal funds, the gay community had to rely upon itself to deal with the crisis. In August 1981, eighty gay New Yorkers gathered in the apartment of novelist Larry Kramer to found an organization to specifically address the lack of public funding for AIDS-related programs. That night they raised $6,635 in seed money for the organization, Gay Men's Health Crisis (GMHC). The New York gay community rallied to GMHC's call for funds and volunteers. Over the next two years, GMHC took in more than $600,000 from its fund-raisers and received a $200,000 grant from New York state and $24,000 from the city.

By 1983 GMHC had become a sophisticated social service organization with growing political power, thirty-two paid staff members, five hundred volunteers and a $900,000 budget. GMHC provided lawyers to help people with AIDS draw up wills and fight evictions and matched AIDS patients with volunteer "buddies" who shopped for groceries, cooked meals, filled out paperwork for social welfare benefits, and, most importantly, provided companionship. One volunteer recalled being asked by a patient, "Can you hold me for a minute? Nobody ever holds me anymore."[7] In two years GMHC had become the largest gay organization in the country and was a model for similar organizations in San Francisco and Los Angeles.[8] Just as the gay community rallied together to confront the political threat posed by the anti–gay rights backlash, it was once again jumping in to address a massive medical crisis that governmental authorities would not even officially acknowledge.

The lack of governmental support for AIDS services in the early days of the epidemic was largely due to the absence of a popular demand for action. The mainstream press was so slow to cover the crisis that most Americans remained ignorant of its seriousness until the mid-1980s. In 1981 two new cases of AIDS were diagnosed in New York each week, and one new case was discovered in the United States each day.[9] But that year the *New York Times* published only two stories on the epidemic while *Time* and *Newsweek* did not run their first stories on the disease until late December. In 1982 only thirty articles on AIDS appeared in the nation's leading news magazines and newspapers, and most of those were in the year's final days. A reporter at the *Wall Street Journal* found his stories on AIDS rejected repeatedly by the editors. Only after he changed tack and submitted an article about twenty-three heterosexuals, mostly heroin users, who were discovered to suffer from AIDS, did the disease make the newspaper with the largest circulation in the United States. Like the other newspapers, the *Wall Street Journal* began giving substantial coverage to AIDS only after it struck people who were not gay.[10]

The disease first became a topic of discussion on network television in December 1981 when ABC's *Good Morning America* host Frank Gifford interviewed the director of AIDS research at the U.S. Centers for Disease Control. Gifford began the interview by reading aloud the shocking numbers of deaths and new cases. "This is a terrible problem," Gifford continued, "How come nobody's paying any attention to it?"[11] When the *CBS Evening News* first covered the story in August 1982, Dan Rather observed, "Federal Health officials consider it an epidemic. Yet you rarely hear a thing about it. At first, it seemed to strike only one segment of the population. Now Barry Peterson tells us, this is no longer the case."[12] Not surprisingly, a major television news organization finally covered the story only after the disease began to affect straights.

The few stories that did make it into the mainstream media tended to reinforce the public's apathy and ignorance. Liberal editors downplayed the threat so as not to cause panic and held back details of how the disease was spread to avoid inflaming homophobes or offending gays. Ironically, well-meaning editors avoided the true story to protect gays from a political and social backlash. Rather than specifically talk about how the disease was transmitted through contact with semen and blood, journalists and editors vaguely referred to the exchange of "bodily fluids."[13] Using the term "bodily fluids" may have spared the delicate sensibilities of the American public but it also fed their fears. After all, saliva was also a bodily fluid.[14]

More than the lack of coverage or the vagueness of the reporting, the most harmful aspect of the early media reports on AIDS was their optimism. Pieces on AIDS usually ended on a positive note—a breakthrough or vaccine was just around the corner.[15] The press and the government seemed to collaborate in a conspiracy of silence redux. Bureaucrats thought they could restrict governmental spending if they downplayed the seriousness of the epidemic and so gave optimistic press releases. Reporters parroted the government's press releases without the slightest inclination to uncover whether the reported "facts" were true. This type of press release journalism had fallen out of vogue in the days of Vietnam and Watergate; it seemed to have made a comeback with the AIDS epidemic.[16]

No municipal government was more negligent about the AIDS crisis than the New York City authorities. Even though New Yorkers accounted for one-half of the nation's AIDS caseload in the early 1980s, there were no city programs to deal with the disease.[17] By the end of

1983 the New York City government's entire contribution to AIDS services was a $24,500 allocation to the Red Cross to provide home-attendant care to AIDS patients.[18] There were two major reasons why AIDS policy in New York remained nothing more than a laundry list of unmet promises and unfunded proposals until the mid-1980s: its negligent press and its negligent mayor.

By contrast, even though San Francisco had a third of the number of New York's AIDS cases, its municipal government put forth a major effort to address the problem. The Institute for Health Policy Studies at the University of California, San Francisco, later analyzed the differences between the municipal responses to AIDS in New York City and San Francisco and concluded that the disparate quality resulted in part from the vast differences in news coverage by the two cities' major newspapers. Between June 1982 and June 1985, the *San Francisco Chronicle* printed 442 AIDS stories, of which 67 made the front page. In the same period, the *New York Times* ran 226 stories, only 7 of which were on page one. From mid-1983 on, the *Chronicle*'s coverage focused on public policy aspects of the epidemic while the *Times* covered AIDS almost exclusively as a medical issue, placing little emphasis on social impact or policy. The University of California study concluded that "the extensive nature of coverage by the *Chronicle*, aside from providing a degree of health education not found in New York, helped sustain a level of political pressure on local government and health officials to respond to the AIDS crisis."[19] Eventually a series of newspaper articles on New York's tepid response to the crisis was published, but not in New York—it appeared in the *San Francisco Chronicle*.[20]

The other major reason for New York City's inaction was Mayor Ed Koch. Long suspected of being a homosexual, Koch was skittish about all gay issues. When confronted by a friend about the lack of municipal support for AIDS programs, Koch shrugged. "What should I do? The gay community doesn't like me. Everybody says I'm gay, and I'm not. I don't know what they want me to do."[21] As late as 1985 the official position of the New York City authorities was that the AIDS epidemic was *not* a crisis, even though the number of New Yorkers afflicted with the syndrome had reached three thousand.[22]

By the end of 1982 it was increasingly clear that the principle method of transmission of the disease was through sexual intercourse without condoms and the use of shared needles by intravenous drug users.[23] For people who engaged in these activities to avoid infection, they would have to modify their behavior. In the absence of substantial media coverage and governmental leadership, the gay community was left on its own to address the pivotal issue of public information. A great debate arose within the gay community about whether groups like GMHC should promote changes in sexual practices. Many leaders of the gay liberation movement like Marty Robinson and Jim Owles resented the suggestion that the disease was a result of hard-won sexual liberation.[24] Frank Kameny was quoted in a *Newsweek* cover story on AIDS defending the right to be promiscuous: "I have never looked upon 'promiscuity' as a dirty word. It is a natural and normal style of living, while monogamy is a deeply entrenched cultural overlay," mere "moralistic baggage society has been dumping for years." Kameny was proud that the gay liberation movement helped promote "the concept of recreational sex" and "opened the possibility of a much more relaxed and open [sexual] life style."[25] *The Advocate*'s publisher David Goodstein and its editor Robert McQueen subscribed to the idea that recreational sex was an integral part of male homosexuality and waited years before publishing articles that called for an alteration of sexual practices in light of the AIDS crisis.[26] Michael Callen, a twenty-eight-year-old with AIDS, complained that "the belief that was handed to me was that sex was liberating. Being gay was tied to the right to have sex."[27]

Another impediment to the critical campaign to change unsafe sexual behavior was the $100 million bathhouse and sex club industry that arose in the wake of the gay liberation movement. Owners of these centers of gay life were often community leaders who supported the financially starved gay political groups.[28] Advertisements for bathhouses were also a major source of income for the gay press. Reports on the cause of AIDS would strike directly at the financial interests of these influential gay community institutions.

Even when gay newspapers did print articles and opinion pieces suggesting a change in sexual practices, many gays were resistant. Steve Schulte, director of the Gay and Lesbian Community Services Center in Los Angeles, surmised that "gay people have been denied their sexuality for so long that this freedom has become very important."[29] Ray Hill, a gay political activist in Houston, told *Newsweek* that "gays have been hearing that sex will kill you for years, and they won't believe it about AIDS."[30]

Two men, however, refused to countenance the conspiracy of silence perpetrated by both the mainstream and gay press. Larry Kramer agitated constantly for a public information campaign that stressed the dangers of promiscuity. Writing in the gay newspaper *New York Native*, Kramer complained that he was "sick of guys who moan that giving up careless sex until this thing blows over is worse than death. How can they value life so little and cocks and asses so much?"[31]

Kramer was so incensed by the reluctance of GMHC to address the issue of unsafe behavior that he wrote an autobiographical play *The Normal Heart*, in which he bashed the New York gay leadership. At one point in the play, Kramer's alter ego asks, "Why didn't you guys fight for the right to get married instead of the right to legitimize promiscuity?" The play also suggested that the reason for Ed Koch's low profile on the issue of AIDS was his fear that his own sexuality would be exposed. Hours before the opening-night performance, Koch called a press conference to announce a $6 million program to provide AIDS patients with hospice care and day care for children. Koch also addressed the issue of his sexuality: "Regrettably in our society, one technique used in order to seek to slander an individual is to simply accuse that individual of homosexuality. These charges are made even more frequently if the person is a single individual over the age of forty and unmarried. It is an outrageous charge because in many cases it is untrue and even if true, irrelevant."[32]

No one did more to address the media silence than Randy Shilts, a reporter for the *San Francisco Chronicle*. Shilts kicked off a firestorm in March 1983 when he published a story about the results of an unreleased report that found that one in every 350 single men in the city's gay neighborhoods had been diagnosed with AIDS. That spring, attendance dropped in the baths, bars, and sex clubs in gay communities throughout the nation.[33] In an April 1983 issue of *The Advocate*, New York writer George Whitmore described how that spring Gotham's gays seemed to be "obsessed with AIDS. We've finally come down off the psychosexual binge of the 1970s."[34]

Shilts's report was a media trigger. The following month *Newsweek* bestowed an unprecedented level of "newsworthiness" to AIDS with a cover story on the disease. The cover displayed a disembodied hand holding a tube of blood ominously labeled, "Caution KS/AIDS."[35] While the gay leadership was reluctant to attribute the rapid spread of AIDS to risky behavior, *Newsweek* was not:

> For Gay America, a decade of carefree sexual adventure, a headlong gambol on the far side of the human libido, has all but come to a close. The flag of sexual liberation that had flown as the symbol of the gay movement has been lowered. Caution and responsibility—to oneself, to one's friends, to the larger and still pressing concerns of gay life in America—are now the watchwords of gay liberation.[36]

The article continued in a sanctimonious vein, observing that "the gays who got AIDS, it turned out, had often had many more sexual contacts (a lifetime average of 1100 partners) than the controls (500 partners). . . . In addition, many AIDS patients had used amyl nitrites, the sexually stimulating inhalants called 'poppers' that have been shown to produce immunosupression." *Newsweek* even suggested that "large amounts of sperm—also a suspected agent of immunosupression—might cause the problem if it were absorbed by the body during frequent oral or anal intercourse."[37] While *Newsweek*'s moralistic reportage failed to mention how the sexual practices of straights were also potentially dangerous, it was the first national publication to offer readers a detailed warning about how the disease was spread.

The *Newsweek* cover story was followed by a flood of stories about AIDS in the mainstream press. In the first three months of 1983, 169 stories about the epidemic ran in the nation's major newspapers and news magazines, more than four times the number of the last three months of 1982.[38] Between July and September 1983, the nation's major print media churned out another 726 stories on AIDS.[39] Even the supermarket tabloid the *Globe* ran an article claiming that AIDS was part of King Tut's curse, which had hit the United States when treasures from his tomb made a national tour.[40]

The media frenzy around AIDS predictably generated widespread popular anxiety. As late as 1983 a substantial minority of the public believed that casual social contact, like shaking hands with AIDS victims, would transmit the disease.[41] *Newsweek* reported that gays had been told to leave restaurants, refused ambulance service, and evicted from their apartments because they were suspected of having AIDS.[42] Fundamentalist preachers in Houston urged city officials to close gay bars as health hazards. A pool in Tulsa, Oklahoma, was drained by recreation officials after word spread that a local gay rights group held its third anniversary party there.[43] Even the San Francisco municipal government issued masks and gloves to firefighters and police officers for use in close contact with homosexuals in emergency situations. In a syndicated column that appeared in newspapers throughout the United States, William F. Buckley proposed tattooing people with AIDS to make it impossible for them to circulate unmarked among the general population.[44] Between 1982 and 1983 a poll found the number of people who thought that homosexuality should be considered an accepted alternative lifestyle had dropped from 58 percent to 51 percent.[45] Polling data also revealed that the number of people who declared that homosexual relations were "always wrong" had climbed from 73 percent in 1980 to 78 percent in 1987.[46] The AIDS epidemic brought all the fears about gay life rushing back. A married gay man struggling with his identity was told by his therapist: "Why leave a life-style for a death-style?" "For many," *Newsweek* concluded, "the closet door is again swinging closed."[47]

Seeing where the political winds were blowing, former Gay Activists Alliance leader Arnie Kantrowitz urged the gay leadership to stop bickering: "We won't need to criticize each other once the Moral Majority gets wind of this. They even blamed us for blizzards and droughts."[48] Kantrowitz was right.

On July 4, 1983, Jerry Falwell took the stage at a Moral Majority rally in Cincinnati to discuss what he dubbed the "plague of the century": "If the Reagan administration does not put its full weight against this, what is now a gay plague in this country, I feel that a year from now, President Ronald Reagan, personally, will be blamed for allowing this awful disease to break out among the innocent American public." Falwell demanded the federal government shut down gay bathhouses and prohibit homosexuals from donating blood. Claiming that he had nothing against homosexuals themselves—only their "perverted lifestyle"—Falwell pronounced AIDS as "the judgment of

God. . . . You can't fly into the laws of God and God's nature without paying the price."[49]

Conservative pundit Pat Buchanan wrote in a 1983 *New York Post* opinion piece, "The sexual revolution has begun to devour its children. And among the revolutionary vanguard, the Gay Rights activists, the mortality rate is highest and climbing. . . . The poor homosexuals— they have declared war upon nature, and now nature is exacting an awful retribution." Buchanan concluded that the Democratic Party's decision to hold their 1984 National Convention in San Francisco would present liberals with a dilemma: "Does [the party] maintain . . . its solemn commitment to federally protected civil rights for active homosexuals, equal access to jobs, housing and public accommodations" or will it expose the children and wives of delegates to restaurants and hotels that employ "active homosexuals who belong to a community that is a common carrier of dangerous, communicable and sometimes fatal diseases."[50] During Anita Bryant's Save Our Children campaign, Americans had heard how gay rights threatened the "health of the family" by offering young people an alternative to family life. With the onset of AIDS, right-wingers like Buchanan asserted that gay rights literally threatened the health of America's families.

The AIDS crisis brought the issue of homosexuality an unprecedented high profile during the 1984 presidential campaign. On the eve of the Democratic Party's convention in San Francisco, Jerry Falwell and Phyllis Schlafly organized a two-day "Family Forum" in the city by the Bay to discuss the "threat of homosexuality." Falwell announced to a fervent audience, "We didn't choose San Francisco—the Democrats chose San Francisco." Appearing on *Face the Nation* after the Democratic convention, Ed Rollins, Reagan's campaign manager, said, "The Democratic Party has been the party of quotas, the party of alternate lifestyles, the party of gay rights." At the Republican convention in Dallas, the rhetoric was filled with references to "family values" and featured Jerry Falwell delivering the benediction the night Reagan was nominated for a second term.[51] The 1984 election was a powerful model for how the Right would exploit the Democratic Party's support for gay rights by playing upon the fears of the electorate.

With the demise of the Gay Activists Alliance, the gay community was bereft of a vigorous activist organization that could act as a media watchdog to counter the unbalanced coverage. On November 14, 1985, six hundred people, led by former GAA member Arnie Kantrowitz, gathered in the Metropolitan-Duane Methodist Church to address the need by forming the Gay and Lesbian Alliance Against Defamation, or GLAAD. The new organization's first target was the paper that printed Pat Buchanan's diatribes against homosexuals, Rupert Murdoch's *New York Post*. Five hundred people assembled at the *Post*'s offices early one December morning holding banners that read, "Close the Post, not the Baths." Ten years after leaving the GAA, having lost a few pounds and a lot of hair, Marty Robinson was once again in front of the crowd leading a chant: "Who lies the most? . . . *The New York Post!*"[52]

The person most responsible for changing the way the media and government handled the AIDS crisis was not a journalist or an activist, he was a victim. *Time* magazine opened an August 1985 article about "AIDS: A Spreading Scourge" with a reference to a story that had shocked Americans the previous week:

> The rumors fed by his wan and wasted appearance had circulated for days. Rock Hudson, it was said, was suffering from liver cancer and slipping in and out of a coma at the American hospital in the Paris suburb of Neuilly. Reality was more shocking than rumor. At the hospital last week a spokeswoman for the actor bluntly announced, "Mr. Rock Hudson had acquired immune deficiency syndrome."[53]

To moviegoers of the 1950s and '60s, no star more completely typified old-fashioned American male virtues than Rock Hudson. *Look* magazine, which named Hudson "Star of the Year" in 1958, described him as "wholesome. He doesn't perspire. He has no pimples. He smells of milk. His whole appearance is cleanliness and respectability—this boy is pure." In the 1950s Hudson was nominated for an Academy Award for his role as a rugged cattle rancher in *Giant* and more recently had seen a revival of his career, playing a suave ladies' man in the 1980s hit television series *Dynasty*.[54] Now, he was the most famous AIDS patient in the world.

Hudson was one of several closeted celebrities with AIDS who had

tried to hide their sickness. Roy Cohn adamantly denied he had AIDS
in a *60 Minutes* interview and attributed his extreme weight loss to
liver cancer. When Liberace was on his deathbed, a spokesman maintained that the pianist was suffering from the ill effects of a water-
melon diet.[55] Rock Hudson, however, sought experimental treatment
in the Pasteur Institute, a French hospital known throughout the
world for treating AIDS. It did not take long for the press to connect
the dots. After the initial reports of Hudson's sickness, a White House
spokesman announced that President Reagan had telephoned his
friend in Paris to "wish him well and let him know that he and Mrs.
Reagan were keeping him in their thoughts and prayers."[56] That
announcement was the closest Reagan had come to publicly acknowl-
edging the epidemic.[57]

At first, gay rights groups and AIDS organizations preferred to let
the world think Rock Hudson was straight so that they would no
longer see AIDS as exclusively a gay disease.[58] But the activists soon
realized that Rock Hudson's revelation brought an unprecedented
amount of sympathetic attention to both AIDS and homosexuality.
When Hudson returned to Los Angeles, news helicopters circled the
airport shooting video of his gaunt form clad in a white hospital gown.
Randy Shilts sadly noted in his monumental history of the AIDS epidemic, *And the Band Played On*, "The television stations could afford
helicopters to record fifteen seconds of Rock Hudson on a stretcher,
but they had never afforded the time to note the passing of the thousands who had gone before him."[59]

The sudden interest in AIDS after Rock Hudson's revelation was
symptomatic of the American cult of celebrity. By the time of Hudson's
announcement, the Centers for Disease Control had counted 11,871
cases of AIDS in the United States and 5,917 deaths.[60] Such facts and
statistics held little power over the American imagination. News about
Rock Hudson, however, struck upon the sappy, sentimental American
connection to silver screen icons. Rock Hudson, according to *Time*,
"put a face on the illness and brought it home to many who could not
have dealt with it two weeks ago."[61]

Once AIDS finally caught the public's attention, governmental
action followed. The revelation that Hudson had to leave the United
States to receive state-of-the art AIDS treatment was a major embar-

rassment for American science and the federal government, which still had not devoted substantial resources to AIDS research and services.[62] Dr. Alvin Friedman-Kien, who spent years treating AIDS patients and trying to break the media silence, told *Time*, "It takes something like this to make the public aware that not enough is being done."[63] Doctors involved in AIDS research called Hudson's announcement the single most important event in the history of the epidemic.[64]

A year later Surgeon General Dr. C. Everett Koop issued a bold report on how the public and the government could combat the spread of AIDS. Ronald Reagan nominated Koop to the position because of the doctor's leading role in the antiabortion movement. But in October 1986, Koop broke the official silence and defied the moralism of the Right when he issued a blistering statement on how "many people, especially our youth, are not receiving information that is vital to their future health and well-being because of our reticence in dealing with the subjects of sex, sexual practices—homosexual and heterosexual." Koop concluded, "Education about AIDS should start at an early age so that children can grow up knowing the behaviors to avoid to protect themselves from exposure to the AIDS virus."[65] Randy Shilts perfectly summed up the significance of the Koop report: "It took a square-jawed, heterosexually-perceived actor like Rock Hudson to make AIDS something people could talk about. It took an ultra-conservative fundamentalist who looked like an Old Testament prophet to credibly call for all of America to take the epidemic seriously at last."[66] At last, the highest-ranking medical authority in the United States was telling the American people what they needed to do to save their lives.

A celebrity revelation and a governmental report were not enough to sustain public interest and governmental action. Throughout the history of the gay rights movement, the most effective tactic for generating media coverage and political support was the zap. In the 1980s, Marty Robinson, who invented the tactic, founded a new organization, Lavender Hill Mob, which brought the zap to the "AIDS awareness movement." To promote federal legislation prohibiting discrimination against people with AIDS, the Lavender Hill Mob stormed the New York offices of Republican Senator Alfonse D'Amato, brandishing mock "arrest warrants." The Catholic Church also became a target of

Robinson's Mob after the Vatican issued a "Letter to the Bishops on the Pastoral Care of Homosexual Persons." Written by the Prefect for the Doctrine of Faith, Joseph Cardinal Ratzinger, known today as Pope Benedict XVI, the letter claimed homosexuals possessed "a more or less strong tendency to behavior which is intrinsically evil from the moral point of view, and should therefore be considered objectively disordered itself." One Sunday, Lavender Hill Mob member Bill Bahlman disguised himself as a priest and joined seven other activists in the first pew of St. Patrick's Cathedral. When Archbishop John Cardinal O'Connor began his sermon, Bahlman and the others stood up holding hands in defiant protest.

In March 1987 members of the Lavender Hill Mob met with hundreds of others to found another organization dedicated to the zap, the AIDS Coalition to Unleash Power—dubbed ACT-UP. Some in the new organization were veteran activists like GLF legend Jim Fouratt, others were new to political activism. Unlike the shaggy, blue-jean clad Gay Activists Alliance members, ACT-UP was made up largely of 1980s-styled, middle class professionals who, according to the *Wall Street Journal*, "look like Yuppies" and "act like Yippies." These "shock troops in America's newest radical movement" used "their clean-cut looks and natty attire to gain entry to the halls of government, finance and religion."[67]

ACT-UP launched its first zap against the pharmaceutical company Burroughs Wellcome Co., which owned the patent to a new drug called azidothymidine, or AZT. At the time, AZT was the only promising AIDS medication on the market, but only for those who could afford the $10,000 yearly price tag, or others, like Roy Cohn, who used their connections to receive the experimental treatment.[68] One morning in April 1989, four clean-cut young men in business suits walked into the North Carolina headquarters of Burroughs Wellcome Co. and chained themselves to a radiator. In good GAA fashion, someone at ACT-UP called the Associated Press and announced the news, "Burroughs Wellcome had been raided by ACT-UP!" A few months later, seven well-dressed young men walked through the doors of the New York Stock Exchange and onto the trading floor. Five of them climbed to a balcony where they handcuffed themselves around a banister and sounded air horns to attract attention.[69] Chanting

"Release the Drugs!" the protestors urged brokers to dump their stock in Burroughs Wellcome.[70] Two ACT-UP photographers snapped pictures and handed the roles of film to a runner, who immediately delivered them to the Associated Press offices. Within an hour, photos of ACT-UP's latest publicity coup were on the AP wire.[71] Less than three years after the founding of ACT-UP, Burroughs Wellcome reduced the cost of AZT. Another ACT-UP target, Dr. Anthony Fauci, the director of the National Institute of Allergy and Infectious Diseases, praised the group's impact on the drug industry: "Did ACT-UP play a significant role in the whole idea of expanded access to experimental drugs? The answer is yes."[72] ACT-UP also forced Northwest Airlines to abandon its policy of excluding AIDS patients from flights by launching a "phone zap," a campaign that flooded the company's switchboard with prank calls.[73]

ACT-UP adopted a symbol that had been initially used by the Study Group during the long struggle over the New York gay rights bill, the pink triangle that the Nazis had stitched to the uniforms of homosexual concentration camp inmates. The ACT-UP triangle was different, however: it pointed up. Its designer claimed "we were trying to disavow the victim role."[74] Throughout the late 1980s, ACT-UP posters appeared throughout New York City bearing the pink triangle on a black background hovering over the slogan "SILENCE = DEATH." The *Wall Street Journal* remarked how on "the streets of New York, it is virtually impossible to miss ACT-UP's militant message" stamped on posters and T-shirts that brought in $150,000 to feed ACT-UP's $500,000 annual budget.[75] By 1990 ACT-UP had chapters in forty American cities as well as several cities abroad.[76]

ACT-UP brought more attention to the unmet needs of people with AIDS than any other organization. Its zaps were featured by all the major media organizations ranging from the *New York Times* and the *Post* to the *Wall Street Journal* and *60 Minutes*. By 1989 ACT-UP members were being invited to sit on the government panels they once attacked. The Food and Drug Administration and the National Institutes of Health sought ACT-UP's advice on how and when some AIDS drugs should be tested.[77] The *New York Times* credited ACT-UP with bringing major changes to the way the federal government tested and distributed experimental drugs, allowing patients to obtain them much faster. "There's no doubt that they've had an enormous effect," said Dr. Stephen Joseph, the former New York City health commissioner who himself was a target of ACT-UP zaps. "We've basically changed the way we make drugs available." In the 1970s zaps forced liberal politicians to embrace gay rights and the psychiatric community to remove the sickness label from homosexuality. ACT-UP's zaps in the 1980s helped prolong the lives of thousands of AIDS victims into the next decade.

Organizations like GMHC and ACT-UP revitalized the political consciousness of the gay community and gave new direction to the lives of many victims. Peter Staley, a twenty-eight-year-old bond trader who was diagnosed with AIDS in 1985, told the *Wall Street Journal*, "Act-Up has been my way of taking control of my life away from the AIDS virus." Many closeted gays who had never thought to become involved in the gay rights movement were mobilized by the AIDS crisis. Dr. Ken Wein, a psychologist who joined the GMHC, told the *New York Times*, "I wouldn't have put myself on the line before. AIDS finally strengthened my will to confront my boss, who was biased against gays, and quit a job at a hospital where I worked. You get enraged at the feeling that the world thinks you're disposable because you're gay."[78] Jeff Levi of the National Gay Task Force informed *Newsweek*, "The number of people AIDS has brought out into the [politically active] community—many of them out of the closet—is very exciting to see. When it's life or death, it's worth risking your job."[79] The *Wall Street Journal* reported how an ACT-UP meeting was packed with lawyers, artists, designers, teachers, writers, and even a few celebrities, including actress Susan Sarandon and artist Keith Haring.[80] Seeing the thousands of gays and straights who volunteered to care for AIDS patients and became active for the first time in the gay political movement, Jim Fouratt thought, "I haven't experienced this kind of caring since the early days of gay liberation."[81]

While only a relatively small percentage of gays and lesbians joined AIDS organizations, the horror of the epidemic and the stridency of right-wing attacks on the gay community convinced an unprecedented number of people to come out to their straight friends, co-workers, and families. A 1985 poll found that only a quarter of Americans had a friend, relative, or co-worker who was openly gay while more than half believed they did not know any homosexuals. Fifteen years later, the number of people who knew someone openly gay had tripled, to three-quarters of the population. Only one-fifth of Americans reported *not* knowing anyone gay.[82] All the revelations prompted millions of Americans to discuss and reevaluate how they related to the homosexuals in their families, their neighborhoods, and their offices. Since the 1980s these discussions have quietly, but significantly, contributed to the growing acceptance of homosexuality in the United States.[83]

AIDS also forced gays and straights to alter their sexual practices. In big cities and small towns across the United States in the late 1980s there was a sharp decline in the rate of anal gonorrhea infections among male homosexuals.[84] Bill Jones, the owner of San Francisco's Sutro bathhouse, told *Newsweek,* "many gays are beginning to see that the party is over. You find more people interested in monogamy and their homes and their health. You go home and get on with your life instead of being part of the wildness that has been going on in the last five years, the dehumanization."[85] Most straights also altered their sexual practices. The rampant promiscuity of the days of disco, when the pill was seen as sufficient protection, gave way to a dramatic rise in condom use and serial monogamy.

The AIDS crisis also sparked the revolutionary movement to gain legal recognition for gay marriage. Gays and lesbians had always formed lifelong, stable relationships that were fully acknowledged and respected by their friends. AIDS, however, suddenly forced tens of thousands of committed gay couples to deal with powerful institutions—hospitals, funeral homes, state agencies—that did not recognize their commitments. Even if AIDS patients were on their deathbeds, their life-partners were often excluded from visiting because they were not officially "spouses" or next of kin. Hospitals were not obligated to consult with gay partners or even inform them about their loved ones' treatment. If a patient died, the life-partner did not automatically inherit estate property that was not in both men's names. Bereaved men lost not only their lovers but also their homes, their mementos, and their property. Responding to a public outcry to address the iniquity, Ed Koch announced that the domestic partners of city employees would henceforth be eligible for bereavement leaves already available to marital spouses. A year later San Francisco voters approved the establishment of a domestic partnership registry. Within two years, six other cities had established similar registries.[86] Over the subsequent twenty years, the movement to secure gay marriage rights has mobilized yet another generation of activists.

In a brutal way, the AIDS crisis had a positive effect on the gay rights movement. For years, activists shared a strange fantasy: What if one day, very suddenly, every homosexual in America turned blue— and the rest of society saw once and for all just how commonplace and how unthreatening homosexuality really is?[87] Donald Webster Cory had a similar thought in 1951. "If only all of the inverts, the millions in all lands, could simultaneously rise up in our full strength!" Three decades later, the AIDS epidemic forced tens of thousands of gay men and lesbians into the open either as activists or victims.[88] By the mid-1980s, for the first time, the gay community and the gay rights movement approached the level of political clout that was roughly commensurate with its size and talents.[89]

Throughout the 1980s and 1990s the AIDS epidemic took an apocalyptic toll on the gay community. By 1988, a little less than a decade since the epidemic first hit the United States, eighty-two thousand Americans had been diagnosed with AIDS; forty-six thousand were dead.[90] Anecdotal evidence from doctors with practices serving a mostly gay clientele suggested that at least half of the gay men in New York and San Francisco born between 1945 and 1960 were probably infected with HIV between the end of the seventies and the end of the eighties. Gay men in Manhattan from the baby-boom generation suffered a 50 percent casualty rate from AIDS.[91] Heroes of this history of the gay rights movement—Bob Martin, Marty Robinson, Jim Owles, Morty Manford, Bruce Voeller, Lenny Matlovich, and Randy Shilts—were all lost to AIDS.

The dream that these men shared, however, was not lost. In 1951 Donald Webster Cory suggested that the way to secure equal rights for gays and lesbians was for homosexuals to be recognized as a minority, for American liberals to embrace their cause, and for the conspiracy of silence to be broken by serious media coverage of homosexuality. Thirty years later, the gay rights movement had achieved these goals and transformed America into a country where most homosexuals could confidently abandon the closet and identify themselves proudly as gay men to their families, friends, and co-workers.

As Cory predicted, all Americans have benefited from the gay power revolution. By establishing a media presence, the gay rights movement was able to reeducate and liberate a majority of Americans. Numerous television programs and news reports showed straights that homosexuals were not threats to society. Parents were no longer told to be embarrassed by their "deviant" children but were encouraged to form loving, honest relationships with them. Employers no longer feared the impact of homosexual workers on office morale but were free to exploit the talents of all their employees. A majority of Americans were freed from the pervasive homophobia that kept generations of gays and straights from becoming friends. The number of people who reported having a gay friend or close acquaintance doubled from 1985 to 1994 (from 22 to 43 percent) and rose to 56 percent by 2000.[92] Having a gay friend or family member was predictive of liberal sentiments toward homosexuals and gay rights. A 1993 survey found that two-thirds of the respondents who had a close gay friend or family member would not worry if their child's teacher were gay or lesbian.[93] While significant portions of the population, most notably televangelists, opportunistic politicians, and government agencies, have continued to resist granting equal rights to homosexuals, a majority of the American population has made great strides toward the day when all citizens can live openly and contribute their talents freely to the wealth and strength of the nation.

ACKNOWLEDGMENTS

Like all histories, this book is a collaboration between its author and a vast number of historians, librarians, teachers, and editors. But without the contributions of several people in particular, this work would have taken an entirely different direction.

I owe a great deal to the groundbreaking research of George Chauncey and John D'Emilio, who both brought academic credibility to the field of gay history. I hope this book demonstrates that the history of the gay rights movement is not only an important subject to be further researched and taught but that it is an essential piece of the political and social history of the United States.

I would like to thank two archivists, Rich Wandel and Rutherford Witthus, who guided me through their archives and, along the way, provided key insights that I incorporated into the book.

There are precious few people on earth who combine vast knowledge and intelligence along with great kindness and generosity. Fortunately for me, two such extraordinary men were my advisers throughout this project: Jim Shenton and Alan Brinkley. This book would never have been written had I not known Jim. Stories about his friends in the gay rights movement convinced me their history must be written. I will always be grateful for Jim's friendship, which, like his spirit, lives on. When I first began writing this book, it was a dissertation about a small number of activists in New York City. Over the subsequent few years, my PhD adviser Alan Brinkley pushed me to place this story within the bigger context of American politics. Under his guidance I began to trace the story of how gay activism altered American liberalism and sparked a powerful conservative backlash that endures to this day. Thanks to Alan, this book demonstrates how the gay rights movement transformed American politics.

I would also like to thank several friends and fellow historians who helped with the key, and sometimes painful, task of editing the manuscript: James Downs, Peter Maguire, and Robert Jakoubek. Thanks also to my dissertation advisers Elizabeth Blackmar, Anders Stephanson, Thaddeus Russell, and Todd Gitlin. Todd provided key assistance in helping me refine my concept of the "media trigger." David Nasaw and Martin Duberman also gave important advice very early on in the project.

Thanks to David Carter and Michael Denneny for helping me get this book published. I am especially grateful to Don Weise at Carroll & Graf for putting faith in an unpublished writer with nothing to offer but a few chapters of a dissertation and a good story. Thanks also to Bettye Lane and Rich Wandel for the use of their amazing photos, which help tell that story.

No one made a greater contribution to this book than my best friend and most talented editor, Stephanie Gangi. When she first started reading my manuscript it was an academic dissertation—heavily researched and footnoted, dry and lifeless. In just a few months, she taught me how to unleash my voice in my writing. The chapters I wrote after she became involved in the project, and in my life, are a testament to her brilliance and her love. Stephanie was my inspiration through the best parts of this book and for that I will always be grateful.

I would like to thank my parents and sister. They have been behind me from the very beginning and will be till the end.

And finally I would like to thank the heroes of the gay rights revolution whom I interviewed for this book. Thank you for inviting me into your homes and sharing your experiences, both happy and sad. Special thanks to Ethan Geto, who took time away from his effort still "fighting the good fight" to help me.

I also want to acknowledge the many heroes who were no longer able to share their stories. A few years ago, Jim Shenton said he was proud that I had decided to tell their story. I hope I have succeeded in doing so.

BIBLIOGRAPHY

Archival Collections

Stephen Donaldson Papers. Rare Books and Manuscripts Division. New York Public Library, New York, NY.

Martin Duberman Papers. Rare Books and Manuscripts Division. New York Public Library, New York, NY.

Pete Fisher Collection. Lesbian Gay, Bisexual & Transgender Community Center National History Archive, New York, NY.

Foster Gunnison Papers. Thomas J. Dodd Research Center. University of Connecticut, Stores, CT.

Richard Inman Papers. Thomas J. Dodd Research Center. University of Connecticut, Stores, CT.

International Gay Information Center Papers. Rare Books and Manuscripts Division. New York Public Library, New York, NY.

Karla Jay Papers. Rare Books and Manuscripts Division. New York Public Library, New York, NY.

Jeanne Manford Papers. Rare Books and Manuscripts Division. New York Public Library, New York, NY.

Morty Manford Papers. Rare Books and Manuscripts Division. New York Public Library, New York, NY.

Mattachine Society of New York Papers. Rare Books and Manuscripts Division. New York Public Library, New York, NY.

National Gay and Lesbian Task Force Papers. Human Sexuality Collection. Cornell University, Ithaca, NY.

Student Homophile League Papers. Columbiana Archives. Columbia University, New York, NY.

Bruce Voeller Papers. Human Sexuality Collection. Cornell University, Ithaca, NY.

Voices of the Oral History Project of GLHSNC. San Francisco Public Library. San Francisco, CA.

Interviews (Author)

Henry Coleman, March 6, 2001.

Arthur Evans, May 11, 2004.

Pete Fisher, August 9, 2003.

Jim Fouratt, January 15, 2004.

Ethan Geto, July 31, 2004 and October 21, 2004.

Ron Gold, July 17, 2004.
Herbert Hendin, July 5, 2004.
Jerry Hoose, January 24, 2004.
Karla Jay, January 26, 2004.
Frank Kameny, December 12, 2004.
Arnie Kantrowitz, July 17, 2004.
Bob Kohler, January 18, 2004.
Mike Lavery, February 13, 2004.
Dick Leitsch, January 19, 2003.
Jack Nichols, November 7, 2004.
John O'Brien, January 31, 2004.
Peter Pouncey, April 3, 2001.
Marc Rubin, August 9, 2003.
Harold Sackheim, March 1, 2001.
James P. Shenton, October 9, 2000.
Charles Silverstein, July 8, 2004.
Robert Spitzer, June 25, 2004.
Rich Wandel, July 26, 2003.
George Weinberg, July 30, 2003.
Allen Young, February 17, 2004.

Periodicals
The Advocate
Bay Area Reporter
Bergen Record
The Catholic News
Change
Christian Science Monitor
Christopher Street
Collier's Magazine
Columbia Owl
Columbia Spectator
Come Out!
Commercial Appeal
Crawdaddy
Daily American
Daily News
Denver Post
The Double F Journal
Esquire
Freedom's Journal
Free Press
GAY
Gay Activist
Gay Books Bulletin
Gay Pride
Gay Sunshine

Gaysweek
Harper's Magazine
Hartford Times
Jersey Journal
Journalism Review
The Ladder
Life
London Daily Mirror
Los Angeles Times
Mattachine Review
Michael's Thing
New Republic
New York
New York Native
New York Post
New York Times
The New Yorker
Newsday
One
The Overseas Weekly
Passaic (NJ) Herald News
Pittsburgh Post-Gazette
Press
Providence Journal
Rome Daily American
San Francisco Chronicle
Screw
The Stanford Daily
Star
Stars and Stripes
Time
Times Herald
Variety
Vector
Village Voice
The Villager
Wall Street Journal
Washington Post

Memoirs
Bell, Arthur. *Dancing the Gay Lib Blues.* New York: Simon and Schuster, 1971.
Hay, Harry. *Radically Gay: Gay Liberation in the Words of Its Founder.* Boston:
     Beacon Press, 1996.
Hoffman, Abbie. *Soon to a Major Motion Picture.* New York: G.P. Putnam's Sons, 1980.
Jay, Karla. *Tales of the Lavender Menace.* New York: Basic Books, 1999.
Rubin, Jerry. *Do It!* New York: Simon and Schuster, 1970.

Books and Articles

Adam, Barry D. *The Rise of a Gay and Lesbian Movement.* Boston: Twayne Publishers, 1987.

Alwood, Edward. *Straight News: Gays, Lesbians, and the News Media.* New York: Columbia University Press, 1996.

Bayer, Ronald. *Homosexuality and American Psychiatry: The Politics of Diagnosis.* New York: Basic Books, 1981.

Berkeley, Kathleen. *The Women's Liberation Movement in America.* Westport, CT: Greenwood Press, 1999.

Brinkley, Alan. *Liberalism and Its Discontents.* Cambridge: Harvard University Press, 1998.

Bullough, Vern L., ed. *Before Stonewall: Activists for Gay and Lesbian Rights in Historical Context.* New York: Harrington Park Press, Inc., 2002.

Carter, David. *Stonewall: The Riots That Sparked the Gay Revolution.* New York: St. Martin's Press, 2004.

Chauncey, George. *Why Marriage?* New York: Basic Books, 2004.

———. *Gay New York: Gender, Urban Culture, and the Making of the Gay Male World, 1890–1940.* New York: Basic Books, 1994.

Cory, Donald Webster. *The Homosexual in America: A Subjective Approach.* 2nd ed. New York: Greenberg, 1959.

Cruikshank, Margaret. *The Gay and Lesbian Liberation Movement.* New York: Routledge, Chapman & Hall, Inc., 1992.

D'Emilio, John. *Sexual Politics, Sexual Communities.* Chicago: University of Chicago Press, 1983.

———. "The Homosexual Menace: The Politics of Sexuality in Cold War America." In *Passion and Power: Sexuality in History,* ed. Kathy Peiss and Christina Simmons. Philadelphia: Temple University Press, 1998.

Duberman, Martin. *Stonewall.* New York: A Plume Book, 1994.

Fisher, Pete. *Gay Mystique.* New York: Stein and Day, 1972.

Fone, Byrne. *Homophobia.* New York: Metropolitan Books, 2000.

Freud, Sigmund. "The Sexual Life of Human Beings." In *Introductory Lectures on Psychoanalysis (1916–1917),* James Strachey trans. and ed. New York: W.W. Norton & Company, 1966.

Gentry, Curt. *J. Edgar Hoover: The Man and the Secrets.* New York: W.W. Norton & Company, 1991.

Gross, Larry. *Up From Invisibly.* New York: Columbia University Press, 2001.

Hendin, Herbert. *The Age of Sensation.* New York: W.W. Norton & Company, 1975.

Hooker, Evelyn. "Male Homosexuality in the Rorschach." *Journal of Projective Techniques,* 21 (1957).

Jezer, Marty. *Abbie Hoffman: American Rebel.* New Brunswick, NJ: Rutgers University Press, 1993.

Johnson, David K. *The Lavender Scare.* Chicago: The University of Chicago Press, 2004.

Kaiser, Charles. *The Gay Metropolis.* San Diego: Harcourt Brace & Company, 1997.

Louys's, Pierre. *Songs of Bilitis.*

Marcus, Eric. *Making Gay History.* New York: Perennial, 2002.

Marotta, Toby. *The Politics of Homosexuality.* New York: Houghton Mifflin, 1981.

McGirr, Lisa *Suburban Warriors: The Origins of the New American Right.* Princeton, NJ: Princeton University Press, 2001.

Miller, Neil. *Out of the Past: Gay and Lesbian History from 1969 to the Present.* New York: Vintage, 1995.

Minton, Henry. *Departing from Deviance.* Chicago: University of Chicago Press, 2002.

Moor, Paul. "The View from Irving Bieber's Couch; 'Heads I Win, Tails You Lose,' "*Journal of Homosexuality* 36, no. 1, The Hayworth Press Inc. (New York: 1998).

Murphy, John. *Homosexual Liberation: A Personal View.* New York: Praeger Publishers, 1971.

Nagourney, Adam, and Dudley Clendinen. *Out for Good.* New York: Simon & Schuster, 1999.

Newton, Esther. *Cherry Grove, Fire Island.* Boston: Beacon Press, 1993.

Onge, Jack. *The Gay Liberation Movement.* Chicago: The Alliance Press, 1971.

Rado, Sandor. *Adaptational Psychodynamics: Motivation and Control.* New York: Science House, 1969.

Sagarin, Edward. *Odd Man In.* Chicago: Quadrangle Books, 1969.

Sears, John. *Lonely Hunters.* Boulder, CO: Westview Press, 1997.

———.*Rebels, Rubyfruit and Rhinestones: Queering Space in the Stonewall South.*

Shilts, Randy. *And the Band Played On.* New York: St. Martin's Press, 1987.

Socarides, Charles. *Beyond Sexual Freedom.* New York: Quadrangle, 1975.

———. *The Overt Homosexual.* New York: Grune & Stratton, 1968.

New Brunswick, NJ: Rutgers University Press, 2001.

Streitmatter, Rodger. *Unspeakable: The Rise of the Gay and Lesbian Press in America.* Boston: Faber and Faber, 1995.

Summers, Anthony. *Official and Confidential: The Secret Life of J. Edgar Hoover.* New York: G.P. Putnam's Sons, 1993.

Teal, Don. *The Gay Militants.* New York: St. Martin's Press, 1971.

Theoharis, Athan G., and John Stuart Cox. *The Boss: J. Edgar Hoover and the Great American Inquisition.* Philadelphia: Temple University Press, 1988.

Theoharis, Athan G. *J. Edgar Hoover, Sex and Crime.* Chicago: Ivan R Dee, 1995.

Weil, Gordon. *The Long Shot, George McGovern Runs for President.* New York: W.W. Norton & Company Inc.

Weinberg, George. *Society and the Healthy Homosexual.* New York: St. Martin's Press, 1972.

White, Theodore H. *The Making of The President 1972.* New York: Atheneum Publishers, 1973.

NOTES

Chapter 1: "The Greatest Homosexual Population in the World"

1   Robert G. Doty, "Growth of Overt Homosexuality in City Provokes Wide Concern," *New York Times*, December 17, 1963.

2   Charles Socarides, "A Sickness Theory," reprinted in *Vector* 6, no. 9, September 1970.

3   Doty, "Growth of Overt Homosexuality in City Provokes Wide Concern."

4   Charles Kaiser, *The Gay Metropolis* (San Diego: Harcourt, Brace & Company, 1997), 82.

5   John D'Emilio, *Sexual Politics Sexual Communities* (Chicago: University of Chicago Press, 1983), 17.

6   Quoted in David K. Johnson, *The Lavender Scare* (Chicago: The University of Chicago Press, 2004), 71.

7   Kaiser, *The Gay Metropolis*, 74.

8   Senate Committee on Expenditures in Executive Departments, *Employment of Homosexuals and Other Sex Perverts in Government*, 81st Cong., 2d sess., 1950, reprinted in Donald Webster Cory, *The Homosexual in America, A Subjective Approach.* (New York: Greenberg, 1951), 269.

9   "Homosexuals' Militancy reflected in Attacks on Ouster from U.S. Jobs," *Washington Post*, February 4, 1965.

10   David K. Johnson, "Franklyn E. Kameny," in *Before Stonewall: Activists for Gay and Lesbian Rights in Historical Context*, Vern L. Bullough, ed. (New York: Harrington Park Press, Inc., 2002), 211; Nicholas Von Hoffman, *Citizen Cohn* (New York: Doubleday, 1978), 129.

11   Quoted in Johnson, *The Lavender Scare*, 77.

12   George Chauncey, *Why Marriage* (New York: Basic Books, 2004), 6.and John Stuart Cox, *The Boss: J. Edgar Hoover and the Great American Inquisition* (Philadelphia: Temple University Press, 1988) 208–12; Athan G. Theoharis, *J. Edgar Hoover, Sex and Crime* (Chicago: Ivan R Dee, 1995) 33–39.

13   Cory, *Homosexual in America,* 93.

14   "Rock: A Courageous Disclosure," *Time,* August 5, 1985.

15   "Liberace Testifies," *New York Times,* June 9, 1959; "Liberace, in Libel
      Suit, Denies Homosexuality," *The Washington Post,* June 9, 1959; "Lib-
      erace Defended Reputation in Libel Action in London Court," *Los Angeles
      Times,* June 9, 1959; "London Article Cut Years From Career, Liberace
      Says," *Los Angeles Times,* June 10, 1959; "Liberace is Accused of Debasing
      Mother Love," *The Washington Post,* June 11, 1959; "Libel Denied in Lib-
      erace London Case," *Los Angeles Times,* June 11, 1959; "Writer Says He
      Held Liberace to Be a Clown," *Los Angeles Times,* June 12, 1959; "Lib-
      erace Suit Turns to Piano-Playing Ability," *Los Angeles Times,* June 16,
      1959; "Liberace Read Wrong Meaning, Says Lawyer," *Los Angeles Times,*
      June 17, 1959; "Liberace Awarded $22,400 for Libel," *New York Times,*
      June 18, 1959, "Liberace Wins $22,400 Sex Status 'Vindicated,' " *The
      Washington Post,* June 18, 1959; "Liberace Wins Libel Suit, $22,400 Dam-
      ages," *Los Angeles Times,* June 18, 1959.

16   Hoffman, 132.

17   Jack Roth, "Nine Seized Here In Extortion Ring," *New York Times,* Feb-
      ruary 18, 1966; Jack Roth, "Nationwide Ring Preying on Prominent Devi-
      ates," *New York Times,* March 3, 1966; Edward Ranzal, "3 Indicted Here
      as Sex Extorters," *New York Times,* June 1, 1966; "Detective Accused As a
      Top Exporter," *New York Times,* July 1, 1966; "Extortion Suspect Surren-
      ders Here," *New York Times,* July 23, 1966; "Blackmailer Gets Five-Year
      Sentence in Homosexual Case," *New York Times,* August 17, 1966;
      "Detective and Two Others Indicted in Extortion Plot," *New York Times,*
      August 19, 1966; "Blackmail Paid by Congressman," *New York Times,* May
      17, 1967; "$25,000 Bail Is Forfeited By an Extortion Fugitive," *New York
      Times,* May 23, 1967; "Extortionist Gets Maximum Five Years," *New York
      Times* July 12, 1967; "2 Found Guilty in Chicago in Extortion of Homo-
      sexuals," *New York Times* December 9, 1967; 3 Guilty in Homosexual
      Case." *New York Times,* January 31, 1968; Murray Weiss, "J. Edgar's Slip,"
      New York Post, February 11, 1993; "Blackmailed Admiral Killed Himself,"
      New York Post, February 11, 1993.

18   Jack Roth "Blackmail Paid by Congressman," *New York Times,* May 17,
      1967.

19   According to the *Times,* the Mafioso "hinted that a few crooked policemen
      cooperated with the gang and issued summonses for violations real or fan-
      cied against a place without mafia protection." Charles Grutzner, "Mafia
      Buys Clubs for Homosexuals," *New York Times,* November 30, 1967.

20   "SLA Cancels 6 Café Licenses Here and Upstate," *New York Times*,
      October 8, 1963.

21   Charles Grutzner, "Mafia Increasing Investments in Business on L.I.,"
      New York Times, October 8, 1967.

22   Norman Sklarewitz, "Caught in the Act Police Don Disguises to Capture
      Criminals," *Wall Street Journal*, April 18, 1967.

23   Charles Grutzner, "Court Annuls SLA Penalty in a Morals Case," *New
      York Times*, March 9, 1967.

24   "State Aids Clean-up of Taverns in City," *New York Times*, October 14,
      1959; "SLA Warns Bars of Bad Clientele," *New York Times*, October 18,
      1959; "3 Liquor Permits Lifted," October 24, 1959; "2 More Bars
      Closed," *New York Times*, October 31, 1959; "SLA Cancels 6 Café licenses
      Here and Upstate," *New York Times*, October 8, 1963; Charles Grutzner
      "SLA to Publicize Bar Suspensions," *New York Times*, December 11, 1963.

25   Eric Pace, "Garelik Urges Public to Report Police Trapping of Homosex-
      uals," *New York Times*, April 2, 1966.

26   Doty, "Growth of Overt Homosexuality in City Provokes Wide Concern."

27   " 'Village' Assured of Added Police: Drive Against Undesirables is Planned
      by Murphy," *New York Times*, October 7, 1964.

28   "Scooter Patrolman Is Added to Force in Washington Square," *New York
      Times*, October 10, 1964.

29   David Burnham, "Police Violence: A Changing Pattern," *New York Times*,
      July 7, 1968.

30   Eric Pace, "Garelik Urges Public to Report Police Trapping of Homosex-
      uals."

31   Cory, 39.

32   Ibid., 32.

33   Ibid., 112.

34   Ibid., 161.

35   Ibid., 192.

36   Ibid., 35.

37   Ibid., 45.

38   Cory, 228.

39   Ibid., 10.

40   Ibid., 54.

41   Ibid., 230.

42   Ibid., 89.

43   Ibid., 229.

44   Ibid., 229–31.

45   Ibid., 157.
46   Ibid., 242
47   Ibid., 235.
48   Stephen O. Murray, "Donald Webster Cory (1913–1986)" in *Before Stonewall: Activists for Gay and Lesbian Rights in Historical Context*. (Harrington park Press: New York, 2002), 337.
49   Donald Webster Cory, *The Homosexual in America: A Subjective Approach*, 2nd ed. (New York: Greenberg, 1959), 39.

Chapter 2: Breaking the Conspiracy of Silence

1   Doty, "Growth of Overt Homosexuality in City Provokes Wide Concern."
2   Harry Hay, *Radically Gay: Gay Liberation in the Words of Its Founder.* (Boston: Beacon Press, 1996), 48–49; Vern L. Bullough, "Harry Hay," in *Before Stonewall: Activists for Gay and Lesbian Rights in Historical Context*, 73–80.
3   See "Mattachine Society Missions and Purposes," in Harry Hay, *Radically Gay*, 131–32.
4   D'Emilio, 64.
5   Ibid., 63–66.
6   Murray, 337–38.
7   Rodger Streitmatter, *Unspeakable: The Rise of the Gay and Lesbian Press in America* (Boston: Faber and Faber, 1995), 20.
8   Quoted in Sears, *Lonely Hunters* (Boulder, CO: Westview Press, 1997), 196.
9   Quoted in Hoffman, 132.
10   D'Emilio, 73–79.
11   Ibid., 82.
12   Streitmatter, 21.
13   D'Emilio, 104.
14   Ibid., 113.
15   Quoted in Streitmatter, 39.
16   Quoted in Sears, *Lonely Hunters*, 200.
17   D'Emilio, 112.
18   Streitmatter, 18.
19   Ibid., 50.
20   D'Emilio, 124–25.
21   Ibid., 123.
22   Ibid., 150.
23   Ibid.

24   David K. Johnson, "Franklin E. Kameny," in *Before Stonewall: Activists for Gay and Lesbian Rights in Historical Context*, 73–80.

25   Johnson, *The Lavender Scare*, 213.

26   Frank Kameny, interview by author, tape recording, Washington, D.C., December 12, 2004.

27   Quoted by James T. Sears, "Jack Nichols: The Blue Fairy of the Gay Movement," in *Before Stonewall: Activists for Gay and Lesbian Rights in Historical Context*, 223.

28   Nichols quoted in Sears, *Lonely Hunters*, 196.

29   Sears, *Lonely Hunters*, 225.

30   Johnson, *The Lavender Scare*, 183.

31   Kameny, interview; Sears, *Lonely Hunters*, 205.

32   David R. Boldt, "They Love Dowdy," *Washington Post*, May 4, 1970.

33   Johnson, *The Lavender Scare*, 213.

34   Quoted in Johnson, *The Lavender Scare*, 187.

35   John M. Goshko, "House Group Continues Homosexuality Hearing," *Washington Post*, April 10, 1963.

36   Josh M. Goshko, "'Morality Talk Shows Sex Hearing," *Washington Post*, August 9, 1963.

37   Johnson, *The Lavender Scare*, 190.

38   "Fund Raising Bill Target for ACLU," *Washington Post*, March 9, 1964.

39   Paul A Schuette, "Dowdy Bill Attacked," *Washington Post*, March 21, 1964.

40   "Legislating Morality," *Washington Post*, 8 August 1964.

41   Jean White, "Homophile Groups Argue Civil Liberties," *Washington Post*, October 11, 1964.

42   Kameny, interview.

43   Johnson, *The Lavender Scare*, 212.

44   D'Emilio, 152.

45   Ibid., 154.

46   Ibid., 156.

47   Quoted in D'Emilio, 152–53.

48   Streitmatter, 62.

49   Quoted in D'Emilio, 158.

50   Milton Bracker, "Homosexuals Air Their Views Here," *New York Times*, July 16, 1962.

51   "Homosexual Group Asks Understanding," *New York Times*, October 18, 1963

52   Jean White, "Homophile Groups Argue Civil Liberties;" "Homosexuals

Militancy Reflected in Attacks on Ouster from U.S. Jobs," *Washington Post*,
February 4, 1965.

53 Quoted in Jack Nichols, "George Weinberg," *Before Stonewall: Activists for
Gay and Lesbian Rights in Historical Context*, 354–55.

54 Quoted in D'Emilio, 169.

55 Kay Tobin Lahusen, "Barbara Gittings: Independent Spirit," in *Before
Stonewall: Activists for Gay and Lesbian Rights in Historical Context*, 244.

56 D'Emilio, 170.

57 Quoted in Lahusen, 244.

58 Streitmatter, 255.

59 Lahusen, 245–46; D'Emilio, 173.

60 Paul Hoffman, "Cuban Government Is Alarmed by Increase in Homosexuality," *New York Times*, May 16, 1965; "Havana University Ousts 40,"
New York Times, May 27, 1965.

61 Kameny, interview.

62 Sears, *Lonely Hunters*, 222.

63 Streitmatter, 63.

64 "Homosexuals Stage Protest in Capital," *New York Times*, May 30, 1965;
D'Emilio, 164.

65 Quoted in Streitmatter, 62.

66 Quoted in Johnson, *The Lavender Scare*, 201–02.

67 Martin Duberman, *Stonewall* (New York: A Plume Book, 1994), 113.

68 Quoted in D'Emilio, 164.

69 Jack Nichols, interview by author, telephone, November 7, 2004.

70 Jack Nichols, interview; Johnson, *The Lavender Scare*, 213; D'Emilio,
165.

71 Sears, *Lonely Hunters*, 211.

72 Doty, "Growth of Overt Homosexuality in City Provokes Wide Concern."

73 Albert J. de Dion letter to *Washington Post*, August 1, 1960.

74 Quoted in D'Emilio, 167.

75 Edward Sagarin, *Odd Man In* (Chicago: Quadrangle Books, 1969), 100.

76 Ibid., 109.

77 Ibid., 108.

78 Ibid., 108.

79 Leitsch, interview.

80 Shortly after the inauguration, the *New York Times* printed a News Analysis
on "Lindsay and the Police." The report asked, "There has been growing
evidence that the police have been increasingly entrapping prostitutes and
homosexuals. If the Mayor believes this practice is wrong, wasteful or both,

should he put an end to it?" Sidney Zion, "Lindsay and the Police," *New York Times*, January 29, 1966.

81   Eric Pace, "Leary's Progress," *New York Times*, June 20, 1966.

82   Duberman, *Stonewall*, 110.

83   Sidney Zion, "Lindsay Placates Coffeehouse Set," *New York Times*, May 5, 1966.

84   Eric Pace, "Policemen Forbidden to Entrap Homosexuals to Make Arrests," *New York Times*, May 11, 1966.

85   Duberman, *Stonewall*, 114–15.

86   "3 Deviates Invite Exclusion by Bars," *New York Times*, April 22, 1966

87   Charles Grutzner, "Court Annuls SLA Penalty in a Morals Case," *New York Times*, 9 March 1967; Charles Grutzner, "SLA Won't Act Against Bars Refusing Service to Deviates," *New York Times*, April 26, 1966.

88   Alfred Friendly Jr., "Police to Review 'Raided Premises,' *New York Times*, May 19, 1966.

89   D' Emilio, 208; Charles Grutzner, "Mafia Buys Clubs for Homosexuals," *New York Times*, November 30, 1967.

90   Duberman, *Stonewall*, 56–57.

91   Ibid., 153.

92   Ibid., 156.

93   "Homosexuals Ask Candidates' Ideas," *New York Times*, August 19, 1968

94   Frank Kameny, introduction to *Rebels, Rubyfruit and Rhinestones: Queering Space in the Stonewall South*, by James T. Sears (New Brunswick, NJ: Rutgers University Press, 2001), x.

95   Kameny, interview.

Chapter 3: Pride of Lions

1   Anonymous to *Columbia Spectator*, May 2, 1967, Student Homophile League Papers, Columbiana Archives, Columbia University.

2   Robert Martin's Personal Notes, undated, Stephen Donaldson Papers, Rare Books and Manuscripts Division, New York Public Library.

3   Lois was later diagnosed with acute intermittent prophyria. She committed suicide in 1979.

4   Robert Martin to Richard Inman, August 23, 1965, Richard Inman Papers, Thomas J. Dodd Research Center, University of Connecticut; James P. Shenton, friend of Martin, interview by author, New York, NY, October 9, 2000.

5   Young Martin's note is in his FBI file, Donaldson Papers.

6   Martin to Inman, March 13, 1965, Inman Papers.

7   Robert Martin to Dan Pinello, undated, Donaldson Papers.

8   "Student Homophile League: Founder's Retrospective," *Gay Books Bulletin*
     9 (Spring/Summer 1983): 30.

9   Martin to Inman. March 13, 1965, Inman papers.

10   "Student Homophile League: Founder's Retrospective," *Gay Books Bulletin*
     9 (Spring/Summer 1983): 30.

11   Martin to Pinello, undated, Donaldson Papers.

12   John D'Emilio, "The Homosexual Menace: The Politics of Sexuality in
     Cold War America," in *Passion and Power: Sexuality in History*, ed. Kathy
     Peiss and Christina Simmons (Philadelphia: Temple University Press,
     1998), 236.

13   Martin to Inman, August 13, 1965, "Columbia saw me as a precedent case
     (1st in 200 year—history to openly admit homosexuality to college),"
     Inman Papers.

14   "Student Homophile League: Founder's Retrospective," *Gay Books Bulletin*
     9 (Spring/Summer 1983): 30.

15   James P. Shenton, interview.

16   Martin to Pinello, undated, Donaldson Papers.

17   Murray Schumach, "Columbia Charters Homosexual Group," *New York
     Times*, May 3, 1967.

18   Martin to Pinello, undated, Donaldson Papers.

19   "Student Homophile League: Founder's Retrospective," *Gay Books Bulletin*
     9 (Spring/Summer 1983): 30.

20   Esther Newton, *Cherry Grove, Fire Island* (Boston: Beacon Press, 1993), 197.

21   Ibid., 196.

22   Martin to Pinello, undated, Donaldson Papers.

23   Martin to Gay People at Columbia, March 6, 1982, Student Homophile
     League Papers.

24   "I saw Columbia as the first chapter of a spreading confederation of stu-
     dent homophile groups." Martin to Pinello, undated, Donaldson Papers.

25   "Statement to other homophile organizations from Steven Donaldson and
     Steele Fredericksen co-chairmen," December 1966, Student Homophile
     League Papers.

26   Martin to Pinello, undated, Donaldson Papers.

27   Karla Jay, *Tales of the Lavender Menace* (New York: Basic Books, 1999), 6–7.

28   Martin to Lige Clark, December 6, 1967, Donaldson Papers. "This
     revealing of myself in public as a leader of SHL is just one by-product of
     the thinking and changes I've been undergoing." In a letter to Dennis,
     Martin wrote "I feel that I have changed inconsiderably in the last six

months, both in personality and in world views, I have switched sides from establishment to anti-establishment, become more relaxed and good natured, etc" Martin to Dennis, January 10, 1968, Donaldson Papers.

29 "I've taken LSD and am quite interested in the psychedelic movement." Martin to Dennis, January 10, 1968, Donaldson Papers. In a letter to Dan Pinello, Martin wrote: "I lost my virginity sexually in 1966 psychedelically in 67." Martin became an experienced "trip guide" for first-time LSD users. He claimed he became a liberal in 1967 in reaction to the Kerner report. Martin to Pinello, undated, Donaldson Papers.

30 Martin to Pinello, undated, Donaldson Papers.

31 "Lois wrote to the Navy and mentioned my homosexuality to them. It is a crushing blow, but I am still determined to get in." Martin diary, May 14, 1966, Donaldson Papers.

32 Martin diary, April 3, 1967, April 4, 1967, Donaldson Papers.

33 Chapel Bulletin of Columbia University by John Cannon, May 21, 1967, Student Homophile League Papers. Announcement by Wesley First, May 3, 1967, Student Homophile League Papers.

34 "The others were concerned about subpoenas: the FBI and others were known to consider the fledgling homophile movement to be subversive." Martin to Gay People at Columbia, March 6, 1982, Student Homophile League Papers.

35 Student Homophile League Statement by Robert Martin, February 13, 1967, Student Homophile League Papers.

36 Student Homophile League Statement of Purpose, February 13, 1967, Student Homophile League Papers.

37 After reading a draft of the entire statement, Gunnison read this line and praised Martin for having "worded exactly right. Grade "A" party line. (Kameny would give you a kiss for that)." Gunnison to Martin, February 17, 1967, Gunnison Papers.

38 Duberman, *Stonewall*, 30–35.

39 Gunnison to Martin, January 19, 1967, Gunnison to Martin, February 7, 1967, Gunnison Papers.

40 Gunnison to Martin, March 21, 1967, Gunnison Papers.

41 Martin to Pinello, undated, Donaldson Papers.

42 Schumach, "Columbia Charters."

43 A memorandum to Andrew Cordier recounts Martin's promise to the Committee on Student Organizations to keep publicity at a minimum. "SHL told the Committee they had support of Mattachine society. They

assured that publicity would be kept at a minimum and that this was not a social organization but a counseling society." Martin to Andrew Cordier, memorandum, July 1969, Donaldson Papers.

44   "Homophile League Criticized for Seeking Excessive Publicity," *Columbia Spectator*, May 4, 1967.

45   Memorandum by Robert Martin, "Form K," April 26, 1967, Donaldson Papers.

46   Memorandum by Robert Martin, "Form J," April 26, 1967, Donaldson Papers.

47   Martin to Gay People at Columbia, March 6, 1982, Student Homophile League Papers.

48   Martin to Pinello, undated, Donaldson Papers.

49   In his Morals column Schumach wrote a piece that praised the decision to recognize SHL. Murray Schumach, "The Third Sex," *New York Times*, May 7, 1967.

50   Martin to Gay People at Columbia, March 6, 1982, Student Homophile League Papers.

51   David Truman to Richard Demmerle, June 9, 1967, Student Homophile League Papers.

52   "Charters would be sought at other schools, including Stanford, University of Chicago, University of California at Berkeley, University of Connecticut, Bucknell and Maryland." Schumach, "Columbia Charters."

53   Schumach, "The Third Sex."

54   Dr. Gerald H. Klingon, MD who opposed SHL saw the lack of objectivity in the Schumach article. "The reports of this story contain elements of glorification of this state [homosexuality]."

55   "New York College Group Bomb to Trinity, UConn.," *Hartford Times*, May 3, 1967.

56   Ibid.

57   "A Campus Society for Homosexuals," *San Francisco Chronicle*, May 4, 1967.

58   Martin to Gunnison, May 23, 1967, Gunnison Papers.

59   "A Strange Thing Happened at Columbia," *Passaic (NJ) Herald News*, May 10, 1967.

60   Editorial, "Columbia's Mistaken Step," *Christian Science Monitor*, May 5, 1967.

61   Ibid.

62   "A Sound Mind in a Sound Body," editorial broadcast on WMRI, May 5, 1967, Student Homophile League Papers.

63   The decision of Columbia University to charter a student group seeking equal rights for homosexuals is commendable for a number of reasons. Editorial, "Recognizing Homosexuals," *Providence Journal*, May 8, 1967.

64   Henry W. Pierce, "Homosexuality—A Disease or Way of Life," *Pittsburgh Post-Gazette*, May 5, 1967.

65   "They say their distress is caused not by any mental or emotional sickness, but by knowing they are considered 'different' many feel ostracized and guilt ridden. Some would like to be made 'like other people' if they thought it were possible." Henry W. Pierce, "Homosexuality—A Disease or Way of Life."

66   Quoted in Eric Marcus, *Making Gay History* (New York: Perennial, 2002), 109.

67   D'Emilio describes the importance of relatively benign news coverage of homosexuals. "Even occasional coverage of the movement's efforts took homosexuality out of the shadowy realm of deviance and criminality and placed it in the light of social reform. Press attention represented more than simple reporting on the day's events. It was reshaping in qualitative way the public discourse on homosexuality and in the process was transforming the self-perceptions of gay men and lesbians." D, Emilio, 218.

68   Marcus, 109.

69   Martin to Gay People at Columbia, March 26, 1982, Student Homophile League Papers.

70   The letters about SHL that the administration received are in the Student Homophile League Papers in the Columbiana Archives, Columbia University.

71   Anonymous to Lowe, May 5, 1967, Student Homophile League Papers.

72   Bertram Selverston to Kirk, May 5, 1967, Student Homophile League Papers.

73   Anonymous to Kirk May 7, 1967, Student Homophile League Papers; Loreto to Kirk, May 5, 1967, Student Homophile League Papers; Propp to Kirk May 5, 1967, Student Homophile League Papers.

74   Anthony Philip to Columbia Spectator, May 9, 1967, Student Homophile League Papers.

75   Frank Pitt to Kirk, May 9, 1967, Student Homophile League Papers.

76   Dr. Gerald H. Klingon to Kirk, May 5, 1967, Student Homophile League Papers; Terry A. Terzakis to John Cannon, May 15, 1967, Student Homophile League Papers; Dorothy Burroughs to Wesley First, May 15, 1967, Student Homophile League Papers.

77   Dr. Bertram Selverstone to Kirk, May 10, 1967, Student Homophile League Papers.

78 Anonymous to Kirk, May 5, 1967, Student Homophile League Papers.

79 Blair again associated homosexuality to criminality in a letter to Reverend Horace Donegan, Bishop Episcopal Diocese of New York. "I can see no more reason for establishing a league for homosexuals than for recognizing the rights of other delinquents in society to organize such as robbers, murderers, or prostitutes." Harrison Blair to Kirk, May 11, 1967, Student Homophile League Papers.

80 Anonymous to Lawrence Chamberlain, telephone message, May 3, 1967, Student Homophile League Papers; McCullen to Kirk, May 8, 1967, Student Homophile League Papers; Blair to Kirk, May 5, 1967, Student Homophile League Papers; Charles A. Fremd to Kirk, Student Homophile League Papers, May 10, 1967, Student Homophile League Papers.

81 R. L. Demmerle to Truman, May 18, 1967, Student Homophile League Papers.

82 Anonymous to Kirk, May 3, 1967, Student Homophile League Papers.

83 On May 5th Frank Joseph clipped the headline of *New York Times* article, attached it to a note on which he wrote in red pencil "Please! Regards, Joseph" and sent it to Kirk. Kirk wrote to Joseph "I can assure you that your exclamation was far more mild than mine upon viewing the front page of last Wednesday's NYT." Kirk to Joseph, May 8, 1967, Student Homophile League Papers.

84 Kirk to McCullen, May 17, 1967, Student Homophile League Papers.

85 Kirk to Pit, May 5, 1967, Student Homophile League Papers.

86 In a letter to Loreto, Kirk referred to SHL as "this distasteful and thoroughly disapproved project." Kirk to Loreto, May 17, 1967, Student Homophile League Papers. In a letter to Propp, Kirk stated, "In response to your letter of May fifth, let me say first that my colleagues and I are also disturbed, deeply so over the establishment of the Student Homophile League." Kirk to Propp, May 17, 1967, Student Homophile League Papers.

87 Henry Proffitt to Helen King, May 5, 1967, Student Homophile League Papers

88 Henry Proffitt to Kirk, June 8, 1967, Student Homophile League Papers.

89 Special Notice to homophile organizations May 1967. Martin wrote in his diary, "being investigated by the Univ's legal firm, also may move to withdraw recognition" Martin diary, May 17, 1967, Donaldson Papers.

90 Grayson Kirk received a note on how Truman presented SHL to angry alumni. "The complaint re establishment of Student Homophile league are based on a formula you approved and which has a 'right out' slant. How-

ever we learned today that Dean Truman is answering his letters injecting
freedom of expression argument; Dean Barett reports that the deans agree
with the freedom 'bit' and today the chaplain came out with the attached.
The freedom of expression argument scarcely seems designed to win
wealthy Texas alumni or mothers of prospective students in Des Moines.
They are a number more like these in the works. Can we coordinate?"
Anonymous to Kirk, note, undated, Student Homophile League Papers.

91   Kirk to Editor of *Christian Science Monitor*, May 27, 1967, Student Homophile League Papers.

92   "Truman Questions Homophile Group's Place at Columbia," *Columbia Spectator*, May 5, 1967.

93   Open letter from Martin to Truman printed in *Columbia Spectator*, May 7, 1967.

94   Murray Schumach, "Criticism by Two Officials at Columbia Angers Leader of Student Homophile League," *New York Times*, May 11, 1967.

95   In the letter to Frank Hogan written on May 12, 1967 Leitsch claimed he was authorized by the MSNY to contact the trustee. Leitsch to Hogan, May 12, 1967, Student Homophile League Papers.

96   Leitsch to Hogan, May 12, 1967, Student Homophile League Papers.

97   "If the Columbia group where [sic] of this type, under different leadership, I'd be supporting it." Ibid.

98   Ibid.

99   Kameny and Gittings to the Board of Directors of the Mattachine Society, Inc. of New York, November 6, 1966, Gunnison Papers.

100 Duberman, *Stonewall*, 224.

101 Leitsch to Hogan, May 12, 1967, Student Homophile League Papers.

102 Statement Escalation: the Student Homophile League, August 10, 1967, Student Homophile League Papers.

103 Martin to Gay People at Columbia, March 6, 1982, Student Homophile League Papers.

104 Ibid.

105 Ibid.

106 D'Emilio, *Sexual Politics, Sexual Communities*, 235.

107 Martin to Gay People at Columbia, 6 March 1982, Student Homophile League Papers.

108 Miller, 372.

109 Student Homophile League to Kameny, invitation, December 4, 1967, Student Homophile League Papers.

110   Tauber, "Columbia Reflects."

111   Martin to Lige Clark, December 6, 1967, Donaldson Papers.

112   Martin to Gay People at Columbia, March 6, 1982, Student Homophile
      League Papers.

113   Martin to incoming freshmen, open letter, June 1967, Donaldson Papers.

114   On June 30 Wesley First sent a copy of the note to Grayson Kirk "Proctor
      Kahn has just informed me that the Student Homophile League is seeking
      to have the attached document made a part of the freshmen packet. Mr.
      Kahn also said that Mr. Truman is aware of this. I thought you ought to
      know about it, too." Wesley First to Kirk, June 30, 1967, Student
      Homophile League Papers.

115   Martin to Gunnison, January 13, 1967, Gunnison Papers.

116   Duberman, *Stonewall*, 224.

117   Ibid., 223.

118   Richard Inman to Gunnison, June 17, 1967, Gunnison Papers.

119   Martin to Gunnison, March 29, 1967, Gunnison Papers.

120   Martin to Gunnison, April 17, 1967, Gunnison Papers.

121   Martin to Gunnison, May 23, 1967, Gunnison Papers.

122   Arthur Kokot, "Chapters at Other Campuses Sought by Homophile
      League," *Columbia Spectator*, November 28, 1967. Martin wrote of
      Berrigan's support in the letter to Gay People at Columbia, 6 March
      1982, Student Homophile League Papers. Mark Shultz, "Gay People Dis-
      cuss Results of 12 Year Rights Struggle," *Cornell Daily Sun*, November 2,
      1980.

123   "Homosexual Group Forms," *The Stanford Daily*, February 2, 1968.

124   Martin to Kirk, February 1968, Student Homophile League Papers.

125   Gay Activist, June 1971, Pete Fisher Collection, Lesbian, Gay, Bisexual &
      Transgender Community Center National History Archive, New York City.

126   Martin to Gay People at Columbia, March 6, 1982, Student Homophile
      League Papers.

127   SHL public statement, March 22, 1968, Student Homophile League Papers.

128   Martin to Gay People at Columbia, March 6, 1982, Student Homophile
      League Papers.

129   Ibid.

130   Ibid.

131   Statement by Student Homophile League, "We Protest the Kolb Panel,"
      April 23, 1968, Donaldson Papers.

132   In *The Gay and Lesbian Liberation Movement*, Margaret Cruikshank cele-

brates the lesbians and gays who disrupted a 1973 session on aversion therapy to discourage homosexuality at a meeting of the American Psychiatric Association. She claims that "neither the homophiles of the 1950s nor the militant homosexual organizers of the early 1960s could have done that because they had no context for the rowdy, noisy demonstrations." Margaret Cruikshank, *The Gay and Lesbian Liberation Movement* (New York: Routledge, Chapman & Hall, Inc., 1992), 61. SHL's protest of the sickness model in 1968 reveals this claim to be inaccurate.

133 Martin to Gay People at Columbia, March 6, 1982, Student Homophile League Papers.

134 Memorandum by Martin, "NROTC and the Homosexual Student" Spring 1969, Donaldson Papers.

135 Memorandum by Martin, "Police and Law Reform," March 14, 1969, Donaldson Papers.

136 Statement by Student Homophile League, March 10, 1969, Donaldson Papers.

137 Statement by Student Homophile League, "The Homosexual and the Draft," March 22, 1969, Donaldson Papers.

138 Memorandum by Martin, "Our Demands," March 18, 1969, Donaldson Papers.

139 Arthur Felson, "Lavender Lion," *Pride of Lions* 1972, Student Homophile League Papers.

Chapter 4: From *Boys in the Band* to *Street Fighting Man*

1 "The Homosexual: Newly Visible, Newly Understood," *Time*, October 31, 1969.

2 Walter Kerr, "To Laugh at Oneself or Cry," *New York Times*, April 28, 1968.

3 Rex Reed, "Breakthrough By 'The Boys In the Band," *New York Times*, May 12, 1968.

4 Sam Zolotow, " 'Boys in the Band' Increases Prices," *New York Times*, November 6, 1968.

5 Lige Clarke and Jack Nichols, "The Band with the Rag On," *Screw*, August 25, 1969. For their views on "Boys in the Band," see also "It's a Big, Big World but I'm Just a Little Guy, *GAY*, April 20, 1970, "That's How Little Boys are 'Made,' " *GAY*, October 27, 1969.

6 Streitmatter, 85.

7 Streitmatter, 84.

8 Sears, *Rebels, Rubyfruit and Rhinestone*, 228–29.

9   Lige and Jack, "Off the Far End," *Screw*, May 2, 1969.

10   Kaiser, 151.

11   David Carter, *Stonewall: The Riots the Sparked the Gay Revolution* (New York: St. Martin's Press, 2004), 8.

12   Duberman, *Stonewall*, 187.

13   Ibid., 193.

14   Ibid., 185.

15   Streitmatter, 119.

16   Duberman, 182.

17   Carter, 80.

18   Ibid., 81.

19   Ibid., 81

20   Duberman, *Stonewall*, 182.

21   Carter, 102–03.

22   In an issue of *GAY* magazine on the tenth anniversary of Stonewall, Bruce Voeller called the police raid on the Stonewall "one of their periodic harassment raids." Bruce Voeller, "Stonewall Anniversary," *The Advocate*, July 12, 1979.

23   Quoted in Carter, 125.

24   Quoted in Carter, 125.

25   Manford, Morty, "Why We Should Postpone New York's Gay Rights Bill," *Gaysweek*, 16 October 16, 1978.

26   "Homo Nest Raided, Queen Bees Are Stinging Mad." *Daily News*, July 6, 1968.

27   Lucian Truscott, "Gay Power Comes to Sheridan Square," *Village Voice*, July 3, 1969.

28   "Queen Power: Fags Against Pigs in Stonewall Bust," *Rat*, July 9–23, 1969.

29   Carter, 147.

30   Howard Smith, "Full Moon over the Stonewall," *Village Voice*, July 3, 1969.

31   Carter, 152.

32   Smith, "Full Moon."

33   Quoted in Carter, 161.

34   Truscott, "Gay Power."

35   Smith, "Full Moon."

36   Smith, "Full Moon."

37   Quoted in Carter, 172.

38   Smith, "Full Moon."

39   Quoted in Carter, 179.

40   "4 Policemen Hurt in Village Raid," *New York Times*, June 29, 1969;
      "Police Again Rout Village Youths," *New York Times*, June 30, 1969.

41   "4 Policemen Hurt in 'Village' Raid," *New York Times*; Dennis Eskow, "3
      Cops Hurt as Bar Raid Riles Crowd," *Daily News*, June 29, 1969.

42   "Cops Injured 5 Seized in Village," *New York Post*, July 8, 1969.

43   Don Teal, "Stonewall: The Riots," *The Advocate*, July 121979.

44   Truscott, "Gay Power."

45   Ibid.

46   Quoted in Carter, 188.

47   Duberman, *Stonewall*, 204.

48   Dick Leitsch, "Police Raid on NY Club Sets Off First Gay Riot," *Los
      Angeles Advocate*, September 1969.

49   Ibid.

50   Ibid.

51   "Homo Nest Raided, Queen Bees Are Stinging Mad." *Daily News*, July 6,
      1968

52   Jay Levin, "The Gay Anger Behind the Riots," the *New York Post*, July 8,
      1969.

53   "Gay Power in New York City," *The Ladder*, October–November 1969.

54   Teal, "Stonewall: The Riots."

55   *Newsweek*'s October 1969 feature on the liberalization of police toward
      homosexuals quoted Ginsberg's comment on the "beautiful" young gays in
      the Stonewall. "Policing the Third Sex," *Newsweek*, October 27, 1969. It
      also appeared in the analyses of the riots that Lige Clarke and Jack Nichols
      wrote for *Screw* and the *Los Angeles Advocate*. Lige Clarke and Jack
      Nichols, "NY Gays Will the Spark Die?" *Los Angeles Advocate*, September
      1969; Lige Clarke and Jack Nichols, "Pampered Perverts," *Screw*, July 25,
      1969, 16.

56   Quoted in Sears, *Lonely Hunters*, 107.

57   Ethan Geto, interview by author, New York City, tape recording, July 31,
      2004.

58   Clarke and Nichols, "Pampered Perverts." .

59   Jim Rankin, "NACHO Upside Down," *Gay Sunshine*, October 1970.

60   "What Makes Mick Mighty?," *GAY*, December 15, 1969

61   Streitmatter, 197; Lige Clarke and Jack Nichols, "GAY Goes Weekly: the
      World's Only Weekly Gay Newspaper!," *GAY*, April 13, 1970.

62   Jonathan Black, "The Boys in the Snake Pit: Games 'Straights' Play," *Vil-
      lage Voice*, March 19, 1970, 61–64.

63   "Jumper's Condition Still Grave," *New York Post*, March 10, 1970.

64   "Patrons Tell of Raid from Inside," *GAY*, April 13, 1970.

65   Philip McCarthy, "Impaled Saved by Fire Docs," *Daily News*, March 9, 1970; Leo Louis Martello, "Raid Victim Impaled on Fence," *Los Angeles Advocate*, April 29–May 12, 1970.

66   "Gays Respond to Hovde's Letter," *Columbia Owl*, October 27, 1971.

67   "500 Angry Homosexuals Protest Raid," *GAY*, April 13, 1970.

68   Quoted in Carter, 252.

69   Black, "The Boys in the Snake Pit."

70   "Gay Power in New York City," *The Ladder*, October–November 1969.

71   Duberman, *Stonewall*, 210.

72   Ibid., 272.

73   Teal, 300.

74   Ibid., 303.

75   Jonathan Black, "A Happy Birthday for Gay Liberation," *Village Voice*, July 2, 1970.

76   Ibid.

77   Carter, 253.

78   Carter, 254.

79   Teal, 303.

80   Kohler, interview by author, tape recording, New York City, January 10, 2004.

81   Duberman, *Stonewall*, 279.

82   Jason Gould, "Out of the Closets and into the Streets," *GAY*, July 20, 1970.

83   Ibid.

84   Lige and Jack Nichols, "Love's Coming of Age: June 28, 1970," *GAY*, July 20, 1970.

85   Jason Gould, "Homosexual Liberation Day 1970," *GAY*, July 27, 1970.

86   Clarke and Nichols, "Love's Coming of Age."

87   Kay Tobin, "Thousands Take Part in Gay Marches," *GAY*, July 20, 1970.

88   Gould, "Homosexual Liberation Day 1970."

89   Jonathan Black, "A Happy Birthday for Gay Liberation," *Village Voice*, July 2, 1970, 58.

90   Robert Liechti, "Of the Day that was: and the Glory of It," *GAY*, July 27, 1970.

91   Cory, 10.

92   Tobin, "Thousands Take Part in Gay Marches."

93   Lacy Fosburgh, "Thousands of Homosexuals Hold a Protest Rally in Central Park," *New York Times*, June 29, 1970.

94   Black, "A Happy Birthday for Gay Liberation."

95   Quoted in Arthur Bell, "Hostility Comes Out of the Closet," *Village Voice*, June 28, 1973.

96   Ibid; Carter, 25.

97   Teal, 310.

Chapter 5: The New Homosexual

1   Tom Burke, "The New Homosexuality," *Esquire*, December 1969.

2   Dick Leitsch "The Hairpin Drop Heard Around the World," Gunnison Papers.

3   Dick Leitsch, interview by author, tape recording, New York City, January 19, 2004.

4   Toby Marotta, *Politics of Homosexuality* (Boston: Houghton Mifflin, 1981), 79.

5   Mike Lavery, interview by author, tape recording, New York City, 13 February 2004.

6   The Action Committee's break with Mattachine may have been a product of personality conflicts as well as disagreement over tactics. In *Out for Good*, Clendinen and Nagourney describe how Dick Leitsch offended many female members of the committee with obscene jokes such as asking "Who opened the tuna fish?" every time a woman walked into the room. Dudley Clendinen and Adam Nagourney, *Out for Good* (New York: Simon and Schuster, 1999), 26. In a 2003 interview with the author Leitsch claimed his joke was not meant to mock or offend but to kid Shelly and others for refusing to douche out of a feminist determination to embrace all aspects of their bodies. Leitsch, interview.

7   Burke, "The New Homosexuality"

8   Jim Fouratt, interview by author, tape recording, New York City, 24 January 2004; Burke, "The New Homosexuality."

9   For a detailed recount of Jim Fouratt's life, see Duberman, *Stonewall*.

10   Abbie Hoffman, *Soon to a Major Motion Picture* (New York: G.P. Putnam's Sons, 1980), 119.

11   Hoffman, 102; For Jerry Rubin's account of the Stock Market protest see Jerry Rubin, *Do It!* (New York: Simon and Schuster, 1970), 117–19. Jerry Rubin later became a stockbroker.

12   Fouratt, interview.

13   Marty Jezer, *Abbie Hoffman: American Rebel* (New Brunswick, NJ: Rutgers University Press, 1993), 128; Fouratt, interview.

14   In an interview with the author Leitsch bragged about his ability to achieve change by working with liberals in "smoke filled rooms." Leitsch, interview.

15   Dick Leitsch, "Homosexuals Don't Really Exist," *GAY*, 27 April 1970.

16   Bob Martin, "The New Homosexual and His Movement," *WIN*, 15 November 1969, 15–16.

17   Bob Martin, "A Statement of Beliefs," undated, Gunnison papers.

18   Adam Nagourney and Dudley Clendinen, *Out for Good*. (New York: Simon & Schuster, 1999), 31.

19   Carter, 218

20   Jonathan Black, "Gay Power Hits Back," *Village Voice*, August 1, 1969.

21   Don Teal, *The Gay Militants* (New York: St. Martin's Press, 1971), 21; Martola, 82.

22   Carter, 217.

23   Pete Fisher, *Gay Mystique* (New York: Stein and Day, 1972), 188.

24   Teal, 35.

25   Ibid., 34.

26   Jerry Hoose, interview by author, tape recording, New York City, January 24, 2004.

27   "Gay was our term." Jerry Hoose, interview by author, tape recording, New York City, January 24, 2004. For an exploration of the origins and significance of the term "gay," see George Chauncey's *Gay New York: Gender, Urban Culture, and the Making of the Gay Male World, 1890–1940* (New York: Basic Books, 1994).

28   Martha Shelly, in Eric Marcus, *Making Gay History*, 133; Fouratt, interview.

29   "Our liberation is tied to the liberation of all peoples," International Gay Information Center Ephemera—Organizations—Gay Liberation Front, Manuscripts and Archives Division, New York Public Library; Clendinen and Nagourney, 32.

30   Louis Hart called GLF a "structureless structure." Lois Hart, "Some News and a Whole Lot's Opinion by the Fumious Bandersnatch," *Come Out*, 3 April–May 1970, 3.

31   Clendinen and Nagourney, 32.

32   Jay, 124.

33   Jack Onge, *The Gay Liberation Movement* (Chicago: The Alliance Press, 1971), 16; Kay Lahusen, quoted in Marcus 135.

34   Arthur Evans, interview by author, tape recording, San Francisco,

May 11, 2004; "On Our Own, Gay Men in Consciousness Raising Groups," International Gay Information Center Collection—Ephemera.

35   Hoose, interview; Kohler, interview; Fouratt; interview.

36   In an interview with the author Jim Fouratt lamented the persistence of the decades old rumor. "You don't know what it's like to live with that label year after year." Fouratt, interview; Despite the lack of evidence of Fouratt's involvement with the FBI the rumor has been repeated by Clendinen and Nagourney and Martin Duberman.

37   John Murphy, *Homosexual Liberation: A Personal View.* (New York: Praeger Publishers, 1971), 78.

38   Martola provides a solid discussion of the New Left countercultural divide in GLF. Marotta, 83–91.

39   For a description of the similarities between Black Power and Pride and Gay Power and Pride, see Marotta, 95–98.

40   Clendinen and Nagourney, 46.

41   Evans, interview.

42   Jay, 80; Allen Young who also became an important writer on gay issues remembered his first GLF meeting gave him a "Strange sensation of being very much at home." Allen Young, interview by author, February 17, 2004.

43   "Proposals for Organization of Gay Liberation Front" July 14, 1970, International Gay Information Center Collection—Ephemera, Gay Liberation Front; Lavery, interview.

44   Minutes of a meeting, May 17, 1970, International Gay Information Center Collection—Ephemera, Gay Liberation Front.

45   Onge, 18; John O'Brien, interview by author, January 31, 2004; "Red Butterfly Cell," *Come Out!* vol. 1, no. 7, December–January 1970; Teal, 85.

46   Arthur Evans, interview by Roland Schembari, transcript, 3 April 1998, Voices of the Oral History Project of GLHSNC, San Francisco, CA; Onge, 16.

47   "Gay Jewish Revolution," January 1971, *Come Out!* vol. 2, no. 8; Fisher, 188.

48   "Gay Youth," *Come Out!* vol. 1, no. 7, December–January 1970.

49   Teal, 136.

50   Quoted in Teal, 88.

51   Evans, interview; Jerry Hoose also thought of GLF as the breeding ground for all subsequent liberation groups, Hoose, interview.

52   Bob Kohler, interview; Hoose, interview; announcement for dance "All

proceeds to legal assistance, housing, clothing, food etc. for street people and other members of the Gay Community, Arthur Bell Papers, International Gay Information Center Papers.

53   Clendinen and Nagourney, 45.
54   Lavery, interview; Murphy, 78.
55   Jay, 92; "Radicalesbians," *Come Out!* 1, no. 7, December–January 1970.
56   Michael Brown, Michael Tallman, and Leo Martello: "The Summer of Gay Power, and the Village Voice Exposed!" *Come Out!*, November 14, 1969; Bob Kohler, interview.
57   Quoted in Marotta, 112–13.
58   Fouratt, interview.
59   Hoose, interview.
60   "Homosexuals in Revolt: The Year the One Liberation Movement Turned Militant," *Life*, December 31, 1971.
61   "Marchi or Procaccino: Jail or Asylum," *Come Out!*, November 14, 1969.
62   "The October Rebellion," *Come Out!* 1, no. 1, November 14, 1969.
63   Arthur Evans, interview by author, tape recording, San Francisco, May 11, 2004.
64   Marotta, 138.
65   Quoted in Teal 90.
66   Hoose, interview; Marotta, 139–140.
67   *Come Out! Is Dead,* undated copy, Manford Papers.
68   Memo from Media Committee, International Gay Information Center Collection Ephemera—Organizations, Gay Liberation Front.
69   Lavery, interview.
70   "The Homosexual: Newly Visible, Newly Understood," *Time*, October 31, 1969.
71   Teal, 81.
72   The leaflets demanded *Time* give the GLF equal space in their next edition. Leaflet, International Gay Information Center Papers, Ephemera- Organizations, Gay Liberation Front, Rare Books and Manuscripts Division, New York Public Library.
73   Kohler, interview.
74   Hoose, interview.
75   Bob Martin also intended to radicalize the entire homophile movement in the fall of 1969. Martin to Marc, November 19, 1969, Gunnison Papers.
76   Marotta, 115.
77   Mattachine Folder, Gunnison Papers.

78   Austin Wade and Madolin Cervantes, "Report to the Board of MSNY Delegates to ERCHO," January 20, 1970, Gunnison Papers.

79   Quoted in Duberman, 229.

80   Duberman, 227–29.

81   Bob Martin, in a letter to *Playboy,* July 1970.

82   Foster Gunnison, in a letter to *Playboy,* August 1970, 46.

83   Barbara Gittings in Marcus, 136; Clendinen and Nagourney, 46.

84   Marotta, 117.

85   "Of course, the new wave frequently tries to put the last wave out of business. Certainly we had our differences with Del Martin and Phyllis Lyon at DOB. We had said to them, 'You're over the hill. Your thinking is out of date.' So GLF did the same to us." Kay Lahusen in Marcus, 136.

86   Karla Jay, interview by author, New York City, January 26, 2004; Fouratt, interview; For a very positive description of the consciousness-raising sessions, see Murphy 86–93; Fisher, 189.

87   Duberman, 221; Marotta, 102.

88   Young, interview.

89   Kohler, interview.

90   Fisher, 189.

91   Marotta, 141.

92   Lavery, interview.

93   Mike Lavery also remembered some consciousness-raising sessions to be destructive and "dangerous." Lavery, interview; Fisher, 189; Teal, 88; Marotta, 142.

94   Barry D. Adam, *The Rise of a Gay and Lesbian Movement* (Boston: Twayne Publishers, 1987) 90; Jay, 137.

95   "Radicalesbians," *Come Out!* 1, no. 7, December–January 1970.

96   Adam, 91.

97   Jay, 143; Onge, 18.

98   Quoted in Alisa Solomon, "Our Hearts Were Young and Gay," *Village Voice,* October 26–November 1, 2005.

99   Jay, Interview; Kathleen Berkeley, *The Women's Liberation Movement in America* (Westport, CT: Greenwood Press, 1999), 50; Adam, 96.

100 For a deeper discussion of lesbian feminism and Radicalesbians, see Marotta, chapter 9.

101 "From Sexual Revolution to Revolutionary Effeminism," *The Double F Journal,* Summer 1972; "Five Notes on Collective Living," *Come Out!* 1, no. 7, December 1970.

102 Marotta, 122.

103   Jay, interview.

104   Evans, interview.

105   O'Brien, interview.

106   Martha Shelly, oral history in Marcus, 137–38.

107   Quoted in Duberman, 258.

108   Arthur Irving, "An Interview with Our President: Jim Owles of GAA," Arthur Bell Papers, International Gay Information Center Collection; Robinson and Owles stuck around GLF to secretly recruit according to Jerry Hoose in Teal, 89 and they unsuccessfully tried to recruit Mike Lavery. Lavery, interview.

109   GLF minutes, May 17, 1970, International Gay Information Center Papers, Ephemera.

110   Quoted in Charles Kaiser, *The Gay Metropolis, 1940–1996*, 206.

111   "Note for a Political Platform and Program for Gay Liberation," Summer 1970, International Gay Information Center Papers, Ephemera

112   What We Want, What We Believe," February 1971, International Gay Information Center Papers, Ephemera.

113   Streitmatter, 133.

114   Kenneth Sherril "Leading the Gay Activists Movement, the Problem of Finding Followers," (paper presented at the annual meeting of the American Political Science Association, New York City, 1973); Edward Sagarin, "Behind the Gay Liberation Front," *The Realist*, May–June 1970; Allen Young, who was a revolutionary Marxist at the time, also agrees that the rhetoric of GLF limited its appeal among most gays. Young, interview.

115   Hoose, interview; Jay, interview.

116   Jay, 223; Lavery, interview; Young, interview.

117   Hoose interview; Lavery, interview.

118   Jay, 253.

119   Sasha Gregory, "Gay Liberation Front," *Gay Pride* (San Francisco), June 25, 1972.

Chapter 6: The Made-for-TV Movement

1   Arnold Hano claimed that every Saturday night between 50 and 60 million Americans watched *All in the Family*. "Can Archie Bunker Give Bigotry a Bad Name?" *New York Times*, March 12, 1972.

2   Quoted in *Harper*'s magazine, February 2000.

3   The GAA held a workshop entitled "The Mass Media as Gay Propaganda." The description reads "using the media to reach the gay community and

society at large; getting TV coverage; tactics for TV and radio appearances; controlling press relations; organizational publications; the gay press." Printed Ephemera, box 22, folder 1, Gay Activists Alliance Papers, Rare Books and Manuscripts Division, New York Public Library.

4   The informal discussions that lead to the creation of GAA began in November 1969. The founders included Jim Owles, Arthur Evans, Kay Tobin, Marty Robinson, Tom Doerr, Richard Flynn, Arthur Bell, Don Teal, Leo Martello, Steve Adams, Fred Orlansky, Garry Dutton, Fred Calellero. "What is GAA?" Printed Ephemera, box 22, folder 1, Gay Activists Alliance Papers.

5   Frank Conner, draft for article entitled "Who has the Power?" for *Gay Activist*, box 18, folder 9–11, Gay Activists Alliance Papers; Arthur Bell, *Dancing the Gay Lib Blues* (New York: Simon and Schuster, 1971) 23; Marc Rubin, interview by author, tape recording, New York City, August 9, 2003; Pete Fisher, interview by author, tape recording, New York City, August 9, 2003.

6   Mike Lavery, interview by author, tape recording, New York City, February 13, 2004.

7   The constitution was worked out by Jim Owles, Marty Robinson, Arthur Evans, and Arthur Bell. Frank Conner, draft for article titled, "Who has the Power?" for *Gay Activist*, box 18, folder 9–11, Gay Activists Alliance Papers; Don Teal, *The Gay Militants* (New York: St. Martin's Press, 1971), 204.

8   "Constitution and Bylaws of GAA," box 22, folder 1, Gay Activists Alliance Papers.

9   Murphy, *Homosexual Liberation*, 145–46; GLFer quote from Teal, 112.

10   Frank Conner, draft for article, entitled "Who has the Power?" for *Gay Activist*, box 18, folder 9–11, Gay Activists Alliance Papers.

11   Quoted in Teal, 117.

12   Bell, 29; Jim Owles praised the *New York Post* in a letter to the editor in 1971. Jim Owles to James A. Wechsler, box 17, folder 9, News and Media Correspondence, Gay Activists Alliance Papers; Rich Wandel, president of the GAA in 1972, wrote in a letter to the editor of the *Post*, "Of all the media the *Post* has been most enlightened and fair in its reportage of aspects of the gay liberation movement and most specifically the Gay Activists Alliance's role in effecting change." Rich Wandel to *New York Post*, February 3, 1972, box 17, folder 9, News and Media Correspondence, Gay Activists Alliance Papers. Pete Hamill would later

emerge as an important ally of the GAA in the Inner Circle Affair (see chapter 7).

13   Ron Hollander, "Gays Picket City Hall," *New York Post*, March 5, 1970.

14   Quoted in Teal, 118.

15   Ibid., 118.

16   Bell, 39.

17   Activist Pete Fisher echoed Donald Webster Cory when he told a *Newsday* reporter, "What has made gay people one of the most oppressed groups in society is that, unlike the black man, they have been able to hide. We've been our own police. . . .Homosexuals are still terribly afraid to do anything in public. It took me a couple of months to get up the courage to go to a demonstration. I always assumed I'd be beaten up, that society was right, that it was very natural I should hide. . . . But getting out on the street in a demonstration was a really revolutionary thing. You find people are not as dangerous, as threatening as you thought. All of a sudden you realize you can be proud of yourself, you can be as good as anybody else, and you've been treated like___for years. You really see people growing and developing as they move beyond dissembling and being frightened." Quoted in David Gelman in "Homosexuals: Out of the Closet," *Newsday*, May 15, 1971.

18   Joseph Epstein, "Homo/Hetero: The Struggle for Sexual Identity," *Harper's* magazine, September 1970.

19   Press Release, "Gay Activists Alliance Invades Harper's Magazine," October 27, 1970, box 17, folder 10, News and Media Relations, Gay Activists Alliance Papers.

20   Bell, 133–34

21   Ibid., 127.

22   Quoted in Teal, 251.

23   Arthur Evans, interview by Roland Schembari, transcript, April 3, 1998, Voices of the Oral History Project of GLHSNC, San Francisco, CA; Evans confirmed this quote in an interview with the author.

24   "Gay Activists Appear on Cavett Show," box 17, folder 10, News and Media Press Releases, Gay Activists Alliance Papers; Larry Gross, *Up From Invisibly* (New York: Columbia University Press, 2001), 44.

25   Evans, interview.

26   Gregory Dawson, "News Briefs," *Gay Activist*, April 1973; Gregory Dawson, "Why We Demonstrate," *Gay Activist*, April 1973.

27   Murphy, *Homosexual Liberation*, 168.

28   Bell, 163.

29 Foster Gunnison Jr. to Pete Fisher, May 3, 1971, Gunnison Papers, GAA-New York Correspondence April 1971–November 1972, Gunnison Papers.

30 Not all gays were pleased with the show. William Edward Beardemphl wrote in the *Bay Area Reporter,* "From New York we were treated to a devastating Dick Cavett program where a desperate host tried to make GAA leader Jim Owles and Mattachine Leader Dick Leitsch look good. Mr. Owles and Mr. Leitsch did everything possible to appear as uninformed, backbiting jackasses. It was embarrassing to say the least." William Edward Beardemphl, "Comments," *Bay Area Reporter* (San Francisco), January 1, 1972.

31 Clendinen and Nagourney, 188.

32 Charles Silverstein, interview by author, tape recording, New York City, July 8, 2004.

33 "Attendance at Thursday night meetings at the Church of the Holy Apostles meeting hall (1800 square feet) soared above 300, boosted by increasing media exposure, such as the appearance of GAA members on the Susskind Show." "GAA Finds a Home," *Gay Activist*, May 1971.

34 "Media Wrap-up," Media Committee, box 18, folder 9–11, Gay Activists Alliance Papers.

35 "Gay Activists Alliance Committees," February 1970, GAA- New York Correspondence, April 1971–November 1972, Gunnison Papers.

36 Video Tape Committee, box 17, folder 17–19, Gay Activists Alliance Papers; Jim Owles, Printed Ephemera 1970–1971, box 22, folder 1, Gay Activists Alliance Papers.

37 Public Service Announcement, News and Media Relations, box 17, folder 10, Gay Activists Alliance Papers. Mike Lavery recalled that there was an attempt to target the stereotypes of the "limp-wristed faggot, the prissy faggot." Lavery, interview by author, New York City, tape recording, June 15, 2004.

38 "It is the cornerstone precept of the movement that Gay is not only Good, it is practically ordinary, and lately, more and more gays have been 'coming out,' as they put it, to submit their ordinariness to public scrutiny. In New York, the leading edge of this confrontation is the Gay Activist Alliance." David Gelman, "Homosexuals: Out of the Closet," *Newsday*, May 15, 1971.

39 Billy Schoell, "Eye on the Media," Media Committee, box 18, folder 9–11, Gay Activists Alliance Papers.

40 Various letters from GAA to media organizations are in News and Media Related Correspondence, box 17, folder 9, Gay Activists Alliance Papers;

Pete Fisher to Bantam Books, box 18, folder 7, Gay Activists Alliance Papers.

41   Gregory Dawson, "Marcus Welby Protestors Found Innocent," *Gay Activist*, April 1973;Albin Krebs, "Welby is Scored by Gay Activists," *New York Times*, February 17, 1973; Ron Gold, interview by author, tape recording, New York City, July 17, 2004; Kantrowitz, interview by author, tape recording, New York City, July 17, 2004.

42   "Bob Hope Still Top Comedian, but Image Shows Some Tarnish," *Free Press* (Burlington, VT), January 20, 1972; Bell, 168.

43   Kantrowitz, interview.

44   Gregory Dawson, "News Briefs," *Gay Activist*, April 1973; Gregory Dawson, "Why We Demonstrate," *Gay Activist*, April 1973.

45   Arthur Bell, "Gay Job Hearings: Palatable for Mom?" *Village Voice*, October 28, 1971.

46   Text of the bill, Pete Fisher Collection, Lesbian, Gay, Bisexual & Trans-gender Community Center National History Archive, New York City.

47   "Intro 475 does have much value in itself, but Gay Liberationists, except for revolutionaries who saw 475 as a way of showing that the system was hopelessly unresponsive, saw Intro 475 as the best way of getting the mes-sage to the community: the closet is built in fear, not shame. In that very real sense, Intro 475 never was and never could be defeated. Many Gays came out of the closet for the struggle and many more will join them as that struggle continues." Marty Robinson, "Trashing of Intro 475 The Closet of Fear," *Village Voice*, February 17, 1972; "The importance of the drive was the issue rather than the actual bill." Ernest Peter Cohen, "475: A Gay Odyssey," *Gay Activist*, March 1972; Rich Wandel claims the GAA leadership did not expect the bill to pass but saw the fight for its passage as "an organizing tool." Wandel, interview.

48   1964 Greitzer and Ed Koch pressed the Police Commission to assign more plainclothes detectives to sweep "perverts" from Washington Square Park and the surrounding streets. The Mattachine Society waged a successful cam-paign against the consequent entrapment campaign. Teal, 113; Ernest Peter Cohen wrote in the GAA newsletter that Greitzer "had been known to be anti-gay." Ernest Peter Cohen, "475: A Gay Odyssey," *Gay Activist*, March 1972.

49   *Gay Activist*, August 1971.

50   Quoted in Clendinen and Nagourney, 68.

51   Three years later Jim Owles became the first openly gay person to run for

city council when he challenged Carol Greitzer for her council seat. See chapter 10.

52 "Councilman Greitzer Yields to Gay Activists," *Gay*, June 1, 1970; Teal, 115; Bell, 69–73.

53 The UPI story about the GAA and civil right legislation was printed in *Daily American* (Naples, Italy) September 21, 1971; *Times Herald* (Dallas, Texas) October 10, 1971.

54 Arthur Evans, interview by author, tape recording, May 11, 2004; Morty Manford and Arthur Evans described zapping in a three part series in *Gay* magazine. Morty Manford and Arthur Evans, "The Theory and Practice of Confrontation Tactics," *Gay*, February 12, 1973; "The Theory and Practice of Confrontation Tactics: Part II, The Political Function of Zaps," *Gay*, February 26, 1973; "How to Zap," *Gay*, March 12, 1973.

55 Wandel, interview; Rubin, interview; Fisher, interview.

56 Pete Fisher, position paper on "A Strategy for Passing Intro #2," February 17, 1974, box 16, folder 1–2, Fair Employment, Gay Activists Alliance Papers.

57 Evans, interview.

58 Rubin, interview.

59 Dennis Altman wrote that "the real significance of zapping a political figure like John Lindsay may lie less in its effect on the policies being challenged than in the new self-confidence and identity the activity provides those who participate and the new model of gayness it offers to those as yet too scared to come out." Quoted in Neil Miller, *Out of the Past: Gay and Lesbian History from 1969 to the Present* (New York: Vintage, 1995), 379. Arthur Bell recalled "Although zaps may not have the long-range therapeutic value of a series of sessions with an analyst, they do tend to release poison gases and clear the head." Bell, 70. Rich Wandel called zaps "a way of bringing the community together." Wandel, interview.

60 Gross, 47.

61 Evans, interview; Fisher, interview.

62 Wandel, interview.

63 Evans, interview.

64 Clendinen and Nagourney, 52–53.

65 Grace Glueck, "For Museum Birthday, Good Cheer and Cake," *New York Times*, April 14, 1970.

66 "Gays Back Mayor's Shield," box 22, folder 12, Gay Activists Alliance Papers; "GAA Confronts Lindsay At Museum," *Gay*, May 4, 1970.

67   Kantrowitz, interview.

68   Sandra Vaughn, "Lindsay & Homosexuals: An Edited Encounter," *Village Voice*, April 23, 1970; Teal, 123; Bell, 54.

69   John Toscano, "Rings a Gay Alarm in Firehouse," *Daily News*, October 19, 1971; Clendinen and Nagourney, 54.

70   "GAA Confronts Lindsay at Channel 5," *Gay*, May 11, 1970.

71   "GAA Confronts Goldberg," *Gay*, June 29, 1970.

72   Statement issued by Arthur J. Goldberg, October 25, 1970, News and Media Relations, box 17, folder 10, Gay Activists Alliance Papers.

73   Bell, 139–40.

74   "3 Candidates Support Rights of Homosexuals," *New York Times*, October 27, 1970.

75   Editorial, *Gay*, November 9, 1970.

76   Jim Owles to GAA membership, 1970, box 18, folder 4–6, Gay Activists Alliance Papers.

77   Lindsay Van Gelder, "Gay Bill of Rights Makes Progress," *New York Post*, November 5, 1970.

78   Barbara Trecker, "The 'Gays' Advocate in Albany," *New York Post*, March 6, 1971.

79   "A clear indication that the militants have made an impression on some local legislators can be found in the fact that 14 separate bills affecting the rights of homosexuals were introduced in the two houses of the state legislature in the last session." Joseph Lelyveld, "Militant Homosexuals to Stage March to Central Park Today," *New York Times*, June 27, 1971. A columnist for the *New York Post* wrote "No one is really quite sure how large the 'hidden' homosexual vote is." James Wechsler, "The Sex Files," *New York Post*, November 11, 1971.

80   "The Department of Consumer Affairs issued licenses for cabarets, dance halls and catering establishments. Prior to Myerson's reforms homosexuals were prohibited from remaining in or being employed in cabarets and prohibited homosexuals or those who pretended to be gay from entering or remaining in food catering places. Any businesses in violating of these prohibitions could be denied a license to operate." Alfonso A. Navaez, "City Acts to Let Homosexuals Meet and Work in Cabarets," *New York Times*, October 12, 1971; Barbara Trecker and George Artz, "Bess Seeks New Deal for Gays," *New York Post*, October 11, 1971.

81   "GAA managed to combine the discipline of nonviolence with militancy, non-violence without Uncle Tomism, and become relevant and even

exciting to many of America's Gay Youth. . . .GAA is neither politically equivalent to the Black Panther Party nor some form of the Southern Christian Leadership Conference. It is a critic-liaison to the establishment, something new, not a reckless happening." Marty Robinson, "Trashing of Intro 475: The Closet of Fear," *Village Voice*, February 17, 1972.

82 Ethan Geto, interview, July 31, 2004.

83 Arthur Bell, "Defeat of the 'Anti-Closet' Bill," *Village Voice*, February 3, 1972.

84 George Douris, "Gay People's Shenanigans Give Mayor New Headache," *Press* (Long Island, NY), February 1, 1972.

85 "Fidelifacts Oppresses Homosexuals," Fair Employment Records, box 16, folder 1–2, Gay Activists Alliance Papers; Gillen's employment investigations always included a look into the personal lives of the prospective employee. In 1966 when Gillen was hired to investigate Ralph Nader, Gillen asked a friend of Nader why the thirty-one year-old lawyer was not married. The friend asked, "Are you asking me if he is a homosexual?" Gillen responded, "Well, we have to inquire about these things. I've seen him on TV and he certainly doesn't look like. . . .But we want to know about such matters." Walter Rugaber, "Critic of Auto Industry's Safety Standards Says He Was Trailed and Harassed; Charges Called Absurd," *New York Times*, March 6, 1966.

86 Onge, 26; Press Release, Fair Employment Records, box 16, folder 1–2, Gay Activists Alliance Papers.

87 Paul Burt, "GAA Initiates Cable TV Program," *Gay Activist*, November 1973.

88 Rudi Stern, "Audio/Video," *Crawdaddy*, August 29, 1971; Stern also wrote Arthur Bell, "Other groups talk about the possibility of being able to see a demonstration the night after it happened but no other group has put the pieces together. Quite impressive." Rudi Stern to Arthur Bell, July 9, 1971, Bell Papers.

89 Video Tape Committee, box 17, folder 17–19, Gay Activists Alliance Papers.

90 "Gay Marriages Are Catching On," *New York Post*, April 14, 1971.

91 "The value of such tape is that they can see their action as a learning experience over which they have control, as opposed to the cultural freak show treatment which network television would present." Rudi Stern, *Crawdaddy*, August 29, 1971.

92 Report by Agitprop Committee, box 19, folder 16, Gay Activists Alliance Papers.

93   Agitprop Miscellaneous, box 19, folder 16, Gay Activists Alliance
      Papers.

94   William Stern, Assistant Principal Brandeis High School to GAA, box 8
      folder 11, Gay Activists Alliance Papers.

95   The figure comes from Morty Manford to Bernard S. Cayne, Editor-in
      Chief of the *Encyclopedia Americana*, January 17, 1974, box 19, folder
      16; Breaking the H.S. Barrier, *Gay Activist*.

96   "Gays Zap Maryland SDS," National Gay Movement Outgoing Corre-
      spondence, box 16, folder 14, Gay Activists Alliance Papers.

97   Julius Johnson, Minister of Information, Gainesville GFL to Morty Man-
      ford, Video Tape Committee, box 17, folder 17, Gay Activists Alliance
      Papers.

98   Frank Kameny to Richard Wandel, National Gay Movement Outgoing
      Correspondence, box 16, folder 14, Gay Activists Alliance Papers.

99   Barbara Trecker, "Homosexuals vs. Small Town Fascists," *New York Post*,
      August 25, 1971; Morty Manford in Marcus, 157–58.

100   National Gay Movement Correspondence, box 16, Gay Activists Alliance
      Papers.

101   David Corcoran, "Homosexuals Demand Equal Rights," *Bergen Record*
      (New Jersey), September 19, 1971.

102   "Homosexuals Plan to Build Political Clout," *Daily News*, November 14,
      1971.

103   "The Militant Homosexual," *Newsweek*, August 23, 1971.

104   "Homosexuals in Revolt: The year the one liberation movement turned
      militant," *Life*, December 31, 1971.

105   Wandel to Charles, April 6, 1971, Gay Activists Alliance Papers.

106   Clendinen and Nagourney, 56.

107   Wandel to Charles April 6, 1971, Gay Activists Alliance Papers; The finance
      committee records for February 1, 1971–January 31, 1972 show the GAA
      spent $1,283.30 making the merchandise and took in $3,269.42 in sales.
      Finance Committee Records, box 16, folder 3–4, Gay Activists Alliance Papers.

108   "The History of the Lambda," *Gay Life*, March 27, 1981, box 146, folder
      26, Bruce Voeller Papers.

109   "It all adds up to a Gay revolution—and GAA's Firehouse, along with its
      lambda, has become one of its most powerful symbols. "Firehouse Festivi-
      ties," *Gay Activist*, June 1971.

110   Joseph Lelyveld, "Militant Homosexuals to Stage March to Central Park
      Today," *New York Times*, June 27, 1971.

111 Press release, June 12, 1972, Printed Ephemera, Gay Activists Alliance
     Papers; Press release, September 2, 1971, Gay Activists Alliance Papers;
     Dick Brukenfeld, "Learn and Live," *Village Voice*, June 22, 1972.

112 Fisher, interview.

113 Alan Bell, "Some Thoughts on the Westside/GAA Dances," *Village Voice*,
     January 3, 1977, box 18, folder 3, Gay Activists Alliance Papers.

114 Kantrowitz, interview.

115 Finances Committee Records, box 16, folder 3–4, Gay Activists Alliance
     Papers.

116 "The Fire House as Political Tool a Talk with Marty Robinson," Media
     Committee, box 18, folder 9–11, Gay Activists Alliance Papers; Gay
     Activists Alliance General Meeting Minutes, December 21, 1972, Gay
     Activists Alliance Papers; Pete Fisher and Marc Rubin both agree that the
     GAA dances were political because just showing up for a gay dance was a
     political act in the early 1970s. Rubin, interview; Fisher interview.

117 Gay Activists Alliance General Meeting Minutes, December 21, 1972, Gay
     Activists Alliance Papers.

118 Wandel, interview.

119 Arnie Kantrowitz, "The Day Gay Lib Died," *New York Native*, November
     2–15, 1981.

120 "The Gay Vote," *New Republic*; GAA leaflet "Senator Muskie Refuses to
     Endorse Civil Liberties for Gay People," box 22, folder 2, Gay Activists
     Alliance Papers; "Muskie Troubled by Issue Critics," *New York Times*, Jan-
     uary 6, 1972; Ted Knap, "Fat Cats Purr for Muskie at $500 Meal," *Press*
     (Pittsburgh), January 16, 1972.

121 Quoted in Theodore H. White, *The Making of The President 1972* (New
     York: Atheneum Publishers, 1973), 76.

122 A column by Victor Riesel ran three newspapers under different headlines.
     "Kennedy's 'Gay' Policy Shows He is Not Serious," *Commercial Appeal*
     (Memphis); "Kennedy Won't Run," *Free Press* (Burlington, Vermont), Jan-
     uary 24, 1972, and "Count Ted Out," *Jersey Journal* (Jersey City), Jan-
     uary 24, 1972.

123 Arthur Bell, "Gay Lib: Gene and Ted Say OK," *Village Voice*, November
     25, 1971; Thomas Ronan, "Senator Kennedy Hints Opposition to Rehn-
     quist," *New York Times*, November 17, 1971.

124 The bill only needed the support of eight of the fifteen council members
     on the General Welfare committee. Only five voted "yes." "Intro 475
     Rides Again," *Press*, June 30, 1972; "Gay Bill Defeated, Irked Activists to

Demonstrate," *Press*, January 28, 1972; "NY Council Kills Bill to OK Homosexuals" *Denver Post–New York Times Wire Service*, January 28, 1972.

125   Edward Ranzal, "Council Kills a Bill Giving Homosexuals Protection on Bias," *New York Times*, January 28, 1972.

126   Silverstein, interview.

127   Edward Ranzal, "Homosexual Bill Argued in Council," November 16, 1971, *New York Times*, November 16, 1971. According to the *New York Post*, "The transvestites, actions no doubt contributed to the bill's defeat." Barbara Trecker, "Homosexuals in New York," *New York Post*, March 29, 1974.

128   Arthur Bell, "Defeat of the 'Anti-closet' Bill," *Village Voice*, February 3, 1972; Ron Gold, "Gay Lib Shouts Down Mayor Lindsay," *Variety*, February 3, 1972; "A Gay Affair," *Newsday*, January 26, 1972; Martin Tolchin, "Thousands of City Employes *sic* Attend Lindsay Benefit," *New York Times*, January 26, 1972; Sam Roberts, "Film Opener Raises 300G For Lindsay," *Daily News*, January 26, 1972; "NY Gay Activists Disrupt Lindsay's Campaign Fundraiser at Music Hall," *Variety*, January 26, 1972; Sandor M. Polster and John Mullane, The Lindsay Bash—Quite a Mishmash," *New York Post*, January 26, 1972; Wandel, interview.

129   "17 in Gay Alliance Held after Protests at Lindsay Offices," *New York Times*, January 27, 1972.

130   Alan Eysen, "For Lindsay, a Chant and a Mishap," *Newsday*, February 18, 1972; "Lindsay is Greeted by 200 at LI Headquarters Opens," *New York Times*, February 18, 1972.

131   "New City Directive Bars Hiring Bias on Homosexuals," *New York Times*, February 8, 1972; Barbara Tucker, "City Bars Homosexual Job Bias," *New York Post*, February 8, 1972.

132   Martin Arnold, "Not Exactly a Banner day for Gay Lib," *New York Times*, February 13, 1972.

133   Clendinen and Nagourney, 140.

134   "The Gay Vote," *New Republic*, September 1972.

135   The statement read in part "It is a basic tenet of our belief that our government should preserve the rights of the individual without presuming to dictate private matters. Independence of religious and political beliefs is a recognized right. Surely this right should be extended to a matter that is as irrelevant to the body politic as sexual orientation. We have found it necessary to spell out in legislation that there shall be no discrimination based

on race, creed, national origin, or sex in housing, employment, and public accommodations. Now we are recognizing that it is unfortunately also necessary to identify yet another group that has suffered harassment and deprivation. I hope for the day when we do not need to specify that 'Liberty and Justice for All' includes Blacks, Chicanos, American Indians, Women, Homosexuals, or any other group. All means ALL." Quoted in GAA press release, "McGovern Supports Civil Rights and Civil Liberties for Homosexuals," box 17, folder 8, Gay Activists Alliance Papers; Barbara Trecker, "McGovern Backs Gay Bill—Applause Halts Hearing," *New York Post*, December 17, 1971.

136 Alan Brinkley, *Liberalism and Its Discontents* (Cambridge: Harvard University Press, 1998), 260.

137 Susan Fogg, " 'Gays' Knock at Democrats' Door," *Star* (Washington D.C), June 12, 1972.

138 Muskie, Hubert Humphrey, and others in the party pushed McGovern to moderate his stance on various issues including gay rights. Jeffrey Antevil, "3 Unity Plank Nailed into the Dem Platform," *Daily News*, June 26, 1972; for a detailed description of the fight for a gay rights plank at the 1972 Democratic National Convention, see Clendinen and Nagourney, 132–36.

139 Geto had decided to support McGovern because of the candidate's commitment to withdraw from Vietnam and his ability to win the nomination. He convinced Robert Abrams, the Bronx borough president to support the little known candidate. The endorsement earned Abrams the chairmanship of McGovern's New York campaign while Geto became directly involved in the McGovern operation. Geto, interview.

140 The GOP national platform chairman was pleased with the radicalism of the Democratic platform and publicly declared Republican plans to use it against McGovern in the fall. "GOP platform leader Criticizes McGovern," *Associated Press*, June 7, 1972. Gordon Weil, a high ranking McGovern campaign official, wrote about the platform fight, "On gay rights, a young woman from the Ohio delegation rose to oppose the minority plank and launched into a most distasteful attack on homosexuals. But, however offensive her remarks might be to some McGovern delegates, we knew that the plank must be defeated." Gordon Weil, *The Long Shot, George McGovern Runs for President* (New York: W.W. Norton & Company Inc., 1973), 126.

141 Geto, interview.

142 George McGovern to Rich Wandel, August 7, 1972, box 22, folder 2, Gay Activists Alliance Papers; George McGovern to Rich Wandel, August 10, 1972, box 22, folder 2, Gay Activists Alliance Papers. Since the letters bear different signatures it is clear they were not both sent by the senator.

143 Geto, interview; Clendinen and Nagourney, 145.

144 "Why We Are Occupying McGovern Headquarters," August 21, 1972, press release, box 22, folder 2, Gay Activists Alliance Papers.

145 Geto, interview.

146 Clendinen and Nagourney, 142.

147 Ron Gold press release, "McGovern Backs Gay Rights," October 12, 1972, box 16, folder 9, Gay Activists Alliance Papers.

148 Thomas P. Ronan, "McGovern Hailed Warmly at Trade Union Rally Here," *New York Post*, October 21, 1972.

149 Evans, interview.

150 Cory, 89.

151 Ibid., 229.

Chapter 7: The Inner Circle Affair

1 Journalists and historians have presented the Inner Circle Affair as a beating of gay activists rather than a fistfight or melee. Interviews conducted for this book revealed that Manford and fellow Activists fought back.

2 Many books use the word "homophobia," but none delve into its origins or its implications. There is nothing about the term in Marotta, Adam, Kaiser, Engel, Clendinen and Nagourney, and the media studies. Cruikshank calls the term an "effective strategy for shifting from the defensive position of having to justify homosexuality to the offensive by forcing opposition to justify its stance." In a book entitled *Homophobia*, Byrne Fone presents the history of antigay laws, governmental policies, and social mores as a history of homophobia. But the word is not just a synonym for antigay discrimination.

3 George Weinberg, interview by author, tape recording, New York, NY, July 30, 2003; In his history of homophobia, Byrne Fone speculated that that term was coined in the 1960s, but the earliest place he found the word was in a 1971 article by K. T. Smith entitled "Homophobia: A Tentative Personality Profile." Fone also cites George Weinberg's 1972 book *Society and the Healthy Homosexual* and claims that Mark Freedman in 1975 in "Homophobia: The Psychology of a Social Disease," added to Weinberg's definition

with his description of homophobia as an "extreme rage and fear reaction to homosexuals." But Manford described these aspects of homophobia in 1972. Byrne Fone, *Homophobia* (New York: Metropolitan Books, 2000), 5.

4   George Weinberg, *Society and the Healthy Homosexual* (New York: St. Martin's Press, 1972), 4.

5   George Weinberg, interview by author, tape recording, New York, NY, July 30, 2003.

6   Geto, interview.

7   Calvin Trillin, "A Few Observations on the Zapping of the Inner Circle," *The New Yorker*, July 15, 1972.

8   Terry Pristin, "The Annual Room 9 Follies," *Journalism Review*, July 1972.

9   Ibid.

10   GAA Press Release, "Gays assaulted at New York Hilton," April 18, 1972, Gay Activists Alliance Papers; Judith Michaelson, "Charge Police Ignored Beatings at Hilton Gala," *New York Post*, April 18, 1972.

11   In *Out for Good* Clendinen and Nagourney assert that Ethan Geto was the one who made the call. Clendinen and Nagourney, 145.

12   The GAA Executive Committee Records at the New York Public Library contain minutes from the meeting in which GAA voted to zap the Inner Circle. "Ethan Geto moved that buses returning from Albany stop at the NY Hilton Hotel at 54th St. and 6th Ave. to zap the news and media people attending the inner circle dinner. Passed." GAA Executive Committee Records, Gay Activists Alliance Papers; "Any Old Jobs for Homos," *Daily News*, April 5, 1972.

13   Geto, interview.

14   Michael Maye's testimony, Criminal Court of New York, June 27, 1972, Morty Manford Papers, Rare Books and Manuscripts, NYPL.

15   John O' Sullivan's testimony, Criminal Court of the City of New York, June 27, 1972, Manford, Papers.

16   Leonard Cohen's testimony, Criminal Court of the City of New York, June 26, 1972, Manford Papers.

17   Ethan Geto's testimony, Criminal Court of the City of New York, June 26, 1972, Manford Papers.

18   Katz, "Inner Circle Affair."

19   David McCormack's testimony, Criminal Court of the City of New York, June 29, 1972; Judith Michaelson, "Charge Police Ignored Beatings at Hilton Gala," *New York Post*, April 18, 1972.

20   Joseph Kahn, "Saw Maye Assault Activist: Official," *New York Post*, April
      28, 1972, Ethan Geto's testimony, Criminal Court of the City of New
      York, June 26, 1972.

21   Michael Maye's testimony, June 27, 1972.

22   Ibid.

23   Jerome Kretchmer's testimony, June 26, 1972.

24   John O Sullivan's testimony, June 29, 1972.

25   Ibid.

26   Orest V. Maresca testimony, Criminal Court of the City of New York, June
      29, 1972, Manford Papers.

27   Fran Palumbo's testimony, Criminal Court of the City of New York, June
      29, 1972, Manford Papers.

28   Although Manford later played the innocent victim to the press, he told his
      friend Ethan Geto that he kicked Maye in the groin. Geto, interview.

29   Manford's notes, Manford Papers.

30   Manford's notes, Manford Papers; Judith Michaelson, "Charge Police
      Ignored Beatings at Hilton Gala."

31   Morty Manford's testimony, Criminal Court of the City of New York, June
      26, 1972, Manford Papers; In court, Mark Sternberg, aid to Mayor Lindsay,
      testified that at the top of the escalator he saw Maye beat a protestor and
      knock him to the floor. Manford was probably that protestor. Mark Stern-
      berg's testimony, Criminal Court of the City of New York, June 27, 1972.

32   Morty Manford's testimony, Criminal, June 26, 1972; Mark Sternberg also
      did not see Maye throw Manford on the escalator. Mark Sternberg's testi-
      mony, June 27, 1972. Leonard Cohen, one of the prosecution's witnesses
      during Maye's trial claimed two gray haired dinner guests lifted Manford
      up and heaved him onto the escalator.

33   Michael Maye's testimony, June 27, 1972.

34   Michaelson, "Charge Police Ignored Beatings at Hilton Gala."

35   Leonard Cohen and Mark Sternberg did not recall a bald man but testi-
      fied that after Manford was thrown on the moving stairs, Maye bounded
      down the escalator and repeatedly stomped on the young man. Leonard
      Cohen's testimony, Criminal Court of the City of New York, June 26,
      1972, Manford Papers; Mark Sternberg's testimony, June 27, 1972; Lacey
      Fosburgh, "Court Told Maye Beat Homosexual," *New York Post*, June 27,
      1972; John Scanlon, who testified against Maye, did not recall Manford
      being thrown onto the escalator. He remembered a police officer
      escorting Morty down the escalator and Maye suddenly leaping down

upon Manford and grinding his heal into the student's groin four or five times. Scanlon worked in the same building as Maye and was certain of his identity. Eric Pace, "Official Accuses Maye of Assault," *New York Times,* April 25, 1972; Lacey Fosburgh, "Maye Kicked Man, Witness Testifies," *New York Times,* June 24, 1972; John Scanlon's testimony, Criminal Court of the City of New York, June 26, 1972; All of the prosecution witnesses agreed that Maye brutally assaulted Manford on the escalator. For other details on the beating, see also Judith Michaelson, "Maye Denies Attack Charge," *New York Post,* April 19, 1972; Judith Michaelson, "3rd Witness Says Maye Attacked 2 Protestors," *New York Post,* April 19, 1972; Judith Michaelson, "Charge Police Ignored Beatings at Hilton Gala"; Manford's testimony, Criminal Court of the City of New York, June 26, 1972.

36   Mark Sternberg's testimony, June 27, 1972.

37   Michael Maye's testimony, June 27, 1972.

38   Ibid.

39   Michaelson, "Charge Police Ignored Beatings at Hilton Gala."

40   Leonard Cohen's testimony, June 26, 1972.

41   Michaelson, "Charge Police Ignored Beatings at Hilton Gala."

42   Ibid.

43   Statement by Ethan M. Geto, May 1, 1972, Manford Papers.

44   Lacey Fosburgh, "Maye Kicked Man, Witness Testifies."

45   Michael Maye's testimony, June 27, 1972.

46   Les L. Ledbetter, "Homosexuals File Assault Charges Against Maye and 6 Others," *New York Times,* April 19, 1972.

47   Michaelson, "Maye Denies Attack Charge."

48   Fosburgh, "Maye Is Held as Harasser in Gay Alliance Outbreak," *New York Times,* May 23, 1972.

49   Maye's brother became a police officer and president of the transit police PBA.

50   Bell, *Dancing the Gay Lib Blues,* 108–9.

51   Nancy Burton, "Lindsay Pestered at NYU Meeting," *The Villager,* September 24, 1970.

52   Terry Pristin, "Golden Gloves," *Journalism Review,* July 1972.

53   Henry Coleman, interview by author, telephone, March, 6, 2001.

54   Arthur Bell, "The Mickey Maye Story: Flashback to Dirty Dicks," *Village Voice,* May 25, 1972.

55   Michael Maye's testimony, June 27, 1972.

56   Joseph Kahn, "Inner Circle: Still No Action," *New York Post*, April 22, 1972.

57   Charles Tiefer, "Gay Leader Severely Beaten at Hilton Dinner Conference," *Columbia Spectator*, April 20, 1972.

58   Kahn, "Inner Circle: Still No Action."

59   Michael Kramer, "The City Politic Fireman's Brawl," *New York*, May 15, 1972.

60   Kahn, "Inner Circle: Still No Action."

61   Judith Michaelson, "3rd Witness Says Maye Attacked 2 Protestors," *New York Post*, April 19, 1972.

62   Katz, "Inner Circle Affair"

63   Peter Fisher letter to editor, *New York Post*, April 20, 1972.

64   "Inner Circle Dinner, New York Hilton Hotel, 4/15/72," FBI Files, box 18, folder 7, Gay Activists Alliance Papers.

65   Geto, interview; Calvin Trillin, "A Few Observations on the Zapping of the Inner Circle," *The New Yorker*, July 15, 1972.

66   James Wechsler, "Good Clean Fun?" *New York Post*, April 21, 1972.

67   In *Straight News: Gays, Lesbians, and the News Media,* Edward Alwood incorrectly claims that like other New York reporters, *New York Post* Columnist Pete Hamill referred to the Inner Circle in his column only in passing. Edward Alwood, *Straight News: Gays, Lesbians, and the News Media* (New York: Columbia University Press, 1996), 122.

68   Gale McGovern, letter to editor, *New York Post*, April 25, 1972.

69   John Mullane, "Gays Say DA Plays Politics," *New York Post*, May 24, 1972.

70   Michaelson, "Maye Denies Attack Charge."

71   Carol Greitzer to Commissioner Patrick Murphy, Gay Activists Alliance Papers.

72   "Maye Denies Attack, Says Gays Invaded" *Daily News*, April 20 1972

73   Joseph Kahn, "Ready Report on Beatings," *New York Post*, April 26, 1972.

74   Judith Michaelson, "Maye Denies Attack Charge"; Gay Activist Charge is Disputed by Maye," *New York Post*, April 20, 1972.

75   Sandy Reichman, *New York Post*, April 25, 1972.

76   "Homosexuals Push Maye Case," *New York Times*, May 4, 1972.

77   "Maye hit with a Rap in Gay Tiff," *Daily News*, May 23, 1972 and Mike Pearl and Judith Michaelson "Arrest May in Gay Beating," *New York Post*, May 22, 1972.

78   William Proctor, "Maye Cleared of Charges in Hilton," *Daily News*, July 6, 1972; Lacey Fosburgh, "Maye is Held as Harasser in Gay Alliance Outbreak," *New York Times*, May 23, 1972.

79   "Maye hit with a Rap in Gay Tiff," *Daily News*, May 23, 1972

80   Lacey Fosburgh, "Maye Is Held as Harasser in Gay Alliance Outbreak,"
      New York Times, May 23, 1972.

81   Councilmen Eldon Clingan, Carter Burden, and Charles Taylor, statement
      regarding the charges against Allen Roskoff, Manford Papers.

82   "Gay Activist Demonstrator Awaiting Arrest at City Hall," Press release
      from the Office of Eldon Clingan, Manford Papers.

83   "Case Against Gay Activist Is Dropped by D.A.," *New York Times*,

84   Manford to Friends (Supporters of Gay People at Columbia) May 17,
      1972, Manford Papers.

85   "New Assault Is Reported by Gay Activist Member," *New York Times*, April
      22, 1972.

86   Michael Blaine, "The Charge of Mayehem," *Village Voice*, May 4, 1972.

87   Michael Kramer, "The City Politic Fireman's Brawl."

88   Ibid.

89   According to Pete Fisher, Manford consciously promoted the word during
      interviews after the Inner Circle incident. Fisher, interview.

90   Press conference statement, May 16, 1972, Manford Papers.

91   Morty Manford's testimony, Criminal Court of the City of New York, June
      26, 1972.

92   Manford to faculty members, July 17, 1972, Manford Papers.

93   "Gay Chief Calls Maye a 'Savage,' " *New York Post*, June 26, 1972.

94   Lacey Fosburgh, "Court Told Maye Beat Homosexual," *New York Times*,
      June 27, 1972.

95   "Maye Called 'Savage,' " *The Long Island Press*, June 27, 1972.

96   Arthur Bell, "Morty Manford & the Flaming Homophobe," *Village Voice*,
      July 13, 1972.

97   "The Charge is Mayehem," *The Voice*, May 4, 1972.

98   Manford to Dwayne, June 16, 1972, Manford Papers.

99   Quoted in Alwood, 150.

100   Geto perjured himself playing the concerned, impartial citizen who was
      outraged by Maye's brutality. When asked if he were Manford's friend
      Geto said no. Geto, Interview; Ethan Geto's testimony, June 27, 1972.

101   "Maye Cleared in Gay Incident," *Jersey Journal*, July 5, 1972.

102   Kramer, "The City Politic Fireman's Brawl".

103   "Morty Manford's National Ambitions," *Michael's Thing*, October 7, 1974.

104   From an undated speech, Jeanne Manford Papers, Manuscripts Division,
      New York Public Library.

105   "For Homosexuals, It's Getting Less Difficult to Tell Parents," *New York Times.*

106   Undated form letter to gay parents, Jeanne Manford Papers.

107   PFLAG newsletter, Winter 1991, Jeanne Manford Papers.

108   Marilyn Goldstein, "Our Child is Gay," *Newsday's Magazine for Long Island*, August 19, 1979.

109   Geto, interview.

110   From an undated speech, Jeanne Manford Papers.

111   "Morty Manford, whose complaint of being beaten by Michael J. Maye, President of the Uniformed Firefighters association has put the union leader on trial, also marched, accompanied by his mother, Jean Manford. Mrs. Manford said "I'm Proud of My son, I'm not ashamed of him," *New York Times,* June 26, 1972.

112   Anna Quindlen, "No Closet Space," *New York Times,* May 27, 1992.

113   Jeanne Manford's notes, Jeanne Manford Papers.

114   Judy Klemesrud, "For Homosexuals' Parents, Strength in Community," *New York Times,* 1984.

115   Cory, 10.

Chapter 8: The Gay Lounge

1   Memorandum by Morty Manford, 1970, Manford Papers.

2   Robert Liebert, "The Gay Student Movement: A Psychopolitical View," *Change*, October 1971.

3   "Gay Group Requests Meeting with McGill about Lounge," *Columbia Spectator*, April 27, 1071

4   J. Michael Marion, "SAS Position Paper Denies That the Lounge Is Exclusionary," *Columbia Spectator*, April 29, 1971.

5   "SAS Public Statement," *Columbia Spectator*, April 9, 1971.

6   Peter Pouncey, interview by author, April 3, 2001, New York City.

7   Liebert, "The Gay Student Movement: A Psychopolitical View."

8   Memorandum by Carl Hovde, "On the Assignment and Use of Lounge Space in Columbia College," May 5, 1971.

9   Editorial, *Columbia Spectator*, May 7, 1971.

10   Marion, "SAS Position Paper Denies That the Lounge Is Exclusionary."

11   "Manford said gay people 'need a place to meet casually in an unoppressed atmosphere.' " J. Michael Marion, "Columbia Homosexual Group Requests Gay Lounge Facilities," *Columbia Spectator* April 25, 1971.

12   Memorandum by Morty Manford, "On the Importance of the Gay Lounge," September 19, 1972, Manford Papers.

13   Manford speech delivered during a UDC meeting, April 21, 1971, Manford Papers.

14   Furnald Hall Undergraduate Dormitory Council to McGill, April 1971, Student Homophile League Papers.

15   "Furnald Hall Undergraduate Dormitory Council Approves Homosexual Lounge Facilities," *Columbia Spectator*, April 29, 1971.

16   Liebert, "The Gay Student Movement: A Psychopolitical View."

17   Marion, "Columbia Homosexual Group Requests Gay Lounge Facilities."

18   Memorandum by Morty Manford, April 26, 1971. Student Homophile League Papers.

19   "Furnald Hall Undergraduate Dormitory Council Approves Homosexual Lounge Facilities," *Columbia Spectator*.

20   John Brecher, "UDC Asserts Rights to Decide on Use of Residence Space," *Columbia Spectator*, April 5, 1971.

21   Omer S. J. Williams to the Committee on Legal Affairs of the Columbia University Trustees, January 31, 1972, Student Homophile League Papers.

22   McGill to editor of the *Columbia Spectator*, November, 3, 1971.

23   Hovde to Marylyn Haft, October 27, 1971, Student Homophile League Papers.

24   "I do not feel, so far at least that I wish to take an action seen by some as endorsing a homosexual orientation in a community where there are many young people of naturally ambiguous drives given their age." Hovde to Haft, October 27, 1971, Student Homophile League Papers.

25   "Hovde Affirms Position Opposing Gay Lounge," *Columbia Spectator*, November 3, 1971.

26   "When I point to the focus on sexuality as disqualifying for the institutional action requested, I of course do not mean by this that sexuality is somehow beneath notice or that it is less important because one cannot see it. It is the most profound and complicated thing about our being, and while obviously social in its reaching out for associations, it is at the same time profoundly private, underlying many characteristics of our individual natures, both powerful and delicate, it is not in my view the proper focus of official action." Hovde to Manford, Sackheim and Others, May 28, 1971, Student Homophile League Papers.

27   Karen Barrey, "Gay People Take Lounge in Furnald," *Columbia Owl*, May 12, 1971.

28   "Defying Ban, Gay Group Grabs Room at Columbia," *New York Post*, May 10, 1971.

29   Karen Barrey, "Gay People Take Lounge in Furnald," *Columbia Owl*, May 12, 1971.

30   "Gay Students and Hovde: Mistrust" *Columbia Spectator*, May 12, 1971.

31   *The Advocate*, 7, no. 20, July 1971.

32   Manford to the summit meeting of the New York area gay community, July 14, 1971 Manford Papers.

33   Manford to the summit meeting of the New York area gay community, July 14, 1971 Manford Papers.

34   Henry Coleman, interview by author, March 6, 2001, New York City.

35   McGill speech at Holy Cross University, September 25, 1971, Student Homophile League Papers.

36   Hovde to Haft, October 4, 1971, Student Homophile League Papers.

37   Manford to Committee to Oversee University Maintenance, undated, Manford Papers.

38   Maureen McGuirl in "Gay Lounge Flourishes," *Columbia Spectator*, November, 30, 1971.

39   Ibid.

40   "ACLU Urges Hovde to Reverse Position Against Gay Lounge," *Columbia Spectator*, October 22, 1971.

41   Edward Ranzal, "Homosexual Bill Argues in Council," *New York Times*, November 16, 1971.

42   "UDC to Appeal Gay Lounge Ruling: First Time in Columbia History," *Columbia Spectator*, November 18, 1971.

43   Henry Coleman, interview.

44   Pouncey, interview.

45   Memorandum by Morty Manford, December 9, 1971. Manford Papers.

46   Gail Robinson, "Two in GPC Stage Sit-In to Protest Lounge Condition," *Columbia Spectator*, December 10, 1971.

47   "Columbia Agrees to Equip Gay Area," *New York Times*, December 10, 1971.

48   Letter to Manford, Manford Papers.

49   Editorial, *Columbia Spectator*, January 4, 1972; Coleman, interview; Pouncey, interview by author, April 3, 2001, New York City.

50   Omer S. J. Williams to the Committee on Legal Affairs of the Columbia University Trustees, January 31, 1972, Student Homophile League Papers.

51   Pouncey, interview.

52   "Briton Named Columbia College Dean," *New York Times*, March 28, 1972.

53 "Gay Lounge Given Approval of Dean Pouncey," *Columbia Spectator*, September 19, 1972.

54 Peter Pouncey, "Statement on the Gay Lounge," *Columbia Spectator*, September 19, 1972.

55 Pouncey, interview.

56 "Homosexuals Allowed Own Columbia Lounge," *New York Times*, September 19, 1972.

57 Cory, 54.

Chapter 9: "It's Official Now: We're Not Sick"

1   Jane E. Brody, "Homosexuality: Parents Are Not Always to Blame," *New York Times*, February 10, 1971.

2   "The Changing View of Homosexuality," *New York Times*, February 28, 1971.

3   Sigmund Freud, "The Sexual Life of Human Beings," *Introductory Lectures on Psychoanalysis (1916–1917)*, James Strachey trans. and ed. (New York: W.W. Norton & Company, 1966), 304.

4   Ronald Bayer, *Homosexuality and American Psychiatry: The Politics of Diagnosis.* (New York: Basic Books, 1981), 21–22.

5   Freud, "The Sexual Life of Human Beings."

6   Jim Fouratt, interview by author, tape recording, New York City, January 24, 2004.

7   Charles W. Socarides, *Beyond Sexual Freedom* (New York: Quadrangle, 1975), 81.

8   Sandor Rado *Adaptational Psychodynamics: Motivation and Control.* (New York: Science House, 1969), 212–13; Jack Dresher, "I'm Your Handyman: A History of Reparative Therapies," *Journal of Homosexuality* 36, no. 1, 1998, The Hayworth Press Inc.; for Rado's oral history see, *Heresy: Sandor Rado and the Psychoanalytic Movement.* (Northvale, New Jersey: Jason Aronson Inc., 1995)

9   Doty, "Growth of Overt Homosexuality in City Provokes Wide Concern."

10 Bieber's discussion of Hooker's work in his work was limited to a glib conclusion that since her findings were at variance with his own, her methods of evaluation must have been flawed. Jean M. White, "Scientists Disagree on Basic Nature of Homosexuality, Chance of Cure," the *Washington Post*, February 1, 1965.

11 Irving Bieber quoted in transcribed debate with Robert Spitzer in "The APA Ruling on Homosexuality: The Issue is Subtle, The Debate Still On," *New York Times*, December 23, 1973.

12   "Homosexuality Is an Illness and Is Curable in Some Cases, Major Doc-
      tors' Group Says," *Wall Street Journal*, May 19, 1964.

13   Paul Moor, "The View from Irving Bieber's Couch; 'Heads I Win, Tails
      You Lose,' " *Journal of Homosexuality*, The Hayworth Press Inc. (New
      York: 1998), 36, no. 1.

14   Charles Socarides, "A Sickness Theory," originally written, "Stay Young
      Newsletter: Review of Medical Fact and Opinion," reprinted in *Vector* 6,
      no. 9, September 1970.

15   Charles Socarides, *The Overt Homosexual* (New York: Grune &Stratton,
      1968).

16   Alix Spiegel, "John Frey, Dr. H. Anonymous," National Public Radio
      broadcast, April 4, 2003.

17   Socarides, *Beyond Sexual Freedom*, 83.

18   Doty, "Growth of Overt Homosexuality in City Provokes Wide Concern."

19   Jane E. Brody, "More Homosexuals Aided to Become Heterosexual," *New
      York Times*, February 28, 1971.

20   "Homosexuality Is an Illness and Is Curable in Some Cases, Major Doc-
      tors' Group Says," *Wall Street Journal*, May 19, 1964.

21   Morton M. Hunt, "A Neurosis Is Just a Bad Habit," *New York Times*, June
      4, 1967.

22   George Weinberg, interview by author, tape recording, New York City,
      June 4, 2004.

23   Brody, "More Homosexuals Aided to Become Heterosexual."

24   Bayer, 44.

25   This quote from Kinsey's book can be found in "Dr. Kinsey Defends State-
      ments In Book," *New York Times*, June 5, 1948 and Alton L. Blakeslee,
      "New Kinsey Book Given Preview," *New York Times*, April 27, 1950.

26   Nate Haeltine, "Experts Evaluate Kinsey Sex Study," *Washington Post*, Jan-
      uary 17, 1954.

27   Hooker became familiar with Kinsey's work at Bryn Mawr when several of
      her students who had been interviewed by Kinsey, "told her hair-raising
      tales of questions about fellatio or cunninlingus and these kids didn't know
      what he was talking about. They would answer questions simply because
      they didn't know what he was talking about. They would simply answer all
      his questions yes." Evelyn Hooker, interview by Bruce Voeller, Bruce
      Voeller Papers, box 36, folder 13, Human Sexuality Collection, Cornell
      University, Ithaca, New York.

28   For a discussion of Hooker's background and research, see Henry Minton

Departing from Deviance Chicago: University of Chicago Press, 2002),
219–32.

29   Evelyn Hooker, "Male homosexuality in the Rorschach," in: *Journal of Projective Techniques*, 21 (1957): 18–31.

30   Minton, 236–37.

31   Jack Nichols, interview; Johnson, 213; D'Emilio, 165.

32   Kaiser, 235.

33   Kameny, interview.

34   "The Homosexual: Newly Visible, Newly Understood," *Time*, October 31, 1969.

35   "A Discussion: Are Homosexuals Sick?" *Time*, October 31, 1969.

36   "The Changing View of Homosexuality," *New York Times*, February 28, 1971.

37   Minton, 254; DeEmilio, *Sexual Politics, Sexual Communities*, 216.

38   Clendinen and Nagourney, 201–3.

39   Stuart Auerbach, "Gays and Dolls Battle the Shrinks," *Washington Post*, May 15, 1970.

40   Kameny, interview.

41   Bayer, 103–5.

42   Minton, 258; Frank Kameny, "Psychiatrists Re-evaluate: Aftermath of Gay Zapping," *Vector* 7, no. 8, August 1971.

43   Clendinen and Nagourney, 207.

44   Marcus, 178.

45   Dr. Ralph Elias, " 'Sickness Theory' Ignored," *Vector*, June 1972.

46   Spiegel, "Dr. H. Anonymous."

47   Kaiser, 236.

48   Clendinen and Nagourney, 208; Minton, 258.

49   Victor Cohn, "Doctors Rule Homosexuals not Abnormal," *Washington Post*, December 16, 1973.

50   Quoted in Bayer, 113.

51   Silverstein, interview by author, tape recording, New York City, July 15, 2004.

52   "Executive Committee Minutes September 20, 1972," Gay Activists Alliance Records, box 15, folder 18.

53   "Therapy Scored by Homosexuals," *New York Times*, October 9, 1972.

54   Ron Gold to Lee Hanna, News Dept. WNBC-TV, undated, Gay Activists Alliance Records, box 15, folder 18.

55   Spitzer, interview by author, tape recording, New York City, June 25, 2004.

56 Quoted in Bayer, 119.

57 Ibid., 120.

58 Spitzer, interview.

59 Silverstein, interview. Before GAA's meeting with the Committee on
    Nomenclature at Columbia medical school, Silverstein enlisted the assis-
    tance of a few sympathetic psychiatrists and psychologists to influence the
    atmosphere of the meeting. Seymour Hallek a widely known critic of psy-
    chiatric authority wrote to the committee that the sickness label should be
    removed because it lacked a scientific basis. Homosexuality he argued was a
    "behavioral variant" not a sickness. Wardell Pomerory, one of Kinsey's
    assistants, stressed how the psychiatric community had been relying on data
    drawn from clinical populations who were not representative of most
    homosexuals. He concluded that psychiatry should have accepted the con-
    clusions he and Kinsey offered a quarter century earlier. Alan Bell of
    Kinsey's Institute for Sex Research at Indiana University cited Evelyn
    Hooker's work in arguing that homosexuality stood "within the normal
    range of psychological functioning" and that well-adjusted gays and
    straights had more in common that disturbed people of any orientation.

60 Bayer interviewed two members of the committee for Bayer, 120 n. 41.

61 Spitzer, interview.

62 Boyce Rensberger, "Psychiatrists Review Stand on Homosexuals," *New
    York Times,* February 9, 1973; Clendinen and Nagourney, 212.

63 Bruce Voeller to A. M. Rosenthal, Managing Editor of the *New York
    Times*, February 15, 1973, Gay Activists Alliance Records New York Public
    Library, box 15, folder 18.

64 "Are Homosexuals Sick?" *Newsweek* 81 no. 21, May 21, 1973.

65 Gold, interview.

66 General Meeting Minutes, May 17, 1973, Gay Activists Alliance Records,
    box 15, folder 18.

67 Gold, interview.

68 Spitzer, interview.

69 Spitzer, interview; Minton, 260.

70 Bayer, 127.

71 Spitzer, interview; Adam, 82; Marcus, 182; Minton, 260.

72 Ibid.

73 Ibid.

74 Spitzer, interview; Bayer, 133.

75 Weinberg, interview; Silverstein, interview.

76 Voeller Papers, box 165, folder 40.

77   According to the minutes of a meeting on October 4, 1973, "Bruce appealed to the membership to stop quarrelling, arguing about power plays and get down to some hard serious work." Later that evening he resigned. Gay Activists Alliance Records, box 15, folder 18.

78   Marotta, *The Politics of Homosexuality*, 113.

79   Clendinen and Nagourney, 189–98.

80   Gold, interview.

81   Clendinen and Nagourney, 189–98.

82   Barbara Trecker, third in five part series, "Homosexuals in New York: 'Coming Out,'" *New York Post*, March 27, 1974.

83   Martin Duberman, "Obit for the Good Dr. Howard Brown," *Village Voice*, February 25, 1975.

84   Marca Chambers, "Ex-City Official Says He's Homosexual," *New York Times*, October 3, 1973.

85   Marcia Chambers, "Doctors Called Ignorant of Sex More," *New York Times*, October 4, 1973

86   Bruce Voeller, "My Days on the Task Force," *Christopher Street*, October 1979.

87   Gold and Rockhil to Gay Brothers and Sisters, December 8, 1973, "Removal of the sickness label can be the best thing that's happened in the history of our movement—but not if nobody knows about it!" Voeller Papers.

88   Gold, interview.

89   Kameny, interview.

90   See Henry Minton, *Departing from Deviance* (Chicago: University of Chicago Press, 2002).

91   Bayer, 135.

92   Victor Cohn, "Doctors Rule Homosexuals not Abnormal," *Washington Post*, December 16, 1973.

93   Marcus, 179.

94   Weinberg, interview.

95   Barbara Trecker, "Homosexuals in New York," *New York Post*, March 29, 1974.

96   *New York Times*, December 16, 1973.

97   Quoted in Bayer, 140.

98   Quoted in Bayer, 142–43

99   Spitzer, interview.

100   Bruce Voeller, "My Days on the Task Force," *Christopher Street*, October 1979.

101 Book of NGTF minutes, box 8, folder 1, National Gay and Lesbian Task Force Papers, Human Sexuality Collection, Cornell University, Ithaca, New York.

102 Bayer, 145.

103 Harold H. Schmeck Jr., "Psychiatrists Approve Change on Homosexuals," *New York Times,* April 9, 1974.

104 Spitzer, interview; Gold interview.

105 Gold, interview.

106 Spitzer, interview; Peter Kriss, "8 Psychiatrists Are Seeking New Vote on Homosexuality as Mental Illness," *New York Times*, May 26, 1974; Psychiatric Unit Upholds Stand That Homosexuality Isn't Illness." *New York Times* June 1, 1975.

107 Kaiser, 240.

108 Quoted in Marcus, 179–82.

109 Bruce Voeller to Dr. Walter Barton, Medial Director of the APA, January 29, 1974, Voeller Papers.

110 Charles Socarides, *Beyond Sexual Freedom* (New York: Quadrangle, 1975).

111 Herbert Hendin, "Homosexuality and the Family," *New York Times*, August 22, 1975; Herbert Hendin, *The Age of Sensation*, New York: W.W. Norton & Company, 1975) 104–18.

112 For an example of how the work of the New York Psychiatrists was used by the religious rights, see David A. Noebel, with Gerald S. Pope and Julian Williams, "The Homosexual Revolution: End Time Abomination" (1977).

113 Herbert Hendin, interview by author, telephone, July 5, 2004.

Chapter 10: Macho Man vs. Miss Oklahoma

1 "Gays on the March," *Time*, September 8, 1975.

2 Barbara Trecker, third in five part series, "Homosexuals in New York: 'Coming Out,'" *New York Post*, March 27, 1974.

3 Nicholas Von Hoffman, "And Now, the Year of the Gay," *Washington Post*, October 15, 1976.

4 John J. O'Connor, "Pressure Groups Are Increasingly Putting the Heat on TV," *New York Times*, October 6, 1974.

5 Tom Shales, "The First Archie Bunker Award, the *Washington Post*, July 31, 1977.

6 Jonathan Mahler, *Ladies and Gentlemen The Bronx is Burning* (New York: Farrar, Straus and Giroux, 2005), 127.

7 Tom Shales, "Macho Mirage: Invasion of the Village People," *Washington Post*, June 24, 1980.

8   John Rockwell, "Pop The Village People," *New York Times*, July 26, 1979.

9   "Pentagon Holds to Anti-Gay Stand," *Advocate*, May 24, 1972; "Sailor
     Given General Discharge," *Stars and Stripes*, March 25, 1972; "Discharge
     Asked for Homosexual Act," *Rome Daily American*, March 24, 1972;
     "U.S. Navy Discharges Seaman," *Daily American*, May 20, 1972; "RAM's
     Unfit Discharge Sticks," *Advocate*, June 7, 1972.

10   "Major Test Being Sought on Navy Homosexuality," *Advocate*, February
     16, 1972; "International Team Helping Sailor Fight Navy," *Advocate*,
     March 1, 1972.

11   Copies of Martin's press releases are in box 8, folder 5, Donaldson Papers.

12   Martin to Arthur C. Warner, February 1, 1972, box 5, folder 6, Donaldson
     Papers; "Sailor Facing Undesirable Discharge to Challenge Navy Regs on
     Homosexuality: Congress Woman, ACLU Join Seaman in Battle," *The
     Overseas Weekly*, April 3, 1972; "Hope to Get ACLU to Take Their Case
     This Time," *Village Voice*, February 10, 1972.

13   "Sam Ervin Intervention Seaman Due General Discharge to Undergo Psy-
     chiatric Test," *Stars and Stripes*, April 23, 1972; *Advocate*, April 12, 1972.

14   "Major Test Seen in Navy Case," *Advocate*, April 26, 1972.

15   "First Gay Naval Vet Gets Discharge Upgrade under Carter Plan," *Gay
     Week*, October 17, 1977.

16   In March 1972 the marine corps ousted Lance Corporal Jeffery Arthur
     Dunbar for homosexuality. After the young man tried to commit suicide,
     investigators searched his wallet and found an affectionate letter addressed
     to a man in Oklahoma. Frank Kameny assisted with Dunbar's defense.
     "Marines Urge Ouster of a Homosexual," *New York Times*, March 22,
     1972. Lenny Matlovich and Vernon Berg also became *cause celebres* of the
     gay rights movement when they were discharged from the Navy in the
     mid-1970s. Peter Kihss; "Homosexual Cites Pentagon View to Back Fight
     Against Ouster," *New York Times*, March 24, 1976; "A Homosexual
     Ensign Receives Other Than Honorable Release," *New York Times*, May
     22, 1976; Rernad Weinraub, "Military, After Appellate Ruling, Starts
     Review on Homosexuality," *New York Times*, December 8, 1978; "The
     Homosexual In Uniform," *New York Times* editorial, December 12, 1978.

17   Box 8, folder 5, Donaldson Papers.

18   Lesley Oelsner, "Homosexual Is Fighting Military Ouster," *New York
     Times*, May 26, 1975; http://www.365gay.com/lifestylechannel/intime/
     months/07-july/matlovich.htm.

19   Quoted in Clendinen and Nagourney, 244.

20   Mahler, 127–28.

21   Laurie Johnson, "Arson Destroys Gay Activist Site," *New York Times*, October 16, 1974.

22   *Advocate*, November 6, 1974.

23   Joe Kennedy, Summer of '77: *Last Hurrah of the Gay Activist's Alliance*. (Westport, CT: PPC Books, 1994), viii.

24   *Advocate*, October 10, 1974; Manford to Bob Cole, news editor Los Angeles Advocate, October 11, 1974, Manford Papers; *Michael's Thing*, November 18 1974; *Michael's Thing*, February 17, 1975; GAA Press release September 14, 1979, "Half of GAA's Executive Committee Resigns over Isolationist Polices," Voeller Papers.

25   Arnie Kantrowitz, "The Day Gay Lib Died," *New York Native*, November 2–15, 1981; GAA press release, September 14, 1979, "Half of GAA's Executive Committee Resigns over Isolationist Polices," Gay Activists Alliance Papers.

26   GAA press release, "Proposals for the January 20th, 1980 Statewide Conference," undated, Gay Activists Alliance Papers.

27   When Liberal Senator Henry M. Jackson, who had called homosexuality "wrong" and "bad," was asked by hecklers how he could justify his stance, Jackson said "go on and have your own rally. Our people want hard work. We don't want gay jobs. You have your gay jobs. You just do your own thing and stay away." Douglas E. Kneeland, "Jackson Salutes 'Amigos' in East Harlem," *New York Times*, April 4, 1976. In response Tom Wicker wrote a column in the *New York Times* criticizing Jackson. "Even so a man who seeks to unify and lead the nation, who proclaims himself, a 'liberal,' who says he is for "human détente and who makes much of what he modestly calls a 'perfect' civil rights record, raises reasonable doubts about his balance and his generosity when he lashes out so intemperately at other Americans, however uncongenial they may be to him." Tom Wicker, "Jackson on Rights," *New York Times*, April 6, 1976.

28   Les Ledbetter, "San Francisco Legislators Meet in Diversity," *New York Times*, January 12, 1978.

29   Roger Ricklefs, "A New Constituency: Political Candidates Seek Out Gay Votes: In Cities Where Homosexuals Are Well-Organized, Risks of Such Campaigns Fade," *Wall Street Journal*, October 20, 1976.

30   Ethan Geto, interview by author, New York City, October 21, 2004.

31   Geto interview, October 21, 2004.

32   Mahler, 165.

33   Richard Goldstein, "Koch and The Gay Vote," *Village Voice*, September 9–15, 1981

34   Maurice Caroll, "Koch Out in Streets for Final Stretch," *New York Times*, November 6, 1977.

35   "Koch Vows to Ban Discrimination by the City Against Homosexuals," *New York Times*, January 3, 1978.

36   Grace Lichtenstein, "Homosexuals in New York Find New Pride," *New York Times*, October 25, 1977.

37   Gays on the March," *Time*, September 8, 1975.

38   Ibid.

39   Ibid.

40   MSGR George E. Kelly, "What Homosexual Activists Demand of Government," *The Catholic News*, May 22, 1975.

41   Alfonzo A Narvaez, "City Backs Homosexuals Bill," *New York Times*, October 19, 1971; Edward Ranzel "Homosexual Bill Argued in Council," *New York Times*, November 16, 1971; "Council Unit's Vote on Homosexual Bill Rejects It 2nd Time," *New York Times* July 20, 1972; Edward Ranzal, Bar Groups Back Homosexual Bill," *New York Times*, February 11, 1973; Jay Levin and Joe Nicholson Jr., "Angry Homosexuals Protest," *New York Post*, April 28, 1973; According to the *New York Post*, "The transvestites actions no doubt contributed to the bill's defeat" in 1971 and 1972. Barbara Trecker, "Homosexuals in New York," *New York Post*, March 29, 1974.

42   Barbara Trecker, "Gay Rights Bill Wins Vital Vote," *New York Post*, April 19, 1974.

43   George Arzt, "Catholic, Firemen Opposition Threatens Gay Rights Measure," *New York Post*, April 29, 1974.

44   "The Committee for the Protection of Family Life in New York City," Voeller Papers.

45   "Forceful Homosexual Bill Return to NY City Council," *The Catholic News*, February 24, 1975.

46   Maurice Carroll, "Council Defeats Homosexual Bill by 22 to 19 Vote," *New York Times*, May 24, 1974.

47   Most of the politicians cited the Church's opposition as the key factor in the defeat of the measure. Maurice Carroll, "Council Defeats Homosexual Bill by 22 to 19 Vote."

48   Quoted in Tom Wicker, "Jackson on Rights."

49   Douglas E. Kneeland, "Jackson Salutes 'Amigos' in East Harlem."

50   Geto, interview, October 21, 2004.

51   "1977: The Year in Review," Voeller Papers.

52   "The White House meeting of March 26 was the culmination of months of quiet planning and negotiating by NGTF, and it was a major step in legitimizing the gay-rights struggle in the eyes of the media, the general public and governmental officials." "1977: The Year in Review," Voeller Papers.

53   Clendinen and Nagourney, 291.

54   "Anita Bryant Scores White House Talk with Homosexuals," *New York Times*, March 28, 1977.

55   One gay rights bill campaign leader quoted in Sears, *Rebels, Rubyfruit and Rhinestones*, 236.

56   Quoted in Clendinen and Nagourney, 299.

57   Theodore Stranger, "Dade Struggle Drawing Nationwide Interest," *Miami Herald*, April 11, 1977.

58   Quoted in Sears, *Rebels, Rubyfruit and Rhinestones*, 244.

59   *People*, June 6, 1977

60   Sears, *Rebels, Rubyfruit and Rhinestones*, 239.

61   Ibid., 241.

62   Ibid., 238.

63   Tom Zito, "The Roasting of Anita Bryant," *Washington Post*, May 13, 1977.

64   Sears, *Rebels, Rubyfruit and Rhinestones*, 243.

65   Tom Curtis, "Mixed Chorus for Bryant," *Washington Post*, June 18, 1977; "3000 in Houston Protest Anita Bryant's Appearance," *New York Times*, June 17, 1977.

66   "Bryant Still Effective?" *Washington Post*, June 20, 1977.

67   Fred Halsted, "Thank God for Anita," *Alternate*, December 1977.

68   Jon Nordheimer, "Miami Homosexuals See a Victory Despite Defeat of Anti-Bias Law," *New York Times*, December 28, 1977.

69   Ibid.

70   Shales, "Macho Mirage: Invasion of the Village People."

71   Ibid.

72   "What do these people have in common?," *New York Post*, June 22, 1978.

73   William Safire, "Now Ease Up, Anita," *New York Times*, June 9, 1977.

74   Quoted in Sears, 245.

75   A year later, Milk became a gay rights martyr when fellow council member Dan White gunned him down in San Francisco's city hall.

76   Clendinen and Nagourney, 310.

77   "Florida Citrus Group Retains Anita Bryant," *New York Times*, July 20, 1977; "Still in Orange Juice Picture," *Washington Post*, June 21, 1977;

"Homosexuals to Boycott Citrus," *New York Times*, August 1, 1977; "A Gay Activist Campaign," *Washington Post*, April 8, 1977.

78   "Anita had Florida Growers in a State," *New York Post*, February 8, 1980.

79   "Anita Bryant's Job Linked by Employer to Sales," *New York Times*, June 20, 1977.

80   Jon Nordheimer, "Miami Homosexuals See a Victory Despite Defeat of Anti-Bias Law," *New York Times*, December 28, 1977.

81   Jay Clarke, "Gay Rights Dispute Stops Bryant's Show," *Washington Post*, February 25, 1977; The Anita Bryant Show, *Washington Post*, March 2, 1977.

82   Quoted in Lisa McGirr, *Suburban Warriors: The Origins of the New American Right* (Princeton, NJ: Princeton University Press, 2001), 258.

83   "After Low-Key Campaigns, Comeback Is Seen for Gay Rights," *Washington Post*, October 27, 1978.

84   "Anita Bryant Says, 'Live and Let Live,' " *New York Times*, November 15, 1980.

85   Clendinen and Nagourney, 421.

Epilogue: The Conspiracy of Silence Redux

1   "Diseases That Plague Gays," *Newsweek*, December 21, 1981.

2   Charles Krauthammer, "The Politics of a Plague Revisited," *The New Republic*, August 1, 1983.

3   Lawrence K. Altman, "Rare Cancer Seen in 41 Homosexuals," *New York Times*, July 3, 1981.

4   Clendinen and Nagourney, 468.

5   Randy Shilts, *And the Band Played On.* (New York, St. Martin's Press: 1987), 171.

6   Shilts, 55; Kaiser, 285

7   Dowd, *New York Times*, December 5, 1983.

8   Shilts, 282.

9   Ibid., 109.

10   Ibid., 126.

11   Ibid., 110.

12   Ibid., 172.

13   Ibid., 268.

14   Ibid., 301.

15   Ibid., 213.

16   Ibid., 173.

17   Ibid., 268.

18   Ibid., 380.

19   Ibid., 385.

20   Ibid., 534.

21   Ibid., 342.

22   Ibid., 533.

23   Clendinen and Nagourney, 477.

24   Ibid., 479.

25   "Gay America in Transition," *Newsweek*, August 8, 1983.

26   Clendinen and Nagourney, 466.

27   "Gay America in Transition," *Newsweek*.

28   Shilts, 19.

29   "Gay America in Transition," *Newsweek*.

30   Ibid.

31   Quoted in Shilts, 245.

32   Quoted in Shilts, 557.

33   Clendinen and Nagourney, 482.

34   Ibid., 483.

35   Shilts, 267.

36   "Gay America in Transition," *Newsweek*.

37   "The AIDS Epidemic: The Search for a Cure," *Newsweek*, April 18, 1983.

38   Shilts, 1267.

39   Ibid., 351.

40   Ibid., 268.

41   "Gay America in Transition," *Newsweek*.

42   Ibid.

43   Clendinen and Nagourney, 486.

44   George Chauncey, *Why Marriage?* 41.

45   "Gay America in Transition," *Newsweek*.

46   Chauncey, *Why Marriage?* 43.

47   "Gay America in Transition," *Newsweek*.

48   Clendinen and Nagourney, 465.

49   Ibid., 488.

50   Patrick J. Buchanan, "Aids Disease: It's Nature Striking Back," *New York Post*, May 24, 1983.

51   Clendinen and Nagourney, 507.

52   Ibid., 526.

53   "AIDS: A Spreading Scourge," *Time*, August 5, 1985.

54   Ibid.

55   Kaiser, 317; Shilts, 578.

56   Shilts, 576.

57   Clendinen and Nagourney, 517.

58   Shilts, 578.

59   Ibid., 581.

60   "AIDS: A Spreading Scourge," *Time*.

61   Ibid.

62   Shilts, 578.

63   "AIDS: A Spreading Scourge," *Time*.

64   Shilts, 579.

65   Quoted in Kaiser, 309.

66   Shilts, 588.

67   Cynthia Crossen, "Shock Troops: AIDS Activist Group Harasses and Provokes to Make Its Point," *Wall Street Journal*, December 7, 1989.

68   Kaiser, 318.

69   Crossen, "Shock Troops: AIDS Activist Group Harasses and Provokes to Make Its Point."

70   Clendinen and Nagourney, 547.

71   Crossen, "Shock Troops: AIDS Activist Group Harasses and Provokes to Make Its Point."

72   Jason deParle, "Rude, Rash, Effective, Act-Up Shifts AIDS Policy," *New York Times*, January 3, 1990.

73   Kaiser, 322.

74   deParle, "Rude, Rash, Effective, Act-Up Shifts AIDS Policy."

75   Crossen, "Shock Troops: AIDS Activist Group Harasses and Provokes to Make Its Point."

76   deParle, "Rude, Rash, Effective, Act-Up Shifts AIDS Policy."

77   Crossen, "Shock Troops: AIDS Activist Group Harasses and Provokes to Make Its Point."

78   Quoted in Dowd, *New York Times*, December 5, 1983.

79   "Gay America in Transition," *Newsweek*.

80   Crossen, "Shock Troops: AIDS Activist Group Harasses and Provokes to Make Its Point."

81   "Gay America in Transition," *Newsweek*.

82   Chauncey, *Why Marriage?* 48.

83   Ibid., 47.

84   Kaiser, 310.

85   "Gay America in Transition," *Newsweek*.

86   Chauncey, *Why Marriage?* 103.

87   "Gay America in Transition," *Newsweek.*

88   Clendinen and Nagourney, 569.

89   Kaiser, 284.

90   Randy Shilts speculated that AIDS arrived in the United States during the 1976 Bicentenial Celebration, Shilts, 3.

91   Kaiser, 283.

92   Chauncey, *Why Marriage?* 48.

93   Ibid., 151.

INDEX